American Militarism on the Small Screen

The military has produced and distributed programs via private broadcasters since the early days of radio, and war and militarism have been popular subjects for commercial television programming from its inception. Despite the historical and social prevalence of military-themed programming on US television, there has been no thorough scholarly investigation of this phenomenon. This volume seeks to identify what television, as a cultural medium, has added to the depictions of war and militarism in the US. Chapters explore a variety of series and engage with the following questions: What are the conventions of the war series? How do fictional depictions of war on US TV operate in dialogue with existing war films? How do they relate to broadcast news coverage of war? Is there anything unique about the way television series, as opposed to films, documentaries, or news stories, depict issues of nationalism and militarism? How do issues of race, class, gender, and sexuality play out differently in the television combat series, for example? How have the conventions of television production, distribution, and reception affected the form, content, and influence of the war story?

Anna Froula is an Associate Professor of Film Studies in the Department of English at East Carolina University, USA. She has published on war and gender for several journals and edited collections and is the Associate Editor of *Cinema Journal,* the journal of the Society of Cinema and Media Studies.

Stacy Takacs is an Associate Professor of American Studies at Oklahoma State University, USA. She has published on the intersections of popular and political cultures for a number of journals and is the author of *Terrorism TV* and *Interrogating Popular Culture.*

Routledge Advances in Television Studies

1 Parody and Taste in Postwar
American Television Culture
Ethan Thompson

2 Television and Postfeminist
Housekeeping
No Time for Mother
Elizabeth Nathanson

3 The Antihero in American
Television
Margrethe Bruun Vaage

4 American Militarism on the
Small Screen
*Edited by Anna Froula and
Stacy Takacs*

American Militarism on the Small Screen

Edited by Anna Froula
and Stacy Takacs

LONDON AND NEW YORK

First published 2016 by Routledge

2 Park Square, Milton Park, Abingdon, Oxforshire OX14 4RN
711 Third Avenue, New York, NY 10017

Routledge is an imprint of the Taylor & Francis Group, an informa business

First issued in paperback 2018

Copyright © 2016 Taylor & Francis

The right of the editors to be identified as the authors of the editorial
material, and of the authors for their individual chapters, has been asserted
in accordance with sections 77 and 78 of the Copyright, Designs and
Patents Act 1988.

All rights reserved. No part of this book may be reprinted or reproduced or
utilised in any form or by any electronic, mechanical, or other means, now
known or hereafter invented, including photocopying and recording, or in
any information storage or retrieval system, without permission in writing
from the publishers.

Notice:
Product or corporate names may be trademarks or registered trademarks,
and are used only for identification and explanation without intent to infringe.

Library of Congress Cataloging-in-Publication Data

Names: Froula, Anna, editor. | Takacs, Stacy, editor.
Title: American militarism on the small screen / edited by Anna Froula
and Stacy Takacs.
Description: New York; London: Routledge, 2016. | Series: Routledge
advances in television studies; 4 | Includes bibliographical references
and index.
Identifiers: LCCN 2016000099
Subjects: LCSH: Militarism on television. | Soldiers on television. | War
television programs—United States—History and criticism.
Classification: LCC PN1992.8.M53 A47 2016 | DDC 791.45/6581—dc23
LC record available at http://lccn.loc.gov/2016000099

ISBN: 978-1-138-92769-8 (hbk)
ISBN: 978-1-138-31943-1 (pbk)

Typeset in Sabon
by codeMantra

This is dedicated to veterans,
whose service is memorialized, sometimes for better,
sometimes for worse, in these fictions.

Contents

List of Figures	ix
Acknowledgments	xi
Introduction: Living Room Wars	1
ANNA FROULA AND STACY TAKACS	

PART I
World War II on the Small Screen

1	"Bilko's Bombers": Anti-Militarism in the Era of the "New Look"	17
	LISA M. MUNDEY	
2	The Long Fight: *Combat!* and the Generic Development of the TV War Drama Series	30
	DAVID P. PIERSON	
3	*12 O'Clock High* and the Image of American Air Power, 1946–1967	46
	SAM EDWARDS	
4	Nervous Laughter: *Hogan's Heroes* and the Vietnam War	63
	ROBERT R. SHANDLEY	
5	*Baa Baa Black Sheep* and the Last Stand of the WWII Drama	77
	A. BOWDOIN VAN RIPER	
6	A Waltz with and for the Greatest Generation: Music in *Band of Brothers* (2001)	93
	TODD DECKER	

viii *Contents*

PART II
Korea and Vietnam on the Small Screen

7 The American Forces Korea Network: "Bringing Troops
a Touch of Home" 111
SUEYOUNG PARK-PRIMIANO

8 "Everybody Here Is Crazy": Images of the Disabled
on Television's *M*A*S*H* 129
KELLY J.W. BROWN

9 Drinking the War Away: Televisual Insobriety and
the Meanings of Alcohol in *M*A*S*H* 144
DAVID SCOTT DIFFRIENT

10 Small-Screen Insurgency: Entertainment Television,
the Vietnamese Revolution, and the Cold War, 1953–1967 162
SCOTT LADERMAN

11 *China Beach* and the Good Series Death 178
CHRISTINE BECKER

PART III
Contemporary Conflicts on the Small Screen

12 Imagining the New Military of the 1990s in
Babylon 5's Future Wars 195
KATHLEEN KENNEDY

13 *JAG*, Melodrama, and Militarism 211
STACY TAKACS

14 Political Amnesia Over Here and Imperial Spectacle
Over There 228
ANNA FROULA

15 *Generation Kill* and the New Screen Combat 245
MAGDALENA YÜKSEL AND COLLEEN KENNEDY-KARPAT

16 "Don't Ask, Don't Tell" and Its Repeal in Showtime's
The L Word and Lifetime's *Army Wives* 261
LIORA ELIAS

List of Contributors 275
Index 281

List of Figures

I.1 From the beginning of television, the military and media have collaborated to tell stories of war. *Victory at Sea*, for example, was created to commemorate WWII and prepare the public for a lingering Cold War. 2

2.1 *Combat!* presented a decidedly bleak image of the war experience. Men often died without cause or recuperation, and death was never particularly meaningful or glorious. 33

5.1 The Black Sheep, like the bomber crews and infantry platoons of classic World War II combat films, are an assembly of archetypal characters. Left to right: Wiley, Gutterman, French, Boyle, Bragg, Casey, Hutchinson, and Anderson. From "Anyone for Suicide?" 84

5.2 Boyington, his deep concern for his men carefully hidden behind a "hard-nosed CO" persona, chews out a pilot whose foolhardy actions endangered himself and his fellow Black Sheep on a mission. From "Five the Hard Way" 89

6.1 Easy Company veteran Carwood Lipton interviewed in the opening moments of episode six. 97

6.2 Donnie Wahlberg as Carwood Lipton in a scene from episode seven included in the opening titles sequence. 99

6.3 "Buck" Compton (Neal McDonough) fades from the scene as Lipton lists Easy's casualties to the sound of a convent choir singing at the end of episode seven. 104

9.1 The pilot episode of *M*A*S*H* establishes Hawkeye and Trapper's proclivity to drink between surgical shifts, as illustrated in this scene. 148

9.2 Near the end of "Too Many Cooks," Colonel Potter and Major Houlihan share a toast at the Officers' Club, a convivial action that is often repeated during the 11-year run of *M*A*S*H*. 150

9.3 Margaret's friend, Captain Helen Whitfield (Gail Strickland), gets "the DTs" when trying to go off the bottle in "Bottoms Up." 154

x *List of Figures*

9.4 When one of the newly arrived female entertainers approaches her table, head nurse Colleen McMurphy (Dana Delany) takes a sip of alcohol and says, "I'm just one of the guys." Like the doctors from *M*A*S*H*, McMurphy is often shown nursing a bottle. From the pilot episode of *China Beach*. 157

11.1 The first season cast of *China Beach* and the cover of the commemorative DVD edition. In its final season, *China Beach* openly memorialized the war and its veterans, thereby providing a "good death" for characters and audience alike. 179

13.1 *JAG* patterned itself after the classic WWII combat film and often featured episodes commemorating those films, as well as the war. Actual footage of the Battle of Iwo Jima provides the backdrop for romance. From "Each of Us Angels" 214

13.2 *JAG* toyed with the romance between its two most prominent characters for 10 seasons before finally consummating the relationship. The series famously ended on a coin toss to determine which of the lovers would resign to facilitate the union. From "Fair Winds and Following Seas" 221

13.3 *JAG* frequently placed its protagonists in peril so that they could rescue one another. Mac (Catherine Bell) was rescuer as often as rescued. From "Gypsy Eyes" 222

14.1 *Over There* explores the controversies surrounding US interrogation policies in "The Prisoner." 236

14.2 In "Orphans," *Over There* contrasted the plight of Iraqi orphan children. ... 238

14.3 .... with the abundance enjoyed by children in the United States. 238

15.1 *Generation Kill* highlights the military's failure to prevent collateral damage in the Iraq War and its consequent wearing down of the soldiers' morale. In one example, members of First Recon witness the annihilation of an Iraqi household that they had determined harmless. 255

Acknowledgments

Collectively, we would like to thank Felisa Salvago-Keyes, Kathleen Laurentiev, and Christina Kowalski at Routledge for their counsel and patience and Andrew Weckenmann and Sofia Buono for editorial assistance. Robert Shandley's chapter "*Hogan's Heroes* and American Militarism" is a greatly condensed version of his argument in *Hogan's Heroes* (Wayne State University Press, 2011). The author and editors wish to thank Wayne State University Press and the TV Milestones editors, Barry Keith Grant and Jeannette Sloniowski, for permission to reuse material from the book. Finally, thanks go to our wonderful contributors who have made this volume possible. We have been wanting to read this book for years, and now we finally get to, thanks to you!

Anna: I would first like to thank Stacy Takacs for agreeing to bring this book to life and for her exceptional work in making it happen. I am also grateful for the institutional support of the East Carolina University English Department and the writing support of my Femidemics: Marame Gueye, Su-Ching Huang, Andrea Kitta, Amanda Klein, and Marianne Montgomery. As ever, my gratitude goes to Sean Morris, who has sustained and nurtured me through this project and beyond.

Stacy: And I would like to thank Anna Froula for having this great idea, which I totally jumped on and ran with. She has been a model of patience and endurance throughout the process, and I apologize for however annoying I know my compulsiveness must have been. Finally, to my colleagues at Oklahoma State University, especially Lu Bailey, John Kinder, David Gray, Louise Siddons, Bin Liang, Laura Belmonte, and Bill Decker, for being a rock-solid foundation for me. As always, Betsy Myers served as a model of devotion throughout the process. My turn next!

Introduction
Living Room Wars

Anna Froula and Stacy Takacs

The television industry in the United States was born of the early military-corporate alliance that resulted in the formation of the Radio Corporation of America (RCA) in 1917. A quasi-private entity created at the behest of the US Navy as a means of centralizing control over the emerging medium of radio, RCA was also a major player in the development of television technologies and forms. Until its demise in 1982, RCA was a regular defense contractor and seated a representative from the US Navy on its Board of Directors.[1] RCA's broadcast wing, NBC, was an early and enthusiastic supporter of the American entry into World War II, and, along with the other commercial networks, it routinely made space in its broadcast schedule available for military messengers.[2] To this day, the major networks and cable channels provide programming (at a fraction of the market rate) to the military's own globe-girdling broadcast operation, The American Forces Radio and Television Service. Thus, the connections between the US military and the otherwise privatized television industry are both long and deep.

The flow of programming across these connections has not been one-way, either. The military has produced and distributed programs via private broadcasters since the early days of radio, and war and militarism would be popular subjects for commercial television programming from its inception. As early as 1949, war documentary series like *Crusade in Europe* (ABC, 1949), *Crusade in the Pacific* (ABC, 1951), and *Victory at Sea* (NBC, 1952)—all based on official military accounts of WWII—offered riveting television. In 1951, the US Army Signal Corps' Pictorial Services division began syndicating its indoctrination materials for commercial viewing via the long-running series *The Big Picture* (1951–1971). Since 1955, the Department of Defense and the various military branches have collaborated with commercial producers to make television series like *Navy Log* (CBS, 1955–1956; ABC, 1956–1958), *West Point* (CBS, 1956–1957; ABC, 1957–1958), *Men of Annapolis* (syndication, 1957–1958), *The Silent Service* (syndication, 1957–1958), and *The Blue Angels* (syndication, 1960–1961). These series aired on NBC, CBS, and ABC affiliate stations throughout the country and overseas and served to increase recruitment and public support for a permanently mobilized military. Since the 1950s, military programming has become legitimate entertainment fare, waxing and waning in popularity as American foreign policy has fluctuated. Most recently, a spate of scripted and unscripted military series has focused on the conduct of the War(s) on Terrorism (*American Fighter Pilot* [CBS, 2002], *Profiles from the Front Line* [ABC, 2003], *Over There* [F/X, 2005], *Generation Kill* [HBO, 2008], and so on). In 2012, NBC even aired the short-lived reality show *Stars Earn Stripes* in which celebrities, such as Terry Crews and Laila Ali, paired with special operations personnel, such as Chris Kyle, author of *American Sniper*, to perform military missions and earn money for different military charities. Hosted by retired NATO Supreme Allied Commander Wesley Clark, the show was canceled after five episodes.[3]

Figure I.1 From the beginning of television, the military and media have collaborated to tell stories of war. *Victory at Sea*, for example, was created to commemorate WWII and prepare the public for a lingering Cold War.

Despite the historical and social prevalence of military-themed programming on US television, there has been no thorough scholarly investigation of this phenomenon. Several volumes have been written about the war film and its various subgenres, and a few works exist on individual television series, but there has been no comprehensive volume dedicated to the study of televisual depictions of the US military and its operations. This anthology seeks to rectify the omission and to identify what television, as a distinct technology and cultural form, has added to the representation of war and militarism within the United States. Given the dearth of scholarship on war series, it seems natural to begin with a definition of the genre as it exists in film scholarship.[4] From there, we may begin to consider the "spin" television has placed on the genre due to its unique industrial and narrative economies.

Hollywood's War Film and Its Influence

One of the defining characteristics of the war genre is that combat shapes the fates and developments of its characters. War films, as David Slocum argues, are concerned with "the motivations, attitudes, and behavior of individuals preparing for or immersed in combat."[5] In this definition, war must be a thematic concern of the narrative, but the action does not have to be *set* in combat to qualify. Film historian Jeannine Basinger, however, insists on a more rigorous definition whereby war is both a theme *and* a setting. Thus, she prefers to speak of the "World War II combat film" as a genre unto itself and to eschew over-generalization based on the narrow subset of films she studies.[6] Yet, her comprehensive study is too rich for scholars—including many of the scholars in this volume—to ignore. It is important, therefore, to lay out a few of her arguments.

According to Basinger, World War II combat films are populated by hardened father-figure heroes who lead a "universal platoon" of men representing the "melting pot" of America in terms of geographic, ethnic, and religious diversity and individuality.[7] Despite their differences and internal conflicts, the men will overcome adversity to become a collective fighting machine in time to fulfill their military and narrative objective: the set-piece battle. Central to the war film's conceit is masculinity—emerging, hardened, conflicted, and beset by debilitating physical and psychological injury—and combat is the threshold and testing ground of manhood. This basic formula is simple enough to foster repetition but flexible enough to admit a range of emotional reconfigurations. As Basinger herself notes, the moral center of the World War II combat film has shifted over time, from justifying the mission and rationale for the fight to exploring the implications of combat in social and moral terms. Some of the films are romanticized and triumphant in tone; others are bleak and nihilistic, but none is particularly critical of the centrality of war in American society; it remains vital to the formation of masculinity and national identity.

As Guy Westwell summarizes, "Hollywood movies tend to show war as necessary, if not essential, and [to] present the armed forces as efficient, egalitarian and heroic institutions."[8] He urges viewers to regard this "cultural imagination of war" with suspicion, for its "myopic view of the past" too easily serves as "justification for wars in the present."[9] In its construction of the enemy as "other," the genre forges national identity in a negative fashion—against those identified as "alien and dangerous."[10] Focusing through the point of view of the heroes, as most films and television shows do, can impede a nuanced understanding of the complexities of war and politics.[11] World War II cinema, in particular, shaped a cultural imagination "predicated on a powerful sense of an integrated America constructed as victim that perceives military action to be a just and necessary response to unwarranted aggression."[12] As the chapters in this volume attest, this imagination would set the tone for depictions of wars to come across a range of media. On US television, especially, war remains the whetstone that hones patriotism and courage, yet it is also, and increasingly, a sore subject, which the medium is eager to work over.

War and the Cultural Logics of Television

The generic definition of the war film fits many televisual iterations quite comfortably. Series like *Baa Baa Black Sheep* and *Twelve O'Clock High*, for example, offer episodic mini-movies that do not depart significantly from the "command dramas" of the Cold War era. They are, as Bow Van Riper argues (chapter 5, this volume), "the last iteration of an old narrative tradition rather than the beginning of a new one."[13]

Yet, other programs seem to offer a specifically televisual twist on the old formulas. The artistic and narrative differences are partially a response to the different commercial logics at play in the different media industries. Whereas the film industry is oriented around the sale of films to audiences, the TV industry focuses on selling audiences to advertisers.[14] The need to promote regular, habituated viewing requires TV producers to adhere to certain well-regulated and predictable formulas. Each program must fit either a 30-minute or one-hour time slot, for instance, and programs must recur regularly (weekly) to encourage repeat viewing and robust sales in the syndication markets (where producers make most of their money). Narratives must also be broken into short narrative "beats," with lots of repetition, to account for the distracted viewing promoted by home reception.[15] Most problematically, stories must accommodate regular breaks for commercial messages. These breaks not only eat into the available story time (such that each 30-minute segment actually works out to about 22 minutes of story telling); they may radically undermine the message or tone of a program (as Anna Froula shows in her consideration of the "flow" surrounding the Iraq War drama *Over There* [chapter 14, this volume]). Put simply, it is difficult to explore complex subject matter and sell shampoo at the same time. Although some of these dynamics have changed with the advent of premium cable channels and sell-through outlets like Netflix and Amazon, advertisers have historically been the primary audience for television programming, and they have not been very interested in courting controversy or exploring complexity. This has made war a tough sell on TV—but not an impossible one. The different political economies simply mean that small screen fictions about war and militarism will assume different poetic forms; as the essays in this volume argue, these differences should not be interpreted as deficiencies.

What might television programs about war and militarism, specifically scripted, entertainment programs about these topics, be said to add to the war genre? For one thing, the domestic setting of television reception, along with the relatively poor visual and audio quality of the set (at least until wide-screen TVs and surround sound arrived in the mid-1990s), have encouraged a certain form of genre recombination. In the early days of television, especially, military comedies like *The Phil Silvers Show* (CBS, 1955–1959), *McHale's Navy* (ABC, 1962–1966), *Gomer Pyle, USMC* (CBS, 1964–1969), *The Wackiest Ship in the Army* (NBC, 1965–1966), *F Troop* (ABC, 1965–1967), and *Hogan's Heroes* (CBS, 1965–1971) ruled the tube. Like other situation comedies, these programs focused less on action or plot development and more on the investigation of the institutions, procedures, and personalities associated with the military setting. As Lisa Mundey points out (chapter 1, this volume), the military bureaucracy is often the butt of the joke on these programs, and the citizen soldiers are the heroes because they resist all attempts to contain their individuality. In the same way that 1950s ethnic family sitcoms helped ease popular anxieties about consumer capitalism, then, these "anti-militarist" sitcoms might be said to have eased fears associated with the move to a permanently mobilized military force after World War II.[16] The likable characters and anti-institutional rhetoric reassured Americans that the military remained firmly in civilian control and would not, therefore, constitute a threat to democracy and the American way of life.

The domesticating influence of the television medium can also be seen in the military dramas of the era. Some of these dramas aspired to be mini WWII films, but, because of the visual and audio constraints of the medium, most were decidedly muted in their presentations of combat. Dramas like *The Blue Angels* (syndicated, 1960–1961), *Twelve O'Clock High* (ABC, 1964–1967), *The Lieutenant* (NBC, 1963–1964), and *Court Martial* (ABC, 1966–1967) were fairly typical command dramas, focused as much on the inner workings of the military hierarchy as on the combat escapades of its soldiers and airmen. Meanwhile, combat programs like *The Gallant Men* (ABC, 1962–1963), *Baa Baa Black Sheep* (NBC, 1976–1978), *Rat Patrol* (ABC, 1966–1968), and *Garrison's Gorillas* (ABC, 1967–1968) catered to a different segment of the household audience—juveniles and their emotionally immature adult counterparts. The simplistic action-adventure formulas in these series undercut the realist ethos of the WWII combat film and replaced it with a war-is-exhilarating bravado designed to thrill, rather than provoke thought (see chapter 5 in this volume for a different take on *Baa Baa Black Sheep*, however). *Combat!* (ABC, 1962–1967), with its gritty style and "war is hell" thematics, may be the lone exception to television's early tendency to domesticate the genre, although it, too, seemed to focus inordinately on interpersonal conflict. As David P. Pierson argues in chapter 2, *Combat!*'s influence on the genre, particularly on the Vietnam War-era drama *Tour of Duty* (CBS, 1987–1990), attests to its lasting legacy as a show that examines the ways war can shatter the lives of those who fight it.

The mid-1980s saw a transformation in the TV industry, as competition from cable fractured and dispersed the mass audience. To recapture some of the lost advertising revenue, networks began to cater to smaller, more lucrative niche audiences using "socially relevant" programming and sophisticated genre recombination strategies.[17] The '80s thus saw the rise of hybrid war programs like *M*A*S*H* (CBS, 1972–1983), a heady combination of sitcom, satire, and drama (see chapters 8 and 9, this volume), and *China Beach* (ABC, 1988–1991), a mix of combat drama, medical procedural, soap opera, and black comedy (see chapter 11, this volume). These series aimed to capture educated, socially liberal audiences whose higher

6 Anna Froula and Stacy Takacs

disposable incomes and upscale tastes could command higher prices from advertisers despite their smaller numbers. The genre innovations should not be dismissed as crass economic calculation, however. They are real innovations with real effects on the ways we, as a society, remember war and explain militarism. Most notably, these innovations enabled new critiques of war to be entertained in prime time. Rather than celebrating the cause of war, programs like these scrutinized the effects of our society's increasing reliance on militarism as a political solution and made the critiques comprehensible by personalizing otherwise abstract geopolitical dilemmas. By encouraging viewers to identify with the complex experiences of the men and women enlisted to fight in our names, such programs opened a space in the culture for a critique of war (if not necessarily militarism) to emerge.

It is no coincidence that both *M*A*S*H* and *China Beach* also embody the mid-1980s shift to more long-form story-telling mechanisms. Like other critically acclaimed shows of the era, these programs mixed episodic plots with open-ended serial story-arcs and allowed the characters to grow and change over time. They expected audiences to be familiar with the lives and backstories of the characters and to keep up with narrative developments without being cued. As Magda Yüksel and Colleen Kennedy-Karpat argue in chapter 15, such long-form story telling promotes ethical contemplation through its slow accumulation of detail and multi-perspectival narration. The "slow-drip" of the narrative, especially its focus on character development, invites viewers to identify with a range of differing points of view and to "immerse themselves in the virtual world of war" in a way that no self-contained film can achieve.[18] Viewers must "lean in" and draw their own conclusions from among the range of perspectives on display. And there is no clear or conclusive ideological outcome to this process. Viewers of *Generation Kill*, a putatively progressive text, might view it as a critique of war or a conservative reaffirmation of the necessity of military professionalism. Likewise, viewers of *JAG*, a supposedly conservative program (see chapter 13), might identify with the honor and integrity of the military life on display or embrace the program's frequent criticisms of military policy and procedure. The narrative openness is radical in the sense that it is reactive and unpredictable (like a "free radical" in chemistry), not in the sense that it promotes the overthrow of existing social structures.

Yet, TV's commercial logics have also imposed a retrospective character on such exercises in ethical contemplation. As an audience, we may be invited to scrutinize war and militarism, but such scrutiny almost always comes too late or is filtered through a displaced allegory that is easily missed. *M*A*S*H* may have been widely perceived as a commentary on Vietnam, but it was set in the earlier Korean context and only overlapped the Vietnam War by a year (the last combat troops had withdrawn from Vietnam by 1973). Viewers certainly could take the show at face value, as a commentary on the Korean conflict; they could also easily ignore its antiwar "edge" in favor of its otherwise conventional sitcom high jinx. As a

Introduction 7

displaced critique, *M*A*S*H* may actually have missed the mark more than it hit it (without deeper reception studies of the program, however, it is difficult to say). Other Vietnam-era war programs eschewed the complexities of that conflict in favor of a nostalgic re-working of the "Good War" (*Combat!*, *Rat Patrol*, *Garrison's Guerillas*). Likewise, *Hogan's Heroes* may have occasionally referenced Cold War politics, but it did so only covertly, by embracing spy craft, rather than war craft (or so Robert Shandley argues in chapter 4, this volume). Finally, although anthology series and episodic dramas sometimes addressed the Vietnam War, the episodes often went without sponsorship or were pushed to the margins of the TV schedule (as Scott Laderman argues in chapter 10, this volume). The expansion of the television universe has not put an end to these problems of displacement, either. While *Over There* and *Generation Kill* tackled the conflict in Iraq as it was happening, they were both consigned to cable where ideological buy-in was mitigated by a literal requirement that viewers pay to access the programs. Given their off-network locations, the reach of these programs was marginal at best.[19] The one exception to the retrospective rule might be *JAG*, which regularly addressed the stakes of the War on Terrorism in weekday primetime, but it has received virtually no critical attention because of its perceived lack of "quality."

What are we to make of this retrospective quality? And what does it suggest about television's unique relation to the processes of commemoration and memorialization? Are small screen military fictions doomed to be nostalgic and elegiac, mourning the loss of an innocence America never possessed? Or might they contribute to a process of working through that is essential to social discourse and societal progress? The chapters that follow take up these and other questions but—in true televisual fashion—offer no definitive conclusions. The answers are open to interpretation, and readers are invited to indulge in such ethical reflection alongside the producers, viewers, and other critics of these series.

Chapter Outline

American Militarism on the Small Screen is organized in a roughly chronological fashion, according to the wars depicted in the series. Thus, it begins with World War II and the Cold War, moves through the wars in Korea and Vietnam, addresses the transformations in the military that occurred during the 1990s, and ends with a consideration of the War on Terrorism. The volume begins with a military sitcom set in the aftermath of World War II. In "*Bilko's Bombers*: Anti-Militarism in the Era of the 'New Look,'" Lisa M. Mundey argues that *The Phil Silvers Show* (CBS, 1955–1959) reflects the persistence of anti-militarism among the American populace. As such, the program expressed and allayed anxieties related to the Eisenhower administration's "New Look" policy of nuclear build-up. In a period when audiences were viewing such dark silver-screen dramas as *From Here to Eternity*

8 *Anna Froula and Stacy Takacs*

(1953) and *The Caine Mutiny* (1954), *The Phil Silvers Show* harked back to a time when Americans were suspicious of permanent mobilization and the use of militarism as a political tool.

Analyzing the longest running war drama on American television, David P. Pierson's "The Long Fight: *Combat!* and the Generic Development of the TV War Drama Series" suggests *Combat!* (ABC, 1962–1967) established many of the conventions of the war drama series. Trading on nostalgia for World War II as a "just war" and speaking to viewers hungry for darker and more haunting portrayals of the foot soldier's experience, *Combat!* sought to distance viewers from the mythic portrayals of individual heroism seen in other war texts. The series' world-weary exploration of combat and its effects resonated with a post-Korean War American society acclimating both to traumatized veterans and to war without victory.

Sam Edwards' "*12 O'Clock High* and the Image of American Air Power, 1946–1967" examines the drama *12 O'Clock High* (ABC, 1962–1967) and its bolstering of American air power and the image of strategic bombing in an era of disillusionment. Edwards argues that, compared to contemporaneous satires like *Dr. Strangelove, Or How I Learned to Stop Worrying and Love the Bomb* (1964), *12 O'Clock High* was a throwback to more conventionally celebratory depictions of air power post-WWII. But, by 1962, it was already out of step with the cultural zeitgeist. Edwards suggests that the program's nostalgia for the decisiveness of World War II speaks to the confusion and dismay wrought by the Cold War conflicts in Korea and Vietnam. In that sense, *12 O'Clock High* reflects the growing disenchantment with the changes in geopolitical realities and alliances.

In "Nervous Laughter: *Hogan's Heroes* and the Vietnam War," Robert Shandley explores similar cultural shifts as the backdrop of *Hogan's Heroes* (CBS, 1965–1971). As the only series to run during the United States' major actions in Vietnam, this World War II comedy reflects changing social attitudes about war, militarism, and authoritarianism while displaying caution regarding Cold War themes. Through the trickster figure of Hogan and the parallels drawn between the German Army and the Pentagon war machine, the series creates a safe space in which viewers might ponder the dynamics of insurgent warfare in a Cold War context. It also hints at—but only hints at—the reasons one might choose not to fight.

A. Bowdoin Van Riper's "*Baa Baa Black Sheep* and the Last Stand of the WWII Drama" considers how *Baa Baa Black Sheep* (NBC 1976–1978) was a final chapter of the open-ended World War II dramas of combat. The show followed the exploits of a small Marine Corps fighter squadron in the Pacific Theater and mined Hollywood's "golden age" of war dramas for both footage and conventions. In this way, the series attempted to recast traditional narratives of military heroism in an era when many Americans had grown weary of mythic portrayals of war. Van Riper reads the series as the ultimate, highly polished version of Hollywood's cultural imagination of World War II.

Introduction   9

Twenty-three years later, *Band of Brothers* (HBO, 2001) sought to capitalize on the nostalgic desire to memorialize the "Greatest Generation" before they disappeared. In "A Waltz with and for the Greatest Generation: Music in *Band of Brothers* (2001)," Todd Decker reads the show through its innovative yet sentimental waltzing score. Its use of a specific musical meter and overall soundscape, Decker argues, builds emotional attachments between the viewers and the characters and helps to bridge the gap between the generations. Broadcast shortly after 9/11, the program could not help but comment on the imminent deployment of US soldiers abroad.

In "The American Forces Korea Network: 'Bringing Troops a Touch of Home'" Sueyoung Park-Primiano shifts the focus from American shows created and broadcast for Americans domestically to the Armed Forces Korea Network (AFKN), which disseminated US television to troops stationed in South Korea (where it generated a large "shadow audience" of Korean citizens, as well). Conceived as a means to boost morale and combat homesickness, the network broadcast such contemporary fare as *The Adventures of Ozzie and Harriet* (ABC, 1952–1966) and *What's My Line?* (CBS, 1950–1967) and provided strategic messaging to address local concerns about the presence of US military bases. This chapter should be viewed as a complement to the others in its attention to military-media relations at the distribution level, not just at the level of program production.

The next two chapters tackle the iconic military satire *M*A*S*H* and speak to different aspects of its anti-war thematics. Kelly J. W. Brown's "'Everybody Here Is Crazy': Images of the Disabled on Television's *M*A*S*H*" focuses on the compassionate ways that the series treated both physically and psychologically debilitating traumas. Rejecting prevalent stereotypes of disability, *M*A*S*H* chose to emphasize the long-term effects of war and injury. In that way, the program provided insight into the realities of traumatic injury and promoted viewer empathy for those disabled—whether physically or psychologically—by war and other traumas. In "Drinking the War Away: Televisual Insobriety and the Meanings of Alcohol in *M*A*S*H*," David Scott Diffrient turns to the 4077th Mobile Army Surgical Hospital staff's use of self-medication to mitigate the traumas and despair of war. This chapter highlights the contradictory messages and ritualistic meanings of alcohol in the series and argues that *M*A*S*H*'s nuanced "alcoholic imaginary" reflects the changing social attitudes about alcohol consumption but does so in a way that is mindful of the challenges that members of the armed forces must endure. Taken together, these two essays draw attention to oft-neglected aspects of the war narrative and show how TV's long-form story-telling structure may be used to inject subtlety and complexity into the cultural imagination of war.

Scott Laderman's "Small-Screen Insurgency: Entertainment Television, the Vietnamese Revolution, and the Cold War, 1953–1967" addresses the gap in critical scholarship about fictional television's wartime treatment of the controversial war in Vietnam. This chapter analyzes the few anthology

10 *Anna Froula and Stacy Takacs*

series that made the rare move of engaging the conflict—such as *Biff Baker, USA* (CBS, 1952–1953), *Navy Log* (CBS, 1955–1956; ABC, 1956–1958), and *Alcoa Premiere* (ABC, 1961–1963). Laderman argues that these series are important primary documents that, if nothing else, reveal how the country's most popular medium was imagining US involvement in Vietnam in the early days of the conflict.

In "*China Beach* and the Good Series Death," Christine Becker discusses one of the two prime-time series (thus far) to reflect directly on the conflict in Vietnam in the wake of the United States' defeat. In contrast to *Tour of Duty* (CBS, 1987–1990), which was a fairly straightforward combat series, aligned with the revisionary cultural politics of the Reagan era, *China Beach* (CBS 1987–1991) focused on the service of military women and foregrounded themes of trauma and loss. Indeed, as Becker shows, the program regularly dealt with issues of memory and memorialization in a complex way and never more so than in its final season. Utilizing a frame narrative and frequent temporal shifts, the final season commemorates, without simplistically celebrating, the experiences of Vietnam veterans. In that way, it achieved a "good death" for both the characters and the spectators.

After the Vietnam conflict, and the social tumult it created, political elites in the US decided to end the draft and professionalize the military. To entice recruits, the military began advertising advanced training and educational benefits, and it opened a range of new opportunities to women interested in serving. The next two chapters address some of the transformations wrought by these policy shifts. Kathleen Kennedy's chapter, "Imagining the New Military of the 1990s in *Babylon 5*'s Future Wars," explores the changing landscape of sex and sexuality in the US military through allegory. Although it was a science fiction fantasy series, writes Kennedy, *Babylon 5* (PTEN/TNT, 1994–1998) showed how the introduction of powerful women and queer characters might influence future wars. By and large, it relieved the audience's anxieties by promising that such soldiers would uphold conventional military values. Anticipating changes that would not take place for two decades, the show offered nuanced characters that could entertain both resistance to and acceptance of sexual difference in the military.

Stacy Takacs' "*JAG*, Melodrama, and Militarism" focuses on the long-running series *JAG* (NBC, 1995–1996; CBS, 1997–2005) and its melodramatic moral calculus. Drawing inspiration and visuals from classic Hollywood war films, Takacs writes, *JAG* encourages viewers to *feel* for service members and equates war and militarism with moral order, although without serving partisan ideological aims. Nonetheless, its narrative structures of good and evil, problem and solution, and peril and security compel its audience to support the increased militarization of the United States. During a time of relative peace (the 1990s), the series sustained popular faith in the soldier-hero and the military values he—and now she—represents.

Unlike the successful *JAG*, which lasted 10 seasons and spawned many spin-offs, other military television shows—and most Hollywood war films—broadcast during the War on Terror have struggled to gain traction with audiences already weary of the wars in Afghanistan and Iraq. As Anna Froula argues in "Political Amnesia over Here and Imperial Spectacle *Over There*," the first series to directly address a war as it was happening, *Over There* (F/X, 2005), over-relied on Vietnam-era conventions and was canceled after only one season. It merits analysis, however, as a primary document revealing national fantasies about the face of the United States at war and its attendant controversies and tragedies, many of which she details in the chapter.

Two years after *Over There*, HBO debuted its own Iraq War drama, which also had trouble drawing a large audience at the time (although it has since done well in DVD and online sales). Magdalena Yüksel and Colleen Kennedy-Karpat's "*Generation Kill* and the New Screen Combat" argues that the miniseries cultivated an "ethos of skepticism" by challenging many of the generic conventions of the war story. *Generation Kill*, they argue, deploys political humor and careful attention to the deaths of civilians to update the combat series for the twenty-first century. Using its ensemble cast to complicate the hero-narrative, the miniseries offers multiple perspectives on the war and studiously refuses to choose sides. The result, the authors argue, is a much more complex and multivalent depiction of war and militarism.

Finally, in "'Don't Ask, Don't Tell' and Its Repeal in Showtime's *The L Word* and Lifetime's *Army Wives*," Liora Elias analyzes two rare instances of military series that explore the lives of gay and lesbian soldiers. While *The L Word* depicts the struggles of a lesbian soldier under the ban and moderately develops the depiction of lesbian identity on television, *Army Wives* presents an idealized vision of lesbian soldiering and service after the ban was repealed. Yet these representations, Elias argues, are still overly limited in their depiction of the difficulties experienced by real-life gay and lesbian soldiers. As such, they contribute to a post-gay politics of homonormativity, which seeks only to assimilate gays and lesbians into social institutions, like the military, rather than change those institutions.

Collectively, these chapters and their intersections reveal the multiple ways entertainment television has grappled with and continues to imagine the face of American militarism. Addressing issues of identity, social stratification, and geopolitical conflict, these series have contributed to the collective cultural imagination of war, but not always in predictable ways. Like war films, they often give us a glimpse of what we *hope* war looks like. They offer shining spectacles of service and heroism, and they continue to connect war and militarism with positive values, like duty, honor, and self-sacrifice. In that sense, they, too, produce a "myopic view of the past" that provides "justification for wars in the present."[20] However, the repetitive, slow-burn nature of television series production, along with the medium's inherent intertextuality, prolongs and complicates the engagement with war, perhaps long enough to foster contradictions, which viewers must then resolve for

12 *Anna Froula and Stacy Takacs*

themselves. As Horace Newcomb and Paul Hirsch argued long ago, television is a meaning-producing machine whose multiplicity may be its greatest strength. Its insatiable need for "more" allows the medium to serve as an open-ended "cultural forum" within which questions about the social order are regularly raised but rarely definitively answered.[21] In regard to the presentation of war and militarism, we can see that there is no single way of depicting the "war story" or the "military message" on TV. It is up to the viewers to decipher these texts and to place them in their cultural, social, and historical contexts. In a similar fashion, this volume is designed to be a conversation starter, and we hope the enclosed essays will inspire a wealth of new research on the subject.

Notes

1. Kenneth Bilby, *The General: David Sarnoff and the Rise of the Communications Industry* (New York: Harper & Row, 1986), 42–47.
2. On these dynamics, see Susan Douglas, *Inventing American Broadcasting, 1899–1922* (Baltimore: Johns Hopkins University Press, 1987); Michele Hilmes, *Radio Voices: American Broadcasting, 1922–1952* (Minneapolis, MN: University of Minnesota Press, 1997); J. Fred MacDonald, *Television and the Red Menace: The Video Road to Vietnam* (New York: Praeger, 1985).
3. Nine Nobel Peace laureates called on NBC to cancel the reality show, describing it as an effort to "sanitize war by likening it to an athletic competition" and arguing that it "continues and expands on an inglorious tradition of glorifying war and armed violence." See Mario Anzuoni, "Nobel Laureates Call for End to TV's *Stars Earn Stripes*," *Reuters*, August 13, 2012, http://www.reuters.com/article/2012/08/14/entertainment-us-starsearnstripes-idUSBRE87C11020120814. Chris Kyle with Scott McEwen and Jim DeFelice, *American Sniper: The Autobiography of the Most Lethal Sniper in US Military History* (New York: Harper, 2012).
4. To be fair, there have been several significant investigations of war on US television, but they have largely taken the form of stand-alone articles or chapters in anthologies devoted mostly to film. See, for example, J. Fred MacDonald, "The Cold War as Entertainment in 'Fifties Television," *Journal of Popular Film* 7, no. 1 (1978); Daniel Miller, "Prime Time's *Tour of Duty*," in *Inventing Vietnam: The War in Film and Television*, ed. Michael A. Anderregg (Philadelphia, PA: Temple Univ. Press, 1991); Peter C. Rollins, "Victory at Sea: Cold War Epic," in *Television Histories: Shaping Collective Memory in the Media Age*, ed. Gary R. Edgerton and Peter C. Rollins (Lexington, KY: University Press of Kentucky, 2001); Sasha Torres, "War and Remembrance: Televisual Narrative, National Memory, and China Beach," *Camera Obscura* 11–12, no. 33–34 (1994–1995); Carolyn Reed Vartanian, "Women Next Door to War: *China Beach*," in *Inventing Vietnam: The War in Film and Television*, ed. Michael A. Anderregg (Philadelphia, PA: Temple Univ. Press, 1991); Rick Worland, "The Other Living-Room War: Prime Time Combat Series, 1962–1975," *Journal of Film and Video* 50, no. 3 (1988); "Sign-Posts up Ahead: The Twilight Zone, the Outer Limits, and TV Political Fantasy 1959–1965," *Science-Fiction Studies* 23, no. 1 (1996). The big exceptions here are MacDonald, *Television and the Red Menace: The Video Road to Vietnam*; Marita Sturken, *Tangled Memories: The Vietnam*

War, the Aids Epidemic, and the Politics of Remembering (Berkley, CA: Univ. of California Press, 1997), and Stacy Takacs, *Terrorism TV: Popular Entertainment in Post-9/11 America* (Lawrence, KS: University Press of Kansas, 2012).

5. J. David Slocum, "General Introduction: Seeing through American War Cinema," in *Hollywood and War: The Film Reader*, ed. J. David Slocum (New York: Routledge, 2006), 8.

6. Jeanine Basinger, *The World War II Combat Film, Anatomy of a Genre* (New York: Columbia University Press, 1986).

7. Ibid., 65–75.

8. Guy Westwell, *War Cinema: Hollywood on the Front Line* (New York: Wallflower, 2006), 115.

9. Ibid., 113.

10. Ibid., 110.

11. Ibid., 109.

12. Ibid., 43.

13. Chapter 5, this volume, 78.

14. Although new technologies have fragmented the mass audience and enabled new production models, especially on premium cable and sell-through outlets like Netflix, the network model of selling audiences to advertisers still drives most of the industry.

15. Michael Z. Newman, "From Beats to Arcs: Toward a Poetics of Television Narrative," *Velvet Light Trap* 58 (2006).

16. On the ideological role of ethnic family sitcoms vis-à-vis consumerism, see George Lipsitz, *Time Passages: Collective Memory and American Popular Culture* (Minneapolis, MN: Univ. of Minnesota Press, 1990), especially chapter 3.

17. Todd Gitlin, *Inside Prime Time* (Berkeley, CA: University of California Press, 2000 [1983]). See also, Aniko Bodroghkozy, *Groove Tube: Sixties Television and the Youth Rebellion* (Durham, NC: Duke University Press, 2001).

18. Chapter 15, this volume, 253.

19. For its 13-episode run, *Over There* averaged only 1.2 million viewers while *Generation Kill* averaged 1 to 1.3 million for its seven episodes. See "FX Will Not Renew *Over There* for a Second Season," *The Futon Critic*, November 1, 2005, http://www.thefutoncritic.com/news/2005/11/01/fx-will-not-renew-over-there-for-a-second-season-based-on-the-series-ratings-performance-over-its-13-epsiode-run—19673/20051101fx01/#dVvDt8swPQ5mQ61C.99 and "HBO's *Generation Kill* Can't Touch *John Adams*," *TV by the Numbers*, July 16, 2008, http://tvbythenumbers.zap2it.com/2008/07/16/hbos-generation-kill-cant-touch-john-adams/4451/.

20. Westwell, *War Cinema*, 115.

21. Horace Newcomb and Paul M. Hirsch, "Television as a Cultural Forum," in *Television: The Critical View*, ed. Horace Newcombe (New York: Oxford UP, 2000).

Part I

World War II on the Small Screen

1 "Bilko's Bombers"

Anti-Militarism in the Era of the "New Look"

Lisa M. Mundey

As the Army platoon shuffled into their barracks to change out of their baseball uniforms and back into fatigues, Master Sergeant Ernest G. Bilko (Phil Silvers) poured out his disapproval. "There they are, 'Bilko's Bombers.' Oh, this is a proud day," he declares sarcastically, "Twenty-four to nothin'! Say, we're lucky at that. The score could have been much worse. Fortunately, they called the game at the end of the fifth inning! Bilko's Bombers?" the master sergeant questions incredulously. "Bilko's Misguided Missiles! This is a day that will live in infamy," Bilko pronounces, echoing the famous words President Franklin D. Roosevelt uttered after the December 7, 1941, Japanese attack on Pearl Harbor. While the soldiers offer excuses for their poor performance, Bilko cannot help but focus on his own reputation: "Well, it's probably all over the post by now. Motor Platoon nothing, WAC [Women's Army Corps] typists twenty-four!" The men lost to the women soldiers at baseball! How could Bilko survive the humiliation? And more importantly, how could he get his men to improve enough to make good on the $50 bet he placed on the next game against fellow male soldiers?[1]

The Phil Silvers Show (CBS, 1955–1959) follows the exploits of the clever, fast-talking, con-artist Master Sergeant Bilko. As a career noncommissioned officer (NCO) who finds a home in the peacetime Army in command of a motor platoon at fictional Fort Baxter, Kansas, Bilko launches countless get-rich-quick plans, which invariably fall apart. Whereas circumstances often turn against Bilko and his plans, his own conscience won't let him go too far either. Bilko's right-hand men are Corporals Henshaw (Allan Melvin) and Barbella (Harvey Lembeck), who help run Bilko's schemes and keep the motor platoon running. Often Bilko's fellow master sergeants, Sowici (Harry Clark), Ritzik (Joe E. Ross), Grover (Jimmy Little), and Pendleton (Ned Glass) fall victim to his plots. Bilko easily manipulates post commander Colonel Hall (Paul Ford) in pursuit of his schemes, and his flattery has Mrs. Nell Hall (Hope Sansberry), the colonel's wife, wrapped around his finger. Bilko's platoon is rounded out by Privates Paparelli (Billy Sands), Zimmerman (Mickey Freeman), and Doberman (Maurice Gosfield).[2] Often referred to as *Sergeant Bilko* after its lead character, *The Phil Silvers Show* inaugurated a nearly 30-year run of military television comedies, which more often than not used the military as a vehicle for laughs.

18   *Lisa M. Mundey*

Notably, the series regularly included women and African-American characters. WAC Master Sergeant Joan Hogan (Elisabeth Fraser) appeared as recurring character, and African-American soldiers routinely appeared in the platoon, as WACs and even as a master sergeant. These characters reflected the reality that the military did include women and had integrated racially; nonetheless, it was rare to see any black characters on television in the 1950s. Some of the black soldiers had speaking parts as well. Indeed, the integration of the series "offended certain Southern stations carrying the program," and one advertiser "requested that the black actors be removed."[3] To the show's credit, the producers and lead actor refused to do so, and the black characters remained (albeit in marginal roles).[4]

The Phil Silvers Show reflects a continuation of America's anti-militarist tradition by refusing to take the regular military seriously, undermining authority, portraying part-time citizen-soldiers as more effective than active-duty regulars and depicting the uneasy relationship between regulars and civilians. There is also an occasional episode that features the "battle of the sexes" between the male soldiers and female WACs. Bilko runs the platoon in rather unmilitary ways and takes advantage of the bureaucracy to further his schemes at every chance. Bilko also tries to fleece his soldiers to fund his gambling. The series focuses on enlisted personnel rather than officers, giving Americans an anti-authoritarian and "working-class" view of the Army. Although Bilko's rank gave him power within the platoon, he regularly turned the tables on all the authority figures on post, particularly by manipulating the post commander. Fictional Ft. Baxter echoes the real-life complications of having a regular garrison set among a civilian population, where the civilians love having the economic boost of an Army post but do not much like soldiers hanging around.

The Phil Silvers Show originated out of a performance by Silvers on February 6, 1954, for a live audience that included President Dwight Eisenhower, Vice President Richard Nixon, and CBS vice-president for pro-gramming, Hubbell Robinson. After witnessing Silvers' quick wit, Robinson paired the actor with Nat Hiken, a well-established writer and producer who had worked with radio comedian Fred Allen, the early TV star Milton Berle, and Martha Raye on her variety show. After brainstorming, Silvers initially rejected the idea of playing an Army con artist, thinking it was too close to material already performed by Bud Abbott and Lou Costello in their comedy film *Buck Privates* (1941). Although Hiken and Silvers presented the network with several options, including Silvers as a baseball manager or stockbroker, CBS executives chose the Army premise.[5]

CBS's selection of a military comedy stood in contrast with what American audiences were seeing on the silver screen. By 1955, the most popular military movies were rather dark dramas, including *From Here to Eternity* (1953), where fellow soldiers mistreat the main character who is killed by friendly fire at the end; *The Caine Mutiny* (1954), about a para-noid captain whose crew takes control of the ship and faces a court martial for doing so; and *The Bridges at Toko-Ri* (1954), a Korean War film that questions the war and ends with the senseless death of the protagonist and beloved supporting characters.[6] Nevertheless, a comedy series certainly fit with the more upbeat and popular television variety programs like *The Jackie Gleason Show* (CBS, 1952–1959) and other sitcoms, such as *I Love Lucy* (CBS, 1951–1957). Of course, there was always the appeal of the built-in audience of veterans, reservists, National Guardsmen, and active duty service personnel.[7]

Hiken drew on his own military experience as well as entertainment industry shenanigans for the comedy premises for the new show. Inducted into the Army Air Forces in September 1943, Hiken served as a publicist for the service during World War II.[8] His unconventional wartime service did not even require him to leave New York City, where he received permission to continue writing for Fred Allen. As Hiken's biographer, David Everitt, explains, "The absurdity of his distinctly unmilitary military service was not lost on Nat."[9]

Hiken created a fictitious Army post in Kansas named Ft. Baxter, based, in part, on Ft. Dix, New Jersey.[10] The show's sets were apparently so realistic that actor Mickey Freeman, who played Private Zimmerman, recalled "you would often find an actor taking a nap in one of the bunks."[11] Hiken did not want his Ft. Baxter to be perfect, however, so he insisted that the soldiers appear disheveled.[12] No one encapsulated the sad sack soldier more than Private Duane Doberman. As Freeman describes him, Doberman was "a loser, a slovenly fat man who shuffled rather than walked, a man who mumbled rather than talked."[13] Doberman was nearly as popular as Bilko, and actor Maurice Gosfield received fan mail to rival that of Phil Silvers.[14]

Like *I Love Lucy*, *The Phil Silvers Show* was filmed initially in front of a live studio audience. The stress of recording live strained the crew, so they shifted to a different technique to get real audience reactions. Crew members took two episodes of the program at a time to an Army post, where "the projectionist would show the episodes while specially placed microphones would pick up the soldiers' responses." The laughter on the soundtrack came from soldiers themselves. In fact, "sometimes there was so much laughter that canned material had to be substituted so that the dialogue would not be drowned out."[15] The series clearly resonated with the built-in audience of GIs, and it turned out to be just as funny for civilians.

Audience reaction, particularly with respect to viewership, indicates whether a series appeals to the cultural sensibilities of a broad audience, and this series proved popular with everyone. *The Phil Silvers Show* shot up the television rating charts. Around 23 million Americans tuned in to watch the show each week, "attracting legions of fans from every demographic group including women and children."[16] Daniel Czitrom asserts that the show "had universal appeal because everyone could identify with the burlesque of authority, particularly in that most disciplined of institutions, the army" and that audiences enjoyed Bilko's attempts "at beating authority in

20   *Lisa M. Mundey*

all its guises."[17] According to Edward Montagne, who helped produce the series, President Eisenhower, a professional soldier who had been the actual Supreme Allied Commander of the Allied forces during World War II, was a fan of the show. Professional media reviewers also responded favorably, including Jack Gould from *The New York Times*. The show even found an appreciative audience in Great Britain.[18]

Individual opinions concerning *The Phil Silvers Show* ranged from positive comments about "funny Army life" to complaints about the gambling and exploitation of the soldiers. Some veterans in the audience grumbled that the depiction of the Army was unrealistic.[19] While most of the soldiers who were recorded on the laugh track clearly enjoyed the humor, one officer denounced Bilko as "a four-flusher, a sharpie, a cad who exploits an oafish colonel and an element of tramps, no-goods, and semi-criminals doing nothing all day."[20] Given that most men in the Army were short-time enlistees or draftees, they clearly brought civilian attitudes with them into the service. Nonetheless, one would expect that some military professionals wanted to see the services respected, not spoofed, and so disliked the comedy. There were similar reactions of military professionals to the popular newspaper comic strip *Beetle Bailey* (Mort Walker, 1950-present) and comic strip and comic book *Sad Sack* (created by George Baker, in newspaper syndication 1944–1957), which also regularly poked fun at the regular Army.[21]

Whereas high audience ratings assured the continuation of *The Phil Silvers Show* beyond a single season, the industry also showered the series with honors. In 1955, Phil Silvers won Emmys for best actor and best comedian, and Nat Hiken picked up awards for best comedy series, best director, and, with his co-authors, best writing. Lightning struck again as *The Phil Silvers Show* won best series and best comedy writing at both the 1956 and 1957 Emmy Awards. In 1956, Silvers and Ford each received a nomination for "best comedian and best supporting actor, respectively," while Gosfield was nominated for best supporting actor for the 1958–1959 season.[22]

Facing burnout, series creator Nat Hiken left *The Phil Silvers Show* in May 1957. The program largely retained its signature comedy after Hiken's departure and aired for two additional years, wrapping up on June 17, 1959. Although there had been a slight dip in the show's ratings, the reason the series ended had to do with issues of sponsorship.[23] Because "sponsors and shows were closely coupled in the public's mind," explains Everitt, no other company wanted to compete with sponsor Camel cigarettes to help underwrite the series. Unfortunately for the cast, Camel did not want to cover the entire cost of the show either, so the network canceled it.[24]

The Phil Silvers Show aired during a military build-up in the United States, which deviated from traditional American defense policy limiting the size of the active duty force during peacetime. During the 1950s, Americans believed there was a clear and present danger of international Communism and feared an atomic war with the Soviet Union. Given these perceived threats, Americans supported military preparedness. When Eisenhower assumed office in 1953, he worried that a large military force structure would stress the American economy but also recognized the necessity of having a credible deterrent. As a result, his "New Look" policy somewhat reduced the size of active-duty forces, increased the part-time citizen-soldier reserves, and relied more heavily on technology, particularly nuclear weapons to deter potential enemies. The United States invested in missile technology and strategic bombers for the Air Force as well as nuclear weapons, submarines, and aircraft carriers for the Navy.[25]

Despite this peacetime military build-up, often associated with militaristic countries, American culture did not meet the typical definition of militarism: valuing the military and its ideals of discipline, obedience, hierarchy, and regimentation above civilian society and democratic principles. It forced scholars such as Michael Sherry to label what was happening in Cold War America as "militarization" instead of "militarism," and Christian Appy dubbed it "sentimental militarism."[26] Even if militarism happened through policy, Americans did not accept it as part of their identity. Anti-militarism is not the same as being anti-military. Anti-militarists understand that a professional military force is essential to fight wars of necessity. During peacetime, however, they believed the military ought to be kept as small as possible so as not to threaten the civil liberties of the population or become a drain on the economy. At all times, the military must remain firmly under civilian control. Anti-militarists value democracy, volunteering, and independent thought; they are not necessarily pacifists.[27]

Although most Americans supported military preparedness, plenty of civilians and the many veterans in society—from World War II, the Korean War, and the peacetime draft—presented a healthy criticism of the military hierarchy, authority, and regimentation. The harsh discipline and caste distinctions between officers and enlisted in the World War II-era military garnered such criticism from veterans that Congress reformed everything from military customs and courtesies to military justice and pay.[28] *New York Times* military correspondent Hanson Baldwin summed up the public view of the military in the early 1950s as "one of slightly patronizing contempt."[29] Young men during the 1950s wanted to avoid military service and disliked the peacetime draft as an unwelcome diversion from their civilian career plans.[30] In this light, it makes sense that *The Phil Silvers Show* played up the anti-militarism of the culture for laughs. The series pokes fun at the regular military and its bureaucracy and hierarchical rank structure. It depicts regulars as incompetent and citizen-soldiers as the truly effective soldiers. It also shows how civilians are not quite comfortable with soldiers in their midst.

Rather than taking the regular Army seriously, countless episodes of *The Phil Silvers Show* get laughs by demonstrating the *un*military nature of how Bilko manages his platoon. Audiences learn that part of the reason Bilko's motor platoon ran smoothly was that he regularly bypassed Army regulations. He traded jeep tires with the local fueling station in order to get parts and grease for the vehicles. When a temporary master sergeant tries to direct the

22   *Lisa M. Mundey*

motor pool according to Army regulations—that is, filing requisitions for equipment—all the vehicles break down while waiting for parts.[31] Of course, Bilko also used the motor pool as his personal auto fleet, entering a Sherman tank in the local stock car race, for example, or stranding Colonel Hall without a staff car so he could take out a platinum blond for a date as he did in "The Transfer."[32]

Unlike what a proper platoon leader ought to do, Bilko tries constantly to fleece his soldiers for money to fund his gambling. A permanent fixture of the set is the bulletin board, which boasts a variety of fund-raising events such as raffles, a football pool, and tickets to the platoon picnic. In "The Recruits," Bilko tries to sell platoon stationary to the soldiers. He rents out his personal vehicle for 10 cents a mile. On countless episodes, there are tickets to some dance, whether a "Welcome Rookies" dance or a dance to "Let Bygones Be Bygones" by celebrating Revolutionary War traitor Benedict Arnold's birthday in "The Transfer." Bilko even managed to sell furlough insurance![33]

On occasion, even Colonel Hall appreciated Bilko's unmilitary methods. In "The Transfer," Bilko's replacement in the motor pool completed an excessive 19 inventories in one month and so swamped Hall with work that he missed dinner with his wife each evening. He actually wanted Bilko back![34] In "The Centennial," when the post's new special service officer, Lieutenant Barry Parker (Al Checco), disbanded all the card games on post—including Colonel Hall's—the post commander supported Bilko's bid to run him out. What comes next is the celebration of Ft. Baxter's "centennial" in the form of a dramatization of key events in the post's history. Both Bilko and Hall know the post's storied past is more embarrassing than heroic, and, with his career riding on a successful show, Parker finally gives up and leaves. "Bilko, you are a conniver, a sharpster, and an operator," Hall lectures sternly, "and sometimes you're almost a blessing," he finishes with a smile.[35] Even the colonel recognizes that some military problems could not be easily solved through proper channels. Sometimes the unmilitary run-around is necessary.

The Phil Silvers Show often undermines military hierarchy and authority. It is significant that it was Master Sergeant Ernest Bilko that really ran Ft. Baxter rather than its actual commanding officer, a point Hall articulated clearly in the episode "Bivouac." The colonel admitted, "for the past eight years I've been laboring under the delusion that I run this post." Shaking his head, he laments, "It's time to face facts: you, Sergeant Bilko, you run this post." Bilko replies, "Oh, sir, I couldn't do it without your cooperation!"[36] Having a noncommissioned officer run circles around the highest-ranking officer on post subverts the very hierarchy of the armed forces. In reality, a motor pool master sergeant would not have ready access to or frequent communications with a post commander, much less be able to manipulate him as Bilko does on the show.

Even as a lowly private, Bilko could turn the tables on all the authority figures on post. In "Army Memoirs" Colonel Hall reduced Bilko's rank as

"*Bilko's Bombers*" 23

punishment. The three other master sergeants were on report for unmilitary behavior: Andy Pendleton, the quartermaster, for requisitioning Air Force jackets; Steve Grover, in Signal Corps, for having a direct phone line to horse races; and Stanley Sowici, the mess sergeant, for unsanitary conditions. Hall takes Bilko's stripes and busts him down to private, but Bilko brags that he will have his stripes back within six hours. He accomplishes this goal by tricking every one of the NCOs into revealing an embarrassing moment that Bilko could then use for blackmail. For instance, Bilko learns that Pendleton outfitted troops going to Africa in World War II with snowshoes and fur coats because he thought they were going to Alaska. One by one, Bilko gets the dirt on all the master sergeants and even on the colonel himself. At "six hours on the nose," Bilko successfully gets his stripes back, demonstrating that he can run circles around authority figures no matter what rank.[37]

Historically, anti-militarists prefer citizen-soldiers to regulars as a way to safeguard the citizens' civil liberties. At the same time, one also expects that full-time active duty soldiers would be more effective than the part-time ones, given that it is their full-time job to train and prepare for war. *The Phil Silvers Show* both pokes fun at the regulars and reinforces the preferred position of the citizen-soldier in America's democracy in the episode "War Games." The audience learns early in the episode that the regular Army units at Ft. Baxter always lose to the Kansas National Guard during the annual war games exercise. Given Bilko's unmilitary nature, he wants nothing to do with the rough life of actually soldiering in the field, so he fakes a leg injury to get out of his platoon's bivouac. To occupy Bilko on post, Colonel Hall assigns him a rookie platoon to train. Bilko easily outmaneuvers the authority of the commanding officer by field-promoting a rookie to sergeant and sits back while the platoon drills itself. To Bilko's horror, the rookies manage to become the top-ranked platoon and are ordered to lead the war games exercise against the Kansas National Guard. Not only does Bilko not want to participate in the war games, he actually needs to get out of the exercise so he can be the best man at a wedding in town. Bilko goes AWOL (away without leave) during the field maneuver, unbeknownst to the platoon. Unfortunately for Bilko, the platoon follows him thinking he is leading the charge. Because the platoon is heading the maneuvers, and the platoon is following Bilko, all Army units converge first at Nick's Diner, then at the flower shop, and eventually at the wedding. There the active-duty troops "capture" the National Guard's Captain Bigelow, the father of the bride. Miscommunication, not skill, gives the regulars their first win against the part-time citizen-soldiers, both poking fun at the peacetime active duty force and elevating the position of the citizen-soldier in American culture.[38]

In a democracy, there is a tension between the active-duty military force and the civilian population. In the United States, civilians have historically looked down upon the regulars and perceived soldiers as joining the Army because they could not be successful as civilians. At the same time, civilian communities often relied on military posts as a source of federal funding

24   *Lisa M. Mundey*

and economic development.[39] The theme that civilians find regulars undesirable and the theme that civilians like to profit from the military are both played for laughs in the episode "Empty Store." The premise of the story is a scheme by Bilko played out on his fellow master sergeants. A broke Bilko had been frozen out of the master sergeants' poker games. Bilko's attempts at raising a new bankroll to get into the game by selling three-dollar tickets to a dance to honor Chester Arthur have fallen flat with the platoon, as they recognize it as a ploy to get their cash. So, Bilko plans a scam on the noncommissioned officers by renting out an empty storefront in town. The other NCOs are convinced Bilko has a plan for the storefront despite Bilko's continued protestations that it is simply an empty store.[40]

Bilko's lease of the storefront needs to be countersigned by Colonel Hall, so the post commander comes face-to-face with the mayor of Roseville, the town outside Ft. Baxter. Hall remarks that "the town has continually slammed doors in the face of Ft. Baxter soldiers," a historically accurate occurrence in anti-militaristic America. Indeed, the mayor is alarmed that "hundreds of soldiers are milling around that empty store" and insists that only the owner of the store can be on the premises, not the servicemen. Soldiers are unwelcome, perhaps even perceived as threatening to the civilians of Roseville. The mayor finally relents when another Roseville businessman comes in to rent the adjoining storefront for an ice cream parlor to take advantage of the servicemen's presence. At this point, Hall sarcastically remarks, "oh, now you like soldiers" when there is profit to be made from them.[41] Whereas the whole skit was written for laughs, it actually contains a fairly accurate portrayal of the relationship between military posts and their surrounding communities: soldiers are often unwelcome, but the posts are good for the local economy.

As the episode "The Reunion" illustrates, civilian life is still more highly valued and preferred than a military career in American culture, even a decade into the Cold War. Describing his World War II combat experience to his sidekicks, Bilko explains, "We were pinned down on a beach in the Marianas, and we swore that if we ever got out of it alive we were gonna meet ten years from that day for the biggest, fanciest banquet at the Waldorf Astoria." Although initially excited to appear in uniform with his master sergeant's stripes, Bilko immediately feels unaccomplished next to what his squad has done with their postwar civilian careers. An ex-truck driver now operates his own trucking company, while a former waiter owns 200 restaurants. Another one works for a big cotton mill, whereas a fourth serves as the chairman of the board of an insurance company. Embarrassed that he is still in the service, Bilko quickly fabricates a story that he is a big government contractor. In the end, he admits that he is still in the Army. Given that the men know and like Bilko and that they are veterans themselves, they embrace Bilko's choice and promptly start reenacting the big battle in the hotel dining room, using the tables and chairs for cover.[42] Thanks to their previous relationship with him, Bilko's veteran buddies can accept his decision to remain in the active duty force, even as they have comfortably moved into civilian lives and careers.

Indeed, with so many veterans in postwar American society, there came some awkward moments when a serviceman's military rank and civilian job were not equivalent. *The Phil Silvers Show* played this for laughs, too, in "The Reunion." As an Army regular, Bilko initially felt pride at achieving the rank of master sergeant. He strode around with his stripes at the hotel, but he soon learned that the hotel valet had been a lieutenant during World War II. Bilko immediately starts calling him "sir." The civilian world had turned the rank hierarchy upside down where lieutenants were now valets and enlisted soldiers had become owners of large companies. The award-winning film *The Best Years of Our Lives* (1946) had made the very same point a decade earlier with a more serious and dramatic tone. In this film, the prosperous upper-class banker had been a sergeant in the Army, and the guy from the other side of the tracks had risen to the rank of captain in the US Army Air Force. Although captain is a respectable rank in the military, the character could not find equivalent employment as a civilian and ended up in his old job as a lowly soda jerk. His military experience had not initially helped him in civilian life.[43] By the time *The Phil Silvers Show* aired in 1955, World War II veterans largely had become successful civilians, and postwar fears of a return to the Great Depression instead turned into abundance and prosperity for many Americans.

Thanks to the 1948 Women's Armed Services Integration Act, women served in the active duty military forces, which led to a variety of supporting WAC characters on *The Phil Silvers Show*. With Master Sergeant Joan Hogan, the series highlighted a popular "battle of the sexes" theme between her and Bilko, which was "the established frame for representing military women in the postwar period."[44] Both in real life and in popular culture, women's presence in the military proved disruptive to men, and they occupied a contradictory space where they were seen as not fully feminine and not fully soldiers either.[45] Yvonne Tasker argues that Hogan is a "female version of Bilko," yet, though she is as clever and skilled as Bilko, Hogan does not scheme and run cons like he does.[46] Ultimately, the *Phil Silvers Show* alleviated the ambivalence toward women in uniform by making Hogan Bilko's girlfriend.

Hogan was initially introduced as Bilko's rival and witty match in the episode "The WAC."[47] The premise of the story is that the post commander needs a master sergeant to volunteer to check doors around post, and this extra duty comes with the use of a jeep. Intensely averse to walking and marching around post, Bilko wants to be the one to get it. Fortunately for him, the other NCOs, who have not bothered to learn all the Army abbreviations, do not realize a jeep comes with the extra duty. Bilko outsmarts all but a mysterious Master Sergeant Hogan, new to Ft. Baxter. Assuming that the new NCO must be male, Bilko prepares to schmooze the new serviceman with a welcome party, a cake, and a date. Sweet, blond, Southern

26   Lisa M. Mundey

Joan Hogan appears instead, and she is not so easily bamboozled. More importantly, she knows that a jeep is at stake, so the war is on between the master sergeants—and between man and woman.

Hogan is as cunning as Bilko, although it is effectively hidden behind her feminine Southern charm. Bilko tries to drown Hogan and the other WAC administrators in paperwork by invoking a regulation established during the Spanish-American War to document missing Army equipment. Although the other WACs—and even Colonel Hall—beg Hogan to withdraw her name from consideration for the jeep, she cheerfully reassures everyone she can handle Bilko. Unflustered, Hogan sweetly explains to Bilko that she is happy to file the report just as soon as she receives his inventory of everything he has ever been issued in his 15-year military career. This regulation, she adds, was put on the books during the even earlier Civil War. In his final attempt to wrangle the jeep from Hogan, Bilko tries the "Bilko Blitz" of getting her to fall for his "lonely heart" routine. Hogan turns the tables on him by one-upping his routine. "What do you think a woman soldier goes through?" she cries, "It's romantic to be a man in uniform, but a woman in uniform? That wall between her and every soft and tender feeling she's got." Not only did Hogan outsmart Bilko at his own con, she also played off the assumption that a woman could not be both a soldier *and* feminine at the same time.[48] Indeed, Hogan became Bilko's romantic partner, thus shifting her identity away from being a soldier to being a woman.

The success of *The Phil Silvers Show* inspired new military comedies, including the successful and anti-militaristic *McHale's Navy* (ABC, 1962–1966) and *Broadside* (ABC, 1964–1965). *McHale's Navy* starred Ernest Borgnine, a navy vet himself, as a PT boat commander in the South Pacific during World War II. *Broadside* featured Navy WAVES (Women Accepted for Volunteer Emergency Service) on an island in the South Pacific, playing out the battle of the sexes with the base commander. Both of these shows were created by Edward Montagne, who had worked on *The Phil Silvers Show* as a producer since the series' beginning.[49] In fact, Montagne intended for *McHale's Navy* to be "*Bilko* at sea—the navy with a bunch of funny sailors."[50] Even more anti-militarist than *The Phil Silvers Show*, the two Navy series followed the exploits of America's citizen-sailors and women volunteers, poking fun at the Navy's bureaucracy, discipline, and regimentation. This anti-militarist trend continued through the 1960s, culminating in the anti-military film (1970) and television series *M*A*S*H* (CBS, 1972–1983). The controversial Vietnam War turned many Americans away from supporting the military, however, so both television and Hollywood shied away from military shows and movies during the 1970s.

During the 1980s, President Ronald Reagan did much to rehabilitate the image of the military and elevate it to a position of honor socially and culturally. Indeed, the America of the 1980s became more militaristic than the America of the early decades of the Cold War had been.[51] For example, in 1955 Army draftees believed "civilians were indifferent or sometimes hostile

"*Bilko's Bombers*" 27

to soldiers."[52] By 2011, in sharp contrast, 91 percent of Americans reported pride in the military, and an additional 76 percent stated "they had thanked someone in the military for serving."[53] Since the late 1980s, the American people have placed more confidence in the military than in any other institution, including churches.[54] Americans now honor the military rather than laugh at it. It is possible that the first television military comedy since 1983, the well-written *Enlisted* (Fox, 2014), failed to find an audience, in part, because Americans today are too militaristic to laugh at soldiers.[55] *Enlisted* actor Chris Lowell surmised that it had been decades since television networks even tried to produce a military comedy because "there's such a sensitivity and fear around mocking or laughing at any public service," and he pointed out that the show's creator was "hell-bent on making sure the military knows we're laughing *with* them, not *at* them."[56]

Notes

1. "Hillbilly Whiz," season 3, episode 3, *The Phil Silvers Show: 50th Anniversary Edition*, aired October 1, 1957 (Hollywood, CA: Paramount Pictures and CBS, 2006), DVD.
2. David Everitt, *King of the Half Hour: Nat Hiken and the Golden Age of TV Comedy* (Syracuse, NY: Syracuse University Press, 2001), 211.
3. Ibid., 116–17.
4. Ibid., 117.
5. Ibid., xii, 99–101.
6. Lisa M. Mundey, *American Militarism and Anti-Militarism in Popular Media, 1945–1970* (Jefferson, NC: McFarland & Company, 2012), 65–67, 70–76.
7. Daniel Czitrom, "Bilko: A Sitcom for All Seasons," in *Popular Culture in America*, ed. Paul Buhle (Minneapolis, MN: University of Minneapolis Press, 1987), 159.
8. Everitt, *King of the Half-Hour*, 29, 102.
9. Ibid., 30.
10. Ibid., 102.
11. Mickey Freeman and Sholom Rubinstein, *Bilko: Behind the Lines with Phil Silvers* (Waterville, ME: Thorndike Press, 2002), 13.
12. Everitt, *King of the Half Hour*, 104; Freeman and Rubinstein, *Bilko*, 13–14.
13. Freeman and Rubinstein, *Bilko*, 18.
14. Freeman and Rubinstein, *Bilko*, 18; Everitt, *King of the Half* Hour, 113–16.
15. Everitt, *King of the Half Hour*, 103, 131.
16. Czitrom, "Bilko," 159.
17. Ibid.
18. Everitt, *King of the Half-Hour*, 116, 134; Jack Gould, "A Nice Guy," *New York Times*, Mar. 4, 1956, in Everitt, *King of the Half Hour*, 106.
19. Public Opinion Surveys, Inc., "Attitudes of 16 to 20 Year Old Males toward The Military Service as a Career," (Princeton, NJ: Public Opinion Surveys, Inc., 1955), 34, 36; Public Opinion Surveys, Inc., "Attitudes of Adult Civilians Toward The Military Service as a Career," (Princeton, NJ: Public Opinion Surveys, Inc., 1955), 23–28.
20. Major Multissimus, "The Wearing of the Army Green," *Army*, May 1957.
21. Mundey, *Militarism and Anti-Militarism*, 105–108.

28   *Lisa M. Mundey*

22. Everitt, *King of the Half-Hour*, 114, 116, 129, 213.
23. Ibid., 132–35. The initial corporate sponsors for *The Phil Silvers Show* were Camel cigarettes and Amana refrigerators.
24. Ibid., 134–35.
25. Allan R. Millett, Peter Maslowski, and William B. Feis, *For the Common Defense: A Military History of the United States from 1607 to 2012* (New York: Free Press, 2012), 453, 460–62, 478–85.
26. Alfred Vagts, *A History of Militarism: Romance and Realities of a Profession* (New York: W. Norton & Company, 1937), 15; Michael S. Sherry, *In the Shadow of War: The United States Since the 1930s* (New Haven, CT: Yale University Press, 1995), xi; Christian G. Appy, "'We'll Follow the Old Man': The Strains of Sentimental Militarism in Popular Films of the Fifties," in *Rethinking Cold War Culture,* ed. Peter J. Kuznick and James Gilbert (Washington, DC: Smithsonian Institution Press, 2001), 76; J. Fred MacDonald, *Television and the Red Menace: The Video War to Vietnam* (Jefferson, NC: McFarland Publishers, Inc., 1985), vii, 114. MacDonald considers the military comedies that aired during the 1950s and 1960s militaristic, including *The Phil Silvers Show*.
27. Arthur A. Ekirch, Jr., "Militarism and Antimilitarism," in *The Oxford Companion to American Military History*, ed. John Whiteclay Chambers, II (New York: Oxford University Press, 1999), 438. A longer introduction to the concept is in Arthur A. Ekirch, Jr., *The Civilian and the Military: A History of the American Antimilitarist Tradition* (Colorado Springs: Ralph Myles, Publisher, 1972). See also Mundey, *American Militarism and Anti-Militarism*, 5–8.
28. Mark R. Grandstaff, "Making the Military American: Advertising, Reform, and the Demise of an Antistanding Military Tradition, 1945–1955," *Journal of Military History* Vol. 60, no. 2 (1996): 306–11.
29. Hanson W. Baldwin, "What's Wrong with the Regulars?" *Saturday Evening Post*, 31 October 1953, 19–20.
30. Public Opinion Surveys, Inc., "Attitudes of 16 to 20 Year Old Males," 3–4.
31. "The Transfer," season 1, episode 20, *The Phil Silvers Show: The First Season,* aired January 31, 1956 (Hollywood, CA: Paramount Pictures and CBS, 2010), DVD, hereafter first season episodes come from this DVD set; "Recruiting Sergeant," season 1, episode 30, *The Phil Silvers Show*, aired April 17, 1956.
32. "The Transfer."
33. "New Recruits," season 1, episode 1, *The Phil Silvers Show*, aired September 20, 1955; "The Transfer."
34. Ibid.
35. "The Centennial," season 1, episode 10, *The Phil Silvers Show*, aired November 22, 1955.
36. "Bivouac," season 1, episode 11, *The Phil Silvers Show*, aired November 29, 1955.
37. "Army Memoirs," season 1, episode 23, *The Phil Silvers Show,* aired February 23, 1956.
38. "War Games," season 1, episode 33, *The Phil Silvers Show,* aired May 8, 1956.
39. For a historic examination as the US Army in the economic development, see Francis Paul Prucha, *Broadax and Bayonet: The Role of the United States Army in the Development of the Northwest, 1815–1860* (Madison: State Historical Society of Wisconsin, 1953; Lincoln: University of Nebraska Press, 1995). Civilian dependence on local military funding greatly increased during and after World War II. See R. Douglas Hurt, *The Great Plains during World War II*

(Lincoln: University of Nebraska Press, 2008). For the place of the regulars in American society see Edward M. Coffman, *The Regulars: The American Army, 1898–1941* (Cambridge, MA: The Belknap Press of the Harvard University Press, 2004). Civilians disliking soldiers dates back at least to the nineteenth century. See Kevin Adams, *Class and Race in the Frontier Army: Military Life in the West, 1870–1890* (Norman, OK: University of Oklahoma Press, 2009), 141. Even today, many service personnel feel this way about the communities outside military bases.

40. "Empty Store," season 1, episode 2, *The Phil Silvers Show*, aired September 27, 1955.
41. Ibid.
42. "The Reunion," season 1, episode 14, *The Phil Silvers Show*, aired December 20, 1955.
43. Mundey, *American Militarism and Anti-Militarism*, 24–26.
44. Yvonne Tasker, *Soldiers' Stories: Military Women in Cinema and Television since World War II* (Durham: Duke University Press, 2011), 7.
45. Ibid., 5.
46. Ibid., 156.
47. "The WAC," season 1, episode 3, *The Phil Silvers Show*, aired October 4, 1955.
48. "The WAC"; Tasker, *Soldiers' Stories*, 5–13.
49. Everitt, *King of the Half-Hour*, 104.
50. Montagne quoted in Freeman and Rubinstein, *Bilko*, 61–62.
51. Andrew J. Bacevich, *The New American Militarism: How Americans Are Seduced by War* (New York: Oxford University Press, 2005), 5–6.
52. "Draftee in a Peacetime Army," *Life*, 11 July 1955, 97.
53. Bruce Drake, "On Memorial Day, Public Pride in Veterans, But at a Distance," *Pew Research Center*, accessed September 27, 2015, http://www.pewresearch.org/fact-tank/2013/05/24/on-memorial-day-public-pride-in-veterans-but-at-a-distance-2/.
54. "Confidence in Institutions," *Gallup*, accessed September 26, 2015, http://www.gallup.com/poll/1597/confidence-institutions.aspx.
55. Emily Yahr, "'Enlisted' Actors Talk Military Comedies, Reaction from Vets, and Going to Real-Life Boot Camp," *The Washington Post*, January 17, 2014, https://www.washingtonpost.com/news/style-blog/wp/2014/01/17/enlisted-actors-talk-military-comedies-reaction-from-vets-and-going-to-real-life-boot-camp/. The series received criticism from soldiers for making mistakes in the pilot episode. Lead actor Geoff Stults made a video apologizing for the errors. Sara Bibel, "Friday Final Ratings," *TV By the Numbers*, March 31, 2014, http://tvbythenumbers.zap2it.com/. The last episode to air before Fox canceled the series, "Paint Car 5000 vs. The Mondo Spider," season 1, episode 2, aired March 28, 2014, had a low rating of 0.4 among the 18–49 demographic with only 1.33 million viewers.
56. Yahr, "Enlisted." My emphasis.

2 The Long Fight

Combat! and the Generic Development of the TV War Drama Series

David P. Pierson

Some of my fondest boyhood memories were the hours spent playing "combat" with the other boys in the neighborhood. Because this took place in the early 1960s, our chosen play model was based on *Combat!* (ABC, 1962–1967), the popular TV dramatic series set during World War II. We took turns playing Sergeant Saunders (Vic Morrow), the squad leader; Doc, the medic (Steven Rogers, Conlan Carter); and the other squad members. Wesley Britton says that the series' popularity with young viewers led to tie-in board games and bubblegum cards.[1] He also relates that one Vietnam veteran told him that many older adolescent males were so inspired by the show that they volunteered for the Army.[2] Regardless of whether the series might have served as encouragement for some young men to join the military, *Combat!* depicts war as a grim, grueling experience with few crucial battles or heroic acts and a place where death is often an arbitrary occurrence.[3]

Combat! is the longest running war drama on American television with 152 hour-long episodes. The series followed a small squad of American soldiers (King Company of the US Army 2nd Platoon) fighting its way across France during the Second World War following the D-Day invasion.[4] *Combat!'s* two main co-stars and squad leaders were Morrow as Sgt. Charles "Chip" Saunders and Rick Jason as Lieutenant Gil Hanley. Both actors rotated as featured performers in individual episodes. During its initial broadcast, *Combat!* was a popular action series that broke into the Nielsen ratings top 10 shows in its 1964–1965 season. The series' first four seasons were filmed in black and white with its final season in color. Besides its regular cast, the series featured numerous notable guest stars, including Charles Bronson, James Caan, John Cassavetes, James Colburn, Robert Duvall, Joan Hackett, Dennis Hopper, Lee Marvin, Sal Mineo, Warren Oates, Louise Rainer, Telly Savalas, Dean Stockwell, Dennis Weaver, and James Whitmore. *Combat!* went into worldwide syndication in the 1970s, which produced a new and attentive audience for its wartime stories.

Veteran Hollywood screenwriter-director, Robert Pirosh developed the concept for the series. As a screenwriter, Pirosh wrote both comedies (*A Day at the Races* [1937], *Up in Arms* [1944], *I Married a Witch* [1944]) and war films (*Battleground* [1949], *Go for Broke* [1951], *Hell Is for Heroes* [1962]).

His first war film, the 1949 *Battleground*, which was about the US Army 101st Airborne Division defending the small town of Bastogne, Belgium, during the Battle of the Bulge, won him an Academy Award for his screenplay. Unlike many Hollywood screenwriters, Pirosh had first-hand experience serving as an infantryman in the European Theater during the Second World War. His experience enabled him to write credibly from the point of view of the common foot soldier. In late 1957, he began working on an idea for a television series based on his wartime diary.[5] After developing the concept for *Combat!*, he took it to Selig Seligman, an ABC-TV vice-president in charge of productions. *Combat!* was produced by Selmur Productions, an independent production company, and shot on MGM's California studio back lots. To orient the series' cast members to the demanding physical life of an infantryman, Seligman sent them through a mock "boot camp."[6]

Although it was not the first war drama on American television (*Navy Log* [CBS, 1955–1956; ABC, 1956–1958], *Combat Sergeant* [ABC, 1956], *Silent Service* [NBC, 1957–1958], etc.), I argue that *Combat!* successfully translated several of the basic features of the combat war film genre to the television medium and in the process established many of the narrative and thematic conventions of the American television war drama series. *Combat!*'s enduring televisual status and generic influence can be seen in subsequent TV war dramas such as *The Rat Patrol* (ABC, 1966–1967), *Garrison's Gorillas* (ABC, 1967–1968), *Tour of Duty* (CBS, 1987–1990), *Band of Brothers* (HBO, 2001), *Over There* (F/X, 2005), and *Generation Kill* (HBO, 2008), which all appropriated features of the series. To understand *Combat's* impact on the TV war drama genre and its legacy, this chapter will examine the emergence and popularity of the 1960s TV war dramas and the relationship between the Hollywood war film and the series. It will also explore how *Combat!*, through its narratives and characters, exemplified America's Cold War politics and policies during the Kennedy-Johnson administrations.

The Emergence and Prevalence of TV War Dramas in the 1960s

In the 1950s, the American military representatives and themes were consistently integrated into popular entertainment. The American military forces received praise and became a part of a range of programming from popular military documentary series of actual battles (the Battle of the Bulge, D-Day) to fictionalized dramas.[7] By the early 1960s, dramatized images of the fighting soldier were even more prevalent on network television. In fact, never in American broadcasting had there been so many war dramas.[8] Most of the series were set during World War II (*The Gallant Men* [ABC, 1962–1963], *Twelve O'Clock High* [ABC, 1964–1967]). There are a number of factors for the increased number of television combat war dramas. One institutional factor was the waning of the popularity of the adult

32   *David P. Pierson*

TV western in the early 1960s. The TV western reached the height of its popularity in 1959, when 31 episodic Westerns were running on prime-time television and seven out of 10 shows were westerns. By the early 1960s, the ratings of TV westerns began to wane, and the genre lost some of its attractiveness with audiences.[9] In response, networks began to explore other action-adventure genres including episodic combat war dramas.

Another institutional factor was that, in the early 1960s, the ABC-TV network, which gained popularity and high-ratings from its action-adventure series like *Cheyenne* (ABC, 1955–1963) and *77 Sunset Strip* (ABC, 1958–1964), came increasingly under attack for its more violence-oriented series such as *The Untouchables* (ABC, 1959–1963). The highly rated crime drama, along with several westerns, became targets of a special Congressional inquiry examining television violence and its possible association with juvenile delinquency. Because of its perceived negative portrayal of Italian-Americans, *The Untouchables* received increasing threats of sponsorship withdrawal.[10] As a possible programming alternative, dramas such as *Combat!*, with their wartime setting and battlefield conflicts, provided some degree of justification for moments of television violence.[11]

In the early 1960s, the Hollywood war film was experiencing its own nostalgic rebirth with the release of expensive blockbuster epics like *The Guns of Navarone* (1961) and *The Longest Day* (1962), which chronicled the allied efforts in the D-Day invasion. Jeanine Basinger, who wrote the definitive account of the World War-II combat war film genre, describes this period as the "fourth wave" of the evolving genre lasting from 1960 to 1970.[12] Other films from this period include the *Battle of the Bulge* (1965), *Battle of Britain* (1969), and *Tora! Tora! Tora!* (1970). These blockbuster war film epics were not about exploring unresolved issues related to the Second World War, but rather they were cinematic efforts to preserve and present the war as a revered memory for posterity. These films re-created the war's great battles, shooting them on actual battlefields and relying heavily on veterans as advisors and even actors. A few of these films intermixed actual WWII footage with their staged dramatic depictions. Basinger argues that in this late evolutionary phase, the conflicted nature of the "true war" was removed and replaced with a historically detailed model that would serve to distance the war and reconstruct it as a mythic and legendary story. She says that, because *Combat!* follows the traditional format of the combat war film and uses some actual battle footage for realism, it is part of this epic fourth wave.[13] I would argue, however, that the series was often cautious about many of the heroic myths and legends associated with previous World War II films. As Rick Worland points out in his analysis of the series, *Combat!* "contained no self-righteous glorification of killing, no sanctified killers in the mold of Sgt. York or Audie Murphy in the ranks of … King Company."[14] In fact, many of the episodes argued that this highly individualistic warrior-type represented a clear threat to the integrity of the squad as a collective fighting force. Unlike the mythologizing fourth-wave films,

Combat! frequently showed men dying without cause or recuperation; it did not depict death as particularly meaningful or necessary to advance the Allied cause.[15] Instead of striving to preserve the war as a courageous legendary account, the series depicted the war as a just but bleak and morally exhausting experience.

Figure 2.1 *Combat!* presented a decidedly bleak image of the war experience. Men often died without cause or recuperation, and death was never particularly meaningful or glorious.

Whereas J. Fred MacDonald asserts that the popularity of *Combat!* and other TV war dramas laid the ideological grounds for the country's budding military involvement in South Vietnam, Worland, who analyzed the relationship between the series and the gradual escalation of the Vietnam War, found no direct correlation between them.[16] Unlike Pearl Harbor, there was no single event that signaled the country's sudden emergence into the Vietnam War. There is no clear Vietnam War analogy to the dramatic increase in Hollywood war films following Pearl Harbor. Unlike Pearl Harbor, and despite the passage of the Gulf of Tonkin Resolution in 1965, there was no event or emotional catalyst that served to rally public support behind the war effort. Instead, America's involvement in the war grew incrementally. The Vietnam War gradually and steadily worked its way into the public consciousness in the early to mid-1960s. Worland theorizes that, perhaps, the expanding commitment of American ground troops and forces inadvertently sparked a renewal of interest in the combat war film, much like the public interest that followed America's entries into World War II and Korea, and this may help explain the popularity of *Combat!* and the multitude of military war dramas and service comedies [*Hogan's Heroes* (CBS, 1965–1971), *McHale's Navy* (ABC, 1962–1966)] of that time period.[17]

Combat! and the Combat War Film

Combat! not only shares narrative and thematic attributes with the combat war film genre, it effectively transformed many of them into the narrative confines of a weekly episodic TV series. To Basinger, the most critical characteristic of the genre is that the wartime characters find themselves (and the audience) completely immersed in an inescapable combat situation with no recourse to long periods of R&R, journeys back home, or extensive flashback sequences of life before the war. For Basinger this trait is crucial because most Hollywood war films prior to the Second World War used "war" primarily as a backdrop for stories more centered on romantic relationships or character biographies than the experience of war itself.[18] With the exception of two Christmas season episodes, *Combat!*'s squad is situated in the contested arena of post D-Day invasion France where they are constantly under the impending threat of enemy attack.[19] Even in the episode "A Day in June," during which Sgt. Saunders reminisces about the events leading to D-Day, the narrative flashbacks show the squad's brutal Omaha Beach assault, which resulted in the death of many of his fellow soldiers.[20] Despite the episode's historic positioning, Worland maintains that the series' narratives tended to remain at the micro level of the small military unit. The squad's assignments were rarely connected to the grand plans of the Allied forces, and "there was little inference anything the squad did could seriously affect the outcome of the war one way or the other."[21] With the exception of taking place in post D-Day France, the series' setting is a place without a firm geographic or temporal dimension. This indefinite setting provides it with the ideal narrative space for the discussion and playing out of moral, social, and political conflicts. *Combat!*'s setting, as with most TV series, is more of a liminal or ritualized space. Horace Newcomb and Paul Hirsch, relying on anthropologist Victor Turner's concept of liminality, argue that popular TV entertainment creates liminal, ritualized dramatic spaces for addressing contemporary moral, social, and political struggles.[22] On the historical level, *Combat!*'s setting defines a period in which Americans were portrayed as liberators in the long fight to retrieve Europe from the grips of Nazi Germany. On the liminal, political level, the series implicitly spoke to the Kennedy-Johnson administrations' efforts to preserve and promote America's image as a democratic alternative in the global struggle against Communism.

Another defining feature of the combat war film is the thematic construction of the military group into a representative social microcosm of American society. With the notable exception of women, the combat fighting group is usually comprised of members from different social, ethnic, and racial backgrounds. The propagandistic intention of this narrative construct is to illustrate to audiences the necessity for all social groups, both military and civilian, to overcome their internal divisions and work together to defeat a common enemy.[23] Following World War II, this feature continued to hold social relevance, especially to an anxious postwar America, which abruptly found itself facing a new type of enemy (Soviet Communists) and war (Cold War). Despite its lack of ethnic and racial diversity, *Combat!*'s squad integrated soldiers from different social backgrounds

The Long Fight 35

and distinct temperaments. K Company regulars include Sgt. Saunders, a tough, experienced, but sensitive soldier from the Midwest who participated in the North African and Italian campaigns and was wounded and received the Purple Heart; the no-nonsense Lt. Hanley, a college-educated, technical sergeant who received a battlefield commission after the D-Day invasion; Pierre Jalbert as Paul "Caje" LeMay from New Orleans, who is of Acadian "Cajun" ancestry, speaks French, and usually acts as a translator; Dick Peabody as Littlejohn, a gentle giant of a man who, before the war, ran a farm with his brothers; Jack Hogan as Private William Kirby, a tough, passionate, and irritable soldier from Chicago who is nonetheless a dependable soldier in a firefight; "Doc" Walton (season one), a gentle, sensitive young medic who is profoundly affected by his battlefield experiences; and Doc Walton (seasons two through five), an easy-going, affable, former Arkansas grocery clerk.[24] As with most television dramas, the episodes usually do not focus their full attention on an individual member (with the exception of the weekly guest star) but rather present the group as another "TV family."[25] In "Point of View" Lt. Hanley remarks that "The first time someone shoots at you. You don't have a command anymore, you got a family."[26] The series lack of emphasis on the individual soldier works to reinforce one of the main themes of the combat war film genre: that any effective fighting group is one that works together as a collective unit.

At the narrative center of the combat war film is the hero protagonist, who is a natural leader with prior wartime experience but who is usually a lower level officer with the rank of sergeant, lieutenant, or captain. The hero is a member of the group but is "forced to separate himself from it because of the demands of leadership."[27] *Combat!'s* Lt. Hanley and Sgt. Saunders both serve as the series' featured performers in individual episodes. Hanley plays two functional roles depending on whether he is the lead performer for the episode. When he is not the lead, he serves as a worldly, efficient, behind-the-scenes administrator calmly dispensing orders to Saunders. But, when he is the lead protagonist, he assumes the tradition of the combat war film hero, a true "man-of-the-people," a field officer with a strong common bond with his men. In keeping with the standard narrative patterns of procedural dramas on US TV in the 1960s and 1970s, both men serve as compassionate, empathetic problem-solvers for the assortment of disaffected soldiers and allies they meet and contend with in their weekly missions.[28] Unlike the composed Hanley, Saunders' brooding, pensive nature endows him with a greater degree of sensitivity to his men's emotional and mental states. For example, in "Mail Call," Saunders sees through a private's easygoing demeanor and exaggerated injuries to help him face and overcome his fears.[29]

The combat war film is narratively structured around the military group's completion of a specific mission objective.[30] *Combat!'s* episodes focus on such duties as blowing up a bridge, taking and holding a hill, taking out an enemy sniper in a church bell tower, and rescuing a French scientist from the Germans. Whereas K Company's actions are generally directed by orders from command, the episode's main dramatic conflict resides within the squad itself and its effects on the group's ability to complete its weekly mission. In the episode "High Named Today," Private Lawson (Dean Stockwell), a soldier who believes he is destined to die, joins the squad, and his fool-hardy penchant for single-handedly charging the enemy and ignoring Hanley and Saunders' orders puts every man's life in danger. Kirby conspires with the other squad members to get Lawson transferred before his "one-man army" tactics get them all killed.[31] The relocating of the central narrative conflict within the American military group, rather than between that group and the enemy forces, had been an ongoing trend with post-World War-II war films (*Twelve O'Clock High* [1950], *From Here to Eternity* [1953]).[32] Whereas the first wave of combat war films was chiefly concerned with providing the rationale for fighting the enemy, subsequent films sought to understand the social and moral implications of the Second World War effort. With the war finally over and the genre's propagandistic intentions no longer required, the combat war film suddenly had the capacity to investigate other pressing postwar social issues, including Cold War politics, military and civilian war fatigue, and internal ethnic and racial conflicts.

As with many of the postwar combat films, *Combat!* can be seen as a somber celebration of the trials and tribulations of the common foot soldier. Pirosh's war films focused on the point of view of the combat infantryman.[33] With images of soldiers walking through snow and mud and expressing anxiety and skepticism about specific orders and the general situation, *Battleground* sought to show the postwar audience the actual conditions of combat life. In *Hell Is for Heroes,* the squad's commander abandons his men near the Siegfried Line in 1944 to go back to the rear echelon, and the small group must determine how to deceive the Germans into believing they are a battalion of men. The film's protagonist is Private Reese (Steve McQueen), an alienated outsider with little respect for command or his fellow soldiers who just happens to be an efficient warrior. *Heroes*, which was produced a year before *Combat!*, expresses the darker postwar notion that despite the public reverence for military command, GIs might become victims of war, their officers or the Army itself more broadly.[34] This belief was expressed in many postwar combat films including *Attack!* (1956) and *Pork Chop Hill* (1959). Andrew Huebner asserts that throughout its five-year run, "*Combat!* perpetuated almost every disquieting aspect of the warrior image percolating in the 1950s and the early 1960s."[35] Huebner's viewpoint contrasts sharply with Thomas Doherty and Basinger who see the series as continuing the traditional themes and tropes of the classical Hollywood combat war film.[36] Yet, it seems clear that *Combat!* blended classic combat war themes with newer themes established in the late postwar period. The later themes, which represented a cynical, world-weary perspective of modern war and its effects on soldiers, resonated with a postwar American public becoming familiar with the traumas associated with returning soldiers and jaded over the stalemated Korean War experience.[37]

The Long Fight 37

One postwar theme is that the extreme stress of combat frequently creates intense and violent rivalries between soldiers that lead to breakdowns in teamwork. This theme is exemplified in the episode, "The Bridge of Chalons," in which Hanley assigns Saunders and his men to serve as escorts for Sgt. Turk (Lee Marvin), an inflexible, demolition expert, to destroy a bridge deep in enemy territory.[38] From the outset, Turk shows his utter contempt for the squad's ineptitude, and a mutual hatred develops between him and Saunders. When Kirby accidentally kicks a rock down a hill that almost alerts a group of Germans, Turk admonishes him for trying to wreck his mission. Later, when Kirby pushes Turk away from Littlejohn, who dropped a detonator cord in the road and alerted a German patrol, Turk threatens to court-martial Kirby. Turk accuses Saunders of over-protecting his men. Saunders' men are either injured or killed until only the two sergeants are left to complete the mission. Back at camp, Kirby is left wondering whether a wounded, but still arrogant, Turk plans to press charges against him. The episode highlights the rising tensions and pressures placed on fighting men on perilous combat missions.

The fact that the sheer brutality of war regularly produces psychological injuries in soldiers is also a regular topic in the series. In the episode, "No Trumpets, No Drums," Caje accidentally kills an innocent French civilian, suffers psychological trauma, and risks charges of insubordination of duty, as a result.[39] Despite Saunders' gentle warning not to "personalize" an impersonal war, the distraught Caje is unable to contend with the effects of his actions. Normally unwavering, Caje begins to break down; he has been emotionally injured by the tragedy of war. When Caje learns that the man had a young daughter, he ignores his regular duties and devotes his time to being the girl's surrogate father. As the Germans attack the town, Saunders' patience with the distressed soldier finally runs out, and he resorts to slapping him and bluntly reminding him that his wartime priorities must reside with the squad. Severe psychological and graphic physical injuries are represented in the Robert Altman-directed episode "Survival," as well.[40] The episode features a haunting image of Saunders with smoking, severely burnt hands walking mesmerized from a burning barn. Separated from his squad and in agonizing pain, he wanders aimlessly in enemy territory. Traumatized, Saunders is convinced a dead German soldier is his brother, and he carries the man across the countryside. When he is finally rescued, Saunders weeps in pain that he was not able to save his brother. The scene of a normally composed Saunders weeping uncontrollably is an unsettling one for audiences raised on seeing their leading men as calm and restrained in demeanor. The narrative confirms that no soldier is immune to the terrors and psychological damages caused by the inhumanity of modern war.[41]

Another recurring theme in *Combat!* is that field officers are often faced with dispensing brutal, merciless orders to their men. In the two-part episode, "Hills Are for Heroes" Hanley receives orders to take and hold, at any cost, a strategic road guarded by two German bunkers.[42] The bunkers' machine guns efficiently cut down the platoon's numbers, and Saunders is wounded. Without any artillery or tank support, Hanley must order his men to advance again and again to take the hill. The repeated attempts to seize the hill extract a heavy toll in lives and morale, even on Hanley. Finally, with help from a tank, the bunkers fall, but the hillside is filled with the bodies of half of the platoon. Before the men can celebrate their victory, they receive orders to abandon their position and move to a new location.[43] Similar to *Pork Chop Hill*, GIs and field officers find themselves the unwitting victims of orders from a distant command post and dying or being maimed for an essentially useless piece of territory. At a time when the US was dramatically increasing the level of its troop commitment in the Vietnam War, this two-part episode served as a none-too-subtle reminder of the ultimate futility of war.

Beyond expressing the senselessness of war, *Combat!* often featured anti-war themes in its episodes. In the premiere episode, "Forgotten Front," directed by Altman, Hanley dispatches Saunders, Doc, Kirby, and Caje to replace a patrol at an observation post that had been providing firing coordinates to knock out a German artillery position.[44] At the post, Saunders discovers Carl Dorfmann (Albert Paulsen), a frightened, middle-age German deserter hiding in the basement. Dorfmann helps the Americans by sending a German patrol away from the post. With the big gun destroyed, the squad begins returning to the lines but suddenly finds itself pinned down by a German tank entering the town. Saunders and the squad are faced with a moral dilemma—they cannot take Dorfmann with them, and, because of his knowledge about the planned Allied advance, they cannot leave him behind. Saunders leaves it to Caje to take care of the German, as they escape one-by-one out of the town. Later back at camp, Caje confesses to Saunders that he could not look the old man in the eye and shoot him. Initially reluctant to hear Caje's heartfelt confession, Saunders assures him that he did the right thing and even if the old man talked, "one piece of information isn't gonna win or lose this war." Caje replies, "Sarge," and Saunders answers "Yeah?"

CAJE: "Don't you think you have to be pretty sure? Awfully positive before you start playing? Playing God with people's lives?"
SAUNDERS: "Yeah, that's for sure."

Because ordering men into battle and waging war against another country is indeed "playing God," the exchange between the two men can be read as an implicit anti-war message. This episode shows that when one personally knows the enemy, as the squad does with Dorfmann, it becomes extremely difficult to de-personalize and kill the enemy.

Combat! and Cold War Politics

A frequent theme expressed in *Combat!* is that US military field officers must retain a cool-headed, tough but intelligent approach to the enemy. Hanley and Sanders have a managerial style that is historically reflective of the "coolness" of President Kennedy's administrative style in both thought and action. In public, Kennedy avoided any extreme emotional displays and tried to maintain calmness.[45] Sorenson, Kennedy's presidential advisor, lauded the President's intellectual pragmatism or his skill at cutting through the cloud of conventional beliefs and prejudices to seize the essential facts of any impending situation. He also admired his toughness in handling and competing with the Soviets.[46] Kennedy's top advisors believed that many of America's enemies were successful because they were tougher and more determined in achieving their worldwide objectives.[47] To Kennedy, the Cold War ultimately came down to a test of whether or not the democratic world was tougher and more decisive in protecting its core beliefs than the Communists.[48]

Saunders often exemplifies the cool, Kennedyesque style in the series. In the episode, "Anatomy of a Patrol," for example, he manages to outwit and outmaneuver a German patrol in a race to recover the pilot of a downed American observation plane and the reconnaissance photos he carries.[49] The German sergeant is similar to Saunders in his intelligence and demeanor; each cares about his men and tries to accomplish the mission while keeping his men alive. But for one to succeed, the other must fail. Even though Saunders loses three of his men, he retains his focus and demonstrates grace under pressure by managing to outsmart the German sergeant and his squad to retrieve and deliver the valuable film to Allied headquarters. The episode illustrates the tough, Cold War gamesmanship required by the Americans to aggressively compete with the Soviets.

Hanley and Saunders' dispassionate, pragmatic approach to fighting the enemy is often contrasted to the hot-tempered partisans they meet who are generally desperate to win at any cost. The episode, "Vendetta," for instance, begins with Hanley and a few men pinned down by German armored cars, then suddenly rescued by a contingent of Greek soldiers under the command of Colonel Kapsalis (Telly Savalas).[50] The Greek squad has been ordered to find and destroy a V-2 rocket base. To strengthen his numbers, Kapsalis orders Hanley and his men to join the mission. But the Colonel's fanatical drive becomes apparent when he orders a critically wounded soldier to be left behind. Hanley considers Kapsalis' repeated failed attacks on the heavily defended rocket base to be ill conceived and hopeless. Kapsalis finally succeeds with a suicidal attack, driving his explosive-filled jeep into a fuel storage tank that destroys the rocket base. The Cold War theme expressed here is that, whereas allies are crucial, they are often irresponsible fanatics; therefore, it is imperative for the rational, level-headed Americans to retain overall command. In some cases, the partisans are confused about the larger dimensions of the war effort. In "Gadjo," Saunders meets a band of French Gypsy partisans who are battling the Germans.[51] The partisans, however, are fighting not for the allied cause but for revenge against the German unit that massacred their village. They are even willing to fight Saunders and his men to kill a German prisoner of war, the officer responsible for the war

40   *David P. Pierson*

atrocities. Saunders must protect the prisoner for the valuable information he may have. To persuade the Gypsies to join the allied cause, Saunders must teach them about the war's Big Picture: "This is your war? You've been pushed around so long you think everybody's your enemy. ... I'm not saying your lives are gonna be any easier but at least you're going to have a chance to live it. Isn't that more important to your people than revenge?" The Gypsies finally accept Saunders' beliefs and pledge to join the Allied war effort. This narrative illustrates the US's paternalistic perspective to assume that it is our prerogative to explain to our allies the ideological rationale for fighting the Cold War struggle against Communists. America's propagandistic position frequently exhibited both arrogance and paranoia over the US's ability to retain its dominant leadership role in global politics.

A general frustration with the French as reliable allies, especially in light of President Charles de Gualle's role as an international political agitator within the Western Atlantic alliance, is exemplified in several *Combat!* episodes.[52] In "The Chateau," K-Company medic Doc Walton, Pvt. Braddock (Shecky Greene), and several wounded soldiers are captured and herded into a chateau owned by French aristocrat, Count De Gontran (Ben Wright), and his daughter Gabrielle (Joan Hackett) and currently under the command of German Major Richter (Dan O'Herlihy).[53] The Germans are using the chateau as an artillery observation post. Whereas Walton hopes that De Gontran will help him and the other Americans escape, the Count is more concerned with the survival of his ancestral home than the outcome of the war. In one scene, the Count consoles his anxious daughter by proudly explaining the family's elitist philosophy of endurance:

COUNT: Oh my dear, listen to me. Five years ago I promised you that we would survive this stupid war because we are intelligent. We are shrewd. We are practical.
GABRIELLE: Father, I don't think I'm very practical.
COUNT: My dear that's what I'm trying to teach you. How do you suppose this chateau has existed for four-hundred-years with the same family in it? We know how to compromise. We know how to judge people and move with the times.

The aristocratic Count is protective of his autonomous position and sees a kindred spirit in the seemingly cultured German commander. The Count, however, does not realize Major Richter has designs on both the chateau's art treasures and his beautiful daughter Gabrielle. Richter betrays the Count's hospitality by forcing him to sign over his valuable antiques, paintings, and sculptures so they can be shipped to the officer's home. Distraught and deceived, the heartbroken Count suffers a fatal heart attack. Gabrielle exploits her father's condition as a ruse to smuggle a weapon to Walton who employs it to free his fellow Americans. Because the chateau has become a vital German outpost and, thereby, an Allied target, it is subsequently shelled

The Long Fight 41

and destroyed by Allied forces. As the bombs drop, Gabrielle sits proudly in her ancestral home. With the French Count's faulty judgment and defiant, self-interested stance, the episode's narrative serves as a cautionary geo-political morality tale about the dangers of Western European leaders, like de Gualle, who overlook the severity of the grand Cold War battle between the Free World and the Communist threat. As with de Gualle, the Count sought to preserve his family's independence and its ancestral cultural influence at the expense of the region's greater security. The episode argues that there is no place for neutrality and nationalistic autonomy in the indomitable struggle for world freedom. In fact, Western European countries must be prepared to sacrifice their arts, cultures, and people in this global fight.

The episode, "The Finest Hour" shares a similar storyline in that a wealthy French Countess and an ailing Count must entertain a chateau full of German officers and decide whether or not to assist a wounded Hanley and a couple of his men.[54] Hanley must persuade the Countess De Roy (Luise Rainer) to help them gather military intelligence and to inform the Allied command that the Germans plan to launch a major offensive from the new headquarters in the centuries-old mansion. To accomplish this task, Hanley must repeatedly remind her about the war's Big Picture. As with the previous episode, the aristocratic family is asked to make the ultimate sacrifice—the destruction of their ancestral home. The aging Count facilitates the destruction by entertaining and distracting the German officers until the chateau is destroyed by Allied bombing. As Hanley consoles the Countess over the loss of her husband and home, the Countess glowingly refers to the incident as her family's "finest hour." The phrase alludes to Winston Churchill's 1940 speech to the British Parliament declaring the Battle of Dunkirk and the mass evacuation of Allied troops to be Britain's "finest hour." Churchill's speech was also a call to strengthen support for the Allied war effort at home and abroad, especially from the United States. A common Cold War political and rhetorical strategy was to allude to the perceived "justness" and solidarity of the Allied effort during the Second World War and to transfer that *esprit de corps* to the new war.

Conclusion

Combat! is probably best remembered for its gritty, haunting portrayal of tired and exhausted WWII infantrymen struggling to complete a vital mission, determined to stay alive and retain their humanity against the impending threat of death. The series seemed to strike a chord for TV audiences partly tinged with nostalgia over America's military exploits in WWII and ready for an unflinching adult view of the grueling experiences and moral quandaries faced by the common foot soldier. Film historian Stuart Galbraith asserts that one of the most significant aspects of *Combat!* was its visual style, which was not produced like the typical TV drama, but was shot and edited like a feature film.[55] The series made use of hand-held camera shots combined

42 David P. Pierson

with expansive wide shots to provide viewers with both a sense of intimacy and a feeling of epic proportion. Selmur Productions regularly sent a second unit camera crew to France to film establishing shots and to capture the French landscape and architecture. The footage was then matched with the first unit scenes that were shot on MGM's massive but decaying studio back lots. Additional elements to the series' realism included archival footage from WWII to provide a sense of "scope to the battles and the unusual (for the time) choice of having all of its European characters (French, German, Greek) speak their own languages without subtitles."[56] *Combat!* was one of the last of the WWII TV war dramas to treat the war without recourse to irony or exaggeration, which would change with the advent of simplistic action-adventure series such as *The Rat Patrol* and *Garrison's Gorillas*. The series' legacy is further evident in its generic influence on the TV combat war dramas that would follow it. Twenty years after *Combat!*, another TV network (CBS) premiered a dramatic combat war series, *Tour of Duty*, focusing on the members of Bravo Company's second Army platoon in the Vietnam War under the command of the inexperienced, Second Lt. Myron Goldman (Stephen Caffrey) and SSgt. Clayton Ezekiel "Zeke" Anderson (Terence Knox), a tough, experienced sergeant on his third tour of duty. *Tour of Duty* ran from September 1987 to April 1990 with a total of 58 hour-long episodes. It was the first TV war drama following the exploits of infantrymen on American television since the late 1960s. In the course of completing their assigned "search-and-destroy" missions, Lt. Goldman and SSgt. Anderson both must encounter and contend with a steady parade of disaffected soldiers, overzealous officers, and war-torn allies and refugees. The platoon itself is a social microcosm of a diverse, young male America in the late 1960s, including a loyal, working-class sergeant; a Jewish-American, college-educated officer and son of a decorated general from Queens, New York; a soldier and former California surfer; an idealistic soldier and war protestor from Chicago; an African American soldier from the South and former son of a sharecropper, a Japanese American medic; a soldier and son of a rodeo star from Billings, Montana; and an African American soldier from Detroit (*Tour* 2011–2012). With a trio of empathetic leaders, weekly missions, and a socially mixed fighting unit, there is little doubt that *Tour of Duty* was influenced by *Combat!*'s narrative conventions and themes. As television's longest running war drama, *Combat!* continues to serve as a powerful influence on the creation and viability of the combat war drama on American television.

Notes

1. Wesley Britton, "DVD Review: Combat! The Complete Fifth Season," *BC Blogcritics*, accessed October 12, 2014, http://www.blogcritics.org/dvd-review-combat-the-complete-fifth-season.
2. Ibid.
3. James F. Dunnigan and Albert F. Nofi claim that US soldiers, who were unprepared for street fighting in the Battle of Hue in 1968, relied on episodes

The Long Fight 43

of *Combat* to learn about urban warfare strategy and tactics. See *Dirty Little Secrets of the Vietnam War: Military Information You Are Not Supposed to Know* (New York: St. Martin's Press, 1999), 97.

4. James Brooks and Earle Marsh, *The Complete Directory to Prime Time Network TV Shows, 1946-Present,* 4th edition, (New York: Ballantine, 1988), 160–61.

5. Steven Jay Rubin, *Combat Films, American Realism: 1945–1970* (Jefferson, NC: McFarland, 1981), 24–25, 173.

6. Brooks and Marsh, *Prime Time,* 161.

7. A few of these military dramas included *Citizen Soldier* (1956–1957), *Combat Sergeant* (1956), *Flight* (Syndicated, 1958–1959), *Steve Canyon* (NBC, 195–959), and *The West Point Story* (CBS, 1956–1957; ABC, 1957–1958). For more information, see MacDonald, "The Military as TV Entertainment," *Television and the Red Menace: The Video Road to Vietnam* (2009), accessed October 14, 2014, http://jfredmacdonald.com/trm/111militarytv.htm.

8. J. Fred MacDonald, "Politicized TV in Wartime America," *Television and the Red Menace: The Video Road to Vietnam* (2009), accessed October 14, 2014, http://www.ifredmacdonald.com/trm/ivtvwartime.htm.

9. J. Fred MacDonald, *Who Shot the Sheriff: The Rise and Fall of the Television Western* (New York: Praeger, 1986), 117–27.

10. According to Jay S. Harris, in 1961, under protests by the International Longshoremen's Association and a call for a public boycott of L & M products, such as Chesterfield King cigarettes, Liggett & Myers (L & M) Tobacco Company dropped its sponsorship of *The Untouchables.* See *TV Guide: The First 25 Years,* ed. Jay S. Harris (New York: Simon, 1978), 153.

11. Ibid.

12. Jeanine Basinger, *The World War II Combat Film, Anatomy of a Genre* (New York: Columbia University Press, 1986), 188.

13. Ibid., 188–97, 201.

14. Rick Worland, "The Other Living Room War: Evolving Cold War Imagery in Popular TV Programs of the Vietnam Era, 1960–1975" (Ph.D. diss., University of California, Los Angeles, 1989), 212–13.

15. Ibid., 213.

16. MacDonald, "Politicized TV"; Worland, "Living Room War," 210–11.

17. Worland, "Living Room War," 210–11.

18. Basinger, *World War II Combat Film,* 42.

19. These episodes are "The Party," season 1, episode 15, *Combat!—The Complete Collection,* aired December 27, 1963 (Los Angeles: Image Entertainment, 2005) DVD, and "The Furlough," season 5, episode 15, aired December 24, 1966. All subsequent references are to this DVD collection.

20. "A Day in June," season 1, episode 11, *Combat!,* aired December 18, 1962.

21. Worland, "Living Room War," 213.

22. Horace Newcomb and Paul M. Hirsch, "Television as a Cultural Forum," in *Television: The Critical View,* 4th edition, ed. Horace Newcomb (New York: Oxford University Press, 1987) 455–70.

23. Basinger, *World War II Combat Film,* 51.

24. Jo Davidsmeyer, "The Cast of *Combat!,*" *Combat! CombatFan.com,* accessed September 22, 2014. http://www.jodavidsmeyer.com/combat/personnel/cast.html.

25. John Ellis, "Broadcast TV Narration," in *Television: The Critical View,* 4th edition, ed. Horace Newcomb (New York: Oxford University Press, 1987), 553–65.

44   *David P. Pierson*

26. "Point of View," season 3, episode 3, *Combat!,* aired September 24, 1964.
27. Basinger, *World War II Combat Film,* 61.
28. Horace Newcomb, *TV: The Most Popular Art* (Garden City, NY: Anchor Press/Doubleday, 1974).
29. "Mail Call," season 2, episode 21, *Combat!,* aired February 4, 1964.
30. Basinger, *World War II Combat Film,* 61.
31. "High Named Today," season 1, episode 31, *Combat!,* aired May 7, 1963.
32. Steven Fore, "The Perils of Patriotism: The Combat/War Film as Genre and *Southern Comfort* as Generic Self-Immolation," *Australian Journal of Cultural Studies* 2, no. 2 (1984): 40–60.
33. Andrew J. Huebner, *The Warrior Image, Soldiers in American Culture from the Second World War to the Vietnam Era* (Chapel Hill: University of North Carolina Press, 2008), 163.
34. Ibid., 149–50.
35. Ibid., 163.
36. Ibid., 311 and Thomas Doherty, *Projections of War: Hollywood, American Culture, and World War II* (New York: Columbia University Press, 1999), 304.
37. Huebner states that these postwar themes included "brutal orders from officers, violent rivalries between soldiers, breakdowns in teamwork, graphic wounds and death, psychological injuries, even episodes devoted to anti-war messages." Ibid., 163.
38. "The Bridge of Chalons, "season 2, episode 1, *Combat!,* aired September 17, 1963.
39. "No Trumpets, No Drums," season 1, episode 32, *Combat!,* aired May 14, 1963.
40. "Survival," season 1, episode 23, *Combat!,* aired March 12, 1963.
41. Paul Fussell describes the "democracy of fear" that would overtake every soldier in military combat. See, "The Real War, 1939–1945," *The Atlantic Monthly* 26, no. 2 (August 1989): 32–48.
42. "Hills are for Heroes, Part 1," season 4, episode 25, *Combat!,* aired March 1, 1966, and "Hills are for Heroes, Part 2," season 4, episode 26, *Combat!,* aired March 8, 1966.
43. Jo Davidsmeyer, "Hills Are for Heroes, Part 1, Hills Are for Heroes, Part 2," *Combat! CombatFan.com,* accessed September 22, 2014. http://www.jodavidsmeyer.com/combat/episodes/hills_are_for_heroes.html.
44. Jo Davidsmeyer, "Forgotten Front," *Combat! CombatFan.com,* accessed September 22, 2014. http://www.jodavidsmeyer.com/combat/episodes/Forgotten_Front.html.
45. Bruce Miroff, *Pragmatic Illusions: The Presidential Politics of John F. Kennedy* (New York: David McKay, 1976), 3.
46. Theodore C. Sorensen. *Kennedy* (New York: Bantam, 1966), 13.
47. Miroff, *Pragmatic Illusions,* 17–18.
48. Robert Dallek, *The American Style of Foreign Policy* (New York: Knopf, 1983), 224.
49. "Anatomy of a Patrol," season 2, episode 11, *Combat!,* aired November 26, 1963.
50. "Vendetta," season 3, episode 2, *Combat!,* aired September 22, 1964.
51. "Gadjo," season 5, episode 17, *Combat!,* aired January 17, 1967.
52. Sebastian Reyn, in *Atlantis Lost: The American Experience with De Gaulle, 1958–1989* (Amsterdam: Amsterdam University Press, 2010), 356, states that

American public disappointment with De Gaulle emerged with his rejection of Kennedy's plan for a multilateral nuclear force in Europe and "the French withdrawal from NATO."

53. "The Chateau," season 1, episode 19, *Combat!*, aired February 12, 1963.

54. "The Finest Hour," season 4, episode 15, *Combat!*, aired December 21, 1965.

55. Stuart Galbraith, IV, "Combat! The Complete Fourth Season," *DVD Talk*, July 16, 2013, http://www.dvdtalk.com/reviews/60858/combat-the-complete-fourth-season/.

56. Ibid.

3 *12 O'Clock High* and the Image of American Air Power, 1946–1967

Sam Edwards

The image was powerful and quickly infamous: Slim Pickens, rodeo performer and star of numerous film and television Westerns, straddles a giant H-Bomb and, with Stetson in hand, rides it to earth and to doomsday. Here was the essence of Stanley Kubrick's film *Dr. Strangelove* (1964), a dark satire on the insanity of a world that could produce a doctrine of Armageddon and, without irony, reduce it to the acronym "MAD" (Mutually Assured Destruction). While provocative, Kubrick's film was merely the "most notorious chapter in this period's assault on the image of air power."[1] With origins in the era of interwar isolationism, and expressed via print media as well as early cinema, this image asserted that American air power provided protection, deterred potential aggressors, and if necessary would deliver victory when war came. In the eyes of many strategists, this image was affirmed by the events and experiences of World War II, a conflict that saw American Air Force commanders loudly proclaim faith in the bomber's ability to secure victory through the *precise* delivery of destruction. These were the ideas celebrated in wartime propaganda and, with some subtle revisions and refinements, postwar cinema, from *Air Force* (1943) to *A Gathering of Eagles* (1963).

By the early 1960s, however, as Cold War tensions increased, this image came under increasing criticism—hence *Dr. Strangelove*, hence, too, Joseph Heller's novel *Catch-22* (1961), adapted as a film in 1970, and John Hersey's *The War Lover* (1959), released in cinemas in 1962. Yet amidst these critiques, one prominent cultural product did seek to sustain a defense of American air power: the Fox Television/QM Productions series *12 O'Clock High* (ABC, 1964–1967).[2] Based upon a novel (1948) and popular feature film (1949) of the same name, the television series first aired just eight months after Kubrick released *Dr. Strangelove*.[3] Set at an American bomber base in World War II England, and focused on the officers and enlisted men of the fictional 918th Bomb Group, *12 O'Clock High* was partly inspired by a contemporary 1940s nostalgia, seen most clearly in another Fox production, *The Longest Day* (1962); it ran for three seasons on ABC before cancelation in January 1967.

This chapter examines the origins of the television series, paying close attention to its place within the visual culture of American air power. I argue that it sought to reclaim and reinstate an "old" image of air power as a

12 O'Clock High *and the Image of American Air Power, 1946–1967*   47

means of countering the critiques provided by the likes of Kubrick, Heller, and Hersey. However, the chapter also shows that this act of reclamation was doomed to fail because the "old" image no longer accommodated the needs of the moment. The year 1964 was not 1949, and the world of the television series was not that of the earlier film. Indeed, the image of American air power had been long since undermined, not just by Slim Pickens, but also by the political and military events that had shaped Kubrick's satirical assault: the Cold War, the war in Korea, and especially the Cuban Missile Crisis. The escalating conflict in Vietnam provided a final blow, ensuring that war in the azure was seen in a radically different light. Thus, when the first episode of *12 O'Clock High* aired in September 1964, just one month after the Gulf of Tonkin Incident, its days were already numbered.

World War II and the Visual Culture of American Air Power

According to historian Michael Sherry, in the aftermath of World War I and in order to demonstrate the significance of military aviation, American air power advocates developed a revolutionary vision of strategic bombing. Drawing upon ideas then being discussed by general Guilo Douhet in Italy and Marshal High Trenchard in Britain, this vision—most famously articulated in the United States by General William 'Billy' Mitchell—declared that air power offered the only means through which to secure the territorial integrity of the western hemisphere as the bomber was powerfully destructive but also attractively progressive and affordable (an important concern during the Depression). If war came, Mitchell said, this technology offered the means to deliver an organized campaign of bombing designed to cripple an enemy's industrial infrastructure and thus secure strategic victory.[4] In American air power doctrine, then, the bomber quickly accommodated itself to a dynamic and largely unresolved tension: it was a machine of scalpel-like precision *and* the delivery vehicle of overwhelming destructive power, the harbinger of Armageddon. By the 1940s, this "Jekyll and Hyde" image had emerged as a potent influence on popular conceptions of air power in the United States.[5]

American entry into World War II provided the perfect opportunity for senior Air Force commanders, all of whom were Mitchell disciples, to implement this doctrine. For these so-called "Bomber Barons"—General Henry "Hap" Arnold, General Ira Eaker, General Carl "Tooey" Spaatz, General Jimmy Doolittle—the role of the bomber was to deliver, in daylight, *precision* strikes on the "choke" points of industrial infrastructure. This idea would be most clearly realized in the "Schweinfurt Raids" of August to October 1943 during which the Eighth Air Force of the United States Army Air Force (USAAF)—the organization responsible for the American contribution to the Allied strategic bombing campaign—targeted German ball-bearing manufacturing plants (because no military machine can run without ball-bearings). In later raids, the Eighth Air Force would similarly attack German oil refineries.[6]

48 *Sam Edwards*

This concept of air power quickly secured a prominent position in American popular culture. Indeed, "Hap" Arnold, who commanded the USAAF throughout the war, and Ira Eaker, in charge of the Eighth Air Force until January 1944, were both more than happy to exploit their contacts among American publishers and press to communicate their visionary agenda (Eaker had a bachelor's degree in journalism).[7] As a result, even one of the most popular novelists of the Depression, John Steinbeck, wrote in support of the Eighth Air Force.[8] As the war continued, Arnold and Eaker also enlisted help from those involved in a communications technology of the same vintage as military air power: cinema.[9] Two of the most successful propaganda films of World War II confirm the point: *Air Force* (1943), directed by aviation enthusiast Howard Hawks and prompted by an idea of General Arnold's, and *The Memphis Belle* (1944), directed by William Wyler, who was fresh from the success of 1942's pro-interventionist *Mrs. Miniver*. With enthusiastic Air Force support, both films celebrated the American bomber, specifically the B-17, the aircraft central to the Allied strategic bombing campaign in Europe.

Following victory in 1945 and after the US Strategic Bombing Survey (commissioned by Arnold) fell short of declaring that the Allied air campaign had been *decisive*, there were several further cinematic efforts supportive of strategic bombing. *Command Decision* (1948), directed by Sam Wood and starring Clark Gable, is a case in point. Based on a play and then novel authored by William Wister Haines, the film tells the story of Eighth Air Force General Dennis (Gable), and his battle to destroy German jet-manufacturing plants in the face of resistance from congressmen concerned by the "cost" of men and machines. As far as Dennis is concerned, and with a clear nod to the ideas of Billy Mitchell, strategic bombing provides the only means to eradicate the threat posed by these new jet aircraft and thus win the war and save lives. For Gable, this film had personal significance: he had flown five missions as a gunner with the Eighth Air Force in order to get material for an Air Force recruitment film (*Combat America*).[10]

Similar in style and content, but more powerful in delivery, was Daryl Zanuck and Henry King's *12 O'Clock High* (1949). Based upon the novel published a year earlier by Eighth Air Force veterans Sy Bartlett and Beirne Lay, Jr., this film provided yet another robust representation of the importance of strategic bombing.[11] The story centers on General Frank Savage, tasked with turning around the performance and morale of the 918th Bomb Group (BG), based at an imaginary East Anglian airfield—Archbury. The commanding officer of the 918th is suffering from combat exhaustion, a fact demonstrated, says the film, by his increasing caution and unwillingness to risk the lives of his men. In contrast, Savage, played by Gregory Peck, is a motivated and forceful disciplinarian. He quickly imposes himself on his subordinates and converts the 918th from a hard-luck outfit to a hard-hitting one. Throughout, the film makes clear that Savage is no cold and calculating killer but a soldier with a job to do. Indeed, just like Gable's General Dennis, he seeks to save lives through the resolute prosecution of the war.

12 O'Clock High *and the Image of American Air Power, 1946–1967*   49

While audiences warmly received these cinematic visions of World War II air power, they were predicated nonetheless upon an idea of the bomber's purpose and potential already "old" by 1949. Even the format of *12 O'Clock High* asserts this point. The film opens with scenes of a derelict American airfield somewhere in the English countryside (scenes partly inspired by the opening frames of Anthony Asquith's 1945 production *Way to the Stars*). As Robert Wohl has noted, this "atmosphere of nostalgia" ensures that "the past is now past and can be revisited only in fond memory."[12] Similar nostalgia for old certainties was even more apparent in Otto Preminger's 1955 picture, *The Court Martial of Billy Mitchell*, which revisited Mitchell's interwar fall from grace due to his strident attachment to the idea of strategic bombing. To be sure, the courtroom drama was engaging, but a decade after Hiroshima the debate between Mitchell and the Army "Top Brass" over the destructive potential of bombing looked rather dated.

Updating the Image of Air Power in the Cold War

Aware that the earlier image of air power had lost its force, General Curtis LeMay—who became head of the newly created Strategic Air Command (SAC) in the same year *Command Decision* was released—was keen to update it for the nuclear age. For LeMay, an Eighth Air Force veteran who earned his reputation directing operations in the Pacific Theater, the best way to do this was by emphasizing that at the heart of SAC lay the idea of calm command and control. SAC, in short, was not the Horsemen of the Apocalypse, but the guardians of global peace. Enter the so-called "SAC Trilogy," a series of films celebrating Air Force professionalism and procedures.[13]

The first of this trilogy, directed by Anthony Mann, and aptly titled *Strategic Air Command* (1955), was inspired by one of the most powerful actors in postwar Hollywood, a man committed by both politics and personal experience to the doctrine of strategic bombing—Jimmy Stewart. Stewart had flown 20 missions as a wartime officer in the Eighth Air Force and, like LeMay, was a personal friend of Beirne Lay, the co-author of both the novel and film versions of *12 O'Clock High*.[14] In conversation with Lay, Stewart suggested the idea for a film about a World War II veteran and Air Force Reserve Officer recalled to active duty in order to help SAC meet the ever-growing demands on its manpower and mission. What followed was a screenplay along just these lines. Stewart plays Dutch Holland, World War II bomber pilot and baseball legend. Set six years after the war's end, we see Dutch recalled to service by a wartime buddy in need of "mature" leaders to help fulfil SAC's mission. Dutch is reluctant; he is recently married and enjoying life as a peacetime ballplayer. But duty calls, and he returns to uniform. Of special interest is the way General Hawkes (clearly modeled on LeMay) wins Dutch over to military service. With very little subtlety, the General tells anyone who will listen why SAC exists: "we're here,"

50   *Sam Edwards*

he informs Stewart, to "to stop a war from starting." The other two constituents of the "SAC Trilogy"—*Bombers B-52* (1957), directed by Gordon Douglas, and *A Gathering of Eagles* (1963), directed by Delbet Mann—address similar themes, and all three pictures involved either one or more of the Bartlett/Lay *12 O'Clock High* team.

However, although intended to revise the image of air power for the nuclear age, even the SAC Trilogy became dated as real world events altered the context in which Americans understood the role and rationale of the bomber. From the Soviet testing of an atom bomb in 1949 to the fears of nuclear escalation that accompanied the Korean War, contemporary events threatened to expose the bomber for what it really was—a destroyer.[15] And then came two incidents that threatened to undermine the very role and reputation of SAC. First, the Gary Powers controversy of May 1960 (when the Soviet Union shot down a CIA spy plane) raised serious questions about whether or not, in the event of hostilities, SAC aircraft would actually be able to penetrate Soviet air space. Second, the Cuban Missile Crisis of October 1962 produced significant public concern about the threat of nuclear holocaust and about the controls in place to ensure the world could not be annihilated by accident or error. Within the context of these two incidents, the image of air power became the subject of a profound challenge.

Take, for instance, Philip Leacock's 1962 picture *The War Lover*, which depicts the B-17 as the weapon of choice for a psychotic bomber pilot—played in the film with charisma and menace by Steve McQueen—who loved war so much that it provided a sexual thrill. For this pilot, and in a perverse twist on the logic of General Frank Savage, bombing is a "job," but one he likes (in one scene he whoops with joy after being given the reconnaissance photographs recording his most recent "work"). John Hersey, of course, was already famous by this point for revealing the horrors of atomic destruction in *Hiroshima* (1945). Elsewhere, Joseph Heller's novel *Catch-22*, published a year before *The War Lover*, offered a biting satire on war and the various degrees of madness that it promotes, demands, and sustains. As such, it provided a diametrically opposed image of air power to that prevalent in postwar cinema. As Steve Call succinctly explains: "[i]f *The War Lover* is a photographic negative of *12 O'Clock High*, *Catch-22* is its demented nightmare version."[16]

The most celebrated critique of air power in this era was Kubrick's *Dr. Strangelove*. Instead of LeMay-inspired General Castle chomping on his cigars as he delivers yet another pronouncement on the absolute necessity of SAC, we have (with a rather different hint of LeMay influence) General Buck Turgidson (George C. Scott) and General Jack Ripper (Sterling Hayden). The former is philistine, delusional, and occasionally manic when contemplating the destructive power of the B-52, one of which has "gone rogue" and is headed for Russia to deliver the "bomb." The latter dispatches said bomber (and several others) after being consumed by the paranoid obsession that communist infiltrators have "polluted his bodily essence." We are a

12 O'Clock High *and the Image of American Air Power, 1946–1967* 51

long way here from the idea of calm command and control that dominates *Strategic Air Command* and *A Gathering of Eagles*.

Such, then, was the image of air power offered in visual culture by the early 1960s. From the propaganda platitudes of *Air Force* to the blunt politics and patriotism of the SAC Trilogy, advocates of American air power used visual culture as a means to secure popular support for their mission. However, the sharp and satirical critiques of Hersey, Heller, and Kubrick, as well as the Cold War tensions of the moment, dealt their efforts a powerful blow. Combined, these "real" and "reel" events ensured that by the early 1960s, and on the "eve of America's most controversial war [Vietnam], air power had experienced a rapid fall from grace in the eyes of the American public."[17]

12 O'Clock High and the Resurrection of Air Power

Steve Call concludes his insightful examination of the ways in which air power has been sold to the American public with this "fall from grace." In cinematic terms, such a conclusion seems apt. Yet to conclude here neglects an important development in the audio-visual canon of air power. For if American cinema largely abandoned the doctrine of strategic bombing in the aftermath of the Cuban Missile Crisis and *Dr. Strangelove*, one American *television* series embraced it. The series was *12 O'Clock High*.

The origins of the series have been well discussed by Alan Duffin and Paul Matheis in their exhaustive study of the various incarnations of *12 O'Clock High*.[18] As they explain, by 1951 movie theaters were closing as the sale of television sets soared—ticket sales were down, audiences had declined, and profits had fallen. In an attempt to respond to this challenge, movie studios tried new and expensive experiments, such as expanding the use of color film and developing better quality picture formats. At the forefront of these experiments was Twentieth-Century Fox, among the studios worst hit by the declining fortunes of the movie industry. Indeed, Fox was struggling to respond not just to the changed dynamics of the moment but also to some of their own poor decisions. For instance, after selling much of their Hollywood real estate in order to raise capital, they then plowed the new funds into a picture that quickly became a byword for excess, waste, and box office failure: *Cleopatra* (1962). Equally important, their founder and talisman, Daryl F. Zanuck, who had built a career on his intuitive ability to deliver what audiences wanted to see, had left the studio in 1956 amid rancor and recriminations. Without him, Fox lost three decades of sharp and savvy decision-making and story-telling expertise.[19]

In 1960, Zanuck returned from his self-imposed exile in France, appointed his son Richard as president of Fox Television and, with *The Longest Day* (1962), quickly reasserted his ability to identify the zeitgeist.[20] The film cost just $7.75 million to make (as opposed to the $42 million price tag of *Cleopatra*) and was a commercial and critical success.[21] Two years later, the

52   Sam Edwards

considerable media attention surrounding the twentieth anniversary of the D-Day landings confirmed Zanuck's skillful reading of the moment.[22]

But saving the company required more than just one successful picture, and so under Zanuck's leadership Fox also invested greater resources in the new medium of television.[23] Following the success of *The Longest Day*, and no doubt inspired by Zanuck's long-running interest in the Air Force (he was a charter member of the Air Power League and had been personally involved in shaping the 1949 film), company executives began searching for suitable World War II-themed stories among their existing copyright properties. They turned to *12 O'Clock High*, a story that also offered the opportunity, two years after the Cuban Missile Crisis, to recreate a positive image of air power by setting the story in World War II Europe. In this historical context, characters would be able to voice the logic and rationale of strategic bombing without invoking Hiroshima, Nagasaki, or the threat of Armageddon. The Department of Defense was approached for support and technical advice, which was soon forthcoming (the DoD remained involved for the duration of the series and had right of approval on the scripts).[24]

The idea for the series' structure came from Quinn Martin, recently the producer of *The Untouchables*, (ABC, 1959–1963) and later a key figure in such productions as *The FBI* (ABC, 1965–1974) and *Green Hornet* (ABC, 1966–1967). Martin, who had served in the Signal Corps throughout the war, formed his own production company—QM Productions—in 1960. With input from writer Paul Monash and *12 O'Clock High* author Beirne Lay, Martin crafted the idea for a series based on "stories of men during war, not always men at war."[25] In the lead role of General Frank Savage, Martin cast the Broadway trained Robert Lansing. Just a year earlier, Lansing had a minor role in the concluding picture in the SAC Trilogy—*A Gathering of Eagles*. Solidifying these links to the SAC trilogy, Master Sergeant James Doherty, who served as technical advisor on *Bombers B-52*, fulfilled the same role on *12 O'Clock High*.[26] Meanwhile, to support Lansing, Martin cast John Larkin in the role of Major General Wiley Crow (Savage's immediate superior and friend) and Robert Overton as Major Harvey Stovall, his Executive Officer (the only character to last all three seasons). The series was filmed in black and white, which allowed for the frequent display of original wartime footage of American bombers in action (much of this footage was taken from wartime documentaries or postwar films such as *Command Decision*).[27]

Season one explored the narrative possibilities suggested by Monash and Lay. The 33 episodes feature stories in which Savage finds love and romance; stories of capture and captivity; stories of resistance, betrayal, and collaboration. Notably, women often feature as either domestic distractions or subversive threats. As in the SAC Trilogy, they are the representatives of peace and domesticity who provide the cause and justification for the male work of war and, when necessary, offer moments of rest, relaxation and recovery. For instance, in Episode 10 (tellingly titled "Interlude") Savage,

12 O'Clock High *and the Image of American Air Power, 1946–1967*   53

exhausted by combat, is ordered on leave. He takes the train to the "end of the line" (Scotland) and duly falls in love with his carriage counterpart, Anne Macrae, played by Dana Wynter, reprising something of the role she played opposite Robert Taylor in *D-Day: The Sixth of June* (1956). But the potential threat that this "interlude" might permanently interrupt Savage's work is disarmed by a cunning plot device: Macrae is only on the train because she is heading home to die (she has terminal carcinoma). Thus, Savage gets to have his cake and eat it, too. He loves, learns (to cry and feel again), loses, and then returns to war, the better man (and warrior) for being reminded why, and for whom, he fights: he fights for peace, picnics, and posies (shortly before Macrae dies, she reveals to Savage her legacy—a flower bed, sown in her garden).[28] Elsewhere, women are depicted according to the other pole of the classic Virgin/Whore dichotomy; that is, they are the cynical, immoral (or amoral) sexual temptresses who threaten to undermine the business of bombing. In "The Hours Before Dawn" Savage is confronted by an English lady so devoid of moral scruples that she declares "neutrality" and refuses to aid his escape after they are both imprisoned by a downed Luftwaffe bomber pilot. In "Soldiers Sometimes Kill" Savage is even drugged and duped by a woman acting on behalf of an English Nazi fifth-columnist.[29]

Nevertheless, amid these various stories of love and loss, domesticity and deceit, season one frequently revisits the theme central to the original novel and the 1949 film: the necessity and utility of air power. In particular, episodes repeatedly rehearse the reasons the 918th BG are in England and the details of how they do their job. It is here that we see most clearly the attempt to hit the rhetorical rewind button and revive the purpose and rationale of American air power.

Episode 6 well demonstrates the point. Titled "Pressure Point," it follows the attempts of General Savage to win over an anti-bombing politician undertaking an inspection of American airfields in England (a plot that was essentially derivative of *Command Decision*). The politician in question, Senator Clayton Johnson (Larry Gates), already distrusts Savage due to a past connection (15 years earlier Savage had wanted to marry Clayton's daughter, but the Senator broke the engagement due to his dislike of military aviators). These feelings are intensified by Clayton's belief that strategic bombing is ineffective and overly costly in terms of American lives. Ultimately, however, Savage converts the Senator to the war-winning effectiveness of his bomber force by delivering a mission in which the target is completely destroyed without the loss of a single American plane.[30]

Even when the doctrine of air power is not foregrounded, it is often in the background or between the lines. In "Decision," for instance, the precision of the B-17 is powerfully demonstrated by the fact that it is able to hit a factory building immediately adjacent to the "cage" in which American POWs have been imprisoned by their German captors so that they might serve as a human shield.[31] On other occasions, the value of strategic bombing is

54 *Sam Edwards*

asserted in the face of the very moral and ethical qualms so central to the attacks leveled in the likes of *The War Lover* and *Dr. Strangelove*. Thus, in "Follow the Leader," Lt. Mellon, the lead bombardier in the 918th BG, is traumatized by the fact that he is responsible for the accidental destruction of a Dutch school. But after discovering that the error was due to mechanical failure rather than human oversight, General Savage orders him on the next mission. Mellon goes, overcomes his moral uncertainties, and drops his bombs. They fall right on target, and there is no suggestion of civilian death. Similarly, in "The Sound of Distant Thunder," another bombardier, Lt. Lathrop (Peter Fonda), a quiet tee-totaling mid-westerner, loses his faith in bombing after his English girlfriend is killed during a German raid on London. Having experienced what it is like on the receiving end, Lathrop declares to Savage that he cannot go on. With words directly inspired by the rhetoric of the wartime bomber barons, Savage counters that in the long run bombing will actually shorten the war and thus save lives. Lathrop listens, learns, and is ready the next day for the mission. Later, in "Faith, Hope, and Sergeant Aronson," the idea that the doctrine of strategic bombing is a sort of "faith" is affirmed by a story in which an airman of deep religious conviction loses his way following the death of his best friend. He returns to the true path only when required to be a blood donor for a wounded General Savage and only after finding love with a local English girl. With his "heart" restored (much like the wounded Savage, after a complicated operation to remove a piece of shrapnel lodged in his chest), Aronson (Sorrell Booke) returns to battle. Indeed, the closing scene actually suggests that he returns to do "God's work." Here, strategic bombing is divine retribution and American bombers merely the tools with which God smites the unrighteous. Little wonder that in "Here's to Courageous Cowards" even a former conscientious objector is won over to the rightness of the cause.[32]

Such was the skill and subtlety of the first season. It does not shy away from the moral and ethical uncertainties of bomber crews, nor does it ignore the fact of "collateral damage." Furthermore, unlike its cinematic forebears, the first season of *12 O'Clock High* is not blunt with its politics. Rather, it veils its ideological commitment to the bomber through stories that ostensibly explore "other" issues—love, trauma, Anglo-American relations. Yet the resolutions to these stories quietly assert that strategic bombing is right, proper, and effective. Love might be lost, but at least the war will be won; civilians might very occasionally be killed but only by accident or mistake; moral uncertainties are raised but only to ensure they can be confronted and silenced.

Throughout, the audience is encouraged to view events—their reason and rationale—from the perspective of wholesome farm boys, mature and sensitive representatives of the American melting pot (episode 19's Sgt. Aronson is a scholarly and devout Jewish American), or knowledgeable commanders. General Savage is the lynchpin of the whole series, and his very name is indicative of the rationale that structures the show. "Savage" is suggestive of the potential for primitive violence and brutality, and, in the novel, we are told that the character is of partly "Indian blood."[33] Yet as the novel, film, and television series all assert, General Savage is no mere barbarian. Like James Fenimore-Cooper's Hawkeye, his capacity for violence, his "Indian" ancestry, his inner Hyde, is always controlled, to be unleashed only when time and circumstance demand.

The public and critical response to the series was mixed. Some critics, like those in *The New York Times, Time*, and *Newsweek*, thought Robert Lansing's General Savage was powerful and engaging. Others were less impressed, finding the performances wooden, the plots facile and overly simple in their conclusions, and the possible scenarios provided by the focus and format far too restrictive.[34] Perhaps these critics had a point, for the ratings certainly proved disappointing. After securing an impressive Arbitron rating of 23.3 for its first episode (which equated to 50.9% share, or over half of US households with the television on at that hour), in subsequent weeks the show settled at a rather more lowly rating of 12.[35] Part of the problem was that the network screening the show—ABC—seemed uncertain about exactly where to place it in their schedules. It first screened at 9:30 pm on Friday evenings but moved to 10 pm halfway through the series. Moreover, after deciding to commission a second season, ABC moved the series again, this time to the earlier slot of 7:30 pm and on Mondays.[36] The network also made a key demand: that General Savage would have to go.[37]

One of the series' screenwriters, Harold Bloom, recalls that central to ABC's demand was their concern that, in the hands of Lansing, General Savage looked like a "brooding villain."[38] Indeed, in his eyes, furrowed brow, and the intensity of his performance, there *is* something reminiscent of Steve McQueen's psychotic bomber pilot from *The War Lover*. In concert with this "problem," ABC also suggested that the show was too focused on the views and opinions of commanders, rather than on the experiences of the young men flying the planes (who it was assumed would be more engaging for the younger, 7:30 pm, audience).[39] After Generals Turgidson and Ripper, moreover, and with the outspoken LeMay now Chief of the Air Staff (in 1965, LeMay would famously declare that he thought North Vietnam should be bombed back to the "stone age"), it was now increasingly difficult to see the commanders of air power as unequivocally "good."

Thus, despite being intended to re-establish the image of strategic bombing, the decision to focus much of the story telling on General Savage actually threatened to do the opposite. This was especially the case because the director of photography, keen to ensure the show had an authentic, gritty quality, consciously chose—like Kubrick—to invoke a film noir style. Shadow, contrasts of light and dark, and grainy combat footage were all employed to assert the seriousness of the subject matter.[40] As a result, Lansing's brooding was accentuated by a brooding set, and the result was dark both aesthetically and in tone. So Lansing was dismissed, and his character, the central figure in the 1948 novel and the clear focus of the 1949 film, was killed in

56   Sam Edwards

the opening episode of season two ("The Loneliest Place in the World"). Significantly, Lansing refused to appear on set simply to receive the *coup de grace*, and so his exit was achieved by a "clean," if less than subtle, sequence: Savage's plane is hit during a bombing mission and falls from the sky. Back at Archbury, a message from the French Resistance confirms his death, and his picture and name are duly removed from the Group's command roster.[41]

Following the abrupt departure of General Savage, season two is different in feel and form, particularly because the other key character who articulated the views of the World War II Bomber Barons—General Crowe—had similarly exited stage left (John Larkin, who played Crowe, died in early 1965 following a heart attack). With Savage and Crowe gone, the differences between season one and two were apparent right from the start and emphasized in the new lead: Paul Burke, as Colonel Joe Gallagher. Gallagher had previously featured in the opening episode of season one as something of an ill-disciplined flyboy. In season two, however, he emerges as a mature and seasoned commander. To be sure, he occasionally lacks Savage's clarity and conviction, but in many respects Gallagher is a more sympathetic and human character. He makes mistakes; he gets drunk; he pursues women with gusto, yet he maintains his moral compass and makes the tough decisions. However, by replacing the character of *General* Savage with that of *Colonel* Gallagher, and by giving the role of support to *Sergeant* Komansky, played by Chris Robinson (as opposed to *General* Crowe), the decisions Gallagher has to make are of a different sort and order. Whereas Savage and Crowe debated the merits of the overall strategic bombing campaign, Gallagher and Komansky foil saboteurs, perform heroics, and argue over women. Consequently, there is much in season two intended for a younger audience—more sky fighting, excitement, and romance. In order to suggest chronological progression, the series also shifts the action to a different point in the war. While season one placed the drama in 1943, a time when the commanders of the USAAF were still making the case for daylight bombing, season two moves the focus to the months leading up to D-Day (another clear nod toward the recent success of *The Longest Day* and also suggestive of the impact of the 20th anniversary D-Day commemorations, which included a popular CBS documentary featuring Dwight Eisenhower wandering the beaches of Normandy with Walter Cronkite).[42]

If the dynamics of the show were altered by the reintroduction of matinee idol Paul Burke, and by the comradeship (and tension) between his character and that of Sgt. Komansky, the show's writers nonetheless remained committed to providing a positive image of air power. In "Which Way the Wind Blows," for instance, Gallagher finds a way of delivering precision attacks even in overcast weather, an idea refined further in "Back to the Drawing Board" following the development of a new specialist piece of equipment, the "Bomb through Overcast" device. In "25th Mission," the writers even reuse, once again, a plot device from *Command Decision*, albeit with a slight twist: Gallagher must lead his group on a mission to destroy a

12 O'Clock High *and the Image of American Air Power, 1946–1967*   57

jet fighter manufacturing plant, but he must do so at *night*. Thus, even darkness cannot deny the precision of the B-17. A similar homage to the past was also apparent in "Angel Babe," clearly inspired by *The Memphis Belle*.[43]

In addition to episodes that continued to assert the value of air power, season two included some striking attempts to disarm the powerful critiques delivered by the likes of Kubrick, Heller, and Hersey. In "Show Me a Hero, I'll Show You a Bum," for example, we see Sgt. Komansky kick loose a bomb that becomes stuck in the bomb bay during a mission, but there is pointedly no rodeo ride to doomsday. "I Am the Enemy," meanwhile, focuses on an officer very similar in motivation and purpose to Steve McQueen's war-loving pilot from *The War Lover*. However, rather than being revealed as a home-grown American psycho, this pilot—Major Kurt Brown, played by a pre-*Star Trek* William Shatner—turns out to be of German ancestry. His desire to kill German civilians is thus translated into a death wish, rather than being indicative of the real purpose (and result) of strategic bombing. In "The Jones Boys" the story pivots on war profiteers and features an American airman selling government equipment for personal profit. In contrast to Heller's Milo Minderbinder, this is not to be understood as the underlying rationale of war revealed. Rather, to pursue profit is commensurate with duty denied and morals corrupted.[44]

Despite these changes, the response of viewers remained mixed. Notably, some of the "old" fans disliked the new format and complained that in making the show more attractive to a younger audience it had lost much of its character depth and gritty realism.[45] There were problems, too, in the form of tensions between the two leads, Burke and Robinson, the latter of whom occasionally scene stole from the former. Then there were the ratings, which remained poor, generally hovering somewhere around 11.5 to 15.2 according to Arbitron (a 24 to 27 share). As a result, when surveyed in September 1965, *12 O'Clock High* was found to be only the 26th most popular show on the schedules. By November 1965, it was out of the top 40.[46]

Despite a new lead, impressive production values ($130,000 per episode by season two), and a shift in the schedules, *12 O'Clock High* was still struggling to live up to expectations. Even a concerted and costly publicity campaign had failed to build the necessary anticipation. Nonetheless, in March 1966 Quinn Martin received news that the show would be renewed for a third season but on a new condition—that it be produced in full color.[47] Not all were convinced that this was the way to go. The film noir-inspired director of photography, William Spencer, remarked that "World War II was in black-and-white. It's hard to make color look down and dirty and grim."[48] Filming the show in color also presented practical problems. Most of the wartime footage of bombers flying and fighting was in black-and-white, and this made splicing difficult if not impossible. However, ABC insisted, and QM Productions finally agreed.

Thus, season three certainly *looks* different from seasons one and two. In full technicolor, the show no longer suggested the gritty quality of

58   Sam Edwards

authenticity that had characterized earlier episodes. Still, action-adventure remained a key focus, and there was more love, loss, and romance, as well as references to contemporary transatlantic relations and Cold War concerns (more than one episode features Russian characters). During planning, the producers also opted to keep the chronology in and around 1944 so that D-Day could again be in the background. Despite the technical challenge, even the familiar imagery of World War II air combat remained present, as *The Memphis Belle* provided plenty of suitable color footage. As if to assert the extent to which the show remained in tune with its roots, ABC also returned it to its original timeslot of 10:00 pm on Fridays.[49]

Cancelation and Conclusion

In spite of these initiatives, *12 O'Clock High* continued to struggle in the ratings, and across a two-week period in October 1966 it was recorded as the 91st most popular show (out of 92).[50] Consequently, a month later, ABC announced they were dropping the show; season three ended in January 1967 after just 17 episodes.[51] At the time, several factors were identified as responsible for the show's poor overall performance. It was, to be sure, competing against many other shows, not the least of which was *Combat!* (see chapter 2 in this volume). Another factor concerned the relatively high production values, a cost that obviously had to be recouped. Perhaps, too, as some critics suggested, the scenario was overly restrictive; a World War II airfield might work well as the focus for a film, but less so for a TV series offering 33 episodes per season. Eventually, the choice of plot lines *would* expire (a point apparent in season three, which saw some episodes revisiting plots from season one).

All of these are certainly explanatory factors in the collapse and cancel-ation of *12 O'Clock High*, but the contemporary political and cultural con-text was the crucial factor. By 1967, the doctrine of air power had seen too many challenges and critiques, too many questions asked and fears expressed, as American "victory culture" commenced its terminal decline.[52] Who, now, could see a bomb kicked out of a plane without thinking of Slim Pickens? Who, after Buck Turgidson, could see in an air power General a calm and clear commander? Who, after *Strangelove*, not to mention Hiroshima, could see in the strategic bomber anything other than the Destroyer of Worlds? Moreover, the answer to the last question provided yet more problems, for the people who did still have faith in the bomber were those *at that very moment* seeking to apply its power in Vietnam. Operation Rolling Thunder, the American air campaign against North Vietnam, officially began in March 1965, just as *12 O'Clock High* was halfway through its first season. The campaign remained ongoing until 1968 and thus provided the real-world air power backdrop to the televisual theatrics of Quinn Martin's production. Significantly, the Air Force officers who planned Rolling Thunder remained, like General Savage, fully committed to the doctrine of strategic bombing.

12 O'Clock High *and the Image of American Air Power, 1946–1967*   59

As historian Mark Clodfelter has explained, in adherence to what had become the "dogma" of this doctrine, Vietnam-era air leaders "insisted that future attacks directed against a nation's capability to fight would weaken its will to resist."[53] Such was the logic, and the ultimate flaw, governing Rolling Thunder. As a concept, strategic bombing assumes that the enemy *must* have vital centers to attack, and the destruction of such targets will, in turn, affect the ability to make war. Neither of these represented an accurate assessment of the nature of the North Vietnamese economy or of the dynamics of the indigenous Viet Cong guerrilla movement. In short, a World War II-era vision of strategic bombing was simply wrong for Vietnam and wrong for the 1960s.[54]

Here was the ultimate reason for the end of *12 O'Clock High*. As both novel and film, it had been successful because its vision of air power met the demands of the moment. By 1964, this vision had foundered. Korea, the Cuban Missile Crisis, the satirical and political attacks of Kubrick, Heller, and Hersey, all had compromised the "old" idea of air power. And then came Vietnam, a conflict in which this old idea was applied to South-East Asia with little success. Furthermore, the extent to which the show and the doctrine were in symbiotic relationship was institutionalized through the advice and support provided to QM Productions by both the Department of Defense *and* the Air Force (the latter even included images from the show in recruitment posters).[55] Thus, as the 1960s progressed *12 O'Clock High*, just like the actual application of air power in Vietnam, stuttered and struggled, before stalling and crashing. Little wonder that the show's producer, Bill Gordon, later remarked, "there was no question about it. The anti-Vietnam protests and general anti-war sentiment worked against *12 O'Clock High* rating-wise, and perhaps the cliché of World War II."[56] Even the one storyline that might have provided a route through the impasse—celebrations of the wartime transatlantic alliance—was nullified by contemporary disputes and disagreements. Britain persistently refused to contribute troops to the fighting in South-East Asia while President Charles de Gaulle declared in June 1965 that the "United States was the greatest danger in the world today to peace."[57] A year later, De Gaulle withdrew the French military from NATO and then demanded the removal of all US troops from French soil. What chance now for stories lingering on the closeness of the Grand Alliance or eulogizing the Anglo-American "ties that bind"? And so ABC's *12 O'Clock High*, a TV series born of a nostalgic return to the imagined certainties of World War II and intimately connected to a 30 year-effort to celebrate American air power, found that it had no place or purpose amid the changes, challenges, and confusions of the late 1960s.

Notes

1. Steve Call, *Selling Air Power: Military Aviation and Popular Culture after World War II* (College Station: Texas A&M University Press, 2009), 158.
2. Quinn Martin Productions, *12 O'Clock High* (LA: Twentieth-Century Fox Television, 1964–1967). 60 min (78 episodes). All 78 episodes can be viewed

60 *Sam Edwards*

here: https://www.youtube.com/watch?v=5_Q7NSR8aZ8&list=PLa9qlKyhih-9blBR_t4bdPpeTJ2jqBsfrI. All subsequent references are to this youtube collection.

3. Beirne Lay Jr. and Sy Bartlett, *12 O'Clock High* (New York: Ballantine Books, 1965).

4. Michael Sherry, *The Rise of American Air Power: The Creation of Armageddon* (New Haven: Yale University Press, 1987), 22–46.

5. Call, *Selling Air Power*, 32–33.

6. Donald Miller, *Eighth Air Force: The American Bomber Crews in Britain* (London: Aurum Press, 2006); and Ronald Schaffer, *Wings of Judgment: American Bombing in World War II* (Oxford: Oxford University Press, 1985), esp. 35–79. Royal Air Force Bomber Command had a policy of night-time "area bombing." For details about how this has been portrayed, see Michael Paris, *From the Wright Brothers to* Top Gun (Manchester: Manchester University Press, 1995), 140–50, and Mark Connolly, "*Bomber Harris*: Raking Through the Ashes of the Strategic Bombing Campaign against Germany," in *Repicturing the Second World War*, ed. Michael Paris (Basingstoke: Palgrave Macmillan, 2007), 162–76.

7. Call, *Selling Air Power*, 26–27.

8. John Steinbeck, *Bombs Away: The Story of a Bomber Team* (New York: The Viking Press, 1942); John Steinbeck, *Once There Was a War* (New York: The Viking Press, 1958).

9. Paris, *From the Wright Brothers to* Top Gun, 108–10; 152–57.

10. Robert Wohl, *The Spectacle of Flight: Aviation and the Western Imagination, 1920–1950* (New Haven: Yale University Press, 2005), 141; Kenneth D. Rose, *Myth and the Greatest Generation: A Social History of Americans in World War II* (New York: Routledge, 2008), 167.

11. Lay and Bartlett, *12 O'Clock High*, 1948. Lay was no stranger to film adaptions.

12. Wohl, *Spectacle of Flight*, 273.

13. Call, *Selling Air Power*, 111–14.

14. Starr Smith, *Jimmy Stewart: Bomber Pilot* (Minneapolis: Zenith Press, 2005).

15. Simon Duke, *US Defense Bases in the United Kingdom: A Matter for Joint Decisions?* (London: Macmillan, 1987), 35–36.

16. Call, *Selling Air Power*, 152.

17. Call, *Selling Air Power*, 172.

18. Allan T. Duffin and Paul Matheis, *12 O'Clock High Logbook: The Unofficial History of the Novel, Motion Picture, and TV Series* (Boalsburg, PA: BearManor Media, 2005), 96–103.

19. George F. Custen, *Twentieth Century's Fox: Daryl F. Zanuck and the Culture of Hollywood* (New York: Basic Books, 1997), 352–60.

20. Custen, *Twentieth Century's Fox*, 360–68.

21. Duffin and Matheis, *12 O'Clock High Logbook*, 97.

22. Sam Edwards, *Allies in Memory: World War II and the Politics of Transatlantic Commemoration, c. 1941–2001* (Cambridge: Cambridge University Press, 2015), 118–27.

23. Custen, *Twentieth Century's Fox*, 317–22.

24. Duffin and Matheis, *12 O'Clock High Logbook*, 128.

25. Ibid., 105.

26. Ibid., 112.
27. Ibid., 121.
28. "Interlude," season 1, episode 10, *12 O'Clock High*, aired November 27 1964.
29. "The Hours Before Dawn," season 1, episode 8, *12 O'Clock High*, aired November 13 1964. "Soldiers Sometimes Kill," season 1, episode 12, *12 O'Clock High*, aired December 11 1964.
30. "Pressure Point," season 1, episode 6, *12 O'Clock High*, aired October 30 1964.
31. "Decision," season 1, episode 7, *12 O'Clock High*, aired November 6 1964.
32. "Follow the Leader," season 1, episode 2, *12 O'Clock High*, aired September 25 1964; "The Sound of Distant Thunder," season 1, episode 4, *12 O'Clock High*, aired October 16 1964; "Faith, Hope and Sergeant Aronson," season 1, episode 19, *12 O'Clock High*, aired January 29 1965; "Here's to Courageous Cowards," season 1, episode 11, *12 O'Clock High*, aired December 4 1964.
33. Lay and Bartlett, *12 O'Clock High*, 23.
34. See, for example, Jack Gould, "ABC's 'Jonny Quest' a series for Young," *The New York Times*, September 19, 1964, 54; "Review," *Newsweek*, September 25,1964; "Review," *Newsweek*, September 28, 1964.
35. Duffin and Matheis, *12 O'Clock High Logbook*, 126–27.
36. Ibid., 146.
37. Ibid., 132–34.
38. Ibid., 131–32.
39. Ibid., 131.
40. Ibid., 113.
41. "The Loneliest Place in the World," season 2, episode 1, *12 O'Clock High*, aired September 13 1965.
42. Edwards, *Allies in Memory*, 111–27; *D-Day Plus 20 Years: Eisenhower Returns to Normandy*. CBS Reports, Columbia Broadcasting Systems, Inc., 1964. 123 min.
43. "Which Way the Wind Blows," season 2, episode 19, *12 O'Clock High*, aired January 24 1966; "Back to the Drawing Board," season 2, episode 21, *12 O'Clock High*, aired February 6 1966; "25th Mission," season 2, episode 22, *12 O'Clock High*, aired February 14 1966; "Angel Babe," season 2, episode 24, *12 O'Clock High*, aired February 28 1966.
44. "Show Me a Hero, I'll Show You a Bum," season 2, episode 7, *12 O'Clock High*, aired October 25 1965; "I Am the Enemy," season 2, episode 9, *12 O'Clock High*, aired, November 8 1965; "The Jones Boys," season 2, episode 13, *12 O'Clock High*, aired December 6 1965.
45. Duffin and Matheis, *12 O'Clock High Logbook*, 131, 147.
46. Ibid., 148.
47. Ibid., 152.
48. Ibid.
49. Ibid., 153.
50. Ibid., 157.
51. The final episode was "The Hunters and the Killers," season 3, episode 17, *12 O'Clock High*, aired January 13 1967.
52. Thomas Engelhardt, *The End of Victory Culture* (New York: Basic Books, 1995).

62   *Sam Edwards*

53. Mark Clodfelter, *The Limits of Air Power: The American Bombing of North Vietnam* (New York: The Free Press, 1989), 36.
54. Ibid., 203–10.
55. Duffin and Matheis, *12 O'Clock High Logbook*, 146.
56. Ibid., 158.
57. Frank Costigliola, *France and the United States: The Cold Alliance since World War II* (New York: Maxwell Macmillan, 1992), 143.

4 Nervous Laughter

Hogan's Heroes and the Vietnam War[1]

Robert R. Shandley

Almost every response to the 1965 premiere of *Hogan's Heroes* (1965–1971) on primetime CBS referred to the show's World War II historical setting. Most reviews found the situation comedy's conceit of a group of prisoners of war conducting sabotage from the confines of a German *Stalag* offensive. One such critic, Jack Gould of *The New York Times*, admitted as much two years later when he gave the series a second look: "The idea of making sport of the Nazis as clownish oafs originally struck this corner as a wildly improbable premise, but the continued run of Edward H. Felman's production speaks for itself."[2] If Gould's assertion is true, what does it say? By 1967, why had the series become more acceptable in the eyes of a New York taste-maker? Gould's own answer is that the series had found a comedic formula that assured continued success, namely by avoiding the kind of topicality associated with other television programming of the day. While Gould is no doubt right that *Hogan's Heroes* had discovered a formula for success, one that would keep it in syndication for decades after its original broadcast run, his own reading of what constituted that formula is underdeveloped. The secret to the success of *Hogan's Heroes* was the series' ability to couch its own topicality within a historical war setting in which the moral stakes were much less contentious than the war that was raging during the show's run.

Hogan's Heroes was an entertaining military sitcom that coincided with the most intense period of American involvement in Vietnam. It would become part of a genre of uniform comedies and dramas and television spy thrillers that dominated the network line-ups in the early to mid-1960s and provided narrative backfill for the Cold War tensions. The spy programs included shows such as *The Man from U.N.C.L.E.* (NBC 1964–1968), *Espionage* (NBC 1963–1964), *I Spy* (NBC 1965–1968), *Burke's Law* (CBS 1963–1966), *Secret Agent* (CBS 1965–1966), and the comedy *Get Smart* (CBS, 1965–1970). Starting in 1962, military sitcoms and dramas such as ABC's *McHale's Navy* (1962–1966) and *Combat!* (1962–1967) began occupying slots in the schedule. *Gomer Pyle, USMC* (1964–1969) was added to CBS's schedule in 1964. ABC kept up its quotient of military related shows with the introduction that same season of *Twelve O'Clock High* (1964–1967). By 1965, with the addition of *Hogan's Heroes*, which initially ran just before

64 *Robert R. Shandley*

Gomer Pyle, USMC on Friday nights, NBC's *The Wackiest Ship in the Navy* (1965–1966) and *Convoy* (1965) and ABC's *F Troop* (1965–1967), uniform comedies and dramas occupied a dominant portion of the prime-time schedule. Both *Gomer Pyle, USMC* and *Hogan's Heroes* made it into the top 10 in Nielsen ratings that season, with *The Man from U.N.C.L.E.* and *Get Smart* cracking the top 20. In the first year of the escalated American engagement in Vietnam, the spy and military genres were indeed a growing force in the prime time schedule.

While, in the immediate CBS line-up, *Gomer Pyle, USMC* provided *Hogan's Heroes* with a model for plot structure, NBC's *The Man from U.N.C.L.E.* offered another important part of its narrative mix. Premiering the previous year on Tuesday night, *The Man from U.N.C.L.E.* was an Ian Fleming project meant to take advantage of the success of the first Bond film, *From Russia with Love* (1963). While *The Man from U.N.C.L.E.* initially struggled to gain ratings in the fall of 1964, by mid-season it began to establish a following. Research showed that audiences liked the mixture of adventure and comedy.[3] In fact, NBC was putting together a prisoner of war comedy to couple with its success with *The Man from U.N.C.L.E. Campo 44* (1967) was to be set in an Italian POW camp. According to a fan book about *Hogan's Heroes*, when its creators, Albert Ruddy and Bernie Fein, caught wind of this development, they quickly set to work to pen a version of this scenario themselves.[4] Of course, the other model for *Hogan's Heroes* was Billy Wilder's acclaimed POW film, *Stalag 17* (1953), from which Ruddy and Fein obviously drew considerable material.

In order to better comprehend how CBS was attempting to position *Hogan's Heroes,* it is productive to understand who the target audience was. To do so, we can look at some of the early decisions the network made regarding the series. Early in 1965, CBS began making incremental gestures toward broader programming in color. A national survey of women in December 1964 showed that owners of color sets were more affluent, better educated, and more urban than the population as a whole.[5] *Hogan's Heroes* was one of the earliest series on which CBS committed to color. Later that year, once it became clear that the sale of color sets was booming, CBS heightened its commitment to color broadcasting. The fact that *Hogan's Heroes* made the earlier list suggests its intended demographic appeal.

CBS's intentions matter because they help dispel the notion that the network first began targeting an educated, urbane audience with the so-called barnyard purge of the early 1970s, in which they canceled all of the programming that they believed alienated their supposedly urbane target audience. It is that assumption that has also led most observers to treat *M*A*S*H* (1972–1983) as the network's sole sitcom response to the Vietnam War. Because of their tremendous range of shared characteristics, *Hogan's Heroes* and *M*A*S*H* offer useful comparisons. Most of the commentary on the latter series starts with the assumption that the sitcom trials and tribulations of the medical unit during the Korean War are in fact thinly

Nervous Laughter 65

veiled commentaries on Vietnam. Yet, premiering on September 17, 1972, *M*A*S*H* had the benefit of conducting its treatment of the Vietnam War at a time when a vast consensus had formed that shared its anti-war sentiments. *Hogan's Heroes*, on the other hand, is an artifact of the uncertainties and tumult that led to that consensus.

Hogan's Heroes premiered exactly seven years before *M*A*S*H* on September 17, 1965, with the pilot episode, "The Informer."[6] As it was used to sell the network on developing the show, "The Informer" can serve as a primer of the series' premise, its characters, and how its audience is to be conceived and addressed. The opening introduces the ironic combination of the signs upon which the series relies, namely the German war machine and a comedic soundtrack. Sergeant Schulz (John Banner) is introduced as he performs what will become his standard headcount routine, one that usually results in a missing prisoner. Just so the viewer does not become alarmed, the guard's initial interaction with Hogan, as well as the appearance of the German colonel, Klink (Werner Klemperer), is accompanied by a laugh track. It is incumbent for the rest of the episode and indeed arguably the entire series, to establish what is so laughable about this situation: the Germans are merely props, and the prisoners are clearly in charge of the camp. Indeed, that is the necessary conceit for every episode.

The rest of the pilot reveals the various gimmicks and tools with which the prisoners will thwart and sabotage the German war machine, each of which summons its own laugh track. Perhaps the biggest difference between the pilot and the subsequent series lies in the makeup of the dramatis personae. The key group of saboteurs includes Americans Hogan (Bob Crane) and Kinchloe (Ivan Dixon); the Frenchman, LeBeau (Robert Clary); and the Brit, Newkirk (Richard Dawson). In "The Informer," actor Larry Hovis appears as a lieutenant trying to escape but is recast as Sergeant Andrew Carter from the next episode onward. Hogan's counterpart and foil, Col. Klink, is a pompous Prussian living with delusions of grandeur in a failed military career. His ego is easily turned against him, and almost every episode includes his falling victim to the pranks of the prisoners. Each story ends with either his frustration that something has been pulled over on him or his happiness that he has managed to keep the German war machinery from punishing his incompetence.

Klink boasts in every episode that no one has ever escaped from Stalag 13. This conceit trumps all others in the *Hogan's Heroes* story line, for it assures that, despite their incompetence, Klink and Schultz will continue their command of the camp. The prisoners depend on Klink's delusion of competence and Schultz's indifference to the outcome of the war to carry out their sabotage missions. Likewise, the prisoners must all stay put in order to maintain the illusion that the camp is secure. Of course, they come and go at will. The entire set up plays as both cartoonish and cyclical. Nevertheless, the series maintained reasonable ratings and a spot in the CBS primetime lineup for six seasons. Faced with the contradictory demands to be both relevant

66   *Robert R. Shandley*

and timeless, *Hogan's Heroes*' writers became adept at a combination of ideological subtlety and broad humor.

As the only series to span major US involvement in Vietnam, *Hogan's Heroes* presents a commentary about war that is more frequently a reaction to the Southeast Asian conflict than to the one a generation earlier in Europe. The series animates the cultural attitudes about the military, war, and authoritarianism as they shifted in the late 1960s American experience. Hogan and his band of saboteurs differ significantly from the received understanding of World War II valor. Although the title might suggest something grander, the "heroism" with which the POWs are credited generally consists of trickery. More importantly, throughout the run of the series, *Hogan's Heroes* gradually develops an image of the solider as a morally complicated subject rather than a hero.

By the time the second season of the series began filming in the summer of 1966, the United States was fully committed in Vietnam. After numerous attempts to overwhelm the Vietcong forces with large numbers of American troops, US commanders were beginning to understand that they were engaged in a different type of war, one for which their training was not quite suited. Despite numerous large deployments, the Americans and South Vietnamese continually failed to engage similarly large Vietcong forces. What the Johnson administration had claimed would be a brief successful military campaign was turning into a much lengthier commitment that was beginning to lose support both domestically and abroad.

While the Americans were experiencing frustration fighting against a combination insurgent and guerilla war in Vietnam, the war sitcom was making light of similar frustration on the part of Germans, by then on primetime Saturday night. A reading of the series as equating the Pentagon with the World War II German brass would certainly be a stretch; yet, *Hogan's Heroes* does draw increasingly frequent parallels between the two military apparatuses. Whether or not the show's writers intended these parallels (and there are plenty of reasons to believe they did), a late 1960s television audience would have been sensitized to notice them. Moreover, *Hogan's Heroes* clears room, not only for a discussion of insurgent warfare but also for the possibility that one might choose not to fight.

The second season of *Hogan's Heroes* offers the first of many episodes in which the topic is the pending transfer of either Klink or Schultz to the Russian front. This conceit allows the episode to mine a number of issues in the cultural terrain at once. In "Don't Forget to Write" Klink is trapped into volunteering for duty on the German eastern front.[7] Given both the high casualty rate and the frozen conditions, the transfer to Russia is always treated as a likely fatal move. Believing that the retention of the incompetent camp commandant is crucial to preserve their mission, the prisoners spring to action to help Klink avoid combat duty.

Act 1 of "Don't Forget to Write" comprises a draft-dodging narrative in which the prisoners attempt to keep Klink from passing his physical examination. Hogan's suggestion of a way to beat the draft reveals the methods as common knowledge:

HOGAN: Of course, there are ways. But that wouldn't interest you. Well tally ho! Go get 'm!
KLINK: Hogan, wait a minute! What do you mean? Wait!
HOGAN: Not passing the physical. Getting yourself in a weakened condition. Starving yourself. Catching a cold. Maybe even pneumonia, if you're lucky. It's been done before.
KLINK: Hogan, I am a German and an officer! Now, what you are suggesting is obviously dishonest, vile, and deceitful. (*Laugh track*) Now, if I am ordered to the Russian front to be shot out of the wild blue yonder and die in the snow, it is what I must do. (*Laugh track*)
HOGAN: Spoken like a true patriot. (*Laugh track*)
KLINK: Thank you (*Laugh track*)
HOGAN: Good Luck! Don't forget to write. (*Laugh track as Hogan leaves Klink's office and shuts the door*)
KLINK: (*No laugh track. Klink proudly walks back toward his desk, sits down, pauses and then ...*) Hogan! Wait! (*Laugh track*).

The placement of the laugh track alone suggests that Klink's patriotic speech is to be understood as ridiculous. When he inevitably agrees to the plan, Schultz and the POWs team up to put Klink on a starvation diet, make him susceptible to pneumonia, and deprive him of sleep, all in the service of both deteriorating his condition and humiliating him. While attempting to keep him awake, Carter recounts how his friend Charlie attempted to avoid the American draft board by hiding underneath a porch. Act Two begins with all of their efforts coming to naught as the doctor informs Klink that only death would keep him from qualifying physically for service on the Russian front. Thus, the prisoners must concoct a different method to save Klink.

Service avoidance comes up again later the same season in "The Swing Shift."[8] The story line consists of the usual industrial espionage conceit found in dozens of episodes. The POWs' tricks result in Newkirk first becoming foreman in a munitions plant and then being conscripted into the German Army. Again, Newkirk feigns an array of ailments from deafness to fainting spells in order to flunk his physical. And again, the doctor claims being alive to be the only fitness the Army requires. As in "Don't Forget to Write," the draft-dodging schemes fail while appeals to other forms of competence succeed in preventing a transfer to the combat zone.

"The Swing Shift" is noteworthy in another regard—namely, its attitude toward the military-industrial complex. The factory the POWs intend to sabotage has been converted from car to cannon manufacturing. When Klink expresses dismay to Gen. Burkhalter at the loss of auto production, the latter blurts out, "Cannons, cannons, cannons, cannons ... that's what we're making now, cannons!" Although intended to express support for the war

68   *Robert R. Shandley*

effort, Burkhalter (Leon Askin) delivers the lines in a way that ridicules the war machine.

Hogan's Heroes is at times rather masterful at deploying signifiers from World War II in a way that is more suggestive of Vietnam-era signification. No episode epitomizes this tendency more than "Colonel Klink's Secret Weapon."[9] The installment itself depicts the prisoners, as well as Klink and Schultz, as suffering under a new camp discipline regime enforced by the well-connected Sergeant Frank (Milton Selzer). The differentiation between the POWs and the Germans breaks down as both sets of protagonists fall under Frank's self-righteous command. Military discipline procedures are lampooned as arbitrary and nonsensical. Moreover, they threaten Hogan's sabotage and espionage operation, which depends on military inefficiency. As is predictable in the series, Hogan concocts a way to humiliate and discredit Frank. Under the watchful eye of the inspector general, who has come to the camp to assess efficiency, Sergeant Frank's uniform comes apart at the seams, leaving him wearing nothing but underclothes decorated with a victory/peace sign—that is, a sketch of a hand raising the index and middle fingers in the shape of a V. Read in terms of World War II, this would be seen as Churchill's famous victory gesture. But in terms of the late 1960s, the gesture had been coopted into war protestors' call for peace. In fact, in March 1967 when the episode aired, the latter iteration of the gesture was more likely to have been recognized. The soldier flashing a peace symbol during a prime-time sitcom reveals the dual valence between World War II and Vietnam with which *Hogan's Heroes* functions.

Given its Cold War context, one of the trickier narrative challenges of the series lies in the portrayal of the various Russian characters who enter the camp. Representing Russians at all sympathetically at the height of the Cold War carried political pitfalls. The most frequent appearance of a Russian came with the recurring role of Marya (Nita Talbot), a Russian spy who generally consorts with German generals. Marya and Hogan's relationship is marked by both strong sexual tension and a high level of mutual distrust. Hogan is always half-expecting Marya to betray him, but Marya is also the only regularly appearing character in the series whose tactical intelligence can match Hogan's.

Marya is first introduced in the second season as a part of an effort to inject more salaciousness into the story line. "A Tiger Hunt in Paris" is a rare double episode.[10] In it another Hogan love interest and fellow spy, Tiger (Arlene Martel), has been captured in Paris and is about to be transferred to Gestapo headquarters in Berlin for questioning. Marya is identified early on as a White Russian and thus supposedly anti-Bolshevik, although that trait is never again pursued. More importantly, the question of her trustworthiness and loyalties arises almost immediately. When pressed as to why Hogan should provide her with vital information, Marya notes that they are "more or less on the same side." She then clarifies the statement further: "More on the same side so that we can work together from time to time, just enough less that I would like the information." As in all subsequent episodes, Marya proves to be at once dangerous and reliable. Her flirtation with LeBeau keeps the Frenchman convinced of her loyalty, despite all evidence to the contrary, thus giving a nod to the widely held Cold War belief that France was often playing both sides against the middle.

The Marya episodes required some of the most complicated narration in the entire series. Nita Talbot, who was nominated for an Emmy for her portrayal of the Russian spy, displays at once flawless timing and excessively accented English in her Marya performances. The episodes always require additional levels of suspense in order to accommodate the multiple layers of deception necessary to bring the plot to a happy conclusion. Just when Hogan is finally sure that she has sold him out, she carries out a plan that results in far greater destruction or deception than Hogan and his men would have been able to achieve without her. Thus, with its most frequent reference to the complicated relationship between Russia and the rest of the Allied forces, *Hogan's Heroes* constructs a view of the Soviets that is much more aligned with the attitudes during World War II than with those that developed in the subsequent decades. The viewer and Hogan both know that this is not an allegiance, but a contingent working arrangement, one that is always likely to break down.

In "The Hostage," Marya has attached herself to a General von Heiner (Theodore Marcuse) who wants to find out what lies behind a rash of sabotage incidents in the area.[11] Upon being tipped off by Marya, he lays a trap for Hogan, telling him about a fuel depot located nearby (about which Hogan already knows). When Hogan tries to find out why Marya has betrayed the prisoners, she simply assures him that her relationship with "Bobo" von Heiner is all part of a plan that Hogan should trust. Convinced that he is doomed either way, Hogan plants a bomb to blow up the fuel depot. Thereafter, upon Marya's suggestion, Hogan is taken hostage at the fuel depot. Marya visits him and convinces him to tell "Bobo" of his plans. Hogan offers a fake plan to the general and is sent away with Marya just before the depot and von Heiner are blown up. Celebrating another successful caper, Marya exclaims: "Beautiful, Hogan! Oh, you're a fun person!"

HOGAN: Why did you make it so hard for me? Why didn't you work with me instead of against me?
MARYA: Who cares about the rocket fuel! They're not bombing Moscow with their rockets, just London. (*Laugh track.*)
HOGAN: Then what were you after?
MARYA: We cannot trust Hitler to shoot all his own generals. Some we have to take care of ourselves. (*Laugh track.*)
HOGAN: Oh, Bobo!
MARYA: Oh, I am desolate. ... Will you kiss me now or later? (*Laugh track.*)
HOGAN: I think I will make it later.
MARYA: Shy, desperately shy! (*She kisses him during laugh track.*)

70 Robert R. Shandley

Marya reveals that hers is a parallel and compatible mission to the one into which she has tricked Hogan and his Western allied prisoners. Yet she remains throughout the run a seductive and dangerous ally.

A few weeks after "The Hostage" aired, "Two Nazis for the Price of One" gives us a picture of how a plot line about World War II intrigue could easily morph into one about Cold War espionage.[12] In the episode, a high-ranking SS officer, Gruppenführer Freitag (Alan Oppenheimer), has heard tell of the American "Manhattan Project" and wants to know more about it from Hogan. Hogan has no knowledge of the project but understands that it must be important. He also realizes that Freitag knows more than he should and will have to be eliminated. The episode begins the kind of irreverence toward the crimes of German history for which the series became famous:

(*Klink and Hochstetter are in Klink's office, Hogan enters.*)
HOGAN: You wanted to see me, Colonel?. ... Oh, I didn't realize you had company.
HOCHSTETTER: The Gestapo is not company.
HOGAN: Frankly, I never thought much of them myself. (*Laugh track.*)
KLINK: Hogan, you will show a little respect for Major Hochstetter.
HOGAN: Just a little, sir? (*Laugh track.*)
KLINK: I mean a lot of ... please, don't twist my words. ...
HOCHSTETTER: Tell me Hogan, what do know about the Manhattan Project? What is it?
HOGAN: Maybe they are selling the island back to the Indians?
HOCHSTETTER: The 504th bomb group was assigned to the Manhattan Project, is that right?
HOGAN: Were they?
HOCHSTETTER: You should know. You commanded the 504th bomb group.
HOGAN: Did I?

When Hogan resists Hochstetter's attempts at interrogation, the latter leans on Hogan with the SS's reputation for torture.

HOCHSTETTER: Of course, we could give you the time to think it over in a special cell we have. It is not big enough to stand up in and it is not big enough to lie down in.
HOGAN: Sounds like a hotel room I once had in Cleveland. (*Laugh track.*)
HOCHSTETTER: During the day the temperature is 140 degrees and at night it is below freezing.
HOGAN: That's the hotel all right! (*Laugh track.*)
HOCHSTETTER: Then if you don't talk, you will be starved, tortured, and shot. Well, Hogan, what do you say?
HOGAN: What can I say? You've made me homesick for Cleveland. (*Laugh track.*)

Nervous Laughter 71

The exchange reinforces the lampooning attitude toward the criminal aspects of the Nazi war machine as well as the deadpan humor that permeates the series' dialogue. It also sets up the double spy narrative that will follow. Hogan realizes that not only have the Germans found out about a top secret American mission, but also that in order to have done so they must have a spy placed high up in the command structure. The task of preventing the SS from finding out more about the secret American nuclear program is much more a Cold War plot than a World War II one.

Fearing that they have been compromised, the prisoners all prepare to disband their operation and flee to England. But before they leave, Hogan decides that he must eliminate Freitag. It is the only episode in which Hogan or the others attempt a direct assassination. Normally, if a character must die, they simply cause him to be in harm's way. As Hogan enters Klink's office, he hears a shot. Freitag's lieutenant, Mannheim (Jon Cedar), resentful of having been treated shabbily by his superior officer, has beaten Hogan to the punch and shot the Gruppenführer through the window. Mannheim then storms into the office to finish the job, whereupon he stumbles across Klink, Hogan, and Schultz. Schultz conveniently loses his weapon at the moment he is asked to use it.

Hogan's Heroes' most convincing addition to the Cold War narrative comes in its formal construction. The very mix of military comedy with a spy narrative pits Hogan's modern techniques of espionage and sabotage, that is, the non-militaristic interventions of the Cold War, against a bloated military machine, the mechanism of the last war. Hogan and his men apply their trickery to prevent the Germans from gaining technological or material advantage, rather than engaging in direct battles. Thus, it is Hogan who is fighting a Cold War while his adversaries are mired in a troop-based conflict.

The tension among the Allies provides the framework for "A Russian Is Coming," which aired originally on November 25, 1967. In this episode, the POWs are hiding a downed Soviet pilot, Igor Piotkin (Bob Hastings), who provides comic schtick through his distrust of his fellow prisoners. Piotkin insists that Hogan return him to the Soviet Union rather than using the usual escape route to England. Hogan then concocts a plan whereby Piotkin is dressed up as a German lieutenant who is to be sent to the Russian front. The Russian is portrayed as an ideological buffoon who talks about grain production and "the fulfillment of the five year plan." The interaction between Piotkin and the Western POWs leaves both sides wondering why it is that they are meant to be allies. The episode ends with Hogan musing: "Wouldn't it be funny if he really wanted to go to the Russian front." The joke not only refers to the caper that the prisoners have just pulled off. It suggests a general ridiculousness on the part of anyone who would voluntarily go to war. Moreover, although Germany is at war with all of the Allies, the diegetic military confrontation that is always mentioned is that between the Russians and Americans.

72 Robert R. Shandley

The fourth season of *Hogan's Heroes* began with a world in much more turmoil than it had been a season earlier. The Tet Offensive and American inability to make progress in Vietnam led esteemed CBS anchorman, Walter Cronkite, to say on *CBS Evening News*, February 27, 1968, "we are mired in a stalemate." As a result of collapsing public support for the war, Johnson chose not to seek reelection. The assassinations of both Martin Luther King, Jr. and Robert F. Kennedy had left the American political world in turmoil. Anti-war and student protests destabilized regimes all over the world.

Judged by the level of political engagement both before and after the season that began in September 1968, the writers kept most of the episodes of that fourth season remarkably neutral. Although the underlying anti-militarism of mocking uniformed (German) authority and the general suggestion that the military brass is filled with incompetent nincompoops pervades each episode, the plotlines themselves are generally formulaic. Given the widespread political turmoil of that year, it is not too surprising that the writers for *Hogan's Heroes* chose to keep their heads down. However, the first episode of the 1968–1969 season, "Clearance Sale at the Black Market," offered a rather remarkable exception to this rule.[13] In this installment, the prisoners are using Schultz (more precisely his wide girth) to transfer messages to and from the underground agents in town. The notes are surreptitiously placed in Schulz's belt, which Schulz's girlfriend at the local bar removes during their embraces. The episode's humor derives from the notion that someone would be attracted to the rotund sergeant. When Schultz mistakenly witnesses a black market transaction in progress between a local saloonkeeper and a Gestapo agent, the Gestapo quickly arranges for Schultz to be transferred to the Russian front, thereby injecting into the episode another draft-dodging narrative.

The scene begins with an establishing shot of Schultz entering Klink's quarters, where the latter is sitting and eating. Klink offers Schultz a drink and refers to him as "my boy," thereby raising Schultz's suspicion:

KLINK: Schultz, I have the pleasure to tell you that you are being transferred to the Eastern front. *(Cut to a shot of Schultz with a quizzical look. [Laugh track.] Schultz takes a drink straight from the schnapps bottle.)* Isn't that thrilling news!

SCHULTZ: Thrilling? I'm out of my mind. *(Laugh track.)* What happened, Herr Kommandant? Did I do something wrong?

KLINK: Of course not! You are just being asked to use your knowledge and experience in the service of the Third Reich.

SCHULTZ: Yeah?

KLINK: You want Germany to win the war, don't you?

SCHULTZ: *(Noncommittally.)* Yeah.

KLINK: Being transferred to the Eastern front, you can make that possible.

SCHULTZ: Would it be so bad if we *lost* the war? *(Laugh track.)*

KLINK: Schultz, we are going to miss your sense of humor around here.

Nervous Laughter 73

Schultz proceeds to list his infirmities.

KLINK: I think at this point you would find almost anything wrong with yourself.

SCHULTZ: Try me! (*Laugh track.*)

KLINK: Well, I realize you are not exactly what we would call a perfect physical specimen. ...

SCHULTZ: Now, you are on the right track. (*Laugh track.*)

KLINK: But you have something much more important than physical perfection. You have a fighting spirit.

SCHULTZ: I'll get rid of it. (*Laugh track.*)

KLINK: In these times, my boy, a man in uniform has two choices: either he fights, or he is called a coward.

SCHULTZ: I'd rather be a coward. (*Light laugh track.*)

KLINK: Do you want to give up the chance for greater glory on the battlefield? Do you want to go on being called a coward?

SCHULTZ: Why not? That's something I understand. (*Light laugh track.*)

Schultz's quizzical, almost indifferent, look when Klink asks him whether or not he wants Germany to win the war, as well as his query about whether or not it would be so bad if they lost, is this bit of dialogue's most direct engagement with the public discourse of the time. Moreover, the audience is sutured into Schultz's point of view through the insertion of the laugh track after each of his excuses for not being sent into combat.

Walter Cronkite's quagmire comments in February 1968 also expressed pessimism about the potential for victory or defeat in Vietnam, thus instigating considerable public and private debate about the war. The troubles in Southeast Asia were at the forefront of the tight presidential campaign between Hubert H. Humphrey and Richard Nixon, which was being waged when the episode aired. Anybody who had watched the evening news an hour before *Hogan's Heroes* came on would have had no trouble assimilating Schultz's query about the consequences of losing the war with the discussions of Vietnam in the news. Moreover, it is noteworthy that Klink finds humor in his sergeant's question rather than defending the war aims of the Third Reich. Wanting to win a war that was understood as unwinnable is the joke of this exchange.

The prisoners question the legitimacy of Schultz having been called up in the first place. Because he is such an unfit soldier, his being called to battle must be a sign of corruption somewhere, they surmise. While we could suggest an allegorical reading in which the Gestapo stands in for the supposedly corrupt Pentagon, we need not go that far to find the episode's political resonance. A superficial reading of Schultz's reaction to the war does enough. Schultz expresses clear indifference to the outcome of the war and his own participation in it. The POWs side with him and expose the Gestapo agent's black market profiteering operation. *Hogan's Heroes* allows the viewer to root for the guy who is trying to avoid the war and mock those who believe

74   *Robert R. Shandley*

in the war effort. Moreover, the show suggests that the continuance of the war is inherently corrupt. This is, of course, done all in the disguise of World War II uniforms.

In a season where the series displayed a cautious approach to the empirical world, "Clearance Sale at the Black Market" both reflects that caution topically and displays a certain political charisma at the level of dialogue. The same can be said generally about the fourth season, in which writers seem unwilling to reveal their critical hand too openly. While far from underground humor, Season Four of *Hogan's Heroes* still feeds off popular sentiments about war, military service, and the incompetence of the military brass.

The recurring guest appearances of Bernard Fox as Colonel Crittendon provided *Hogan's Heroes'* writers another opportunity to develop story lines that mine cultural attitudes about, among other things, military rank and ceremony. Crittendon, the bumbling member of the Royal Air Force who outranks Hogan by a technicality, is the Allied version of Klink. The technical outranking is an important plot device because it forces Hogan and his men into idiotic adventures concocted by the inept and incorrigible colonel. Moreover, Crittendon's arrival in the first season's "The Flight of the Valkyrie," allows writers to introduce a number of factors into the plot mix that will remain throughout the series.[14]

Most importantly, "The Flight of the Valkyrie" defines the difference between a soldier and a spy and explicitly values the latter over the former. Crittendon insists that a soldier's first duty is to escape and rejoin his unit. Indeed, when Hogan asks "hypothetically" what he would say were a sabotage ring being run out of a prison camp, Crittendon insists that the Geneva Conventions and his honor as a soldier would require him to turn the saboteurs over to the Germans. Here, as well as at other points, the series admits that the heroic escapades of Hogan and his band were technically criminal and, were they caught, the Geneva Conventions—to which Hogan frequently appeals in disputes with Klink—would license their execution. But Crittendon's desire to return to combat is what sets him up as the idiot, whereas Hogan's abilities as a spy are what make him the smart one.

By the fifth season of *Hogan's Heroes* from 1969–1970 the idea of combat avoidance was so well established that its necessity literally goes without saying. In "The Sergeant's Analyst," Schultz is caught by Burkhalter sleeping on the job and is punished by being ordered to the Russian front.[15] Without consulting Schultz and without discussing it with the other prisoners, Hogan immediately begins to scheme to have the order reversed. Their plan involves convincing Burkhalter that Schultz is still useful to the camp, primarily by bribing the general with goods he finds in the prisoners' barracks. This only reinforces the broader sociological suspicion that one could buy oneself out of military service.

It is broadly accepted that middle America of the late 1960s was conflicted about the war in Vietnam. What I have tried to do here is insist

Nervous Laughter 75

that popular television did not wait until the era of "quality television," that is, until after the Vietnam War had slipped from the headlines, to weave these conflicts into sitcom narratives.[16] All of this is done in the form of primetime comedy that seems to have flown under the political radar. Far from a radical example of socially critical television, I offer *Hogan's Heroes* as a prime example of how commercial television was shaped by the tumultuous period in which it was made. Whether we are talking about *The Flintstones* (ABC, 1960–1966), *The Andy Griffith Show* (CBS, 1960–1968), *Gilligan's Island* (CBS, 1964–1967), *All in the Family* (CBS, 1970–1979) or *Hogan's Heroes*, any long-running television show must sift through the grains of its cultural context to find narrative material, attitudes, and commonly held values with which to make itself relevant. Rather than claiming more literacy or psychological depth for one type of program over another, we do better to consider where each show invests itself and how it speaks to its moment. When we do that with Hogan, Klink, Schultz, and company, we find a show that taught America to laugh at its own martial foibles and political unease long before *M*A*S*H* taught us to cry about them.

Notes

1. This is a much shorter version of my argument in *Hogan's Heroes* (Detroit: Wayne State University Press, 2011).
2. Jack Gould, *The New York Times,* Dec. 17, 1967.
3. Jon Heitling, "*The Man from U.N.C.L.E.*" *Book: The Behind-the-Scenes Story of a Television Classic* (New York: St. Martin's Press, 1987), 49.
4. *Campo 44* never made it into production. For further information, see Brenda Scott Royce, "*Hogan's Heroes: Behind the Scenes at Stalag 13*" (Los Angeles: Renaissance Books, 1998).
5. "Color Set Owners Advertiser's Best Prospects" *Broadcasting,* June 21, 1965, 29.
6. "The Informer," season 1, episode 1, *Hogan's Heroes: The Complete Series,* aired September 17, 1965 (Hollywood, CA: Paramount Home Entertainment, 2009) DVD. All subsequent references are to this DVD collection.
7. "Don't Forget to Write," season 2, episode 13, *Hogan's Heroes,* aired December 9, 1966.
8. "The Swing Shift," season 2, episode 21, aired February 3, 1967.
9. "Colonel Klink's Secret Weapon," season 2, episode 28, aired March 24, 1967.
10. "A Tiger Hunt in Paris, Part 1," season 2, episode 10, aired November 18, 1966; "A Tiger Hunt in Paris, Part 2," season 2, episode 11, aired November 25, 1966.
11. "The Hostage," season 3, episode 15, aired December 16, 1967.
12. "Two Nazis for the Price of One," season 3, episode 17, aired December 30, 1967.
13. "Clearance Sale at the Black Market," season 4, episode 1, aired September 28, 1968.

14. "The Flight of the Valkyrie," season 1, episode 5, aired October 15, 1965.
15. "The Sergeant's Analyst," season 5, episode 23, aired March 6, 1970.
16. Quality television was the term used to describe the move by the networks to capture younger audiences by introducing more urbane programming that was more responsive to the political and social sensibilities of the times.

5 *Baa Baa Black Sheep* and the Last Stand of the WWII Drama

A. Bowdoin Van Riper

In World War II, Marine Corps Major Greg "Pappy" Boyington commanded a squadron of fighter pilots. They were a collection of misfits and screwballs who became the terrors of the South Pacific. They were known as the Black Sheep.

—Opening title card for each episode of the series

Eight World War II drama series premiered on American television in the five years between 1962 and 1967, and the three most successful—*Combat!* (ABC 1962–1967), *Twelve O'Clock High* (ABC, 1964–1967), and *The Rat Patrol* (ABC, 1966–1968)—aired for a total of 11 seasons.[1] All eight, however, were gone by the spring of 1968, casualties of changing tastes and the rapid escalation of the war in Vietnam. *Baa Baa Black Sheep*, which premiered on NBC in September 1976, was the first such series to be broadcast in nearly a decade. It was, for all practical purposes, also the last. When it left the airwaves in April 1978—having been canceled, revived, retitled, partially recast, and canceled again—the once-flourishing subgenre it represented died with it. A television-series adaption of the 1967 film *The Dirty Dozen* aired on the nascent, program-hungry Fox network in 1988. It lasted only eight episodes before being canceled. World War II continued to be refought on television in the decades that followed, but in limited-run miniseries like *War and Remembrance* (ABC, 1988–1989), *Band of Brothers* (HBO, 2001), and *The Pacific* (HBO, 2010) rather than in open-ended weekly dramas.

Baa Baa Black Sheep was a heavily fictionalized version of the exploits of a US Marine Corps fighter squadron—VMF-214, nicknamed the "Black Sheep"—fighting the Japanese in the South Pacific. Its unlikely title came from the book that ostensibly inspired it: the memoir of squadron commander Major Gregory "Pappy" Boyington.[2] The long gap separating the series from earlier World War II dramas has caused it to be read, then and now, as fundamentally different from them. The *Washington Post*'s review called it a "war-is-swell series [aimed] at anyone who remembers World War II as a rousing, blowzy, fraternity turkey-shoot."[3] Frank E. Walton, the squadron's former intelligence officer, called it "as phony as a three-dollar bill" and likened its handling of the squadron to "putting a Patek Philippe watch in a Mickey Mouse case."[4] R. J. Thompson, in his study of *Baa*

78 *A. Bowdoin Van Riper*

Baa Black Sheep's creator, Stephen J. Cannell, compares the series to its contemporary *M*A*S*H* (CBS, 1972–1983): an anti-authoritarian comedy pitting anarchic, rule-breaking heroes against a hidebound military establishment.[5] These characterizations, though valid to a point, overlook *Baa Baa Black Sheep*'s comparative seriousness about the war and its principal source of inspiration: the hundreds of World War II combat films turned out by Hollywood between 1942 and the show's premiere in 1976.

The "golden age" of the World War II combat film lasted longer than that of any other Hollywood genre. It began with morale-boosting wartime productions such as *Wake Island* and *Destination Tokyo* in 1942 and ended in 1977 with *A Bridge Too Far*—an elegiac chronicle of a failed 1944 airborne assault that failed to live up to expectations at the box office. The films released in the intervening 35 years depicted the war in every imaginable style, but certain modes of story telling predominated in certain eras: small-unit dramas in the 1940s, command dramas in the 1950s, and sprawling epics with all-star casts in the 1960s and 1970s. *Baa Baa Black Sheep*—created as the golden age of the World War II combat film was drawing to a close—looted all three for plot and character tropes, repackaging them to fit the rigid formulas of 1970s TV drama series. Although it appeared amid the post-Vietnam disillusionment of the mid-1970s and featured a rule-bending hero and a cast of unruly individualists, *Baa Baa Black Sheep* marked the last iteration of an old narrative tradition rather than the beginning of a new one.

Hollywood's World War II

Since 1939, Hollywood studios have released well over a thousand films that touch, in some significant way, on World War II. Not all of those films deal directly with the war, and not all that do focus on members of the uniformed services in combat, but the substantial minority of films that meet both criteria still numbers into the hundreds. Any classification system imposed on such a body of work—films produced over multiple decades, in diverse social and political contexts, and for widely varied purposes—will accommodate some examples better than others and leave classification-defying exceptions strewn around its margins. It should go without saying, therefore, that not every small-unit drama was conceived as a wartime morale-booster, not every 1950s war drama revolved around the "loneliness of command," and not all of Hollywood's all-star battle epics lumbered onto the screen in the 1960s and 1970s, but each of those types of World War II combat film enjoyed its own decade-long "golden age" within the larger one.

Small-unit dramas—films focusing on the experiences of a single infantry platoon, ship's company, or bomber crew—defined the World War II film in the wartime and immediate postwar era. They represent a minority of the war-related films released in the 1940s but a substantial majority of those recognized as genre classics, from *Wake Island* and *Destination Tokyo* in 1942 to *Battleground* and *The Sands of Iwo Jima* in 1949. Even after more than

Baa Baa Black Sheep *and the Last Stand of the WWII Drama*   79

half a century, their cultural influence is substantial. Twenty-first-century World War II dramas such as *Red Tails* (2012), *The Monuments Men* (2013), and *Fury* (2014) consciously imitate them.[6] The concept is so familiar that "bomber crew movie" has become film-fan shorthand for any film about a conspicuously diverse group of characters who learn to work together for a common purpose.[7]

The characters in a small-unit drama are not individuals, but archetypes. The wisecracking New Yorker fights alongside the good-naturedly boastful Texan and the painfully innocent Midwestern farm boy. The middle-aged family man from Pittsburgh shares a foxhole with the skirt-chasing musician from California. The idealistic lieutenant who left college (or law school) to fight for democracy turns for advice to the gravel-voiced sergeant who has spent his life in uniform. The sole non-white member of the unit—Black, Latino, or Native American, depending on the film—blends easily with his comrades and is in turn accepted as "one of the guys." The "universal platoon," as Jeanine Basinger calls it, is an idealized American society in microcosm, and its members—standing shoulder-to-shoulder against the enemy, their differences laid aside "for the duration"—are offered to audiences as models to be emulated.[8] The battles depicted in a small-unit drama are, in the same way, a microcosm of the larger war. Where, when, and why they are happening is, in dramatic terms, virtually irrelevant. The films use real battles and campaigns as context and background, but their plots are not defined by the ebb and flow of actual events.[9] Their purpose is not to recount history, but to dramatize sacrifice, teamwork, and heroism.

The commanding officer—the "skipper," or "old man," or just "CO," depending on the film—is a significant but not central figure in the small-unit drama, whose heroes are invariably enlisted men. The "command drama" subgenre, which emerged in the late 1940s and came into its own in the 1950s, inverts the relationship. The CO is—if not the hero in a conventional sense—the central figure in the story, and interpersonal conflicts are as likely to drive the plot as military ones. *Twelve O'Clock High* (1949), the story of a general (Gregory Peck) sent from 8th Air Force headquarters to shape up the under-performing 918th heavy bomber group, set the pattern for many such dramas to follow. The general, aptly named "Savage," is established in an early scene as a quiet, humane leader with a deep affection for the men under his command. In order to carry out his assignment, however, he presents himself to the 918th as a heartless, unyielding autocrat whose only concern is combat readiness. Savage gradually transforms the 918th into a proud, highly effective unit but at great personal cost: Unable, because of his position, to express the anguish he feels over combat losses, he suffers a mental and physical breakdown. The squadron commander who relieves him—once his harshest critic—adopts his "heartless" leadership style and shoulders the burdens that go with it.

Dramas about the "loneliness of command" were not new in 1948–1949, nor were they limited to films set in World War II. Howard Hawks told similar stories about air-freight pilots in *Only Angels Have Wings* (1940) and cowboys in *Red River* (1948), and John Ford's postwar "cavalry trilogy" explored similar issues in the context of the nineteenth-century Indian Wars. The World War II combat films of the 1950s, however, embraced such stories with particular enthusiasm and—perhaps because they were made in the early Cold War when the survival of freedom and democracy was thought, once again, to be at stake—put particularly sharp edges on the issues they raised. The "tough love" story played out among bomber crews in *Twelve O'Clock High* was transposed to the marines in *The Halls of Montezuma* (1950), navy underwater demolition teams in *The Frogmen* (1951), and submariners in *Run Silent, Run Deep* (1958). Robert Taylor's character puts his marriage at risk to train the crews that will drop the atomic bomb in *Above and Beyond* (1952), and Glenn Ford's submarine captain literally sacrifices his family—drifting in lifeboats after he (unintentionally) sinks the Japanese ship carrying them—rather than expose his submarine to attack in *Torpedo Run* (1958). The moral, in every film, is the same: duty before family, duty before friendship, duty before personal safety ... duty before everything.

The richly developed characters of the small-unit drama and the complex moral dilemmas of the command drama gradually faded from World War II films in the early 1960s, replaced by a new emphasis on spectacle. Producers' willingness to marshal large quantities of men and materiel created new opportunities to recreate large-scale combat onscreen. *Battleground* (1949) had used a cast of less than a dozen to tell the story of a single infantry platoon caught in the Battle of the Bulge. *The Battle of the Bulge* (1965) used a cast of thousands to tell the whole story (purportedly) of the last great German counterattack of the war. All of the characters and many of the events in *Battle of the Bulge* were fictional, but the plot contained enough real historical touchstones to give the film an air of authenticity. Other battle epics were more historically scrupulous. Each of the stars in *The Longest Day* (1962) played an actual participant in the D-Day invasion, and the script was derived (via Cornelius Ryan's bestselling 1959 book) from hundreds of interviews with Allied and Axis veterans.[10] *Tora! Tora! Tora!* (1970), which retold the story of the Japanese attack on Pearl Harbor, was filmed in a straightforward docudrama style and cast with character actors such as Martin Balsam and Jason Robards, rather than A-list stars.

With the possible exception of *Tora! Tora! Tora!,* the World War II battle epics of the 1960s and 1970s were exercises in simulation rather than recreation. They were designed to mimic the look and feel of the battles they depicted, rather than document the precise sequence of events. John Wayne, Peter Lawford, and Red Buttons bore no particular resemblance to the characters they played in *The Longest Day*, but their established star personas—with which contemporary audiences would have been intimately familiar—acted as shorthand for their roles in the battle. The early scenes in *The Battle of the Bulge*, showing column after column of German tanks rolling across the screen, conveyed the scale and power of the attack, if not the actual tactics, landscape, or weather conditions. The Japanese "Zero" fighters swarming over Hawaiian airfields in *Tora! Tora! Tora!* were imitations manufactured from war-surplus American training aircraft, but they immersed audiences in the chaos that prevailed on the morning of December 7, 1941.

Midway and *A Bridge Too Far,* the last two significant films in the "battle epic" cycle that began with *The Longest Day*, were released in June 1976 and June 1977, respectively. The first season of *Baa Baa Black Sheep*—the only serious attempt to reproduce the battle epic's characteristic mixture of visual spectacle and historical specificity in a weekly television drama— aired during the intervening year.

The Illusion of Reality

The setting of *Baa Baa Black Sheep*—like that of theatrical battle-epic films but unlike that of earlier World War II dramas made for television—was both geographically and chronologically specific. *Rat Patrol* took place in an abstract version of the North African desert in which endless stretches of sand separated landmarks with invented names, and the occupied France of *Garrison's Gorillas* was as lightly sketched as *Mission: Impossible*'s interchangeable East European dictatorships. *Baa Baa Black Sheep*, however, took place during the Solomon Islands campaign.

The Solomon Islands lie in the southwestern Pacific Ocean, due east of New Guinea. Japanese forces invaded and occupied them during the first six months of 1942 as part of a larger strategy to cut Allied supply lines linking Australia and New Zealand to the United States. Allied efforts to recapture the islands began in August of the same year. The first major operation of the Solomons campaign, the recapture of Guadalcanal, led to some of the most intense land, sea, and air fighting of the Pacific War, and the bitter Japanese resistance there was repeated, on island after island, until July 1945. Under Boyington's leadership, the pilots of VMF-214 served two tours in the Solomons between August 1943 and January 1944. They were based on the island of Vella Lavella, near New Georgia and under the operational control of the US Marine headquarters located on Espiritu Santo.

The geographic setting of the series is established primarily by casual references to real locations in the Solomons. Plot points and snippets of dialogue throughout the series make reference to the islands of Bougainville, Rendova, and New Georgia (along with its largest settlement, Munda). When Boyington discusses strategy with a senior officer in the episode "Last One for Hutch," for example, the wall map they refer to shows the actual Solomon Islands, and the pins marking known enemy bases approximate those of actual Japanese positions in late 1942, including Buka and the heavily fortified harbor at Rabaul.[11] New Georgia Sound—a narrow interisland channel dividing the Eastern Solomons, which was the site of fierce naval and air battles during 1942—is mentioned throughout the series, under the nickname given to it by American sailors and marines: "the Slot."[12] The islands occupied by the Black Sheep's home base and the nearby Allied

82   *A. Bowdoin Van Riper*

headquarters—identified, by overlay titles, in nearly every episode—are given transparently fictitious versions of their real-world names: Vella La Cava and Esprito Marcos, respectively.[13]

Similar touchstones tie the series to individual characters from the real war. The pilot episode shows Boyington arriving in the Solomons after fighting—as he did in the real world—for Chiang Kai-shek's nationalist government of China as a member of the American Volunteer Group (the famous "Flying Tigers") commanded by General Claire Chennault (George Gaynes).[14] Frustrated by the failure of the Marine Corps to reinstate him at his former rank of major and give him a combat assignment, he enlists the support of Admiral Chester Nimitz, commander of Allied forces in the Central Pacific. General Douglas MacArthur, who commanded Allied operations in the Southwest Pacific from his headquarters in Australia, figures (off-screen) in "Five the Hard Way."[15] Both Nimitz and MacArthur are invoked (though never shown) in later episodes, along with First Lady Eleanor Roosevelt and "Washing Machine Charlie," the generic name given to Japanese pilots whose solo night attacks disrupted the sleep and frayed the nerves of marines on Guadalcanal.[16] Boyington, of course, appears under his real name, and his real-world superiors under transparent pseudonyms: General James Moore (Simon Oakland) as "General Thomas Moore" and Lieutenant Colonel Joseph Smoak (Dana Elcar) as "Colonel Lard," Boyington's nickname for him.[17]

Baa Baa Black Sheep's chronological references are just as frequent but considerably more vague. The first season of the series corresponds roughly to VMF-214's time in combat under Boyington's command: it begins with him returning from China and forming the squadron from a pool of unattached pilots and ends with him awaiting rescue after being shot down by a Japanese adversary. It stretches the time between those events well beyond five months to seven, however, and moves them nearly a year earlier in the war than they actually took place.[18] The series pilot, "Flying Misfits," shows Boyington leaving the still-operational American Volunteer Group, which ceased operations on July 1, 1942, and the opening narration of "Last One for Hutch" refers to the capture of Rabaul as a major Allied objective, which it no longer was by mid-1943.[19] The B-17E Flying Fortress bombers featured in "Trouble at Fort Apache" were used in the Pacific Theater in mid-to-late 1942, but were phased out in favor of B-24 Liberators in the first half of 1943.[20] Likewise, the second-season episode "The Hawk Flies on Sunday" involves the Black Sheep in a secret mission to intercept and shoot down the transport plane carrying Admiral Isoroku Yamamoto, which was successfully carried out in April 1943. The seven months of season one, then, presumably take place sometime between June 1942 and March 1943.

This exercise of chronological license—which increased the dramatic potential of the series by setting the action of season one at a time when control of the Solomons was still up for grabs—would not have been

Baa Baa Black Sheep *and the Last Stand of the WWII Drama* 83

obvious, however, even to the small minority of viewers familiar with the real-world history of the Black Sheep. The 22 episodes that make up the first season are all carefully vague about the passage of time, mentioning neither dates nor datable events such as Christmas or the World Series. The chronological touchstones, like those that link the series to historical figures and real-world geography, are meant to create the illusion of realism, not realism itself. They are designed to anchor the story to real-world events, even when the events that comprise the story are entirely fictitious. They create the impression that the (comparatively) small stories shown on screen fit seamlessly into the larger story of the Solomon Islands campaign and the still-larger story of the Pacific War. The audience is invited to imagine that off-camera—on other islands and in other parts of the Pacific—the war that they remember from history books is unfolding simultaneously.

The "newsreel" snippets that open virtually every episode of *Baa Baa Black Sheep*, appearing between the opening credits and the beginning of the story proper, reinforce the sense of temporal and spatial continuity. They mix period footage of ships and aircraft from the actual Pacific War with contemporary footage designed to establish backstory or introduce key characters from of the episode's supporting cast. Voiceover narration, supplied by an uncredited contemporary actor mimicking the cadences and intonations of a 1940s newsreel announcer, links the two. It also bridges the visual gulf created by the fact that the modern footage (like the rest of the series) is in vivid color and the period footage is in washed-out, 35-year-old color or grainy black and white. Occasionally, as in "Last One for Hutch," the final black-and-white scene of the newsreel fades to color and becomes the first scene of the story proper, visually asserting that the series chronicles a small part of a larger story. *Baa Baa Black Sheep*'s impressionist evocation of the Solomon Islands campaign was not an end in itself but an exercise in creating an authentic-feeling historical backdrop against which to set its story of a small, close-knit unit in action.

America in Microcosm

The golden age of the World War II "small unit" film was 30 years gone by the time *Baa Baa Black Sheep* premiered. *Bataan, Sahara,* and *Air Force* (all 1943) and other landmarks of the genre had long since become period pieces, relegated to film-society screenings and late-night television broadcasts. Beginning with its first episodes, however, *Baa Baa Black Sheep* deftly captured the spirit of the moribund subgenre by recreating its two defining elements: a predictably diverse cast of archetypal characters and a plot arc showing their gradual transformation from a ragged collection of individuals into a disciplined, capable team.

Each of the seven pilots who form the core of the squadron represented a "type" familiar from dozens of wartime films. Jim Gutterman—the executive officer, played by second-generation actor James Whitmore, Jr.—is the requisite pugnacious Texan, complete with a tattered cowboy hat pushed back on his head, and a pearl-handled Colt .45 automatic protruding from his regulation shoulder holster. T. J. Wiley (Robert Ginty) is the smooth-talking ladies' man who woos Navy nurses with promises of moonlit beach picnics and makes improbable pick-up lines ("Do you know how to play strip checkers?") sound charming. Larry Casey (W. K. Stratton) is their collective opposite: a gangly Southerner with the mannerisms of a young James Stewart, as respectful of the rules as Gutterman is dismissive of them and as virginal as Wiley is libidinous. In "The Deadliest Enemy of All," after T. J. proposes strip checkers to his would-be female conquest, the camera cuts to Larry—two tables and a world away—earnestly (and happily) arguing about baseball with his own date.[21] The rest of the central cast falls into similarly well-worn slots: Bob Boyle (Larry Manetti), the scrappy product of the city streets; Jerry Bragg (Dirk Blocker), the stolid Midwestern football hero; Don French (Jeff MacKay), the rebellious son of a wealthy father, and Bob Anderson (John Larroquette), the college-educated rich kid. Chief mechanic John David "Hutch" Hutchinson (Joey Aresco), swarthy despite his WASP name, rounds out the "universal platoon" as VMF 214's token "ethnic" character.

Figure 5.1 The Black Sheep, like the bomber crews and infantry platoons of classic World War II combat films, are an assembly of archetypal characters. Left to right: Wiley, Gutterman, French, Boyle, Bragg, Casey, Hutchinson, and Anderson. From "Anyone for Suicide?"

Small-unit war dramas, especially those made during the war itself, rarely presented their characters as anything *but* lightly sketched archetypes. Embroidering them with more details and more elaborate backstories was neither necessary (given their shared *e pluribus unum* message) nor practical (given their relatively brief running times). The serial nature of television drama removed the latter restriction, however, allowing the characters to be developed, a line or scene at a time, over multiple episodes. For example, Anderson's background of wealth and privilege is revealed not by direct exposition but by the slow accretion of detail. He is the only member of the squadron who sleeps in pajamas rather than government-issue boxer shorts, the only one who calls Gutterman "James" rather than "Jim," and the only one who uses (let alone pronounces correctly) words like "cretin." Hutch's working-class background is sketched the same way, in a series of small moments underscoring the social gulf that exists between officers and enlisted men even in the relatively egalitarian world of the Black Sheep. The final, posthumous glimpse of his background, in the closing narration of "Last One for Hutch," ties together all those that came before. Boyington, without elaboration, identifies his hometown as Flint, Michigan: a blue-collar suburb of Detroit dominated by a sprawling General Motors plant.

Beneath these embroidered details, however, the characters remain their archetypal selves, familiar from scores of small-unit films. Even Gutterman and Lard, who are given more complex character arcs than any of the other supporting characters, are still just minor variations on "the Cocky Texan" and "the Officious Boss."[22] The series-long story that *Baa Baa Black Sheep* tells about the unit is also archetypal. The (fictional) Black Sheep live up to their billing as colorful "misfits and screwballs": Gutterman wears an aloha shirt, Casey's horse-trading skills rival those of Sergeant Ernie Bilko (Phil Silvers) of *The Phil Silvers Show* (CBS, 1955–1959) and Corporal "Radar" O'Reilly (Gary Burghoff) of *M*A*S*H*, and the crash-prone Wiley (as Boyington jokingly puts it) has wrecked enough planes in the space of a few months to qualify as a Japanese ace.[23] They drink scotch, chase women, and fight with brother officers to an extent that wartime filmmakers—whose small-unit dramas mixed entertainment and propaganda— would have rejected as unseemly. Yet, over the course of the first season, they make the same journey as their counterparts in Hollywood's classic small-unit dramas. Beginning as a ragged group of individuals, they emerge as a fearsome, disciplined, capable fighting force.

The events that weld the Black Sheep into an effective fighting force are, broadly speaking, the same as those that drive similar transformations of "universal platoons" on the big screen: encounters with the enemy on the battlefield and interactions with one another in the hours and days in between. The former teaches them to exploit the enemy's weaknesses while minimizing their own and to recognize that missions vital to the war—close air support in "Anyone for Suicide?," anti-ship attacks in

86 A. Bowdoin Van Riper

"The Meatball Circus," and bomber escort in "Trouble at Fort Apache"—
may involve significant risk and little possibility of personal reward.[24]
The latter teaches them to function as a team, developing the absolute,
unwavering trust in one another that combat requires. These transformations are guided and overseen, in classical small-unit drama fashion,
by a hard-nosed commanding officer (as in *Twelve O'Clock High*) or a
tough-minded veteran sergeant (as in *Sahara* and *The Sands of Iwo Jima*).
Boyington, the authority figure (and central character) in *Baa Baa Black
Sheep*, combines elements of both.

Boyington and the Drama of Command

Pappy Boyington's 1956 memoir gave the series its initial inspiration, its
problematic title, and its basic structure. Both the casting of Robert Conrad—
an established star with two hit series on his resume—and the narrative
structure of the series reflect the fact that *Baa Baa Black Sheep* is Boyington's
story.[25] He is the central figure in virtually every episode, the principal
architect of every mission the squadron flies, and the only character whose
thoughts the audience is privy to. Conrad's voiceover narration opens most
of the first-season episodes, closes many of them, and comments on the
unfolding action in several. Looking back on the events of the story from
an undefined "afterward," Conrad-as-Boyington adds squadron-specific
details to the large-scale historical context provided by the faux-newsreel
footage but also interprets the events of the story with the benefit of hind-
sight. Viewers thus see VMF-214's war through Boyington's eyes, and the
central drama in many first-season episodes is rooted not in the combat mission *du jour* but in the challenges that Boyington, as squadron commander,
confronts in the process.

"Five the Hard Way," for example, finds Boyington coping with a visit
from Don French's father, a wealthy newspaper publisher eager to celebrate—
and exploit—the impending fifth aerial victory that will make his son an ace.
Initially cordial, Boyington grows impatient with the elder French, ordering
him to leave Vella La Cava when it becomes clear that his troubled, over-
bearing relationship with his son is compromising Don's effectiveness as a
pilot. The distraction thus removed, Boyington counsels French in an effort
to snap him out of his anxiety over his impending fifth victory. "What if it
took ten victories to become an ace?" he asks. "How hard to do you think
it'd be to get number five? ... I almost got myself killed trying to get number
five because somebody told me it was the big one." The B-plot of the same
episode involves a new pilot, Carter (Frederick Herrick), whom the other
pilots deride as a "hotdog," a "loudmouth," and "a jerk." Here, too, Boyington
functions less as a combat commander than as a stern-but-wise mentor, telling Bragg, the most vociferous complainer: "That's none of your business ...
whether you like him or not, that man is a member of this squadron, until
someone says he isn't."

Baa Baa Black Sheep *and the Last Stand of the WWII Drama* 87

Boyington assumes the role of protective father-mentor to his men throughout the series. Asked by French's father if he has any children, he replies: "A whole squadron of them." His counseling of French in "Five the Hard Way" echoes earlier conversations with Wiley (about whether his flying skills are adequate for a particularly dangerous mission) in "Anyone for Suicide?" and Gutterman (about his shattered self-confidence) in "Devil in the Slot." In "Last One for Hutch," he lashes out at a staff officer who suggests that the squadron's beloved mechanic—killed the day before in a Japanese strafing attack—should be buried on Vella La Cava, rather than returned to his family in the States. Later in the episode, as Hutch's body is loaded onto a transport plane, Sergeant Micklin—the squadron's chief mechanic and Boyington's rough contemporary—observes that "He was good … too damn young." Surveying the pilots, who have assembled as an informal honor guard, Pappy replies, "They're all too damn young."

Hutch is the only member of the central cast killed in the course of the series, but guest characters and (generally unnamed) members of the squadron die with surprising regularity. These losses, and the emotional toll they take on the surviving Black Sheep, account for the grimness that often pervades Boyington's voiceover narration. Describing the effect of relentless Japanese raids on Vella La Cava in the opening of "Last One for Hutch," he notes that "every day the enemy was at full strength while we were being whittled away," as the camera pans across bomb craters, burnt-out tents, and demolished equipment. "Trouble at Fort Apache," in which he witnesses the death of a B-17 squadron commander he has come to respect, ends with him musing: "What are we doing out here? We must all be crazy." Even in victory, Boyington's narrative voice is often bitter and subdued, weighed down by his knowledge of what it has cost. He breaks down, weeping, while writing a letter to a dead pilot's family in "The Greatest Enemy of All" and ends the episode reflecting that "we would always remember what we'd lost" as he thinks about a Navy nurse killed in a Japanese raid. Summing up a particularly brutal mission in the closing narration of "New Georgia on my Mind," he delivers an exhausted benediction: "All you could say about it was: We won."[26]

The central conflict that Boyington faces in these episodes—he cares deeply about his men but must put them in harm's way in order to carry on the war—is the same one faced by big-screen commanders such as Sergeant John Stryker (John Wayne) in *The Sands of Iwo Jima*, and General Frank Savage in *Twelve O'Clock High*. Boyington deals with the all-but-insoluble conflict in much the same way they do: by projecting toughness while slowly dying inside from the strain. A parallel set of episodes enmeshes him in the other principal narrative thread of postwar "command drama" films: clashes over methods and objectives between the hero and his own superior officers.

Conflict between the maverick, unconventional Boyington and the staid military brass represented by Colonel Lard was planned, from the outset,

88   *A. Bowdoin Van Riper*

to be a central element of the series.[27] The opening narration of the first post-pilot episode, "Best Three out of Five," sets the tone for the series: "I have a thing about regulations—I like to break them."[28] Over the course of the series, Boyington falsifies paperwork, steals classified intelligence files, redirects other units' supplies, impersonates officers (including a doctor and a chaplain), engages in fistfights with officers and enlisted men alike, and commits endless acts of insubordination. Much of this is played as comedy or light-hearted adventure, with Boyington cast as a trickster figure whose offenses against military decorum are forgiven by his superiors (notably General Moore) because they serve the greater cause of winning the war. Occasionally, however, the stakes are conspicuously higher and the issues less clear-cut, moving individual episodes into the dramatic territory staked out by films such as *Command Decision* (1948) and *Torpedo Run*.

"Fort Apache," for example, leaves Boyington trapped between two conflicting sets of orders: one issued by an Army brigadier general who is adamant that the Black Sheep *not* escort his heavy bombers into enemy territory and the other by General Moore who insists that they do. Unable to consult with Moore, who is unreachable in Washington, or find a loophole in the morass of regulations governing the situation, he is obliged to choose between loyalty to Moore and obedience to the Army general's lawful (but unwise) orders. The command dilemma in "The Last Mission over Sengai" is even more acute.[29] A courtroom episode loosely modeled on the climax of *The Caine Mutiny* (1955), it takes place in the aftermath of a mission where gunfire from one of the Black Sheep's planes killed and injured friendly forces on the ground. Boyington suspects that Lieutenant Carter, the son of a powerful Kennedy-esque family, is responsible, having made the tragic error while suffering from combat-induced stress. Accused by Carter of firing the fatal shots himself and lying to clear his name, and unwilling to accept Moore's offer of "eagles within a year" (that is, a fast-track promotion to full colonel) if he resigns his command, Boyington insists on a court-martial to clear his name. Armed with exculpatory evidence gathered by the Black Sheep, he saves his career and his honor but at the cost of having to watch his own attorney question the mentally unstable Carter—of whom he still feels protective—until the young pilot suffers a breakdown on the witness stand.

"The Last Mission over Sengai" twice touches, in passing, on a far darker road not taken. In a flashback scene depicting the ill-fated mission, Boyington threatens (by radio) to shoot Carter down if he does not instantly cease fire. Back at Vella La Cava, in the scene that opens the episode, he tells Carter that "You're lucky to be alive. Any of these men [the other Black Sheep] could have planted you, with my blessing." The idea that such an action would be morally justified, implied in both scenes, would never have been countenanced (or even raised) in the command-drama films of the 1940s and '50s, but it resonated with American culture's growing post-Vietnam ambivalence toward war.[30]

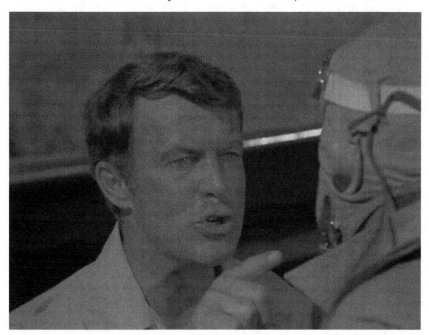

Figure 5.2 Boyington, his deep concern for his men carefully hidden behind a "hard-nosed CO" persona, chews out a pilot whose foolhardy actions endangered himself and his fellow Black Sheep on a mission. From "Five the Hard Way"

Conclusion

The public's growing disenchantment with conventional war stories likely contributed to *Baa Baa Black Sheep*'s cancelation at the end of its first (1976–1977) season. It was brought back the following year as a mid-season replacement, but the abbreviated second season—13 episodes aired between December 1977 and April 1978—was a very different series in tone. Gutterman, the darkest and most complex character in the series besides Boyington, was written out. His place in the cast was taken by Lieutenant Jeb Pruitt (Jeb Adams), an improbably talented and conspicuously under-aged pilot, who represented an attempt by NBC—third among the broadcast networks in the ratings and consistently beaten by ABC in the crucial 18–29 age demographic—to broaden the show's appeal to younger viewers.[31] Further network tinkering was evident in the addition of "Pappy's Lambs," four attractive nurses intended to help the revived series compete against *Charlie's Angels*, the ABC hit opposite which it was scheduled.[32]

Collectively, the changes gave *Black Sheep Squadron* (as it was renamed) a lighter tone, highlighting adventure, romance, and comedy and deemphasizing the relentless grind of the war. They took place, ironically, at a time when

90   A. Bowdoin Van Riper

M*A*S*H was moving in the opposite direction, deemphasizing the anarchic comedy of its early seasons and experimenting with darker themes and episode-long character studies.[33] Over the next five years (1978–1983), *M*A*S*H* cemented its status as the most acclaimed war story ever told on American television, its poignant two-and-a-half-hour finale becoming one of the most-watched programs in the history of the medium.[34] The retooled *Black Sheep Squadron*, in contrast, was quietly canceled. *Tales of the Gold Monkey*, a spiritual successor produced by *Black Sheep* story editor Donald P. Bellisario, lasted only one season (ABC, 1982–1983) before it, too, was canceled.[35]

Baa Baa Black Sheep is remembered today—if it is remembered at all—as a light-hearted adventure series that (like *Tales of the Gold Monkey*) told stories of roguish heroes, beautiful women, and vintage airplanes, set against the backdrop of the wartime South Pacific. Such memories, though accurate to a point, are incomplete. They overlook the historical specificity and surprisingly dark undertones of the first season and thus fail to recognize the cultural context in which the series was created and received (during its initial broadcast run). *Baa Baa Black Sheep* adapted for television narratives that Hollywood had used for decades to present World War II to American movie audiences: narratives that had played a key role in shaping the image of World War II in American culture.[36] It was the series' misfortune to appear when those were rapidly fading—or already gone—from the silver screen and to disappear long before turn-of-millennium nostalgia for "the Greatest Generation" led to their revival in films like *Saving Private Ryan* (1998) and *Pearl Harbor* (2001). *Baa Baa Black Sheep* thus represents the final, highly polished expression of a vision of World War II, formed in wartime and steadily refined over the next three decades: one of flawed heroes worn down by combat, but determined to keep fighting until the job was done.

Notes

1. The eight were, in order: *The Gallant Men* (ABC, 1962–1963), *Combat!* (ABC, 1962–1967), *Twelve O'Clock High* (ABC, 1964–1967), *Convoy* (NBC, 1965–1966), *Jericho* (CBS, 1966–1967), *The Rat Patrol* (ABC, 1966–1968), and *Garrison's Gorillas* (ABC, 1967–1968). On *Combat!* and *The Rat Patrol*, in particular, see Rick Worland, "The Other Living Room War: Prime-Time TV Combat Series, 1962–1975," *Journal of Film and Video* 50, no. 3 (1998): 3–23 and David P. Pierson's chapter in this volume.
2. On the genesis of the series, see Robert J. Thompson, *Adventures on Prime Time: The Television Programs of Stephen J, Cannell* (Westport, CT: Praeger, 1990), 74–75.
3. Tom Shales, "'Black Sheep': Oh What an Unlovely War," *Washington Post*, September 26, 1976.
4. Frank E. Walton, "Baa Baa Black Sheep Is Pulling the Wool over Our Eyes," *TV Guide*, April 23, 1977, 15–20; "Question: Settle a Dispute ..." *TV Guide*, March 31, 2005. http://www.tvguide.com /news/question-settle-dispute-66510.aspx.
5. Thompson, *Adventures on Prime Time*, 76–78.
6. Scattered homages appeared in earlier decades—notably *The Big Red One* (1980) and *Memphis Belle* (1990)—but the subgenre was revived in earnest

during the wave of nostalgia created by Stephen Spielberg's *Saving Private Ryan* and Tom Brokaw's hagiographic bestseller *The Greatest Generation* (both 1998).

7. Examples of the term applied in this sense include: Pauline Kael, "The Boys in the Band," in *5001 Nights at the Movies* (New York: Holt, 1998), 98; writers_reign, "Sub-Standard? On the Contrary," *Internet Movie Database,* December 18, 2008, http://www.imdb.com/title/tt0039615/reviews-2; and Paul Maher, Jr., "Bayonets in Paradise," *All Things Shining: The Terrence Malick Blog,* May 21, 2014, accessed July 13, 2015, http://terrencemalick.me/2014/05/21.

8. Clayton R. Koppes and Gregory D. Black, *Hollywood Goes to War* (Berkeley and Los Angeles: University of California Press, 1990), 259; Jeanine Basinger, *The World War II Combat Film: Anatomy of a Genre* (Middletown, CT: Wesleyan University Press, 2003), 65–75.

9. The marine rifle platoon in *Sands of Iwo Jima* (1949), for example, witnesses the famous flag-raising on Mt. Suribachi from a distance, and the paratroopers in *Battleground* (1949) hear about General Anthony McAuliffe's famous response to a German demand for surrender ("Nuts!") by word-of-mouth.

10. Cornelius Ryan, *The Longest Day: June 6 1944* (New York: Simon and Schuster, 1959).

11. "Last One for Hutch," season 1, episode 21, *Black Sheep Squadron: Volume 2,* aired March 8, 1977 (Universal City, CA: Universal Pictures Home Entertainment, 2007) DVD. All subsequent references to season 1, episode 11–22 are to this DVD collection.

12. Samuel Eliot Morison, *The Two-Ocean War* (Boston: Little, Brown, 1963), 168.

13. The name change is variously attributed to "convenience" and sometimes to "legal reasons" in the secondary literature but never clearly accounted for.

14. Daniel Ford, *Flying Tigers: Claire Chennault and His American Volunteers, 1941–1942,* revised edition (New York: HarperCollins, 2007).

15. "Five the Hard Way," season 1, episode 16, *Baa Baa Black Sheep,* aired February 1, 1977.

16. The name "Washing Machine Charlie" comes from the practice of deliberately de-tuning the engines of planes used for nighttime harassment missions, causing them to run rough and making them simultaneously more irritating and harder to ignore. See Bruce Gamble, *The Black Sheep: The Definitive History of Marine Fighting Squadron 214 in World War II* (New York: Presidio Press, 1998), 81.

17. Bruce Gamble, *Black Sheep One: The Life of Gregory "Pappy" Boyington* (New York: Presidio Press, 2000), 411, 431.

18. The seven-month figure is established in "The Fastest Gun" season 1, episode 22, *Baa Baa Black Sheep,* aired March 22, 1977, when an outsider asks one of the pilots how long the squadron has been together.

19. Morison, *Two-Ocean War,* 292. "Flying Misfits," season 1, episode 0, *Black Sheep Squadron: Volume 1,* aired September 21, 1976 (Universal City, CA: Universal Pictures Home Entertainment, 2005) DVD. All subsequent references to season 1, episodes 0–10 are to this DVD collection.

20. Eric M. Bergerud, *Fire in the Sky: The Air War in the South Pacific* (New York: Basic Books, 2001), 294. "Trouble at Fort Apache" season 1, episode 18, *Baa Baa Black Sheep,* aired February 15, 1977.

21. "The Deadliest Enemy of All," season 1, episodes 13 and 14, *Baa Baa Black Sheep,* aired January 11 & 18, 1977.

92　*A. Bowdoin Van Riper*

22. Gutterman's bravado is gradually revealed, in "The Meatball Circus" season 1, episode 6, *Baa Baa Black Sheep*, aired November 9, 1976 and "Devil in the Slot" season 1, episode 15, *Baa Baa Black Sheep*, aired January 25, 1977, as compensation for a troubled past and a crippling fear of failure, and his loss of confidence in the latter episode leads him to the verge of a breakdown. Lard—who, according to "Cat's Whiskers" season 1, episode 10, *Baa Baa Black Sheep*, aired December 10, 1976 saw combat in China as a junior officer—laments in "Trouble at Fort Apache" that his staff job prevents him from winning the glory and honor that come to "fighting Marines" like Boyington.
23. Boyington makes the "Japanese ace" quip about Wiley in the pilot episode, "Flying Misfits."
24. "Anyone for Suicide?," season 1, episode 8, *Baa Baa Black Sheep*, aired November 23, 1976.
25. *Hawaiian Eye* (1959–1963) and *The Wild, Wild West* (1965–1969).
26. "New Georgia on My Mind," season 1, episode 9, *Baa Baa Black Sheep*, aired November 30, 1976.
27. Gamble, *Black Sheep One*, 484–85.
28. "Best Three Out of Five," season 1, episode 1, *Baa Baa Black Sheep*, aired September 23, 1976.
29. "The Last Mission Over Sengai" season 1, episode 17, *Baa Baa Black Sheep*, aired February 8, 1977.
30. Unsanctioned actions taken against officers seen as dangerous to their own men, part of the folklore of the Vietnam War, also figured in the feature films *The Dirty Dozen* (1967) and *M*A*S*H* (1970), and in "Preventive Medicine" (1979), a seventh-season episode of the *M*A*S*H* television series.
31. "Struggling to Leave the Cellar," *Time,* May 14, 1979; Todd Gitlin, *Inside Prime Time* (1983) Berkeley and Los Angeles: University of California Press, 2000), 56–58.
32. Thompson, *Adventures on Prime Time,* 77.
33. James H. Wittebols, *Watching M*A*S*H, Watching America: A Social History of the 1972–1983 Television* (Jefferson, NC: McFarland, 2003), 107–26. A similar shift was taking place on movie screens, where the conventional *A Bridge Too Far* (1977) performed tepidly, while *The Deer Hunter* (1978), *Apocalypse Now* (1979), and *The Big Red One* (1980) achieved critical and commercial success.
34. "Finale of *M*A*S*H* Draws Record Number of Viewers," *The New York Times*, March 3, 1983: C17. See chapters nine and 10 in this volume for more on *M*A*S*H*.
35. *Gold Monkey* chronicled the adventures of pilot-for-hire Jake Cutter (Stephen Collins) with spies, warlords, treasure-hunters, and the Japanese military on and around the fictional South Pacific island of Boragora in 1938. Cutter's backstory makes him an ex-fighter pilot who fought the Japanese over China in 1936–1937 (anachronistically, as part of the Flying Tigers, who were not formed until 1941).
36. In addition to Basinger, *World War II Combat Film* and Koppes and Black, *Hollywood Goes to War*, see Bernard F. Dick, *The Star Spangled Screen: The American World War II Film* (Lexington: University Press of Kentucky, 1996) and Robert Fyne, *Long Ago and Far Away: Hollywood and the Second World War* (Lanham, MD: Scarecrow Press, 2008).

6 A Waltz with and for the Greatest Generation
Music in *Band of Brothers* (2001)

Todd Decker

Soldiers move together in time, sometimes to the sound of music: attacking in unison at the bugle's call to charge; stepping smartly forward to the four-square rhythmic cadence of a march. A masculine musical genre emerging alongside combat innovations in sixteenth-century Europe, the march coordinated the movement of armies and gave a musical identity to the armed forces of nation-states. In Hollywood war movies and television series about World War II made before about 1980, pre-existing and newly composed marches accompanied stories about soldiers and gave the combat genre a musical signature. Film scores for movies about the Marines almost invariably used the "Marines' Hymn"—a smart, universally known march—as primary musical material. David Lean's epic film *The Bridge on the River Kwai* (1957) turned the "Colonel Bogey March," defiantly whistled by Allied prisoners, into a pop music hit.[1] On television, the assertive, aggressive march theme for the long-running series *Combat!* (ABC, 1962–1967) included sound effects of explosions detonating on the beat during its opening titles. Such marches imparted a jaunty confidence and masculine bravado to the men who fought and won World War II.

And so, it comes as a genuine generic innovation that upwards of 40 percent of the narrative musical score for the HBO limited series *Band of Brothers* (2001) is in triple meter or waltz time. The music for the series' opening and closing titles—heard in three-minute chunks before and after each of the 10 episodes—is also in triple meter and, indeed, sounds like a danceable waltz. Furthermore, not a single musical cue taps into the conventions of the march. The score's only heroic theme is heard but eight times in the series' over 10 hours: always at a tempo too slow to qualify as a march, on occasion played by a solo flute. In *Band of Brothers*, the men of World War II waltz instead of march.

Since around the turn of the twentieth century, the waltz has served as a reservoir of nostalgia—at once old-fashioned, sentimental, feminine, and domestic. The waltz carried these connotations in the 1940s, when most American soldiers were fans of big-band swing, the driving four-beat style of popular music at the time. Composer Michael Kamen's decision to make the score for *Band of Brothers* waltz instead of march or swing—a choice no doubt made in consultation with executive producers

94   Todd Decker

Steven Spielberg and Tom Hanks—adds a precisely calibrated sentimental element to the series' telling of the combat journey of the men of Easy Company, 506th Regiment, 101st Airborne. Popular historian Stephen Ambrose profiled this group of paratroopers in his book on which the series is closely based.[2] Ambrose's approach to historical research and his view of how the US prevailed in the war profoundly shapes not only *Band of Brothers'* version of history but also its use of music to build emotional connections between generations. This chapter considers the series and its score, lending an ear to how music in triple meter works in a variety of ways to build emotional attachments across a generational divide, using musical idioms historically marked as feminine to bring sons and grand-sons—the series' target audience—to knowledge of what grandpa did in the war. Music—in waltz (not march or swing) time—builds a sentimental bridge between old veterans (some of whom appear in the series), the young actors playing them, and the audience watching in living rooms attached to the quasi-elite, pay-to-view space of premium cable.

Band of Brothers premiered to impressive audience numbers on Sunday, September 9, 2001. Expectations were high for the series, which cost $120 million to produce with a further $10 to $15 million spent on a feature film-sized publicity campaign.[3] *Band of Brothers* opened strongly: episodes one and two, shown back to back, garnered some 10 million viewers—the strongest numbers for a long-form program in HBO's history to that point.[4] But as one critic noted soon after, on September 9, 2001, "television was still just a way of passing the time."[5] With the terrorist attacks of September 11, the context for television watching, especially around issues of war and combat, changed profoundly. And while *Band of Brothers* ran as scheduled for the next eight weeks, just three days after the attacks HBO stopped air-ing promotional spots, allowing the series to find its own audience at a time when national attention was absorbed in televised coverage of the imme-diate aftermath of 9/11 and the probable deployment of American troops overseas.[6] By the airdate of the final episode, the United States had "boots on the ground" in Afghanistan.

This radically changed media climate inevitably shaped the ratings and the critical reception of *Band of Brothers*. A second-week drop off in view-ership of 26 percent still left the series better than average for the network on Sunday nights, and in its third week *Band of Brothers* was capturing 13 percent of the audience, "a staggering amount" for a cable series accord-ing to one foreign critic.[7] By the end of the run, HBO reported the series had reached some eight million homes weekly (based on combined view-ership from several airings of each episode each week).[8] Still, the critical consensus was that *Band of Brothers* had "relatively little public impact."[9] Explanations ran the gamut, from a lack of viewer interest in "graphic re-enactments of US soldiers getting killed or maimed" to a sense that "for all its virtues, *Band of Brothers* feels an irrelevance in the current climate … the world it portrays of fighting a known enemy, with clear objectives and a well-defined end in sight, was lost forever the day New York's twin towers crumpled to the ground."[10]

The critics were correct in sensing that *Band of Brothers* hailed from an earlier era in the history of the American soldier as represented in popular culture. Produced before but viewed mostly after 9/11, *Band of Brothers* was made to function within a larger cycle of remembrance of the World War II generation occasioned by the 40th and 50th anniversary seasons of the war in the 1980s and 1990s and given a branding of sorts by Tom Brokaw's 1998 book *The Greatest Generation*.[11] The movies proved an especially potent site for expression of this cultural obsession with World War II. The 1998 film *Saving Private Ryan*, directed by Spielberg and starring Hanks, was widely received as more than just a movie, seeding discussion of the war and those who fought it in the op ed and feature pages of newspapers, not just the entertainment sections. Spielberg and Hanks joined forces to produce *Band of Brothers* as an extension of their work on *Saving Private Ryan*, and, on a more practical level, *Band of Brothers* was shot in part on re-dressed sets built for *Saving Private Ryan*. Hanks directed one episode; media stories told of his fighting back tears on returning to the sets where *Saving Private Ryan* had been shot.[12]

Composer John Williams' musical score for *Saving Private Ryan* does not include waltz-time music, but neither does it use marches, opting instead for a restrained, reserved music that encourages quiet reflection on the costs of war rather than a noisy rallying around the flag. The music for *Saving Private Ryan*'s end titles, a cue titled "Hymn to the Fallen," exemplifies the sober aesthetic of Williams' score, using full orchestra and wordless chorus (as does Kamen's main theme for *Band of Brothers*). "Hymn to the Fallen" features a moderately paced, tuneful, too-slow-to-march-to melody, mostly in the violins and voices, full of expressive sighs offset, in the words of the film's press pack, by "a haunting cadence of military drums." Spielberg, on hearing this music, was reportedly "so moved ... that he could imagine the audience just sitting ... listening in a darkened theater."[13] Williams' "Hymn to the Fallen" and most of the score for *Saving Private Ryan* offer a music of commemoration, not action. In an interview, Spielberg argued that his film demanded a special response from the viewer: "This isn't the kind of movie you see and then go to a bistro and break bread talking about it—you have to go home and deal with it privately. I think the audience leaves the theater with a little bit of what the veterans left that war with, just a fraction."[14] *Band of Brothers*, its music deployed in similar fashion, effectively put the entire experience—war film narrative and post-film reflection—into the private space of the living room.

The music for the other prestige World War II film of 1998—director Terrence Malick's *The Thin Red Line*—overflows with triple-meter themes for strings, which underscore the highly reflective soldiers who people this nuanced hybrid of the combat genre and global art cinema. But composer Hans Zimmer's equivocal, at times tentative score for Malick's film does not

96 Todd Decker

anticipate the sentimental waltz idiom of Kamen's for *Band of Brothers*. Instead, Zimmer uses triple meter to express the soldiers' suspended state, their position in a battle zone where existential questions rise to the surface again and again, often articulated in vaguely assigned, vaguely philosophical voiceovers behind which Zimmer places gently rocking but not particularly tuneful musical support.

The scores for *Saving Private Ryan* and *The Thin Red Line* alike reflect a shift in war movie music dating to the 1980s cycle of films about the Vietnam War. Central to this aesthetic is director Oliver Stone's use of *Adagio for Strings*, composer Samuel Barber's well-known classical piece from 1938, to score much of his 1986 film *Platoon*.[15] The replacement of jaunty marches with slow, serious, reflective music featuring strings over brass occurred first in the Vietnam cycle where such music expressed grief over meaningless sacrifices and lost innocence in a war the US lost. The scores for *Saving Private Ryan* and *The Thin Red Line* brought this innovative war movie music into the cinematic representation of World War II, where it signified differently as sober reflection on meaningful sacrifices and dignified, stoic manhood gained at great cost. *Band of Brothers* brought this new sort of post-Vietnam movie music to television but with a distinctly domestic cast. Indeed, no war film or television series prior to or since *Band of Brothers* reached so directly for the idiom of the waltz.[16]

The content of *Band of Brothers*—including its use of music—can only be understood within the framework of popular military historian Stephen Ambrose's 1990s trio of bestselling books: *Band of Brothers* (1992), *D-Day* (1994), and *Citizen Soldiers* (1997).[17] In Ambrose's telling, American victory in World War II "depended on the junior officers and NCOs on the front lines": "a bunch of eighteen-to-twenty-eight-year-olds. They were magnificently trained and equipped and supported, but only a few of them had ever been in combat. Only a few had ever killed or seen a buddy killed. ... They were citizen-soldiers, not professionals."[18] For Ambrose, these men—who took initiative and were given freedom to improvise on the battlefield—demonstrated America's "moral superiority" over the Germans, a matter of "better training methods, better selection methods for command positions, ultimately [creating] a more open army reflecting a more open society. Democracy proved better able to produce young men who could be made into superb soldiers than Nazi Germany."[19] Ambrose's narratives rely on the recollections of veterans gathered in more than 1,200 oral history interviews. Late in *Citizen Soldiers*, Ambrose briefly mentions a group of recent former soldiers who befriended him during his junior high years in Whitewater, Wisconsin. He recalls their scarred bodies seen during shirts-and-skins games of basketball and overnight hunting trips where they told him his first war stories. Writing some 50 years later, Ambrose confessed, "I've been listening ever since. I thought then that these guys were giants. I still do."[20]

A Waltz with and for the Greatest Generation 97

Ambrose's personal interaction with and sense of awe for the men who, in his view, won World War II was transferred to the actors during the making of *Band of Brothers*. Individual actors corresponded or spoke on the phone with the men they were playing. On one occasion, three surviving members of Easy Company visited the set. *The New York Times* described the scene, where "young actors were being called by the veterans' names," as "a surreal high school reunion without the name tags: older and younger selves meeting and exchanging suspicious but affectionate glances."[21] In line with Ambrose's perspective, one actor characterized *Band of Brothers* as "about a type of man that's no longer created."[22] The theme of generational obligation resounded in the comments of actor Donnie Wahlberg: "I can safely say I speak for 98 percent of the guys in the show—this role was a two-year payback to the veterans of World War II."[23]

The model of oral history and personal contact with veterans as a source for authentic information about the past is built into the formal structure of *Band of Brothers* from its start. The series opens cold on documentary-style interviews with unidentified old men in civilian clothes, a veritable "visual figure for [Ambrose's] research methodology" (Figure 6.1).[24] They speak of the war as "a different time," saying they signed up because "It's what had to be done." Mention is also made of the extra $50 a month earned by those willing to jump out of airplanes onto the battlefield. After almost two minutes of interviews, *Band of Brothers*' opening credits begin, a two-and-a-half minute sequence seen at the start of every episode. The impact of repeated exposure to this musical opening can hardly be overemphasized.

Figure 6.1 Easy Company veteran Carwood Lipton interviewed in the opening moments of episode six.

98   *Todd Decker*

For all of its cinematic production values, in formal terms *Band of Brothers* remains a television show, and so the musical theme that sticks most persistently in the ear is that heard over the opening title sequence—a crucial formal element of many television series, which proves especially important in *Band of Brothers*. This waltz-time main theme is heard again during each episode's lengthy closing credits, which scroll in the manner of a feature film. In both sequences, music alone fills the soundtrack, in spite of several explosive, by implication noisy, images seen in the opening credits. The main theme is also used for dramatic scoring across the series. This music, which critics heard as "lyrical" and an example of musical "ennoblement," provides an overarching emotional continuity to *Band of Brothers*.[25] Seven writers, seven directors, and two cinematographers divided the duties of writing, directing, and shooting *Band of Brothers*. Only Kamen's creative voice runs across the entire series, unifying the whole by means of a medium—music— that specializes in expressing that which cannot be put into words. Here, music is put to the task of supporting a larger sentimental project of transgenerational bonding.

A brief musical analysis of *Band of Brothers'* main theme suggests how precisely Kamen controlled the emotional work done by the score. The theme is entirely diatonic—every pitch in the tune is in the F major scale—a compositional choice that yields a deceptively simple, perhaps even naive tune. Dissonance—nudging the theme toward elegiac pathos—is created by means of pedal tones in the bass and sigh figures in the melody that give this generally harmonious music an underlying tint of longing. The moderately paced theme played by an orchestra of mostly strings has a ceremonial, public quality, indicating the collective address of the series as a representation of the nation during a past period of crisis. But Kamen's melody is audibly waltz-like—it's not too slow to dance to—and retains a certain tenderness, however grand the arrangement. Dance music, after all, is at once public and private: the waltz is a partner dance normally done in the midst of a crowd of dancers with rather intimate embraces sanctioned by the social space of the ballroom. Like many waltzes, Kamen's theme can be translated into the home. It works nicely as a piano solo and has been marketed as sheet music; more than a few amateur pianists offer their versions on YouTube. Subtly mixed wordless choral voices doubling the strings on the tune encourage the listener to understand the melody as a song. It's easy to fall into the habit of singing or humming along with the theme on its return at the start and finish of every episode, especially when binge watching the series with friends or family. This aspect of Kamen's theme has the potential to bond viewers with each other in the act of impromptu musical performance done *with* the show while also letting each individual supply his or her own meaning to a tune that comes with no lyrics attached.

Visually, *Band of Brothers'* opening titles function as a stylized scrapbook of images culled from the series that is always viewed to music. The viewer catches glimpses of battle but spends most of the title sequence peering into the

Figure 6.2 Donnie Wahlberg as Carwood Lipton in a scene from episode seven included in the opening titles sequence.

faces of young men, actors who we understand from the start are embodying the wartime experiences of the old men from the interviews (Figure 6.2). Crucially, the meaning of the images in the opening titles changes as the series progresses. What begins as an assemblage of faces reacting to sights unseen gradually morphs into a memory book of important moments from the series captured in evocative stills. Watching the series provides the sights these men are looking at: the viewer's memory supplies the eyeline matches missing from the opening titles, most of which are moments of intense experience or emotion. As the episodes go by, the credits gain in their density of meaning, offering reminders of scenes already encountered, keeping alive the faces of characters who die or depart from the front line before the close of the series. Kamen's hummable theme accompanies this entire process, always present to usher the committed viewer back into the community of Easy Company. Preserving signal images in a sort of musical amber—reflected visually in the distressed or "antiqued" quality of the images, most presented in a blue-ish wash—the main theme, heard musically whole, orders the characters and events of *Band of Brothers* under the sign of triple-meter motion that commits to no specific historical time period (this is not music of the 1940s) and that avoids excessive or melodramatic sentimentality by means of harmonic and melodic restraint. Kamen's tune serves from the start and throughout as an essential aspect of the series' construction of a lyrical masculinity, forming a sentimental, musical bridge between generations.

Only at the close of episode 10 are the veterans named—allowing the viewer to match each old man with his younger counterpart in the narrative—and only here does music play behind their words (The interview segments are otherwise unscored).[26] The score withholds music from

100 Todd Decker

the old faces until the very end when, at last, they too are bathed in the waltz that has repeatedly supported the actors playing their parts. Not until our final encounter with the veterans do we—the viewers—have the feeling of coming fully to know them, matching their story as embodied by young actors in the series to their actual old faces and voices by now also grown familiar, all happening to the sound of a melody ingrained in our ears over many hours spent watching *Band of Brothers*. This moment of sentimental recognition—finally knowing who's who—is crucially supported by the addition of music. As one critic said of the series' final moments, "I guarantee that composure will be maintained only through extreme effort."[27] Film historian Thomas Schatz has described the inclusion of the veterans as "at once personalizing the narrative and injecting a sense of documentary realism," adding "as the series wears on, both the aged veterans and their dramatic 'characters' become increasingly familiar, and in an odd sense the older and younger versions of the Easy Company warriors gradually fuse."[28] Kamen's music and the sustained visual attention given to old and young faces at the start of each episode works a kind of alchemy in this "fusing" process.

Withholding the names of and music from the veterans packs a tremendous punch at series' end, allowing the viewer to slowly and lastingly absorb the fact that actual men—*these* men, Ambrose's "giants"—lived through the intense experiences of combat portrayed in the show. Smaller-scale strategies of recognition and reflection also inform the series' approach to narrative time, and music and sound play important roles. Each episode of *Band of Brothers* employs an approach to narrative that mixes in-the-moment, life-or-death urgency with reflection on the experience of combat, a flexible formula that might be succinctly described as action in retrospect. By definition, the veteran interviews heading eight of the 10 episodes set all that follows in the historical past. But further narrative devices enhance the sense of the story as always set within a reflective frame. The men of Easy, especially the officers, are consistently presented as introspective by nature—not in the manner of Malick's philosophical soldiers in *The Thin Red Line* but instead as men of action who think over their actions in concrete terms, reviewing what they did and what they lived through. (Eliciting such reflection is, of course, the task of the oral historian. In that sense, Ambrose's methodology found its perfect subject in the voluble men of Easy Company, who also happened to have survived together through a fairly complete narrative of the American war in Europe.) Episodes one and nine are both structured around extended flashbacks with opening and closing scenes framing a narrative understood to have occurred in the recent past.[29] Episode five recounts a series of combat actions as remembered by Captain, later Major, Dick Winters (Damian Lewis) while he types detailed after-action reports.[30] Sound plays a role throughout the episode, as repeated cuts between past and present are matched by way of sound effects: gunshots on the battlefield become the sound of Winters' typewriter. The process of turning combat action into combat narratives—and, by further extension, military history and audiovisual narratives representing combat—is expressed at the level of form, with the sonic rendering of gunfire and typing by way of the same sound effect. First person voiceovers in past tense are sprinkled across the series as well: Winters in episodes two and 10, First Lt. Carwood Lipton (Donnie Wahlberg) in episode seven, and Private David Webster (Eion Bailey) in episode eight, respectively, offer words that help the viewer step back from the immersive, intense narrative.[31] Gentle, often triple-meter music supports most of Winters' and Lipton's voiceovers, turning their words into a species of melodrama where the meaning or mood of spoken language is directed or enhanced by musical content. Such voiceovers sonically soften the visual style of the series, which remains relentlessly earthbound. An article in *American Cinematographer* noted that the ground rules for shooting *Band of Brothers* laid out by Spielberg, including minimal use of cranes, German POV shots, and slow motion. David Frankel, director of episodes seven and nine, said of these limits: "I think Steven wanted the series to reflect the American soldier's subjective experience. That meant [making it] experiential for the audience as well. By using a crane—in effect, stepping back and seeing things in context—you make it too objective."[32] In such a visual context, past-tense voiceovers and reflective music function, by synesthetic analogy, as sonic crane shots, lending a kind of distance to the series' representation of Easy's at times difficult progress.

Only episode six entirely lacks reflective scoring and/or a retrospective narrative strategy.[33] Among the longer episodes in the series, lasting almost an hour and a quarter, episode six tracks medic Eugene Roe (Shane Taylor) on his endless rounds between frozen foxholes and an overburdened hospital during the Battle of the Bulge, a long standoff in the winter of 1944–1945 that Ambrose puts at the center of *Band of Brothers* and *Citizen Soldiers*. Roe is never granted a voiceover: His occasional prayers and gradual slide into physical and emotional exhaustion are presented without a frame. By episode's end, Roe's effectiveness is pushed to the limit, yet he survives. Episode six, the first of two portraying the Bulge, is all the colder for the lack of warm music pulling the viewer back from the freezing woods. Ambrose noted, "More than once in interviewing veterans of the January fighting, when I ask them to describe the cold, men have involuntarily shivered."[34] The long, music-less episode—the cold, unrelenting heart of any binge-viewing of *Band of Brothers*—goes some distance toward communicating the Bulge as described by Ambrose, an opportunity opened up by the limited-series format, which allows for the creation of a contrast between music-filled and musically empty episodes.

Also lacking musical support are the vast majority of the series' combat sequences. Combat unfolds as a strategic enterprise led (well or not) by means of hand signals, radio lingo, and shouted technical terms—the cry "suppressing fire" being a favorite throughout. The lack of music removes any artificial sense of adrenaline or musical signals of impending victory and casts the effort of interpreting the progress of the fighting onto the viewer, who must keep track of Easy's progress (or not) on a second-to-second basis.

102   Todd Decker

There are only a few instances of conventional action or combat scoring in the series. For these moments, Kamen uses a heroic theme in duple meter or march time. As noted, it's heard only eight times in the series and goes unheard in the opening and closing credits.[35] After episode eight, where the theme is heard in restrained orchestration behind the awarding of several battlefield promotions, this heroic music departs the series altogether. The theme gets its fullest expression, complete with brass and drums, at the close of episode one as accompaniment for the Allied aerial armada taking off to initiate the D-Day attacks. Here, at a juncture when some viewers might be deciding whether to stick with the series or not, *Band of Brothers* looks and sounds the most like a World War II movie from the 1960s when the scale and splendor of the war and its materiel were featured in grand fashion in films such as *The Longest Day* (1962) and *The Battle of Britain* (1969). The tempo of Kamen's heroic theme, however, is too slow to be a march and has none of the can-do jauntiness of those films of a previous generation. A singular moment in the series uses the heroic theme to accompany a single battlefield act framed as especially heroic in a conventional sense. In the final moments of the taking of Foy, Lt. Col Ronald Spiers (Matthew Settle) dashes back and forth across open ground held by the Germans to communicate with US forces approaching from the other side of the village. Ambrose quoted Easy veteran Carwood Lipton on Spiers's "dash": "Damn, that was impressive."[36] In the series, Spiers's run earns an action movie music tribute of the heroic theme complete with solo trumpet and drums that is fundamentally at odds with the entire expressive approach of the score. Arrangements of Kamen's score into concert suites on the *Band of Brothers* soundtrack CD do, however, offer the heroic theme as unabashed action movie music in a manner never heard in the actual series.

Episodes six and seven form a pair: Both present the Bulge, and their combined length is equal to a feature film on the long battle. As described above, episode six follows a medic on his rounds and explores the inertia of the Bulge. Episode seven tags along with Lipton and is filled with significant incidents. The episode opens with the needless loss of Corporal Donald Hoobler (Peter McCabe), who accidentally shoots himself with the German luger he finally acquires after months of looking. As the episode unfolds, five more major characters depart the battlefield and leave the series: two are killed in their foxhole, two others lose their legs in an instance of graphic bodily mutilation forthrightly pictured for the cable television audience, and First Lt. Lynn "Buck" Compton (Neal McDonough) succumbs to battle fatigue in a narrative turn showing how even the strongest men collapsed under the strain. The episode concludes with the successful taking of Foy, climaxed by Spiers's dash.

Episode seven, in a further contrast to episode six, is full of music, using throughout a new theme introduced, uncharacteristically for the series, during the title cards naming the episode. Kamen borrows the eighteenth-century French popular song "Plaisir d'Amor," a triple-meter tune quite similar to his own *Band of Brothers* main title: both favor a moderate, danceable tempo; both melodies are diatonic, mixing smooth stepwise and easy triad-based leaps; both circle around the same scale degrees, climaxing at the top of the singer's range; both are, in essence, singable tunes. Indeed, the choice of "Plaisir"—made during pre-production—may have influenced Kamen's theme, which was likely composed during post-production. "Plaisir d'Amor" is heard in several guises as scoring behind Lipton's many voiceovers, most notably in an unsettled, minor-mode, duple-meter version played when Buck finally succumbs to stress. The tune fairly permeates the episode, which also features some of the noisiest combat sounds of the series when German mortars destroy the Ardennes forest in a series of tree-burst attacks.

After the taking of Foy, Easy finally moves indoors, resting in the chapel of a convent. The girls of the convent choir sing "Plaisir d'Amor" in French without instrumental accompaniment, recreating a concert described by Ambrose, who gives the program as "French and Belgian songs, several in English, and the German marching song 'Lili Marlene.'"[37] Given this historical information from Ambrose, the makers of *Band of Brothers* opted for a gentle, sweet, triple-meter tune sung in French, rather than anything in English or a German march. This choice falls squarely within the overall tone of the series and its score. The untranslated "Plaisir" functions as a wordless tune lacking in historical specificity and placing a fresh veil of sentimental reflection over the scene, which serves as a needed relief for the men and the viewer alike. As the choir sings, Lipton counts the casualties sustained by the company during the Bulge. In a rare symbolic shot, the camera ranges across the full company—the dead and the wounded included—sitting in the chapel's choir stalls. As Lipton, in voiceover, names Easy's casualties, the named men's bodies fade out of the image, their figures removed a second time from the story, this time leaving an empty space behind (Figure 6.3). Easy's losses, most already witnessed during the narrative, are rendered visually a second time in a musical sequence that re-configures the essential elements of the opening titles: sweet, waltz-time music and men's faces. When the choir concludes its musical offering, "Plaisir d'Amor" is again taken up by strings in the score, where it plays to the close of the episode, when the main theme's signature cadence melody is tacked on to its end as a coda. Kamen effectively ties one waltz tune to another and puts the series' musical seal of closure on a piece of borrowed music, which may have been the seed for the series' theme itself.

The only articulation of why the men of Easy are fighting comes in episode nine when the series detours away from Easy's story and toward the work of Holocaust remembrance, a task that is underlined by musical means. Borrowed European classical music and a pathos-heavy music by Kamen heard nowhere else in the series—all of it in triple meter—distinguishes this episode from the rest of *Band of Brothers*.

The episode begins with a title card: "April 11, 1945; Thalem, Germany." A strange sound effect comes in: soft, distant, a bit like wind through the trees, a hushed sound that has the odd effect of intensifying the silence. The first image is an extreme close up of a violin, already in motion toward the chin of

Figure 6.3 "Buck" Compton (Neal McDonough) fades from the scene as Lipton lists Easy's casualties to the sound of a convent choir singing at the end of episode seven.

an unseen violinist. The tip of a bow appears and after a rather long wait the violinist begins to play, joined by three as yet unseen others: another violinist, a violist, a cellist. The camera reveals a string quartet made up of German civilians playing the sixth movement of Ludwig van Beethoven's *String Quartet Op. 131*—a slow, triple-meter movement—while a group of other German civilians slowly cleans up a town center catastrophically destroyed by Allied bombs.[38] *Band of Brothers*' casting directors invested in making this musical moment as real as possible. The players onscreen are clearly real musicians playing in convincing synchronization with the music. In a virtuoso Steadicam shot, the camera loops around and among the somber-faced Germans, finally coming to rest on a group of familiar American faces from Easy observing, guns at the ready, from a bombed out second-floor perch above the mess. The men discuss the music—NCO Joseph Liebgott (Ross McCall), a Jewish member of the company, thinks it is Mozart; Capt. Lewis Nixon (Ron Livingston) corrects him, identifying the composer as Beethoven. The scene fades out with the end of a phrase in the music. A title card moves the story back in time one month. The bulk of the episode is a flashback.

More than half way through the episode, some men from Easy, patrolling the forest outside a German town they have just occupied, come upon a sight that is, for the viewer, initially represented only in sonic terms: the hushed, wind-like, heightened silence that opened the episode returns as our only clue to what the men see. One of the men rushes back to town and, having found Winters, says "We found something." On these words, an almost 10-minute cue—the longest stretch of continuous music in the series—begins with a pulsing, in context ominous triple-meter bass figure—a

A Waltz with and for the Greatest Generation   105

long-short, long-short pattern—that might suggest a heartbeat. To the sound of this rhythmic murmur, the patrol's discovery is finally revealed: a forced labor camp, recently abandoned by its guards, filled with starving and dead prisoners. Derek Paget and Steven N. Lipkin note, "When we are allowed to see what has given the entire group pause—the gates and fence of a [work] camp with its emaciated survivors staring back—the moment has been made 'momentous.'"[39] Sound effects and music prove crucial to this effect.

Unlike any previous World War II film or television series, *Band of Brothers* invests narratively in the representation of the encounter between American soldiers and the German forced-labor system. The pictured camp is small but is examined in close detail over a nine-minute period—all to the sound of music. The men of Easy individually explore and respond to the emaciated prisoners, all of whom are male. Many of the encounters are intensely personal. NCO Frank Perconte (James Madio) responds with a dignified salute to a prisoner who raises his hand in an expression of soldierly resilience. A fresh-faced young American soldier, a minor character shown earlier in the episode enthusiastically having sex with a German girl, finds himself embraced and kissed by an elderly prisoner; he returns the embrace, fear and utter bewilderment in his eyes. Liebgott is called upon to translate a prisoner's explanation of the camp and must deliver the news that the prisoners are there because they are Jews.

The pulsing beat continues at the same deliberate tempo across the entire camp sequence. Subtle changes to the texture and melodic content above the triple-meter bass mark moments or revelations along the way. Pairs of descending stepwise, sustained chords in the high strings are heard on the first images of the prisoners behind the camp gates. These chords are very familiar by this point, having been heard in the narrative score many times, usually marking moments of pathos (for example, when the men board the plane for the D-Day jump). An extended version of these chords is also heard between complete playings of the main theme during the end titles, forming an ABA structure where the main theme (A) offers sentimental comfort, and the stepwise chords (B) trigger solemn reflection.

As Easy Company moves into the camp, the paired chords fall away and a new musical theme slowly emerges. It's first heard during the translated conversation with the prisoner—a descending, stepwise melodic line in the piano, an intimate touch that keeps the scale of the score small. A solo oboe ushers in a fuller treatment by the strings when the prisoner reveals the camp contains mostly Jews imprisoned for being Jews. On this news, a jagged extension of the melody unfolds, full of angular leaps and suspensions but harmonically "pure," without a trace of melodramatic Hollywood scoring, in the vein of the main theme but notably more serious in affect. This restrained yet pathos-filled music plays over shots of piles of emaciated dead bodies, observed by the men of Easy and, of course, the viewer in the cold light of day. Slowly developing across many minutes as the horrors of the camp are revealed, Kamen's long cue recalls Barber's *Adagio for Strings* as

106   *Todd Decker*

used, for example, in the burning of the village scene in *Platoon*. In *Platoon*, this music marks war crimes perpetrated by American soldiers in the scene itself. In *Band of Brothers*, this music sounds over a war crime perpetrated by unseen German soldiers, discovered by sympathetic American soldiers who respond with great emotion. Once again, a musical topos innovated in the 1980s Vietnam combat film cycle for one expressive end is repurposed in the 1990s World War II combat film and cable television cycle.

The camp sequence in episode nine ends with Nixon walking through the camp, supervising German civilians who have been tasked with burying the dead. Nixon walks to an instrumental, all-strings version of "Dido's Lament," an aria from Henry Purcell's seventeenth-century opera *Dido and Aeneas* played at the slowest pace of any triple-meter music in the score.[40] The aria's English text begins "When I am laid in earth" and includes the repeated phrase "Remember me," an expression mirroring the phrase "never forget" associated with Holocaust remembrance. Viewers who know Purcell's piece will, perhaps, make these connections, but the qualities of Purcell's music, heard in series context with other, less solemn triple-meter tunes, make the point in itself. The borrowed music comes to a close and, on a cut, the episode returns to the opening scene of Germans clearing up the town square to the music of Beethoven. Nixon announces that Hitler is dead. The Beethoven concludes. The image track fades to black on the violin seen at the start returned to its case. Then, a series of informative title cards flash onscreen, educating viewers on the basics of Holocaust history. The distant shushing sound heard earlier accompanies these cards.

And the task of Holocaust remembrance continues into the end titles. The music accompanying the credit roll for episode nine differs from every other episode in the series. Here, the ABA structure of the end titles cue is reversed into a BAB form: the descending stepwise chords associated with sorrow throughout the score (B) surround a single playing of the comforting main theme (A). This version of the end titles music appears as the last track on the series' soundtrack CD under the title "Band of Brothers Requiem." If end titles music is meant to direct our reflection, as Spielberg said of *Saving Private Ryan*, the changed music for the titles closing "Why We Fight" strives to direct the viewer, for one out of 10 episodes, toward thoughts on the Holocaust, shifting the series' sentimental bridge from the "Greatest Generation" to the "Six Million."

The triple-meter music heard across *Band of Brothers*—most prominently in the lengthy opening and closing credits—is not the music of a jaunty, victorious American militarism but rather a reflection on the human cost of war refracted through a transgenerational lens. This harmonious music works to support the inner lives of the young men who fought the war and to honor in intimate tones the old men who survived to offer living witness. Commemoration of the Holocaust as the reason for the war comes late in the series: the score folds this topic into the larger whole by, again, using triple meter music. While unaccompanied combat action gives evidence for

A Waltz with and for the Greatest Generation   107

these soldiers' bravery and resilience, the score works overtime to present them as also gentle and reflective. In their guise on television and especially in the music that surrounds them and those who watch, Ambrose's "giants" are granted a lyrical, restrained, even beautiful masculinity. Made before the start of the so-called Global War on Terror and televised across a profound juncture in American history—when the nation turned abruptly toward sustained military engagement overseas—*Band of Brothers* was dated from its third episode. In the context of the US's twenty-first-century wars, fought by warrior-professionals such as the Navy SEALs, the waltzes of *Band of Brothers* resound today as nostalgic reminiscences of a different kind of American soldier, man, nation, and century.

Notes

1. The author extends thanks to Gaylyn Studlar, William Paul, and Erin McGlothin. Kenneth J. Alford, *March: "Colonel Bogey"* (London: 1914).
2. Stephen Ambrose, *Band of Brothers: E Company, 506th Regiment, 101st Airborne from Normandy to Hitler's Eagle's Nest* (New York: Simon and Schuster, 1992).
3. Allison Romano, "On HBO, War Is Hype," *Broadcasting & Cable*, August 13, 2001.
4. John Dempsey, "HBO's *Band* Still Playing Well," *Variety*, September 19, 2001.
5. Thomas Sutcliffe, "America's Nostalgic Desire for a Cleaner Kind of Heroism," *The Independent* (London), September 17, 2001.
6. John Dempsey, "*Brothers*' Blurbs Benched," *Variety*, September 14, 2001.
7. Ibid.; Andy Dougan, "Show That Has United America after Attacks," *Evening Times* (Glasgow), September 21, 2001.
8. Adam Buckman, "*Bands*' Quiet Victory," *New York Post*, November 1, 2001.
9. Charlie McCollum, "HBO's *Brothers* Never Attracted a Big Following," *San Jose Mercury News*, November 2, 2001.
10. Ibid.; Sarah Crompton, *Daily Telegraph* (London), September 29, 2001.
11. Tom Brokaw, *The Greatest Generation* (New York: Random House, 1998).
12. "Tom Back on Set of *Saving Private Ryan*," *Belfast Telegraph*, August 29, 2000.
13. Press pack, *Saving Private Ryan*, Margaret Herrick Library, Academy of Motion Picture Arts and Sciences, Hollywood.
14. Bill Higgins, "*Ryan* Leave Them Speechless." *LA Times*, July 23, 1998.
15. Samuel Barber, *Adagio for Strings*, Op. 11 (New York: G. Schirmer, 1939).
16. Clint Eastwood's main theme for *Flags of Our Fathers* (2006) is a waltz, although it lacks the singable quality of Kamen's theme for *Band of Brothers*. The 2010 HBO-Hanks-Spielberg series *The Pacific*, a follow up to *Band of Brothers* with a score credited to Hans Zimmer, Blake Neely, and Geoff Zanelli, does not use music in triple meter.
17. Ambrose, *Band of Brothers* (1992); Stephen Ambrose, *D-Day: June 6, 1944, The Climactic Battle of World War II* (New York: Simon and Schuster, 1994); Stephen Ambrose, *Citizen Soldiers: The U.S. Army from the Normandy Beaches to the Bulge to the Surrender of Germany, June 7, 1944, to May 7, 1945* (New York: Simon and Schuster, 1997).
18. Ambrose, *Citizen Soldiers*, 21; Ambrose, *D-Day*, 25.
19. Ambrose, *Band of Brothers*, 219.

108 *Todd Decker*

20. Ambrose, *Citizen Soldiers*, 471.
21. Kristin Hohenadel, "Learning How the Private Ryans Felt and Fought," *New York Times*, December 17, 2000.
22. Ibid.
23. Richard Huff, "Actors and Vets Bond in *Band of Brothers*," Daily News (New York), September 9, 2001.
24. Derek Paget and Steven N. Lipkin, "'Movie-of-the-Week' Docudrama, 'Historical-Event' Television, and the Steven Spielberg Series *Band of Brothers*," *New Review of Film and Television Studies* 7/1 (March 2009), 103.
25. Caryn James, "Intricate Tapestry of a Heroic Age," *New York Times*, September 7, 2001; Todd McCarthy, Television Reviews, Variety, September 4, 2001.
26. "Part 10—Points," episode 10, *Band of Brothers*, aired November 4, 2001 (New York: HBO Home Video, 2006) DVD. All subsequent references are to this DVD set.
27. Adam Buckman, "*Bands*' Quiet Victory," *New York Post*, November 1, 2001.
28. Thomas Schatz, "Old War / New War: *Band of Brothers* and the Revival of the WWII War Film," *Film & History* 32/1 (2002), 77; reprinted with slight revisions in *The Essential HBO Reader*, ed. Jeffrey P. Jones and Gary R. Edgerton (Lexington: University Press of Kentucky, 2008), 125–34.
29. "Part One—Currahee," episode 1, and "Part 9—Why We Fight," episode 9, *Band of Brothers*, aired September 9 and October 28, 2001.
30. "Part Five—Crossroads," episode 5, *Band of Brothers*, aired September 30, 2001.
31. "Part Seven—The Breaking Point," episode 7, and "Part 8 – The Last Patrol," episode 8, *Band of Brothers*, aired October 14 and 21, 2001.
32. Jean Oppenheimer, "Close Combat: HBO's Intense 10-part Miniseries *Band of Brothers*," *American Cinematographer*, September 2001.
33. Episode three has no retrospective narrative devices, but it does have reflective scoring. The episode toggles between the heat of close battle with the Germans and the inner life of Pfc. Albert Blithe (Marc Warren), an Easy man struck with temporary blindness upon parachuting into Normandy who finds himself reluctant to fight and mentally out of place on the battlefield. Kamen wrote a tentative theme, heard only in this episode, expressing Blithe's state of mind. "Part 3—Carentan," episode 3, and "Part 6 – Bastogne," episode 6, *Band of Brothers*, aired September 16 and October 7, 2001.
34. Ambrose, *Citizen Soldiers*, 375.
35. Cues using the heroic theme can be found in episode one (1:06:50); two (19:50, 48:25); four (54:53) and five (50:41), in both cases bringing the narrative to a close; seven (59:47); and eight (51:56, 54:42). The theme is hinted at briefly in episode one (18:30) during a training run up Mount Currahee.
36. Ambrose, *Band of Brothers*, 211.
37. Ibid., 220.
38. Ludwig van Beethoven, *String Quartet Op. 131* (Mainz, 1827).
39. Paget and Lipkin, "'Movie-of-the-Week,'" 100.
40. Henry Purcell, *Dido and Aeneas* (first performance: Chelsea, 1689).

Part II

Korea and Vietnam on the Small Screen

7 The American Forces Korea Network

"Bringing Troops a Touch of Home"

Sueyoung Park-Primiano

With television's ascendancy as the dominant mass medium in postwar America, there was much experimentation with its programming as a platform for communicating and shaping socio-cultural and political views. The rapid rise of television's popularity between the years of 1948 and 1955, to claim nearly two-thirds of the nation's homes, drew focused attention from powerful corporations and cultural institutions who would become its new sponsors based on their faith in it as a tool for indoctrinating the masses.[1] According to Anna McCarthy, DuPont, the Advertising Council, and The Ford Foundation, among others, turned to television to redefine American "citizenship" by promoting neoliberal "concepts of self-regulation, voluntarism, and entrepreneurial initiative" as the requisite "rights and responsibilities of both individual and corporate citizenship" in a democratic government.[2] Not to be outdone by civilian institutions, the US military also adopted the new medium as a governing tool.

In recognition of television's potential to disseminate information and propaganda, in 1946 the newly established Army Information School in Carlisle, Pennsylvania, installed a visual aids workshop on the campus to test the effectiveness of televising the school's curriculum.[3] While this early interest in television as a tool for militarization was aborted, one service of the US Army became more concerned with popular television's potential to construct a surrogate home for its soldiers and personnel. This shifting focus to domesticate the military population overseas was in response to more troops and their families being stationed abroad for extended periods to safeguard allied territories against Communism. The long, often isolated deployments warranted greater concern for soldier morale and homesickness. The different approach was also fueled by the popular perception of television in the 1950s, "a decade that invested an enormous amount of cultural capital in the ability to form a family" and used television as a central symbol of family life.[4] In addition to its shared belief in television as a family-oriented medium, the military also had experience employing radio to link the troops with "back home."[5] Thus, in 1953 television broadcasting was integrated into the existing radio programming to form the Armed Forces Radio and Television Service (AFRTS). The mandate of this service was to provide troops with access to stateside programming

112 *Sueyoung Park-Primiano*

and "a touch of home" wherever they might be stationed. In time, the service would become America's fourth television network (albeit non-commercial and government-controlled) and the one with the largest geographical reach in the world. The role of the military's network, however, was not entirely benevolent, and claims to recreate stateside programming were not always an attainable, or even a desirable goal, as we shall see below.

This chapter examines the early operations of the US military's television service to discuss how TV was used to domesticate and govern American troops and civilians stationed away from home, with a specific focus on the network established in South Korea.[6] I provide a brief history of AFRTS to contextualize its service mission in the Korean peninsula and identify programming unique to the Korean situation, in which a Communist threat mere miles from the 38th parallel necessitated a prolonged occupation by American servicemen. The hostile circumstances in South Korea, I argue, predisposed the military network to intensify its customization of programs as just one example of the US military's investment in television to serve "as a tool of Cold War cultural and political nationalism" in the many military fronts overseas as well as at home.[7]

History of the AFRTS

Although the US military did not adopt television for its own use until 1953, American servicemen were among the first audience of the new medium a decade earlier. In October 1943, wounded soldiers and sailors under care at New York City hospitals were privy to initial programs offered by NBC, courtesy of the Radio Corporation of America (RCA).[8] Despite the four-hour daily broadcast restriction set by the federal government, the RCA station in New York, WNBT, offered a mix of programs including sporting events, news, and coverage of the 1944 national party conventions. The station was a veritable "arm of the war effort, airing training films for air wardens," newsreels, and shows like *The Red Cross Program* early in the war before adding cultural programs such as Arturo Toscanini and the NBC Symphony's performance of Verdi's "Hymn to the Nations" in April 1944.[9] In return for RCA's generous donation of the receivers to military hospital recreation rooms, recovering veterans offered feedback on their preferred programming of sporting events, which led to a weekly broadcast of at least one baseball game beginning on Memorial Day 1945.[10] This perfect symbiosis between the US military and RCA, which began with radio manufacturing in 1917, would continue in South Korea, along with the soldiers' preference for sporting events.

When television was integrated into AFRTS, it was extending the US military's long tradition of providing morale-boosting activities to its troops, including live entertainment and athletic activities. Once radio was popularized, San Francisco's radio station, KGEI, began transmitting shortwave broadcasts to American soldiers in the Philippines in 1939. The station became the chief source of information for General MacArthur and his men in 1942 when its programs were rebroadcast by a group of American troops from a makeshift station in Bataan, later branded "The Voice of Freedom" by MacArthur.[11] Even earlier in 1940, the radio station in Panama, PCAC, was established to aid communication with soldiers in jungle positions to protect the Canal. The station quickly added music programming into its regular schedule to encourage troops to tune in to the radio as well as improve their morale.[12] Around the same time, a group of lonely American soldiers in Kodiak, Alaska, succeeded in assembling a low-power radio transmitter to launch station KODK, which would evolve into the first official Armed Forces Radio Service (AFRS) station.[13]

The popularity and success of these early efforts and the need to maintain the morale of American soldiers stationed overseas led to the birth of AFRS as a coordinated Army information medium on May 26, 1942. The service was given the directive to "provide education, information and orientation for our Armed Forces overseas by means of entertainment and special events broadcasts."[14] Headquartered in Los Angeles, for its proximity to available talent and recording facilities, the AFRS was directed by the War Department's Morale Services Division, concerned with the mental health of the servicemen. The Division was the second of two units of the Special Service Branch, formerly known as the Morale Branch, with the first unit based solely on the recreational needs of the servicemen. In late 1942, the "all-service complexion of the AFRS emerged when the Navy assigned personnel to Los Angeles, followed by Marine, Coast Guard, and Army Air Corps personnel."[15]

By the end of the Second World War, there were 177 transmitters and over 54 foreign broadcast stations.[16] During this rapid growth, the AFRS remained under the Morale Services Division until the Troop Information and Education Division was established in late wartime to improve the supervision and coordination of information programs. Subsequently, as a result of the National Security Act of 1947 and its amendment in 1949 that merged the military departments, the Armed Forces Information and Education Division (AFIED) was created in 1951. Renamed the Office of Armed Forces Information and Education (OAFIE) one year later, it assumed responsibility for all information and indoctrination services in the Department of Defense (DoD).[17] According to a memorandum from the General Council of the Department of Defense,

> Troop information and education programs attempt to assist service personnel in understanding their responsibilities overseas, in appreciating the role and cultures of our allies, in understanding the basic policies of our government and in developing high morale and esprit. Essentially, these programs are of two types. The first is educational, providing information on such diverse matters as Code of Conduct, the Cold War Areas, the Communist Menace, etc. The second is designed to boost morale; it tries to make the serviceman feel part of the US news reports, radio and television shows, and the like.[18]

114 *Sueyoung Park-Primiano*

In this way, what began innocently as a form of diversion and entertainment "by soldiers for soldiers" was infused with Cold War priorities and incorporated into the US Army's larger political indoctrination machine.[19] Despite the Defense Department's pronouncements, however, its information officers apparently saw themselves as "explainers rather than persuaders," and their "conflicting impulses to inculcate patriotism and to shun propaganda as un-American" kept the indoctrination campaign relatively mild.[20] Indeed, military records have proven even the "best-crafted propaganda, such as director Frank Capra's World War II *Why We Fight* films, failed to budge soldiers' opinions on issues closest to their immediate self-interest."[21] Instead, it was families, peers, schools, and civilian political culture that proved to be a greater influence over the soldiers. Moreover, as acknowledged in the *Army Information Officers' Guide*, "Soldiers and civilians no longer live in isolation from each other. They share community interests and problems and have access to the same sources of information. What the Army says to the public reaches the soldier promptly, and much of what the soldier hears and sees becomes public knowledge."[22] In this regard, then, AFRS, and its successor AFRTS, likely played a more significant role in shaping soldiers' opinions than any indoctrination campaign, for its programming focused on providing access to the same commercial programs transmitted to living rooms back home. The aim was to entertain the troops and, thus, to maintain the soldiers' familial and national ties, as well as to help form and strengthen new bonds between soldiers with shared viewing preferences and habits, particularly sports events. At the very least, the offering of the familiar diversion was undeniably one means for the Defense Department to structure the soldiers' leisure time in an effort to buoy morale and avoid disquiet, or worse, among the ranks.

From 1946 to 1950, as US troops returned from World War II battlefronts, the number of overseas radio transmitters decreased to forty-five, but the outbreak of hostilities in Korea resulted in an increase of the number of outlets to seventy-nine.[23] It was also during the Korean conflict that television was integrated into AFRS to become AFRTS, a time when the new medium was fast becoming a typical household appliance in the US itself. What is more, in response to Cold War priorities, the US Military Service's buildup of career forces in peacetime created a greater need for television to alleviate boredom and connect the troops and their families to life in America. Indeed, the Korean conflict and the Cold War insured the continuing need for and existence of the AFRTS.

The mission of AFRTS was "To provide United States Armed Forces personnel overseas, and in specified military and veterans' hospitals in the United States, as well as certain isolated areas here at home, where US commercial radio and television are not available or adequate, with programs of information, education and entertainment."[24] A 1955 DoD directive issued by OAFIE, on the other hand, made more explicit the ideological goals of AFRTS:

A balanced fare of information and education programs will be furnished [to] all Armed Forces Radio and Television Stations.

These programs will be written (or selected), produced, and distributed on the basis of their contribution toward the accomplishment of the following information and education objective: To foster in the serviceman attitudes conducive to military efficiency by inculcating belief in:

The importance of the individual,

The mission of the Armed Forces,

American democratic principles, and

Increasing knowledge of national and international affairs.[25]

The first military television outlet was established in Limestone, Maine, in 1953, with program material supplied from the New York office. With the assistance of RCA engineers, the studio was furnished with the best production equipment for its size and budget, and the program structure was patterned after what was already regularly seen "at home." Limestone, later renamed Loring Air Force Base, was chosen for its isolated location, large military population, and absence of civilian recreational outlets, including a commercial TV station. It was also thought to be a good indication of the types of problems to be encountered in establishing an Armed Forces Television Service overseas, including poor community-base relations, low morale problems among dependents, poor radio reception in the area, and harsh winters that created difficulties for both military personnel and their dependents.[26]

With the success of the Loring station experiment, the number of television outlets soon grew to be established in Tripoli, Saudi Arabia, Azores, Iceland, Bermuda, Panama, and Alaska, as well as in South Korea. These so-called Strategic Air Command (SAC) bases were primarily film facilities, transmitting unedited content provided by commercial networks, advertisers, and producers. In March 1959, AFRTS established procedures for removing all advertising and sponsors' messages from the telefilms, although discussion to remove them began in late 1954 despite commercial networks' strong objections.[27] The decommercializing practice, an obvious departure from the home front experience, was necessary to maintain the service's non-competing, charity status with "American networks, sponsors, entertainment unions, and so on, [who] have contributed programming and performance rights without [or at low] cost."[28] It also prevented unplanned military endorsement of products and sponsors and was in keeping with the wartime policy for radio transcription "when commercials were omitted under the assumption that soldiers in combat zones would think them trite and in poor taste."[29] Beginning in 1954–1955, the service also began producing and distributing short films worldwide under OAFIE's direction, including local spot announcements to replace the deleted commercials.[30] Sequences from documentaries of local activity with potential national appeal were also accumulated by the US Army Signal Corps for the US Army Pictorial Center's production of the documentary television program, *The Big Picture*, conceived during the Korean War and designed to

116 *Sueyoung Park-Primiano*

run for 13 weeks in late 1951 with each broadcast devoted to the Korean War. The program was later syndicated by the Army and aired on 366 television stations until 1971.[31]

AFRTS Programming

In July 1958, television operations were relocated from New York to Los Angeles (AFRTS-LA), which became responsible for overseeing 27 television stations for the Air Force, Army, and Navy.[32] Based on the performance and ratings of programs at home, the AFRTS-LA would select programs, secure clearances from networks, purchase prints, decommercialize, supervise film processing, package, and air ship an average of 55 hours of television programs to these stations each week. Generally, 50 hours of the weekly schedule consisted of popular purchased television shows such as *Gunsmoke* (CBS, 1955–1975) and *Perry Mason* (CBS, 1957–1966) or of filmed live or taped shows such as *The Dinah Shore Chevy Show* (NBC, 1956–1963), *The Ed Sullivan Show* (CBS, 1948–1971), and *Fight of the Week* (ABC, 1960–1963).[33] The remaining five hours were reserved for more sports, news, and special events of current and local interest. To be sure, the programming of popular entertainment fare was a continuation of the standard operating procedures for the radio network, which sought to follow, as closely as possible, the familiar stateside content, including popular music and big band shows (such as Woody Herman's Orchestra), popular comedies (such as Abbott and Costello), and successful in-house productions such as *Mail Call* and *Command Performance* that relied on voluntary participation by Hollywood heavyweights, including Clark Gable and Bob Hope.[34]

The Weekly TV Film Units were mailed to the lead station on each standard circuit, programmed throughout a given week, and shipped to the next station. The last station in each circuit would then return the Units to AFRTS-LA for recirculation, destruction, or return to the original owners. At any given point, there could be as many as 30 separate Units circulating among six stations, and it would take from five to 10 months for a Unit to complete its scheduled circuit.[35] Special events took precedence over regular programming, and they were shipped as Priority TV Film Units and Special TV Film Programs with a one-week turnaround time. Specials included major presidential addresses, events of immediate worldwide importance, and *The Hearst Weekly News Digest,* which was shipped to every station.[36]

A non-circulating studio film library was also established at each station from which it could draw supplemental program material and whose collection underwent periodic changes and improvements by AFRTS-LA.[37] Each AFRTS station also received Tele-Tips that contained detailed program notes, scheduling information, and suggestions for effective distribution of materials as part of the weekly shipment. To assist in local production, each radio and television station was provided a complete set of transcribed program aids, including sound effects.[38]

Upon selection, all material was screened by AFRTS-LA for both technical and content quality prior to shipping. The inspection of the technical quality and the maintenance of the library was the responsibility of the "film technician." The approval of program content, however, came under the purview of the "program director" in consultation with the "station manager" who was the Officer-in-Charge.[39] As part of the decommercializing procedure, content review included removing "hard sell" commercials and references that would date the material, as well as editing programs to conform to DoD policies and special restrictions.[40] Standards of security, propriety, and good taste "as they are at home" had to be strictly adhered to and expanded to include the following factors:

> Federal Communications Commission Regulations; agreements or memorandum of understanding/record with the host government; Department of Army directives; prohibitions against identification with advertising; commercial interests in programming material; proprietary rights of artist and authors; union interests in the rights and financial interests of their membership; US political sensitivities at home; political and cultural sensitivities of the host country; US diplomatic and military sensitivities of the moment, and others.[41]

Insofar as any agreement or understanding with host countries, AFRTS stations were permitted to operate by US allies based on the theory that they were primarily for the use of American troops stationed overseas. However, for the supporting members of the Congress, to whom AFRTS had to answer as an operation of the DoD, the services' effect on soldiers was of less significance than the influence they had on the shadow audience of foreign civilians, which was estimated to be much greater than the audiences tuning in to the propaganda programs of the Voice of America or Radio Free Europe. An awareness of the large foreign audience led the US State Department to seek "closer coordination" between its political positions, aired through the Voice of America, and those represented by the American Forces Network, Europe (AFN). The Department of the Army complied, albeit begrudgingly, "as long as AFN was not under any formal obligation to be guided by State Department policy."[42]

Nevertheless, although AFRTS was made aware of and sensitive to the foreign population as its audience, its primary concerns were the American men and women serving the country in or out of uniform. And it was precisely this position, or the appearance of indifference toward the host country, that made AFRTS more "credible" to the shadow audience who tuned in.[43] For the information officers working in the field, programming duties included routine monitoring of the daily habits of the American soldiers and their families and audience analysis to ensure viewer satisfaction. To accomplish this, they were steered to think and plan as commercial advertising men and "know the product—know the audience!"[44] The reference to the commercial quality of AFRTS is further extended by Air Force Lt. Col. Larry Pollack, the deputy commander of AFRTS at the newly located headquarters in Sun Valley, California: "We're similar to ABC, NBC and CBS, in that they're not creating programs from the goodness of their hearts, but to sell things. So are we. Our primary job is getting information to the troops and their departments, wrapped up in entertainment so it sells."[45] Indeed, despite its dominance in programming, entertainment was relegated to a lower rung on the mission ladder. According to the DoD, "We operate on the idea that entertainment frequently is the vehicle necessary to insure regular listeners—thereby making them readily available to hear items of greater mission importance. We recognize entertainment as a legitimate mission, though not the Central Mission."[46]

A variety of methods were deployed to measure a station's and audience's coverage, including field strength surveys, mail response, ballots, telephone surveys, personal interviews, diary methods, and the use of automatic devices such as the "Audimeter" introduced by the A.C. Nielsen Company.[47] To determine the personality of the audience, each outlet, in consultation with the representative of the major command, developed questionnaires that were routinely conducted every three years to accommodate the change in military personnel and personality:

> Which military services are represented? Which service is predominant? Other than radio and television, what sources of information are available? What are the working hours of the installation? Of leisure time, which periods are most popular for listening to radio or watching television? Generally, what category of programs is preferred? Specifically, which program titles are favorites? What type of music is desired? What is the dependent population? How many children, by age group, are involved?[48]

Once the audience personality was identified, the field officers then ascertained the availability of desired information and entertainment materials from AFRTS-LA. Hence, programming decisions required cooperation between the field outlets and the stateside office allowing for customization of content and scheduling according to local audience expectation and preference. Among the diverse types of information and entertainment programs were news, sports, music, comedy, religious programs, shows for children, and features for women, along with popular TV genres such as the Western, drama, variety show, and live sporting events. Again, sports features were an integral part of AFRTS programming because so many of the servicemen were fans, and athletic culture was believed to be crucial in developing the military's desired values, such as loyalty and duty.[49]

News programs were largely obtained from private newsgathering organizations, although these were scrutinized for balance and accuracy. For example, any story failing to name its source, no matter how compelling

The American Forces Korea Network   119

the story, was to be strictly avoided. Political news with any appearance of partisanship was also to be avoided, unless it was balanced with a statement from the opposition. Moreover, all news, political or otherwise, was to be free from trivia, commentary, editorializing, interpretation, rumor, supposition, and speculation by all AFRTS outlets.[50] Complementing the private news programs were local spot announcements relating more directly to specific aspects of troop information, including special news releases advanced by the Department of the Army's Office of Chief of Information (OCINFO). Despite these ideal operating guidelines, however, there is no denying the lack of objectivity. One military production staff with 17 years of experience with AFRTS professed, "Of course AFRTS-generated news is biased. We're an arm of Public Affairs." He continued, "I don't think we try to hide the fact that we do news biased for the military."[51]

As for religious programs, they too were to be balanced to cover Protestant, Catholic, and Jewish faiths with equal time given to each faith as part of the standards observed by all personnel connected to each AFRTS network or outlet.[52] Equally guided by program standards were subjects of race, color, nationality; marriage and family; sex; crime and punishment; physical and mental afflictions; alcoholism and narcotic addiction; and profanity and obscenity, reminiscent of the Production Code adopted by major motion picture studios in Hollywood in 1930 and upon which the US network television code was patterned.[53] Good taste, restraint, and decency provided that, "No program will be accepted which represents, ridicules or attacks races, colors or nationalities."[54]

As for examples of unique, locally produced content, an examination of the American Forces Korea Network shows a variety of information and entertainment programs, many of which were live productions that were all but canceled for many of the territories at the end of the Korean War due to DoD budget cuts.[55] Among the discontinued programs was the aforementioned popular musical variety production *Command Performance*, which had been a feature of the service since World War II and included top performers who appeared at the "command" of the troops. Korea's exemption in the programming of live productions may be in response to the greater number of Americans deployed there, and, subsequently, a greater need to continue popular entertainment programs for American troops and families to make more "palatable" the "long service" in an "undesirable" territory where the local culture was unfamiliar and alienating.[56]

Among the television programs produced by AFKN-TV were *Tonight in Korea*, a half-hour weekly variety show that featured USO performances and local GI talents, including a popular ventriloquist and his dummy á la Edgar Bergen and Charlie McCarthy; *The DMZ-A Special Report*, an hour-long film and live program "showing the men and the situation of the units concerned with keeping the peace in Korea"; *Concert on the Hill*, a monthly, 30-minute concert performed on Sundays by the Eighth Army Band; *Teen Canteen*, an hour-long dance show presented every Saturday afternoon

120 Sueyoung Park-Primiano

during school season for American teenagers of Seoul; a Saturday morning children's program that combined the show *Jaspers* [sic] *General Store* with AFRTS cartoons and interviews with children in the Seoul area; *Journey's End*, an hour-long adaptation of the play by R. C. Sheriff, performed and produced entirely by AFKN personnel; coverage of the national election in the "same manner familiar with stateside TV viewers"; and *Stereo Simulcast Band Program*, which involved a traveling musical group, the Porterville California Studio Band, comprised of 19 high school and junior college students performing in a stereo broadcast-telecast over AFKN Radio and TV. This was all in addition to the station's regular live productions, such as news, religious programs, a weekly news round-up, and five-minute filler spots.[57] While stateside programs connected American troops and civilians to what was familiar from back home, these unique, local shows served to acculturate them to their new surroundings by developing new viewing habits or routines and creating a virtual home away from home for them to invest in and become attached to.

History of the AFKN

Prior to AFKN-TV becoming a major broadcasting center, American troops occupying the Korean peninsula in the aftermath of the Pacific War were first provided news and special events programming from AFRS facilities in Japan as part of the Far East Network (FEN). In 1947 there were 16 AFRS stations in the Far East Command, including three AFRS stations located in the Korean cities of Seoul, Chŏnju, and Pusan. After the formation of the First Republic of Korea on August 15, 1948, and the subsequent withdrawal of most US troops, only the Seoul station remained in service. With the outbreak of the Korean War, however, American troops returned to the peninsula, and the single AFRS station continued its service in Seoul until it was forced to flee southward to Taegu, then to Pusan, and back to Taegu as a mobile operation dubbed "Kilroy" (as in "Kilroy was here") for its multiple, temporary locations.

On September 27, 1950, AFRS stations in Korea officially became the American Forces Korea Network according to General Order Number 84 that placed it under the command of the 8th US Army (EUSA).[58] Its primary mission in wartime was to assist with emergency information, including warnings of air raids and surprise attacks, and to aid the commander in disseminating command subjects (e.g., combat maneuvers), news, and entertainment. This included accommodating the multinational troops represented in the United Nations Command in action, which meant widening the AFKN target audience by, for example, providing news in multiple languages, including French, Greek, Dutch, Turkish, and Flemish.

On October 4, 1950, the internationalist and nomadic AFKN-Kilroy went on the air. By June 1951, Kilroy was joined by AFKN-Vagabond in Seoul and AFKN-Gypsy in Kŭmhwa. In response to the greater need for communication with troops in remote locations during the escalation of the Korean conflict, the two new stations were joined by AFKN-Homesteader in Pusan, AFKN-Troubadour in the eastern front, and AFKN-Rambler, Nomad, and Mercury, as well as AFKN-Mercury for Air Force personnel at Kŭnsan Air Force Base on the southeastern coast. In August 1953, AFKN was awarded a Meritorious Unit Citation for its "exceptionally meritorious conduct in performance of outstanding service."[59] More significantly, evidence of AFKN's successful wartime service in boosting troop morale was personally provided by US troops returning for a second tour of duty in Korea whose expression of nostalgic attachment to "Gypsy," "Kilroy," and "Vagabond" forced the reinstatement of the older, peripatetic names despite the stable nature of AFKN in the postwar years.[60]

With continued US military presence in Korea following the Armistice Agreement on July 27, 1953, which left the two Koreas permanently on the brink of war, AFKN prepared for its long-term existence by deactivating four of the mobile stations and building new studios with newly acquired equipment, including a new 300 ft. radio tower, antennas, and transmitters.[61] Its mission also reverted to a more internal focus to help improve the morale of US troops and families by approximating a stateside environment, including duplicating US network program times, as a palliative remedy for homesickness. Located in the Yongsan Military Reservation in Seoul that served as Headquarters for the EUSA, AFKN was one of many morale-boosting facilities at the compound, which boasted a Post Exchange; theaters; chapels; enlisted men's, officers', and non-commissioned officers' clubs; and a library, bowling alley, gymnasium, and craft shop. By mid-1957, there were six AFKN radio stations in Korea that began broadcasting 24 hours a day to entertain and inform Americans serving from the 38th parallel to the southernmost tip of the peninsula.

On September 15, 1957, AFKN increased its operations to include television, and the first television broadcast was aired over AFKN-TV-Seoul, Channel 3, making Korea the first combat zone in AFRTS history to have television programming. This operation was made possible by the construction of a 170-foot antenna on Mt. Nam San in Seoul and a 400-watt transmitter that permitted AFKN-TV to serve a 20-mile radius. It was also made possible by the establishment of South Korea's first commercial television station on May 12, 1956, by RCA, whose aggressive effort to create a new market and demand for its television sets was facilitated by the US military.[62] A new distribution company, KORCAD, was co-founded by RCA and a Korean agent, and initiated the operation of the TV station HLKZ. Not surprisingly, the organization and programming policy were similar to those already established in the US; the high cost of production and RCA's focus on attracting a large audience meant the bulk of the content on HLKZ (and its successors) was entertainment programs and motion pictures imported from the US. The dominance of American and American-influenced entertainment programs would continue into the

122   Sueyoung Park-Primiano

1960s, which counted *Combat!* (ABC, 1962–1967) and *Bonanza* (NBC, 1959–1973) among the many American imports. Such US influence declined in the 1970s after President Park Chung Hee proclaimed the *Yushin Constitution* that wrested control of all media, including the local television networks, to promote pro-government, anti-Communist programs.[63] Ironically, however, the oppressive control over media provoked greater interest in American popular culture; for the many Koreans who lived near US military bases, AFKN-TV provided an escape from the stifling political dogma.[64] Nevertheless, HLKZ failed to show a profit at the time, and the TV station was eventually sold to Hankook Daily Newspaper (*Hankook Ilbo*) in May 1957 and renamed Daehan Broadcasting Company (DBC). From March to June 1957, HLKZ (and DBC) turned over its studios and equipment to AFKN-TV personnel for training, a favor that would soon be returned by AFKN-TV when a fire destroyed DBC's studios in 1959.[65]

The failure of RCA's initial enterprise could have been predicted because the cost of television sets would remain prohibitive for the majority of the local population throughout the 1960s, and few businesses were willing to buy advertising time. However, HLKZ did pioneer the development of the new medium in South Korea and paved the way for the addition of television by AFKN, which eventually established a second television broadcasting station by May 1959. This was followed by the construction of four rebroadcasting stations and a microwave relay center at Mt. Madison near Suwŏn that greatly expanded access to AFKN-TV-Seoul's signals.[66]

While policy control of AFRTS was then exercised by OAFIE in Washington, the establishment and operation of radio and television stations was a function of the Commander-in-Chief, Pacific Area Command, who, in turn, delegated control of all networks in Korea to the Commanding General of 8th US Army. Placed under the local control of the EUSA Information Office in Seoul, AFKN-TV headquarters was responsible for conducting training in television production, floor direction, lighting, and allied fields. Although in most instances AFKN-TV personnel tended to have prior experience in television production, training was also coordinated with Nippon Television in Tokyo, an alliance that predates the 1965 Normalization Treaty between South Korea and Japan. Moreover, AFKN-TV hired a number of Korean citizens and KATUSAs (Korean Augmentation to the US Army) in its early years, providing television broadcasting experience and opportunity to locals. In October 1961, for example, 42 Korean nationals and three KATUSAs were among the 210 AFKN personnel that also included five American officers, 130 enlisted men, and six Department of the Army civilians.[67]

The Seoul headquarters was also responsible for coordinating, handling, programming, and scheduling all military television broadcasts in Korea as the lead station in the 3rd, "Pacific-African," circuit, relaying the aforementioned Weekly TV Film Unit to the next receiving station in Japan and on to stations in the Philippines, Saudi Arabia, and Asmara.[68] Like other newly installed US military television stations overseas, all initial programs were on film provided by AFRTS in Los Angeles and New York. One month after its launch, AFKN-TV's operation began with approximately 36 hours of weekly television broadcasting, and by the end of 1961 the figure nearly doubled to 61 hours. On January 4, 1959, the first live television broadcast debuted with a three-hour special telecast entitled *Lively Look* that included a tour of the studio, musical entertainment, interviews with high ranking Army officials and the American ambassador to Korea, and an AFKN produced documentary film (*In the Beginning*) featuring the network's news gathering operation.[69] The number of hours of live broadcasting also increased over this period from 19 percent in September 1959 to 30 percent in December 1961.

In recognition of the broadcasts' reach beyond the local target audience, the general standards of good taste proposed by OAFIE were complemented with local practice. While there were no specific "do" or "don't" lists related to entertainment programs, there was an AFKN news policy addendum to AFRTS's general guideline requiring adherence to balance and accuracy. Prior to airing, news items were vetted for local insensitivities when they involved members of South Korean government; US military leaders, policies, or maneuvers; and Japanese-Korean or US-Korean relations. Stories that could aid or comfort the enemy and stories conflicting with command policy had to be cleared by the Information Officer of the EUSA and the News Non-Commissioned Officer-in-Charge. Not only the news but AFKN-TV in general was "careful to delete anything of a derogatory nature dealing with Orientals and material which may tend to prolong the bitterness between Koreans and the Japanese." Also black-balled were filmed cartoons showing American minority groups in an unfavorable light and programs the Communists might use for propaganda purposes.[70] The subject of Japan among the list of sensitive targets was, of course, in response to Korea's strained relationship with the neighboring nation since its occupation and colonization by Japan (1910–1945). In any case, the local practice was yet more evidence of the US military's awareness of the shadow audience. They clearly made adjustments for that audience, thereby compromising the effort to supply troops and their families with the same information and entertainment programs experienced in living rooms across the United States.

As in military radio and US network television programming, entertainment shows made up the greatest percentage of AFKN-TV's schedule, totaling 66 percent in December 1961, with news and sports programming registering 18 percent, information and education programs 11 percent, religious programs 4 percent, and children's programs 2 percent.[71] In addition to the locally produced entertainment programs listed earlier, popular stateside programs were regularly featured by AFKN-TV, including *The Many Loves of Dobie Gillis* (CBS, 1959–1963), *The Adventures of Ozzie and Harriet* (ABC, 1952–1966), *Playhouse 90* (CBS, 1956–1961), *The Lawrence Welk Show* (ABC, 1955–1971), *What's My Line?* (CBS, 1950–1967), *The*

Bob Newhart Show (NBC, 1961–1962), and *The Andy Griffith Show* (CBS, 1960–1968). Again, these popular shows were selected to approximate the living room at home and boost US troop morale. In doing so, local commanders were hoping to negate or dispel the fact that the viewing experience was framed by an unfamiliar culture and environment. Indeed, most commanders and production personnel held a favorable opinion of the television service's ability to transmit a "touch of home," viewing it as "essential to service members and their families' well being."[72] At the same time, most commanders strongly disagreed that stateside programs accurately depicted the United States. Even the one commander in South Korea who did agree declared, "AFRTS reflects the exceedingly low standards of US commercial television. Prime time is almost totally devoted to stupid sitcoms that are of no earthly value. ... I am tired of being treated like a 78 IQ slob. AFRTS should not shuffle along in a mindless regurgitation of the worst of US culture."[73] Apart from the strong disapproval of vapid content by commanding officers, however, there was no discussion of its possible ill effects on the ranks, much less any concern about viewing stateside programs out of context.

Conclusion

In short, AFKN-TV combined unique, customized programs with popular stateside shows to address local concerns and threats, as well as entertain American soldiers and civilians who served for extended periods in South Korea to combat Communist influence and infiltration. To perform this mission, AFKN-TV served as a significant indoctrinating tool for the US military to safeguard the loyalty and citizenship of American troops and personnel by providing access to and nurturing a growing pastime stemming from home. Since its inception in 1957, AFKN-TV has become a robust military project programming comfort and military ideals and has thereby ensured American citizens' cultural and national identities vis-à-vis foreign exposure and influence. The contribution of television in the domestication of American servicemen and women in Korea has only multiplied with the increase in broadcasting time from 36 hours a week in 1957 to 19 hours a day in 1984 and with full-time access to the AFRTS Satellite Network (SATNET), which permitted more timely news and quality sports broadcasting. With SATNET in place, in 1988 AFKN became the first military network to work with a major US network to cover the Summer Olympic Games in Seoul, yet another example of the reverse flow of television content—from the military to civilians—discussed in this volume. In 2000, AFKN entered the digital age and acquired non-linear video server technology and digital news and post-production systems. On April 2, 2001, AFKN was renamed AFN-Korea to correspond with changes in the branding and naming conventions of AFRTS. In 2004, AFN-Korea expanded its operation to launch a Korea-specific website as another venue to inform Americans overseas.

In 2007, AFN-Korea launched its own YouTube site, and in 2008, it consolidated operations under the Defense Media Activity Center to streamline military media operations into "a single, joint, integrated multimedia communications organization."[74]

While the addition of new media technology further expanded AFN's presence from local and regional to global, the progress was far from seamless or free from public censure. Rather, it was equally met with stringent restrictions for American residents living off base. In late 2007, under pressure from American media corporations and the US military, Korean cable companies were forced to cease unauthorized broadcasting of the AFN channel.[75] For the Americans settled in off-post residences unable to pick up over-the-air signal, it meant that AFN-Korea's broadcasting was only accessible with a decoder box and a Direct to Home (DTH) satellite dish, available at the Post Exchange. While the halt in local cable service was an inconvenience for American service personnel and families, it also meant a greater restriction on the native population, alleviating prior concerns about Korean reactions to AFKN (and AFN) television broadcasting that shifted from tacit approval in the 1960s to public outrage decades later. In the 1980s, amidst the rising tide against American influence—stoked by the political fallout from the Chun Doo-hwan regime's military coup and violent suppression of the popular democracy movement—there were many debates and articles by Korean leaders and journalists decrying American cultural imperialism and demanding a halt to "living room pollution" by AFKN. The main objections centered on programs containing excessive sex and violence and other "poisonous" influences.[76] These concerns may have been buttressed by the around-the-clock satellite programming of AFKN and a local survey that reported 82 percent of Korean youth and many educated elite were routine viewers of AFKN-TV.[77] Indeed, with students and the educated elite leading the popular uprising, the clamor from the press to shut down AFKN may be interpreted as a reflection of and response to the political pressure from the Chun regime. Around the same time, public remonstrations against AFKN-TV also came from the home front. In 1987, for example, members of the US Congress and the Assistant Secretary of State for East Asian and Pacific Affairs protested AFKN's censorship within an 18-month period of 17 news items that criticized the South Korean government or activities of opposition leaders; portrayed South Korea as dependent on the US; or appeared to be favorable to North Korea.[78] In other words, AFKN was condemned for adhering to local guidelines established at its onset but poorly understood by US politicians. Despite these setbacks, military television has continued to grow and remains an important medium for providing "a touch of home" to American soldiers in South Korea whose numbers were increased by 800 in January 2014 to *rebalance* the threat from North, and even as its effect on Americans overseas is muddled in this age of media-saturation and information explosion.

Notes

NB: A very special thanks to the editors, Stacy Takacs and Anna Froula, for their generous guidance and insightful suggestions with this and several early drafts of the chapter.

1. Lynn Spigel, *Make Room for TV: Television and the Family Ideal in Postwar America* (Chicago and London: The University of Chicago Press, 1992), 1.
2. Anna McCarthy, *The Citizen Machine: Governing by Television in 1950s America* (New York, London: The New Press, 2010), 3–4.
3. Christopher DeRosa, *Political Indoctrination in the US Army: From World War II to the Vietnam War* (Lincoln, NE: University of Nebraska Press, 2006), 86.
4. Spigel, *Make Room for TV*, 2, 39.
5. Ovid L. Bayless, "The American Forces Network—Europe," *Journal of Broadcasting* 12, 2 (1968): 167.
6. For the impact of AFRTS in Korea, see Jeonghwa Choi, "Uses and Effects of Foreign Television Programming: A Study of an American Armed Forces Television in Korea," (PhD diss., Michigan State University, 1989).
7. Kathleen A. Feeley, "US Television as Cold War Cultural Missionary," *Reviews in American History* 39 (2011): 506.
8. James L. Baughman, *Same Time, Same Station: Creating American Television, 1948–1961* (Baltimore: The Johns Hopkins University Press, 2007), 29.
9. Ibid., 29–30.
10. Ibid., 30–31.
11. Department of Defense. *History of AFRTS: "The First 50 Years"* (Alexandria, VA: American Forces Information Service and Armed Forces Radio and Television Service, 1993), 6.
12. Ibid., 7.
13. Ibid., xxi–xxii.
14. Ibid., 19.
15. DoD, *Armed Forces Radio and Television Broadcast Guide* (Los Angeles, CA: Armed Forces Radio and Television Service, 1961), xxi.
16. DeRosa, *Political Indoctrination*, 30.
17. OAFIE was succeeded by the Directorate of Armed Forces Information and Education (DAFIE) in 1962 and then by the Office of Information for the Armed Forces (OIAF) under the Office of Assistant Secretary of Defense, Manpower and Personnel (ASD [MP]) in 1968. See DeRosa, *Political Indoctrination*, 91, 166, 213–14.
18. DoD, Directorate for Armed Forces Information and Education, "Armed Forces Radio and Television World-Wide Programming Conference Report" (World Wide Radio and Television Programming Conference, Los Angeles, California, August 21–25, 1961): 18–19.
19. DoD, *History of AFRTS*, 5.
20. DeRosa, *Political Indoctrination*, xi–xii.
21. Ibid.
22. Department of the Army, *Army Information Officers' Guide* (Washington, DC: Headquarters, Dept. of the Army, 1968), 1–1.
23. DoD, "AFRTS World-Wide Programming Conference Report," 65.
24. Ibid., 63.
25. Earl James Collins, "A History of the Creation, Development and Use of a Worldwide Military Non-Commercial Television Network for the United States

Military by the Armed Forces Radio and Television Service" (MA thesis, The Ohio State University, 1959), 20.

26. DoD, *History of AFRTS*, 79.
27. Ibid., 81–82.
28. Collins, "A History of the Creation," 69–72.
29. R. Stephen Craig, "American Forces Network in the Cold War: Military Broadcasting in Postwar Germany," *Journal of Broadcasting & Electronic Media* 32, no. 3 (1988): 313.
30. DoD, *Armed Forces Radio and Television Broadcast Guide*, xxii.
31. Nancy E. Bernhard, *U.S. Television News and Cold War Propaganda, 1947–1960* (Cambridge: Cambridge University Press, 1999), 142.
32. The US military's move to Los Angeles parallels the commercial networks' move out West, beginning with *I Love Lucy* (CBS, 1951–1957) and the decline of live broadcast shows.
33. DoD, "Armed Forces Radio and Television," 67, 71–72.
34. Craig, "American Forces Network," 310–11.
35. Ibid., 63.
36. Ibid.
37. Ibid.
38. Ibid., 73.
39. *History of AFRTS*, 37–45.
40. DoD, "Armed Forces Radio and Television," 72.
41. *Army Information Officers' Guide*, 17-1-17-2.
42. Craig, "American Forces Network," 312; R. Stephen Craig, "The American Forces Network, Europe: A Case Study in Military Broadcasting," *Journal of Broadcasting & Electronic Media* 30, no. 1 (1986): 33–46.
43. Ibid. See also Ovid L. Bayless, "The American Forces Network-Europe," *Journal of Broadcasting* 12, no. 2 (1968): 161–67.
44. DoD, *AFRTS Broadcast Guide*, 63.
45. T. W. McGarry, "Armed Forces Worldwide Broadcast System: Sun Valley Home to One of the Biggest Radio, TV Networks," *Lost Angeles Times*, November 19, 1987, accessed April 25, 2014, http://articles.latimes.com/print/1987-11-19/local/me-22363_1_armed-forces-radio-service.
46. DoD, "Armed Forces Radio and Television," 106.
47. DoD, *AFRTS Broadcast Guide*, 125–35.
48. Ibid., 53.
49. DeRosa, *Political Indoctrination*, 105–106.
50. DoD, *AFRTS Broadcast Guide*, 66.
51. Thomas D. McCollum, "A Survey of the Roles and Functions of Armed Forces Radio and Television Service," (MA thesis, Marshall University, 1993), 44.
52. Ibid., 57–78.
53. Motion Picture Association of America, *Movies and Self-Regulation: A Responsible Industry Governs Itself* (New York: 1955).
54. DoD, *AFRTS Broadcast Guide*, 57.
55. Collins, "History of the Creation," 15.
56. Ibid., 18. See also Tim Kane, "Global US Troop Deployment, 1950–2003," accessed July 15, 2015, http://www.heritage.org/research/reports/2004/10/global-us-troop-deployment-1950-2003.
57. DoD, "Armed Forces Radio and Television," 97–98.

58. Jerry L. Priscaro, "An Historical Study of the American Forces Korea Network and Its Broadcast Programming: 1957–1962," (MS thesis, Boston University, 1962), 15.
59. Ibid., 19.
60. Ibid., 27–28.
61. Ibid., 22.
62. Tae-Jin Yoon, "Mass Media and the Reproduction of the International Order: Presentation of American Culture by American Television Programs Aired in Korea, 1970 to 1989" (PhD diss., University of Minnesota, 1997), 141.
63. Ibid., 143–45.
64. Christina Klein, "The AFKN Nexus: US Military Broadcasting and New Korean Cinema," *Transnational Cinemas* 3, no. 2 (2012): 19–39.
65. Ibid., 141–42.
66. Priscaro, "An Historical Study of the AFKN," 98.
67. Ibid., 53.
68. Ibid., 141.
69. Ibid., 31, 100.
70. Ibid., 56–57, 138–39.
71. Ibid., 99, 119.
72. McCollum, "A Survey of the Roles," 21.
73. Ibid., 43.
74. "Recent AFKN Data," accessed May 21, 2014, http://www.smecc.org/recent_afkn_data.htm.
75. T.D. Flack, "Korean Cable Firms to Stop AFN Broadcasts," *Stars and Stripes*, November 7, 2007, accessed October 13, 2015, http://www.stripes.com/news/korean-cable-firms-to-stop-afn-broadcasts-1.70882.
76. See J. K. Yoon, "AFKN-ŭi anbang gonghae" [AFKN's living room pollution], *Kyŏnghyang sinmun*, December 14, 1983; and Jeonghwa Choi, "Uses and Effects of Foreign Television Programming: a Study of an American Armed Forces Television in Korea," (PhD diss., Michigan State University, 1989), 12–28.
77. Choi, "Uses and Effects of Foreign Television Programming."
78. McGarry, "Armed Forces Worldwide Broadcast System."

8 "Everybody Here Is Crazy"
Images of the Disabled on Television's *M*A*S*H*

Kelly J. W. Brown

In December 1973, television's *M*A*S*H* (CBS, 1972–1983) aired the first of 40 episodes that tackled the disabling effects of war, the prime-time program capping a year of increased disability awareness and activism in the United States. By then, the Vietnam War had entered its final years of cease-fires and troop withdrawals, and the national media had started to focus on what *Newsweek* termed the "permanent prisoners of war"—the hundreds of thousands of physically and psychologically wounded veterans created in Vietnam.[1]

In September 1973, President Richard Nixon had signed the Rehabilitation Act, the first federal bill to recognize the civil rights of disabled individuals. Over the next decade, while the United States continued to grapple with its own perceptions and understanding of disability, *M*A*S*H* constantly blurred the lines between the fictional 1950s Korean War *set* and the reality of post-Vietnam *America* in its attempts to vocalize the experiences of wounded soldiers alongside the stories of the doctors and nurses who treated them.

When the show's creators, Gene Reynolds and Larry Gelbart, were first approached to translate *M*A*S*H* from a novel and big screen hit to the small screen, they understood *M*A*S*H* would not be a typical military sitcom: "The movie had played the war for fun-and-gaminess, but Reynolds and Gelbart scrupulously refused to jest at scars without also acknowledging the wounds of war."[2] Drawing on real-life stories of Mobile Army Surgical Hospital (MASH) doctors and veterans, as well as William Lindsey White's *Back Down the Ridge*, a historical account of the experiences of wounded casualties in Korea, Reynolds and Gelbart explored both the physical and psychological wounds of battle in their half-hour sitcom about doctors and soldiers trying to make sense of war.[3] *M*A*S*H* proved not to be the typical sitcom. Incorporating multiple plotlines, both humorous and dramatic, within a single episode, *M*A*S*H*'s serial storytelling prompted cultural critics and scholars to label the sitcom television's first "dramedy."[4] *M*A*S*H* even manipulated the laugh track, removing the canned laughter from the operating room and, later, from entire episodes. As a result, between the pratfalls and hijinks of the series' main character, doctor Benjamin "Hawkeye" Pierce (Alan Alda), the show could interject

130   Kelly J. W. Brown

contemporary social commentary on war, sexuality, politics, race, gender, and, especially, disability.

The use of disabled individuals in American visual culture has been a common occurrence since the nineteenth century when "sideshow freaks" became a mainstay of traveling carnivals and circuses.[5] With the advent of film at the turn of the century, disabled characters appeared first as a comedic trope and then as stock villains, a stereotype that continues to be utilized in films and on television today.[6] Writing in the 1980s, disability journalist Lauri E. Klobas, who has produced the only comprehensive analysis to date of disability images on American television, argued that television more than movies had the power to either change or perpetuate disability stereotypes. After extensive research Klobas found that despite the growing awareness of disability rights and the activism of disabled individuals and organizations, stereotypes persisted: "Viewers seldom see disabled characters as multifaceted human beings for whom physical limitations are a fact of nature. Disability is not depicted as being integrated into a busy and full life. ... Given ... the mostly stereotypical nature of these characterizations, the ramifications of erroneous messages are enormous—and frightening."[7] Rarely are disabled characters shown taking advantage of advancements in rehabilitation techniques and technology in order to live lives that are more independent. Instead, according to Klobas, television programs continued to rely on outdated language, tropes, and plots. As a result, television images typically only reinforced the "Otherness" of people with disabilities.

In addition, prior to the debut of *M*A*S*H* in 1972, very few films—and even fewer fictional television programs—specifically addressed the experiences of the disabled soldier. Both television programmers and Hollywood filmmakers were reluctant to recognize the negative effects of war, especially disabilities incurred "over there." The one notable exception was the World War II television drama *Combat!* (ABC, 1962–1967). Robert Altman, who worked on *Combat!* during its first season and who would later direct the movie version of *M*A*S*H* (1970), said in a 1963 interview, "I wanted to do the war stories you couldn't do in 1946."[8] As Andrew J. Huebner describes it, *Combat!* featured "brutal orders from officers, violent rivalries between soldiers, breakdowns in teamwork, graphic wounds and death, psychological injuries, even episodes devoted to anti-war messages."[9] Over the course of five seasons (152 episodes), the eight main characters were physically wounded 144 times, and the program dealt with psychological injuries 15 times (still only six episodes featured physical wounds with long-term disabling effects, such as blindness, paralysis, or amputation).[10] *Combat!* was not the only military drama to appear on television in the late 1950s and early 1960s—*The Gallant Men* (ABC, 1962–1963), *Twelve O'Clock High* (ABC, 1964–1967), and *The Lieutenant* (NBC, 1963–1964)—all had brief television runs during this period, but *Combat!* was the only episodic prime-time program to repeatedly address the physical and psychological effects of war—until *M*A*S*H*.

"Everybody Here Is Crazy"   131

Ultimately *M*A*S*H* rejects the disability tropes that had been so prevalent in American visual culture until the 1970s, including the use of disabled characters as either comic relief or villains; the infantilizing and/or emasculation of disabled men; the silencing of disabled voices; and the use of able-bodied characters to help disabled characters cure or overcome their disability. The entire premise of *M*A*S*H* complicates this latter stereotype, as the able-bodied doctors and nurses who staff MASH 4077 may treat—but never cure—disabled patients and recognize their role as only temporary mediators between the disabling battlefields and the appropriate care and recovery that ultimately awaits those patients away from the front lines of Korea. So, for example, in "Lend a Hand" when Hawkeye injures his arm, he still continues to operate, as his job outranks his status as an abled or disabled individual. In fact, by having Hawkeye experience numerous physical injuries and psychological breaks, *M*A*S*H* demonstrated that even the strongest of characters was susceptible to the disabling effects of war.[11]

When the first episode of *M*A*S*H* that addressed disability aired in 1973, the last of the combat troops and the remaining prisoners of war were beginning to return home. In Vietnam, the wide-scale use of MASHs, combined with "new medical procedures and new drugs," ensured that more wounded were saved during the Vietnam War than in any previous war during the twentieth century.[12] However, that meant the numbers of both short- and long-term physically and psychologically disabled veterans increased as mortality rates decreased. For example, the *US News & World Report* noted, "twenty per cent of the amputees [who survived] lost more than one limb, as compared with five per cent of World War II amputees."[13] In addition to the increased number of wounded returning home from Vietnam, there was an increase in veteran visibility and activism throughout the 1970s. Organizations like Vietnam Veterans Against the War (VVAW) and National Veterans Resource Project brought together veterans and psychiatrists in order to discuss the psychological effects of war in both private and public forums. Books, such as Robert Jay Lifton's *Home from the War* and Charles R. Figley's *Stress Disorders among Vietnam Veterans*, as well as popular magazines, publicized the struggles Vietnam veterans faced in trying to reintegrate into civil society.[14]

Unlike previous military sitcoms and dramas on television, *M*A*S*H* underscored the long-term, life-altering physical disabilities that could be caused by war, including amputation, facial disfiguration, nerve damage, paralysis, blindness, and deafness. *M*A*S*H* also differed from previous film and television representations of disabled veterans in its emphasis on the initial diagnosis and treatment of wounded soldiers, rather than on the themes of recovery and reintegration. As Hawkeye puts it: "I know how it's supposed to go for them. Shock. Anger. Readjustment. But all we ever see is the shock and the anger."[15] For most soldiers who experience a physical disability, the shock and anger are central to their readjustment process.

132 *Kelly J. W. Brown*

Instead of denying or covering up this resentment, $M*A*S*H$ makes it palpable for viewers. When told he must return to the front, Tom (Michael O'Keefe) in "War of Nerves" tells psychologist Sidney Freedman (Allan Arbus), "I'm never going to forgive you for as long as I live. ... And I'll never forget how much I hate you."[16] In "End Run," all-American football player Billy Tyler (Henry Brown) tells Hawkeye and B. J. Hunnicutt (Mike Farrell) to "Go to hell" upon hearing his leg has been amputated.[17] Finally, in "Morale Victory," Private David Sheridan (James Stephens) who believes that permanent nerve damage in his hands has ended his career as a pianist, weeps in the face of a proud Major Charles Winchester (David Ogden Stiers), who believes he has saved the patient from a more disabling amputation.[18] By aiming the patients' vitriol toward main characters, with whom viewers already have an established connection, the shock and anger is amplified and personalized.

In addition to shock and anger, $M*A*S*H$ also showcased soldiers' fears of emasculation as a result of their injuries. Following World War II and the return of the "Greatest Generation," the military became a crucial aspect of not only American society but also the American male identity. As a result, soldiers who acquired a disability often perceived their physical and psychological wounds as emasculating due to the supposed loss of their sexual ability and/or attractiveness. As disability scholar Paul K. Longmore argues, American society often perpetuates this fear of emasculation: "In a sexually supercharged culture that places almost obsessive emphasis on attractiveness, people with various disabilities are often perceived as sexually deviant and even dangerous, asexual, or sexually incapacitated either physically or emotionally."[19] According to Michael Lee Lanning, a platoon leader during the Vietnam War, "a wound to the genitals was the most feared injury in this war, as in any other conflict. A man's first question to the medics was not 'Am I going to make it?' but rather 'Do I still have my balls?'"[20] On $M*A*S*H$, one of the first questions recently disabled patients like Saunders (Jordan Clarke) ("The Smell of Music") and Tom Straw (Tom Sullivan) ("Out of Sight, Out of Mind") ask the doctors is how they should tell their significant others about their injuries.

While $M*A*S*H$ acknowledges these fears of emasculation, the show outright rejects this (mis)perception of the wounded soldier. The doctors reassure both Saunders and Tom Straw that their women will not reject them; patients whose physical and psychological disabilities prevent them from fighting are granted the same recognition for their heroism, courage, and strength as their able-bodied comrades; and Hawkeye, who suffers from both physical and psychological wounds over the course of the show, is repeatedly held up as $M*A*S*H$'s masculine ideal. The most explicit rejection of emasculation occurs in the episode "UN, the Night, and the Music." A visiting Swedish United Nations delegate, Per Johannsen (Dennis Holahan), admits to Hawkeye that a jeep accident a year earlier left him impotent. He enlists Hawkeye's help in trying to evade "an embarrassing and frustrating situation" with nurse Major Margaret Houlihan (Loretta Swit), who keeps attempting to be alone with him.[21] Despite Johannsen's efforts to conform to his new asexual status as prescribed by the nature of his disability—as well as the larger cultural and social perceptions of disability—Margaret convinces him to spend the night with her in spite of his injury. Although Margaret suggests the two will only talk, the long good-bye kiss she and Johannsen share the next morning implies a more intimate night. This episode of *M*A*S*H* asserts that even men with disabilities that leave them impotent can be sexually attractive and develop romantic relationships.

M*A*S*H also demonstrated that reactions to physically disabling injuries could be met with acceptance and humor, rather than shock and anger, consequently embracing disability as a positive marker of identity and character rather than something to be ashamed of, embarrassed by, or feared. For some soldiers, just knowing they were alive could offset any negative reactions or emotions they might have to a physical injury, which is the advice Colonel Sherman T. Potter (Harry Morgan) offers Hunnicutt after a marathon round of incoming wounded and "meatball surgeries":

HUNNICUTT: I gotta tell him I removed his leg.
POTTER: Start it off with, "Son, you're alive."[22]

In the *Newsweek* article "The Permanent War Prisoners," Marine Lance Corporal Terry Holder recalls the conversation he had with his doctor following a surgery to remove a bullet from his spinal cord: "After they'd taken the bullet out, a solemn Navy doctor said, 'Terry, it looks like you will be paralyzed for the rest of your life.' 'Is that all?' I asked. He looked at me stunned. 'Is that all? Am I going to live?' When the doctor nodded yes, I told him that's all I needed to know. I adjusted to the fact so quickly that they sent me to a psychiatrist to find out if I was okay."[23] Like Terry Holder, the character of Lieutenant Pavelich (Jeff East) in "Settling Debts" also adjusted well to the news of his paralysis, even discouraging the other men in his platoon from taking revenge on the sniper whose bullet severed his spinal cord. Private Lumley (David Packer) even shared a joke with Hunnicutt about his new disabled status:

HUNNICUTT: Is there anything I can do?
LUMLEY: Yeah, Can you do me a favor?
HUNNICUTT: Anything.
LUMLEY: Don't tell my wife, okay. See, I love to go out dancing on Saturday nights. She likes to stay in. And if she ever found out I had a wooden leg, she would hide it just to keep me at home.[24]

In the case of Holder, Pavelich, and Lumley, each man suspected his respective injury would lead to a physical disability long before the doctor told

134 *Kelly J. W. Brown*

him so. As a result, in these instances, the disabled men do not seek a cure or a helping or healing hand from their able-bodied doctors but instead take the proverbial steps toward acceptance and readjustment on their own, without anger or fear.

M*A*S*H featured over twice as many episodes on the psychological disabilities of war than on the physical disabilities, including episodes that addressed hysterical paralysis, combat reaction disorders, psychological breakdowns, psychosomatic reactions, addiction, identity loss, self-harm, and even suicide attempts. This contrasts sharply with previous military television shows and films where the psychological consequences of war are minimized or absent. For example, on *Combat!* the occurrence of physical injuries and disabilities outnumbered psychological traumas 10 to one.[25] The invisibility of most psychological disabilities also contributes to their absence from disability analyses of visual culture, including Lauri Klobas' study, *Disability Drama in Television and Film*. Yet the prominence of psychological disabilities on *M*A*S*H* more accurately reflected the large number of psychologically disabled soldiers who were returning from Vietnam. *US News & World Report* cited in 1973 that more than half fully disabled Vietnam veterans suffered from psychological trauma, a statistic that would increase in the years and decades following the war, as the disabled veterans who did not self-report or whom the Army did not recognize began to materialize.[26] As a result, *M*A*S*H*'s recognition of the high rate and wide range of psychological disabilities, as well as its depictions of the causes and consequences of those traumas, validated both the suffering and significance of the psychologically disabled soldier.

M*A*S*H used the character of Major Frank Burns (Larry Linville) to denounce the outdated and politically incorrect language commonly utilized when discussing psychological disabilities. Frank's hypocrisy, narcissism, and strict adherence to military protocols made him the show's primary antagonist, and his ignorance and indifference toward every psychiatric patient that came through the tents of MASH 4077 only furthered viewer empathy for those wounded. For example, in the episode "Deal Me Out," Frank yells at an emotionally distraught patient: "There's nothing wrong with you, see! It's all in your head. But don't get the idea it's psychological. I'm not buying that old combat fatigue dodge. No, you're going back into the front line soldier. The army doesn't care about your head. Just get the enemy in your crosshairs and blast away."[27] That patient, Private Carter, played by guest star John Ritter, would later take Frank hostage, declaring "I'm not going back up to the line. The noise is terrible." Carter's desperation and Frank's comeuppance both serve to substantiate the severe extent of Carter's psychological wounds. Also, Frank's actions toward the psychologically disabled throughout his five seasons on the series repeatedly drew upon the same outmoded language and attitudes:

FRANK: Corporal Travis, Richard. To Tokyo. Typical psycho case. Shell shock.
CAPTAIN "TRAPPER" JOHN McINTYRE (WAYNE ROGERS): Frank, that's straight out of World War I. Nobody thinks shell shock anymore.

> FRANK: Oh what's the diff. Too much action gets them in the ole' brain box, makes even the best soldier gaga.
>
> TRAPPER: Frank, I defy you to show me a medical book that lists the word "gaga."[28]

In addition to the derogative nickname "psycho case," Frank also refers to psychologically wounded patients as "cry babies," "slug-nutty," "nervous nellies," and "yellow-backs." Two observations can be made from Frank's use of these terms: first, he represents older attitudes that categorized these men as weak, verbally perpetuating societal and cultural fears of the disabled's supposed emasculation; second, and more importantly, because Frank is not intended to be taken seriously by either the other characters or the viewers, his phrases and attitudes toward the psychologically disabled should equally be dismissed. Overall, *M*A*S*H* approached the disabled soldier with patience, empathy, and understanding—all characteristics Frank lacked and Hawkeye (along with the rest of the cast) exemplified.

Upon their return from Vietnam, many veterans isolated themselves within civilian life, a numbness psychologist Robert Jay Lifton described as a "refusal to talk or think about the war."[29] Even two decades after the official end of Vietnam, psychiatrist Jonathan Shay noted the persistence of this asocial behavior: veterans were opening up within support groups and to medical professionals but remained reluctant to reveal their wartime experiences to loved ones.[30] Yet, on *M*A*S*H*, the clinical environment of the recovery tents provided a safe place for patients to reveal the stressors that caused their psychological crises. So, while actual veterans may not have been able to tell their own stories at home, families and friends of wounded soldiers could gain some insight into their soldier's psychological realities through these fictional reenactments.

Some *M*A*S*H* patients exhibited what Lifton referred to as anxiety due to their "death imprint ... the indelible images of death, dying, and suffering."[31] For example, Jimmy Danielson (Jim Reid Boyce) reveals to Colonel Potter, "I've never seen a guy die before. I've only been here a couple of weeks, I still haven't stopped shaking."[32] Death imprints affect even the doctors, especially after endless streams of casualties, bombing runs, or near-death experiences. In "Dreams," none of the doctors is able to sleep as the images of lost limbs, the wounded, and the dead keep creating nightmares. Sensory triggers also create psychiatric episodes, like Hawkeye experiencing a psychosomatic reaction to the smell of a patient soaked in lake water and a patient, Corporal Howard Owens (Dennis Kort), hearing the enemy everywhere: "When I hear a twig snap, I think it's a North Korean creeping up on me to slit my throat. ... [And] when they send me back to the evac hospital, all the nurses there wore rubber-soled shoes. At night, it sounded just like the sneakers the Chinese wear. ... I never sleep in the hospital."[33] As Howard reveals, even supposedly safe spaces and innocuous sounds could morph into a fatal threat for traumatized soldiers.

136 *Kelly J. W. Brown*

The most common psychological trigger on $M*A*S*H$ exhibits as survivor's guilt, either having lived when others died or killed in order to live. In "Quo Vadis, Captain Chandler," bombardier Captain Arnold T. Chandler (Alan Fudge) disassociates from his soldier identity and professes himself to be Jesus Christ after his 57th bombing run proved to be one too many. Corporal Gerald Mullins (Joe Pantoliano) played dead among the bleeding bodies of his buddies in order to avoid the same fate in "Identity Crisis." And Corporal Richard Travis (Michael O'Keefe) admitted in "Mad Dogs and Servicemen," "I didn't fire my rifle. I didn't throw my grenade. I didn't do anything" while he watched a battalion of enemy tanks destroy his unit.[34] Other patients revealed their guilt to be based on moments of pure luck: Lieutenant Tom Martinson's (Charles Frank) sergeant stepping on the mine first instead of him ("What's Up, Doc?"); Private Danny Fitzsimons (Brian Byers) sneaking off to the latrine at the exact moment a sniper picked off the four other men in his foxhole ("Mulcahy's War"); and Private Scala (Richard Lineback) deciding to return to the chow line for Thanksgiving seconds just as an artillery burst kills his comrades: "When I ran back to the foxhole, my buddies were dead. Every one of them. [Starts crying] They all looked so surprised. I'd be dead too if I hadn't been such a pig."[35] Much like the therapeutic rap groups formed by Vietnam veterans during this same time period, wounded soldiers sharing their experiences could be cathartic for both the characters on $M*A*S*H$ and the individuals watching at home.[36]

In order to try and avoid the onset of guilt, psychological treatments for battle fatigue on $M*A*S*H$—or combat exhaustion or reaction, all terms used interchangeably throughout the series—were congruent with how doctors in real battle situations treated fatigue. As Sidney Freedman iterates to Hawkeye, "we used to send these cases home. We'd found the problem just stuck with them all their life. But now if the trauma is recent enough, and the defenses haven't built up to the point where they'll resist treatment, it'll yield to talking. But you gotta get them right back to their unit."[37] This was consistent with the Army's protocol for treating fatigue—PIES, or proximity, immediacy, expectancy, and simplicity.[38] Both Sidney and the doctors employed PIES in multiple episodes with mixed results. In "Mad Dogs and Servicemen," Hawkeye uses tough love methods in order to break a patient out of his hysteria-induced paralysis while Sidney's use of PIES in "War of Nerves" causes resentment within a patient whose immediate return to his unit allowed him to participate in a firefight that left his legs mangled by bullets. The anger this patient espouses complicates the notion that psychological wounds can be easily cured through PIES or other methods—especially within the context of a half-hour sitcom—and hints at the long-term effects these wounds have on some soldiers. Even Sidney Freedman at the end of "War of Nerves" admits he will never know the fate of the patient he thought he had been helping.

The open-ended nature of most of the dramatic storylines on $M*A*S*H$ defied the structure of the traditional sitcom and contributed to the show's

"Everybody Here Is Crazy" 137

realism. One of the few scholars to write extensively on M*A*S*H, James H. Wittebols, criticized the program for tidying up plotlines and producing positive resolutions by the end credits:

> M*A*S*H could solve the problems of these [wounded] men in a half-hour episode. Families and relatives of Vietnam veterans were discovering that it would take years for some men. Obviously, the format of television speeds up the resolution of problems in a way that leaves out long-term pain or implications. ... a "quick-fix" from Sidney Freedman or a kind visit from Father Mulcahy was a deceptively simple resolution to what was often a long-term affliction.[39]

However, what Wittebols misses is that very rarely does a disabled patient receive a "quick-fix," and Hawkeye is the only patient Sidney Freedman ever diagnoses and "cures" within a half-hour episode. Although the viewer knows or can guess that for many of the show's disabled patients, both psychological and physical, their immediate fate is the military hospital in Tokyo; but how these fictional patients will cope with the long-term ramifications of their disability is purposefully left unknown and unresolved. As Hawkeye put it, readjustment does not happen in the M*A*S*H tents or even in the warzone.

Sidney also explicitly avoids the trope of the able-bodied character healing the disabled character, as he repeatedly tells patients only they are responsible for and capable of fixing themselves. In "Mad Dogs and Servicemen," Sidney instructs Hawkeye and Trapper John that the Corporal suffering from hysterical paralysis cannot be told he is not paralyzed but must come to that realization on his own. And in "The Billfold Syndrome," field medic Jerry Neilson (Kevin Geer) suffers a complete amnesiac episode. After using hypnosis to discover the trauma that triggered Jerry's amnesia, Sidney tells him: "You're sergeant Jerry Neilson, and you're from Hartford, Connecticut. It's okay to remember. We're going to talk a lot about this. We're going to help you, and you're going to help yourself."[40] The assertion by Sidney that Jerry is going to help himself underscores the point that the able-bodied Sidney will offer the psychological support Jerry needs, but the success of his rehabilitation ultimately lies with Jerry.

After "The Billfold Syndrome" aired, a minister wrote a lengthy letter to the show's producers praising the cast and writers for how well they depicted the psychologically disabling effects of war:

> Oh, I read the statistics which told us that so many died or had been wounded, so many bridges destroyed, and so much of the enemy's supply destroyed, but very few of those statistics ever dealt with the awesome construction of the human mind. ... The scenes depicted Sergeant Neilson's withdrawal and B.J., Hawkeye, and Major Freedman's attempt to reach him. What came through to me was the extraordinary

138   *Kelly J. W. Brown*

> compassion of the three and the deep need of that one. My prayer is
> that those who saw this will see that it is all right for men to cry. There
> is nothing wrong with hugging and being hugged. There is nothing
> inherently dirty in needing to be understood and to be touched in a
> caring way.[41]

In his letter, the minister praises the new understandings of masculinity the show avidly advocated and acknowledges the importance of empathizing with those who suffer from psychological disabilities, especially as a result of war. This letter is important for two reasons. Not only does it show that *M*A*S*H* embodied the social, political, and cultural context of the time period, but it also confirms that the disabled soldiers on *M*A*S*H* were being depicted and received in a positive way.

In addition to the episodic case studies of injury, *M*A*S*H* also temporarily injures or disables at least eight of its main characters and kills another throughout its 11 seasons. By demonstrating the susceptibility of doctors to psychological breakdowns and physical injury, it makes clear to viewers that war could permeate beyond the front lines and that no one was safe from its disabling effects. When a visiting Army Surgeon Steven J. Newsome (Edward Herrmann) suffers a psychological break during surgery, Hunnicutt laments, "He was as strong as any of us." To which Hawkeye replies, "That's what scares me."[42] To emphasize the main characters' vulnerability to the traumas of war, Hawkeye suffers two physical injuries and four psychological crises over the course of the show. In three episodes, Sidney "cures" Hawkeye's psychological breaks, characterized by the previously mentioned nightmares or psychosomatic manifestations, by the end of each episode. However, the arbitrary onset of his psychological breaks as well as their quick resolution is consistent with real life cases of battle fatigue. Yet two episodes stand out for not only the disabling extent of Hawkeye's injuries, but also for their refusal to rely on traditional disability tropes.

In "Out of Sight, Out of Mind," Hawkeye is involved in an accident that leaves his eyes scarred. As a result, he is forced to wear bandages covering his eyes for a week in order to let them heal, thus experiencing temporary blindness. However, Hawkeye discovers his disability to be a blessing rather than curse. As he tells Hunnicutt,

> One part of the world has closed down for me but another part has
> opened up. Sure, I, I, I keep picturing myself sitting on a corner with
> a tin cup selling thermometers, but I'm going through something here
> I didn't expect. This morning I spent two incredible hours listening to
> that rainstorm. And I, and I didn't just hear it, I was part of it. I bet
> you have no idea that rain hitting the ground makes the same sound
> as steaks when they're barbequing. Or that thunder seems to echo
> forever. And you wouldn't believe how funny it is to slip and fall in

"*Everybody Here Is Crazy*" 139

the mud. ... BJ this is full of trap doors, but I think there may almost be some kind of advantage in this. I've never spent a more conscious day in my life.[43]

Although Hawkeye makes reference to many disabled men's fears of the economic consequences of disability, he makes no mention here or throughout the episode to any concerns about the loss of his sexual prowess or playboy reputation. And despite being blind, Hawkeye's other senses allow him to hear the incoming choppers before everybody else, and in the operating room, to smell a perforated bowel while standing over a patient. These new skills affirm his continued usefulness to his profession and colleagues. Lauri Klobas also praised this episode for its progressive and positive approach to a physical disability: "Hawkeye's discoveries excited him in the midst of his depression. He was realizing that there was an existence after disability. Fortunately for him, his vision was retained—but he had truly acquired some valuable perceptions from the difficulty. ... 'Out of Sight, Out of Mind' dealt with a temporary disability quite fairly and with both poignancy and humor."[44]

Another important aspect of "Out of Sight, Out of Mind," is the casting of blind actor Tom Sullivan in the part of blind patient Tom Straw. In the 1970s, as a result of disability activists, it became more common (but still rare) for films and television programs to cast disabled actors in disabled roles.[45] As Klobas argues, "Not only does this add a sheen of authenticity to a production but the inclusion of these performers sometimes permits them to make small improvements for the better in the script or staged action."[46] One of the actresses who played a nurse on the show recalled the following interaction between Sullivan and two of the show's leads: "Alan [Alda] and Mike [Farrell] were having a conversation with him when he bragged that he could 'see'! 'What do you mean?' they said. ... He explained that since he was totally blind his other senses had been heightened and he was able to 'see' ... by body heat."[47] This idea of the other four senses compensating for the loss of the fifth sense is incorporated into Hawkeye's own experience with blindness on the show. The casting of Tom Sullivan, the blinded Hawkeye's reassured worth as both a man and a doctor, and both characters' ultimate acceptance of their disabled status all contributed to the positive representation of the physically disabled on the small screen.

The two and a half hour series finale of *M*A*S*H*, "Goodbye, Farewell, and Amen," also challenged traditional tropes of disability in progressive ways. In the episode, it is revealed that Hawkeye has been sent to a psychiatric hospital in Tokyo. Despite his repeated assertions that he is okay, Sidney continues to work with him in order to uncover the traumatic event that caused his psychotic break. Between the flashing images of Hawkeye's memory and his current containment within the green-gray walls of the hospital, the trigger event is slowly revealed to the audience—and to Hawkeye

140   *Kelly J. W. Brown*

himself. In his flashbacks, Hawkeye and the rest of the 4077 are on a bus with a group of itinerant South Koreans whom they had picked up. In Hawkeye's memory, there is a woman at the back of the bus with a noisy chicken. He yells at her to make the chicken be quiet.

HAWKEYE: Then I went back towards the front of the bus.
SIDNEY: Then what happened next?
> [The chicken is making noises then goes quiet. The woman holding the chicken is crying]
HAWKEYE: There's something wrong with it. It just stopped making noise. It just stopped.
> [The woman on the bus continues crying]
HAWKEYE: She killed it. She killed it. [Hawkeye becomes increasingly upset]
SIDNEY: She killed the chicken?
HAWKEYE: Oh my god. Oh my god.
> [The woman is no longer holding a chicken, but a baby. Hawkeye just stares at her]
HAWKEYE: I didn't mean for her to kill it. I just wanted it to be quiet. [Hawkeye becomes increasingly more hysterical] It was a baby. She smothered her own baby. You son of a bitch, why did you make me remember that?
SIDNEY: You had to get it out in the open. Now we're halfway home.[48]

Unlike the positive experience Hawkeye has when blind, $M*A*S*H$ demonstrates the wide range of responses patients can have to disabling traumas by showcasing Hawkeye's own shock and anger at what he has been through, not only on the bus but throughout the war. And in contrast to previous episodes, Hawkeye's hospitalization also gives the viewers greater insight into the rehabilitation process beyond the tents of $M*A*S*H$ where patients still have not found a "quick-fix" to their problems. Even when Hawkeye returns to the 4077, in accordance with PIES policies, he is not cured and struggles to readjust throughout the remainder of the episode.

Although set during the Korean War in the 1950s, neither the people who worked on $M*A*S*H$ nor the viewers who watched it saw the show as anything but an allegory of the modern war in Vietnam. $M*A*S*H$ utilized social realism, cinematic filming techniques, and character development in order to contemporize its storylines and redefine the traditional structure, content, and purpose of the television military sitcom. By focusing more on the psychology, morality, and maturation of its characters than the absurd situations they might find themselves in (as in a traditional sitcom), $M*A*S*H$ could allow itself to explore the physical and psychological effects of war in new and more personal ways. Having the injured patients articulate their stories, and the doctors experience similar traumas, allowed the viewers to gain greater empathy and insight into the disabling experiences of war without ever seeing a battlefield. But by analyzing $M*A*S*H$

through the lens of disability, a completely different commentary, albeit one just as important but rarely critiqued upon, emerges to offer another crucial insight into Vietnam-era society and culture.

Notes

1. Malcolm MacPherson, "The Permanent War Prisoners," *Newsweek*, March 5, 1973, 23.
2. Brad Darrach, "Tribute: *M*A*S*H*," *People*, March 7, 1983, 100–103, 102.
3. William Lindsey White, *Back down the Ridge* (New York: Harcourt, Brace and Company, 1953).
4. James H. Wittebols, *Watching M*A*S*H*, *Watching America: A Social History of the 1972–1983 Television Series* (Jefferson, NC: McFarland & Company, Inc., 1998), 9; Ed Solomonson and Mark O'Neill, *TV's M*A*S*H: The Ultimate Guide Book* (Albany, GA: BearManor Media, 2009); Jeff Shires, "*M*A*S*H**," *Encyclopedia of Television,* Museum of Broadcast Communications, accessed July 16, 2015 <http://www.museum.tv/eotv/mash.htm>.
5. See Robert Bogdan, *Freak Show: Presenting Human Oddities for Amusement and Profit* (Chicago: The University of Chicago Press, 1988).
6. Martin F. Norden, *The Cinema of Isolation: A History of Physical Disability in the Movies* (New Brunswick, NJ: Rutgers University Press, 1994), 33. For example, in television's *The Walking Dead*, the Governor wore an eye patch after being maimed, and, in the 2013 film *Hansel and Gretel: Witch Hunters*, the coven of evil witches includes conjoined twins and a witch with no legs.
7. Lauri E. Klobas, *Disability Drama in Television and Film* (Jefferson, NC: McFarland & Company, Inc., 1988), xiii–xiv.
8. Altman as quoted in Andrew J. Huebner, *The Warrior Image: Soldiers in American Culture from the Second World War to the Vietnam Era* (Chapel Hill: The University of North Carolina Press, 2008), 163.
9. Ibid. See also chapter 2 in this volume.
10. Numbers compiled from information provided in Jo Davidsmeyer, Combat!: *A Viewer's Companion to the WWII TV Series* (Tallevast, FL: Strange New Worlds, 2002).
11. Hawkeye would not be the only main character to experience the disabilities of war over the course of the show. In the episode "Dreams," each main character suffers from nightmares and insomnia during a particularly intense barrage of casualties. Two visiting doctors, as well as the psychiatrist Sidney Freedman, all suffered psychological breakdowns. And, in the final episode, Father Francis Mulcahy (William Christopher) worries about his future after a shelling attack leaves him partially deaf.
12. Kyle Longley, *Grunts: The American Combat Soldier in Vietnam* (Armonk, NY: M.E. Sharpe, 2008), 166.
13. "Home From Vietnam—For 2.3 Million US Veterans: a New Way of Life," *US News & World Report*, February 12, 1973, 23.
14. Robert Jay Lifton, *Home from the War: Vietnam Veterans: Neither Victims Nor Executioners* (New York: Simon and Schuster, 1973); *Stress Disorders Among Vietnam Veterans: Theory, Research, and Treatment, ed.* Charles R. Figley (New York: Brunner/Mazel, 1978); And in the first half of 1973 alone, the following articles were published: "The Vets: Heroes as Orphans," *Newsweek*, March 5,

142 *Kelly J. W. Brown*

1973; "The Permanent War Prisoners" *Newsweek*, March 5, 1973; MacPherson, "Veterans: Forgotten Warriors?" *Time*, March 12, 1973; "Home from Vietnam," *US News and World Report*, February 12, 1973; and "Vietnam Veterans: Shocking Report on Damaged Lives," *Redbook*, May 1973.

15. "End Run," season 5, episode 17, *M*A*S*H*, aired January 25, 1977 (LA: Twentieth-Century Fox Home Entertainment, 2003), DVD. All subsequent references are to this collection.

16. "War of Nerves," season 6, episode 5, *M*A*S*H*, aired October 11, 1977.

17. "End Run," *M*A*S*H*.

18. "Morale Victory," season 8, episode 19, *M*A*S*H*, aired January 28, 1980.

19. Paul K. Longmore, "Screening Stereotypes: Images of Disabled People in Television and Motion Pictures," in *Images of the Disabled, Disabling Images*, ed. Alan Gartner and Tom Joe (New York: Praeger, 1987), 72.

20. Michael Lee Lanning as quoted in Peter S. Kindsvatter, *American Soldiers: Ground Combat in the World Wars, Korea, and Vietnam* (Lawrence, KS: University Press of Kansas, 2003), 81.

21. "UN, the Music, and the Night," season 11, episode 10, *M*A*S*H*, aired January 3, 1983.

22. "Post Op," season 5, episode 23, *M*A*S*H*, aired March 8, 1977.

23. MacPherson, "Permanent War Prisoners," 23.

24. "UN, the Music, and the Night," *M*A*S*H*.

25. Numbers compiled from information provided in Davidsmeyer, Combat!.

26. Jonathan Shay writes that the Army reported only a five percent psychiatric casualty rate following Vietnam, a "low rate [that] did not reflect the true incidence of major psychological injury but instead reflected a multilayered institutional illusion, denial, and fiat." Jonathan Shay, *Achilles in Vietnam: Combat Trauma and the Undoing of Character* (New York: Scribner, 2003), 203.

27. "Deal Me Out," season 2, episode 13, *M*A*S*H*, aired December 8, 1973.

28. "Mad Dogs and Servicemen," season 3, episode 13, *M*A*S*H*, aired December 10, 1974.

29. Robert Jay Lifton, "The Scars of Vietnam," *Commonweal*, February 20, 1970, 554–56, 556.

30. See Shay, *Achilles in Vietnam*, especially chapter 10.

31. Lifton, "The Scars of Vietnam," 554.

32. "Promotion Commotion," season 10, episode 17, *M*A*S*H*, aired March 1, 1982.

33. "Smilin' Jack," season 4, episode 21, *M*A*S*H*, aired February 3, 1976.

34. "Mad Dogs and Servicemen," *M*A*S*H*.

35. "Trick or Treatment," season 11, episode 2, *M*A*S*H*, aired November 1, 1982.

36. See Arthur Egendorf, "Vietnam Veteran Rap Groups and Themes of Postwar Life," *Journal of Social Issues*, 31, no. 4 (Fall 1975): 111–24.

37. "War of Nerves," *M*A*S*H*.

38. Kindsvatter, *American Soldiers*, 168–69.

39. Wittebols, *Watching* M*A*S*H, 68.

40. "The Billfold Syndrome," season 7, episode 5, *M*A*S*H*, aired October 16, 1978.

41. David S. Reiss, M*A*S*H: *The Exclusive, Inside Story of TV's Most Popular Show* (New York: The Bobbs-Merrill Company, Inc., 1983), 158.

42. "Heal Thyself," season 8, episode 17, *M*A*S*H*, aired January 14, 1980.

43. "Out of Sight, Out of Mind," season 5, episode 3, *M*A*S*H*, aired October 5, 1976.

"Everybody Here Is Crazy"   143

44. Klobas, *Disability Drama*, 47.
45. Twenty years earlier, director William Wyler cast Harold Russell, a World War II veteran who lost both hands in a training accident, in the role of Homer Parish in *The Best Years of Our Lives* (1946). A groundbreaking decision at the time and one rarely emulated. And as a direct result of the lack of acting roles for double amputees, Russell would subsequently quit Hollywood to advocate on behalf of veterans and the disabled.
46. Ibid., xvi.
47. Enid Kent Sperber as quoted in Solomonson and O'Neill, *TV's* M*A*S*H, 346.
48. "Goodbye, Farewell, and Amen," season 11, episode 16, *M*A*S*H*, aired February 28, 1983.

9   Drinking the War Away
Televisual Insobriety and the Meanings of Alcohol in *M*A*S*H*

David Scott Diffrient

> Us infantry guys, we were a bunch of alcoholics.
> > —Gonzalo Baltazar, a private serving with 2/17th
> > Cavalry (Airborne Division) in Vietnam[1]

One of the few television series of its generation to consistently tackle the issue of alcoholism, the Korean War dramedy *M*A*S*H* (CBS, 1972–1983) showcases the humorous as well as harmful effects of intemperance in spaces where sobriety and more than a small measure of good judgment are called for. Although the men and women of the 4077th Mobile Army Surgical Hospital refrain from such activities in the makeshift operating room where incoming wounded arrive around the clock, they sip martinis and down shots of whiskey nearly everywhere else, including inside "the Swamp." As one of the main settings in the series, this temporary home away from home for Benjamin "Hawkeye" Pierce (Alan Alda), "Trapper John" McIntyre (Wayne Rogers), and the other spiritually drained surgeons is little more than a small tent outfitted with standard military-issue cots. However, the Swamp's centerpiece is a homemade distillery, which on more than one occasion is used as a plot device driving the medical staff toward insobriety, a state of mind and body that gives the doctors and nurses temporary respite from the war.

As indicated in a line of dialogue spoken by B. J. Hunnicutt (Mike Farrell) in the season five episode "End Run," alcohol is "supposed to make you feel nothing."[2] Many devoted fans of *M*A*S*H* will be accustomed to hearing this sentiment, which is expressed repeatedly throughout the 11-season run of the series. For example, the Emmy-nominated episode "Alcoholics Unanimous" shows the lengths to which Major Frank Burns (Larry Linville) will go to bring prohibition to the camp in his role as temporary Commanding Officer. Ultimately, by the end of that episode, the teetotaling party-pooper discovers what everyone—even Father Mulcahy (William Christopher), who "takes a few snorts to get his nerve up" before a temperance sermon—already knows: that hard drink softens the senses and thus dulls the pain of war.[3]

In this chapter, I explore the multiple functions and meanings of alcohol in *M*A*S*H*, looking at specific episodes that deploy drinks and drunkenness in thematically significant ways. Key case studies include season six's

Drinking the War Away   145

"Fallen Idol," season eight's "Bottle Fatigue," and season nine's "Bottoms Up," which collectively highlight the fact that almost everyone in the camp turns to beer, wine, cocktails, and other spirits as a means of relief.[4] More importantly, these episodes also contain scenes in which the main characters confront the reasons for, and effects of, periodic drinking. The bulk of this chapter examines the interrelatedness of alcohol and war, taking into consideration the reasons why Hawkeye and other characters might turn to the bottle from time to time. I also reiterate what James Wittebols and other media scholars have argued about *M*A*S*H*: It is a cultural production of social and political relevance that not only entertains but also enlightens, serving an edifying role even as its controversial content and tonally schizophrenic form (shifting from comedy to drama and vice-versa) disturb some audiences.

But I seek to go one step further in pinpointing the series' slippery, sometimes contradictory messages about drinking, which is alternately scrutinized as a negative practice and celebrated as a social activity conducive to community-building and stress-reduction. Such paradoxes contribute to US popular culture's "alcoholic imaginary," an expression that I have coined by modifying the concept of the "social imaginary." Like the social imaginary, the alcoholic imaginary circuitously projects and reinforces dominant ideologies, the seemingly unshakable, ultimately dubious "truths" that ironically beg questioning from sheer repetition as cultural representations. Positive outcomes of drinking are frequently depicted in *M*A*S*H*, as in "Local Indigenous Personnel."[5] Near the end of this season two episode, a racist investigator from I-Corps finally approves the marriage of an American GI and his Korean girlfriend after the Swamp-mates have gotten him drunk, as if alcohol not only can whittle away at one's social inhibitions but can also bring moral clarity to matters of intercultural and cross-generational bonding. As I will later explain, the show's many toast scenes, often depicting medical personnel raising their glasses after a long stint in the OR, best highlight the constructive, cathartic, and ritualistic dimensions of drinking. But less positive aspects of drinking are also on view in this series, indicating that its messages about alcohol consumption shifted alongside changing societal attitudes and political campaigns during the late 1970s and early 1980s.

Compulsively Consumptive: *M*A*S*H*, Korea, and the Alcoholic Imaginary

> Korea was the easiest place in the world to become an alcoholic.
> —a US commanding officer to a junior pilot,
> quoted in *Officers in Flight Suits*[6]

In his brief overview of drinking on American television, David Pratt explains, "From the late 1960s through the early 1970s, producers like Norman Lear created sitcoms that reflected the tense social and political debates of the Vietnam era." Because alcoholism "did not rank among the

146 *David Scott Diffrient*

major controversies of the era," writers and producers "exercised freer rein in showing alcohol use on sitcoms primarily concerned with more volatile topics like race, poverty, and the Vietnam War itself."[7] A bevy of TV comedies from that time period, including *The Mary Tyler Moore Show* (CBS, 1970–1977), *Maude* (CBS, 1972–1978), *Barney Miller* (ABC, 1975–1982), and *WKRP in Cincinnati* (CBS, 1978–1982), occasionally broached the subject of drinking (and drunkenness) in the workplace, turning a harsh light on characters who, despite their foibles, nevertheless remain "lovable" in the eyes of audiences. For Pratt, however, "*M*A*S*H* is singular among Vietnam-era sitcoms for the central role that convivial heavy drinking plays in the series."[8]

It is significant that *M*A*S*H* debuted around the same time that the Department of Defense commenced a series of policy directives to reduce or eliminate substance abuse among members of the US armed forces (a campaign that the Armed Forces Vietnam Network threw their support behind, with talk-show episodes devoted to the subject).[9] Initially, emphasis was placed on rehabilitation and preventative measures that could be integrated with existing education and law enforcement procedures, so that "detection and early intervention" were parts of a two-pronged approach. In 1971, at the behest of President Richard Nixon, the plan accommodated a urinalysis-testing program, which was random and mandatory for service members returning to the United States from the Southeast Asian theater of war. Controversial from its inception, the testing program was soon challenged in the courts (US v. Ruiz, 1974) and eventually discouraged by members of Congress who argued that it was not a cost-effective means of addressing the problem of substance abuse in the military. The rhetoric of alcohol- and drug-prevention in the military died down for a period during the 1970s, only to reemerge at the beginning of the next decade, coinciding with the broadcast run of *M*A*S*H*'s final seasons.

Although launched on September 17, 1972, during the final stages of the Vietnam War, the series—created by Larry Gelbart and Gene Reynolds—is set during the Korean War, an earlier international conflict (or "police action") that took place between June 25, 1950, and July 27, 1953. Because "officers in the 1950s were less well informed about the dangers of drinking and operating aircraft" than today's soldiers and would sometimes fly drunk, the Korean War turned several pilots and other military personnel into "lost souls." That is, they left the theater of war as alcoholics due to their frequent exposure to liquor during the lulls between fighting.[10] In her recently published study of Americans who fought in the Korean War, *In the Shadow of the Greatest Generation*, Melinda Pash cites veterans of that conflict who resorted to substance abuse during and after the fighting, using alcohol to "numb the pain, and keep the nightmares away." Alcoholism, Pash states, "particularly plagued Korean War veterans who participated in combat, at rates somewhat elevated above those of their contemporaries."[11] While this and other studies have begun bringing

Drinking the War Away   147

attention to previously overlooked aspects of the "Forgotten War," the social and psychological role of drinking in the lives of medical personnel has yet to receive the same critical and historical treatment, a surprising fact given that M*A*S*H—a mainstream television program adored by millions of fans—brought the issue to the forefront of popular discourse during the 1970s and early 1980s.

Much has been made of M*A*S*H's long broadcast run (1972–1983), which surpassed the duration of that mid-century war by eight years and attests to the syndicated television show's appeal. In each of its 11 seasons, M*A*S*H adopted an irreverent yet impassioned mode of satirical anti-war discourse that distinguished it from earlier military-themed sitcoms, including Gomer Pyle (CBS, 1964–1969) and Hogan's Heroes (CBS, 1965–1971). Tackling touchy subjects such as xenophobia, racial discrimination, sexism, and the often-dehumanizing bureaucracy of the US military, the TV program—much like the 1970 Robert Altman-directed feature film of the same title—lent a realistic air to a genre that was normally devoid of progressive political commentary.[12] Gelbart and Reynolds also appear to have been inspired by Altman's iconoclastic interest in rebellious personalities, who take the form of martini-sipping draftee surgeons making the best of a bad situation by engaging in libation, foreplay, and other forms of hedonistic activity. In particular, Alan Alda's Captain Benjamin "Hawkeye" Pierce, a role the actor inherited from Donald Sutherland (in Altman's film), stands out for his anti-authoritarianism and low tolerance for "regular army clowns." In the words of Michael B. Kassell, Hawkeye "fought the insanity of war with not only his surgical skills but also his humor, alcohol abuse, and women chasing"—attributes and activities that were first brought together in the show's pilot episode.[13]

Originally broadcast on September 17, 1972, the pilot (written by Gelbart and directed by Reynolds) establishes not only the show's principal setting but also the main character's reliance on recreational spirits to lift his morale. Returning to his tent after putting in a grueling shift at the OR (where he casually dropped sexist one-liners while operating on patients), Hawkeye relaxes in his cot while nursing a martini prepared for him by the Korean "houseboy" Ho-Jon (Patrick Adiarte) (Figure 9.1). He takes a sip and says to Swamp-mate Trapper John, "You know, we gotta do it someday: Throw away all the guns and invite the jokers from the North and the South in here for a cocktail party. Last man standing wins the war." Although Ho-Jon is a minor character slavishly assisting his "masters" in their makeshift home-away-from-home, he serves as a visible sign of the show's cultural-historical context, reminding audiences that the war-torn country of Korea is its principal setting, despite the young actor's Filipino ethnicity. He also provides demonstrable evidence of Hawkeye and Trapper's paternal benevolence, for they ultimately raise $2000 to send the young Asian to the United States where he will attend Hawkeye's alma mater, Androscoggin College, and presumably gain a "better life."

148 David Scott Diffrient

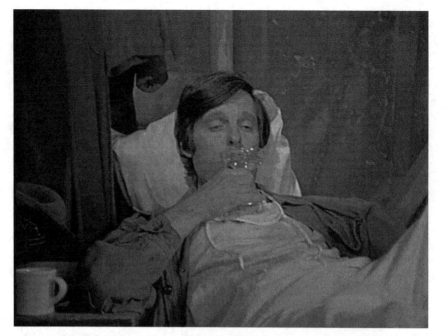

Figure 9.1 The pilot episode of *M*A*S*H* establishes Hawkeye and Trapper's proclivity to drink between surgical shifts, as illustrated in this scene.

Hawkeye and Trapper are able to come up with that money thanks to the "generosity and thirst" of the camp; they charge "ten bucks a head" in an all-you-can-drink raffle, the winner of which will be given a weekend pass to Tokyo in the company of an attractive nurse, Lieutenant Dish (Karen Phillip). Ironically, the raffle winner is Father Mulcahy, a man of the cloth who abstains from both sex and alcohol for much of the series (with the notable exception of the episode "Alcoholics Unanimous"). The festivities come to an abrupt end once helicopters filled with Canadian soldiers land, bringing a fresh supply of dying bodies to the receiving ward in the episode's penultimate scene. One might pause to consider the ethical implications of medical personnel undertaking surgical practices only minutes after imbibing mixed drinks. Regardless, the pilot's foregrounding of drinking culture lays the foundation for ensuing moments in the series when two seemingly unholy alliances—war and comedy, exploitation and charity—are shown to be ripe for narrative and thematic development. Alcohol is thus central to the show's representational polarities, *M*A*S*H*'s tendency to "have it both ways" both generically and ideologically.

For instance, in the season three episode "Rainbow Bridge," the doctors and nurses of the 4077th are invited by Lieutenant Colonel Henry Blake (McLean Stevenson) to have a drink, "Dutch treat," after they have put in 36 straight hours of surgical work (handling 473 cases, including

Drinking the War Away 149

18 laparotomies, 21 busted femurs, and 16 bowel resections).[14] "I think that's an all-timer," Trapper remarks as he pops open a bottle of alcohol, pouring it into a coffee cup. The incongruity of that beverage container and its liquid contents is metaphorically aligned with what transpires later in the episode, when the American doctors—having been sent a communique from the Chinese, who have nine shot-up US soldiers on their side requiring medical attention—cross the front line and meet with the Communists at the titular pickup point, Rainbow Bridge (some 50 miles inside the enemy's territory). "You're doing something decent in the middle of a giant indecency," Hawkeye tells one of the English-speaking Chinese officers (Mako), a comment about heretofore unthinkable cultural mixing and international cooperation that had been anticipated by the doctors' earlier combining of liquor and coffee.[15] Not insignificantly, this episode ends with Trapper and Hawkeye sleeping in their cots, exhausted after performing another 16 hours of surgery and thus unable to make their planned R&R trip to Tokyo. The final image is both humorous and solemn (in keeping with the show's contradictory discourses concerning drinking): A half-filled martini glass is propped up in Hawkeye's hand, as if to remind audiences that alcohol is central to *M*A*S*H*'s hybrid combination of pathos and comedy, sentimentality and satire.[16]

Alcohol is also shown to be part of the healing process, a therapeutic means of overcoming personal pain or professional setbacks, as exemplified in season eight's "Old Soldiers."[17] Unlike Hawkeye and Trapper in the above episode, Colonel Sherman Potter (Harry Morgan), Blake's replacement, takes off for that most privileged of travel destinations, Tokyo, following a "late-night call." The reason for his trip is not, however, rest and recuperation. Instead, he is visiting a sick friend, whose passing makes Potter the last surviving member of a group of tightly knit World War I veterans. When the heartbroken commanding officer returns from Japan to the 4077th, which has become overrun by Korean orphans (war refugees being cared for by their benevolent American overseers), he asks his medical staff to share four bottles of French wine—one for each deceased man—and a toast in their memory. Fans of *M*A*S*H* might find their own memories of earlier episodes triggered by such a toast, which was offered up with slight variation in the eighth season's premiere episode, "Too Many Cooks"; the penultimate scene of which shows the main characters gathering at the Officers' Club and sharing a bottle of Scotch after Potter has read a touching letter sent by his wife, Mildred (Figure 9.2).[18] Scenes showing the characters raising their glasses in a toast recur throughout the history of *M*A*S*H*, as highlighted in episodes such as "Aid Station," "The Grim Reaper," "Stars and Stripes," and "Heroes."[19] These moments—social rituals that are contained within an oft-repeated, equally ritualistic narrative structure unique to a half-hour television comedy-drama—attest to the healing power of alcohol, which serves an important role in the lives of medical personnel as well as soldiers.

Figure 9.2 Near the end of "Too Many Cooks," Colonel Potter and Major Houlihan share a toast at the Officers' Club, a convivial action that is often repeated during the 11-year run of *M*A*S*H*.

Related to its ability to strengthen bonds between people from different social classes and cultural backgrounds, liquor can also reveal otherwise submerged aspects of character, as evidenced in "Hot Lips and Empty Arms."[20] Besides featuring a toast scene, this episode shows the inebriated head nurse Major Margaret Houlihan (Loretta Swit) doing something that she rarely does: opening up about her personal feelings to express her dissatisfaction with Frank Burns (her on-and-off lover). This would be echoed in "Major Ego," an episode from *M*A*S*H*'s seventh season that shows the same loose-lipped woman confiding in B. J., who learns of her pent-up sexual desires and readiness to move forward after her break-up with the money-grubbing Donald Penobscott (Beeson Carroll).[21] Despite the fact that her mother is an alcoholic kleptomaniac (something we learn in the episode "Bulletin Board"), Margaret's willingness to toss back the bottle contributes to her newfound respect for and friendship with the perpetually soused Swamp-mates.[22] In particular, she opens up in a more honest, forthcoming way with Hawkeye, who is only half joking when he says that he has "taken gin intravenously."[23] Gradually, after an initial period of antagonism, the two become close friends, and alcohol—a narrative device that sometimes halts episodic plot progression for the sake of "character-building" and

Drinking the War Away 151

interpersonal connection—contributes to this developing camaraderie, one that is often capped with a toast.

A toast brings the season eight episode "Mr. and Mrs. Who?" to an end, providing narrative symmetry to a story that begins with the sight of Major Charles Emerson Winchester III (David Ogden Stiers) returning to the camp with a hangover.[24] The Harvard graduate's disheveled and unshaven appearance is at odds with his typically refined demeanor, suggesting that he did other things during his weekend trip to Tokyo besides attending a medical seminar. Once he ambles away from the jeep and makes his way to his cot, he unpacks his bag to reveal black stockings and rolls of undeveloped film. "I attended some sort of party at the hospital," Charles sputters, concluding that he must have fallen victim "to the insidious blandishments of a rowdy surgical staff." However, he is unable to recall anything specific about his excursion. It is only thanks to Corporal Max Klinger (Jamie Farr), who develops the rolls of film showing "Major Disaster" wearing a lampshade on his head (a cliché of public drunkenness) and dancing with an unknown woman, that Charles is able to piece together the puzzle of that weekend. Because he drank too many bowls of sake punch, he apparently got married to a woman who is now expected to arrive at the 4077th in pursuit of her husband. Once "Mrs. Winchester" (Claudette Nevins), gets there, though, she explains that they are not really married because the ceremony was performed by the hotel bartender. This information brings a sigh of relief to the man who has undergone serious "bottle fatigue" over the course of this episode.

Although they share hot tea while recalling their time in Tokyo, the episode concludes with the image of the main characters toasting their success in figuring out the solution to a patient's mysterious bout with Korean Hemorrhagic Fever, a disease that attacks the kidneys and, ironically, makes the sufferer (in this case, a man named Shaw) thirsty. "Please, don't say 'drink,'" Charles had earlier said to Shaw, who then asked, "You got it too, Doc?" Charles's reply—"No, my pain, regrettably, is self-inflicted"—would seem to indicate that liquor brings anguish rather than comfort to the men and women of the 4077. However, as they raise their glasses in the final scene, a celebratory mood settles over the camp, suggesting once again that the social experience of alcohol injects levity and goodwill into a space otherwise laden with death and misery. As a bookending device, and following the narrative logic of the sitcom form/formula, the toast scene in this and other *M*A*S*H* episodes ensures a return to the "natural" state of things. That is, what might be seen by some commentators as a potentially disruptive activity is in fact the glue that keeps the social status quo intact, bringing "equilibrium" back to a narrative premised on the mental and physical disequilibrium unique to the wartime experience—an experience that sometimes necessitates the use of alcohol for "self-medication" and "trauma-buffering."

152   *David Scott Diffrient*

It is only when Hawkeye's alcohol dependency interferes with either his professional duties or his romantic liaisons that he begins to seriously reassess its role in his life. For instance, after a drinking binge leaves him hungover in the season six episode "Fallen Idol," he is unable to operate on Corporal Walter "Radar" O'Reilly (Gary Burghoff), who was wounded en route to Seoul. And why was the company clerk undertaking such a perilous journey to the South Korean capital? Because Hawkeye had encouraged Radar to see the city, where he might sow his oats and "become a man." That idea recalls a similar comment in *Gomer Pyle U.S.M.C.* when Sergeant Carter (Frank Sutton) enthusiastically remarks that the childlike Private Pyle (Jim Nabors) has "grown up" upon graduating from vanilla malts to alcohol in the episode "Show Me the Way to Go Home." Such refrains demonstrate the persistence of television's "alcoholic imaginary." Once a hero to Radar, the guilt-ridden Hawkeye is now seen in an entirely new light. Only at the end of this episode, when both men order grape Nehi soft drinks from the bar, are the two able to see eye-to-eye. Equally troubling for Hawkeye is his inability to sustain an erection in bed, one of the many subplots presented in season four's "Some 38th Parallels."[25] Recalling the Painless Pole's predicament in Altman's 1970 film, this development—referred to by Hawkeye as "the big couldn't"—nevertheless differs insofar as the onus for such a failure falls on the hero's heavy drinking. It also provides Hawkeye, who has been "getting nasty notes from [his] liver," one of his many reasons to give up alcohol on the show.

Another nasty note—his previous month's bar tab of $38.20—compels Hawkeye to go off drink for a week in season eight's "Bottle Fatigue." From its first scene until its final moments, this episode devotes a significant amount of screen time to the topic of alcohol consumption and thus deserves special consideration. It begins with Hawkeye, B. J., Charles, Margaret, and Colonel Potter trudging in to the officers' club at a "quarter past catatonic." Physically drained after a full night of OR work, the gang attempts to "synchronize [their] exhaustion" through alcoholic means. As in so many previous episodes, images of drinking establish this episode's point of narrative equilibrium. Potter remarks, "At times like this, I feel a debt of gratitude to that old Kentucky gent who discovered that you can do more with barley than make soup." Charles, ever the blueblood, tells his commanding officer that bourbon is "the grape Nehi of alcoholic beverages." In keeping with his fastidious demeanor, he prefers something more "elegant," such as cognac, to which Potter replies, "Who gives a rat's hat? So long as it numbs the noggin." Igor, the bartender, promptly passes a double Scotch to Margaret while B. J. receives a gin and tonic, and Potter gets his bourbon neat. When Hawkeye first lays eyes on the bar tab that Igor gives him, he says, "I can't be responsible for this. I must have been drunk at the time." In fact, this is "just the tip of the ice cube," for he also has to worry about the charges that have accrued at the camp's other watering hole, Rosie's bar. Winchester tries to calm Hawkeye, telling him that even his "own alcoholic consumption's

Drinking the War Away 153

been elevated since [he] landed in this leper colony." The others, however, cannot help but laugh when the surgeon says that he is giving up alcohol for a week, telling them in earnest, "I want to prove to myself that I can do it." The scenes that follow thus bring narrative *disequilibrium*, or a disruption of the typical state of affairs at the 4077, something that only alcohol can set right by episode's end.

Against the expectations of his friends, the doctor's experiment in sobriety actually succeeds, but not without driving everyone crazy with his "teetotaling tantrums." Ironically, being on the wagon ruins cleanly shaven Hawkeye's chances of getting Nurse Mendenhall (Shelley Long) into bed, for his ill-timed temperance lecture brings their romantic dinner to a premature end. The penultimate scene, coming after an intense situation in the OR (where a North Korean patient brandished a grenade in fear), shows the beleaguered bunch of doctors and nurses once again bellying up to the bar in the Officer's Club, where—recalling the episode's first scene—they order glasses of bourbon and gin and tonic. However, even as this scene adheres to the standard sitcom formula of coming full circle, bringing "order" to a diegetic universe temporarily filled with "disorder," it breaks from narrative tradition in a subtle yet significant way. Having given up his sanctimonious attitude in light of their dangerous standoff with the Communist soldier, Hawkeye holds a glass of Scotch in his hand and pauses before putting it back on the bar, saying that he will drink again when he wants to, not when he needs to.

Episodes shown prior to "Bottle Fatigue," particularly "Period of Adjustment" and "A Night at Rosie's," had already established the fact that almost everyone in the camp turns to alcohol as a means of personal relief and bonding with others.[26] In the aforementioned "End Run," Radar proclaims his masculinity in Rosie's Bar by telling B. J. that his liver is no longer a "virgin" (a comment that recalls an earlier episode, "Springtime," in which the company clerk, having just lost his virginity, says, "I think I've just been slaked!").[27] Even Potter follows the path of his younger predecessor, Blake, sharing several swigs of Hawkeye's whiskey-filled canteen in "The Colonel's Horse" and getting so drunk in "Last Laugh" that he falls down like a fool.[28] More dignified is the colonel's aforementioned toast to his World War I buddies in "Old Soldiers," an episode in which drinking to the memory of fallen friends is deemed an acceptable act for an old-timer like Potter, who somehow manages to maintain the dignity of the Service and the decorum of the OR without ever sacrificing his humanity or sense of humor.

Less acceptable, at least in the eyes of many doctors and nurses in the 4077, is the inability of Margaret's friend, Captain Helen Whitfield (Gail Strickland), to stay sober in "Bottoms Up." Written by Dennis Koenig and directed by Alan Alda, this episode from season nine is significant in many ways. It begins by establishing the long friendship between the two nurses, who play cards in the women's barracks and reminisce about their younger days. One of the best medical personnel in camp, Helen (who used to be a "party girl") reverts back to the habit she gave up years ago, turning to alcohol as an escape from the daily grind. This begins to affect her work in the OR where—suffering from a hangover—she makes mistakes in front of Potter and the others. After being found by Klinger in the supply tent downing a bottle of whiskey, the closet drinker is eventually "outed" by Margaret, who yells, "People's lives are at stake!" (Figure 9.3).

Figure 9.3 Margaret's friend, Captain Helen Whitfield (Gail Strickland), gets "the DTs" when trying to go off the bottle in "Bottoms Up."

Besides showing the challenges involved in going off the bottle (Whitfield gets "the DTs," melting down in the mess tent before finally cleaning up her act), "Bottoms Up" also allows Margaret to turn the tables on Colonel Potter, a man she so admires and respects that she typically assumes a subservient position with him. Here, however, she barks in Potter's face that he has employed a "double standard" with regard to drinking in the camp, meaning that it is "naturally" assumed to be okay for men but unpardonable for women. In a scene that recalls the final moments in "Fallen Idol," Houlihan and Potter put aside their temporary differences and order Scotch and water at the bar. "Hold the Scotch," Margaret quickly adds, reflecting the way that the socially conscious television series became a more sobering depiction of sobriety throughout the late 1970s and early 1980s—a time when the drinking age in most states was raised following news reports about teenage traffic fatalities and increased drug use in high

Drinking the War Away 155

schools. Originally airing in March 1981, "Bottoms Up" is indicative of the tonal shift that had begun occurring in *M*A*S*H* as the series moved away from outright comedy toward serious drama. The strong presence of alcohol in this episode suggests that literal and figurative intemperance was the order of the day.

In his book *Watching M*A*S*H, Watching America*, Wittebols argues that alcohol is integral to this television show's comical yet socially conscious storylines, which would become less satirical, more politically cautious, near the end of its 11-year broadcast.[29] He points toward late-run episodes such as "Taking the Fifth" and "Blood and Guts" (from the series' ninth and tenth seasons, respectively), which indicate that the textual linkage between drinking and sexist attitudes in the military had not dissipated since the 1972 pilot episode. In "Taking the Fifth," Hawkeye the seducer goes so far as to use a rare bottle of Bordeaux to lure one of the camp's nurses into his arms, a form of sexual bribery and questionable foreplay that ultimately fails.[30] Similarly, "Blood and Guts" focuses on a visiting UN war correspondent, the gregarious, Hemingway-like Clayton Kibbee (Gene Evans), who woos the camp's women and writes romanticized, fabricated accounts of American bravery on the battlefield after drinking one too many bottles of Scotch. Initially resentful of Kibbee's encroachment on his territory, Hawkeye is forced to put aside his jealousy once the legendary journalist is wounded and requires medical attention. Kibbee's alcohol-induced irresponsibility not only leads him to embellish dishonest stories of wartime adventure for an oblivious readership back in the States, but also causes him to steal and crash B. J.'s motorcycle while on a drunken binge. Bleeding profusely but too hung over to feel the full extent of the pain, the character falls from grace and becomes a figure of pity rather than envy. Chastened from his humiliating experience, Kibbee ultimately makes amends by writing what the characters believe to be a more honest, *more sober*, account of military life for the daily newspaper *Stars and Stripes*.

As Wittebols points out, prior to that episode's January 18, 1982, broadcast, several American newspapers and magazines (e.g., *Parents* magazine, *US News and World Report*, etc.) had begun running alarming accounts of teenage alcoholism and the increase in traffic fatalities resulting from drunken driving. Into the early 1980s, such reports flamed parental paranoia and fed into legislative and public health attempts to regulate alcohol use among young adults, many of which were couched in the simplistic rhetoric of Nancy Reagan's "Just Say No" anti-drug crusade.[31] Moreover, television writers began exploiting this hot-button topic, as evidenced by "DUI," a 1981 episode of the NBC medical drama *Quincy, M.E.* (1976–1983) in which the title character (Jack Klugman) leads an anti-drunk driving campaign after a lawyer kills a pedestrian while speeding through Los Angeles in a Rolls-Royce.[32] If the "meatball surgeons" in *M*A*S*H* had been loveable lushes during the early-to-mid-1970s, TV increasingly turned "lousy drunks" into figures of public condemnation during the late

156   David Scott Diffrient

1970s and early 1980s, a trend summed up in the words of a police officer in *Quincy, M.E.* who wishes "there were some way we could stop them ... once and for all." Thus, by the time the season 11 episode "Trick or Treatment" was broadcast (on November 1, 1982), the image of a soldier dealing with wounds coming not from combat but from a drunk-driving incident (an untoward collision with a chicken coop, which leads Corporal Hrabosky to run from military police) provided evidence of the television series'—and the nation's—changing attitudes toward alcoholic revelry.[33]

Significantly, the early 1980s witnessed a concerted effort on the part of government officials and military leaders to strengthen existing preventative measures while implementing harsher punitive responses to alcohol and drug use among enlisted men and women. Military historians have argued that this policy change was in part a response to the crash of a jet on the USS Nimitz's flight deck on May 26, 1981, which killed 11 sailors and three marines. Autopsies of the dead showed evidence of marijuana use among some of the sailors and nonprescription antihistamine use by the Navy pilot.[34] In response, the Department of Defense created a 10-point program "to control drug abuse that called for increased drug testing, discharge of repeat offenders, improved rehabilitation programs, and a massive education effort."[35] Existing policies, which were primarily aimed at rehabilitating substance abusers, underwent revisions that indicated greater emphasis on prevention and disciplinary actions. Besides instituting tests to measure the presence of alcohol in individuals seeking entrance into the armed forces, the US military began mandating that on-base driving privileges be revoked if a serviceman or servicewoman was convicted of driving while intoxicated (DWI).[36] The DoD's "zero tolerance" policy, which, in its harshest form, could lead to the discharge of soldiers, was highlighted in December of 1981, when the US Navy launched its own "War on Drugs," the rhetoric of which suggested that military branches were toeing the line drawn by members of the Reagan administration.[37] Not coincidentally, two meetings were convened by the Deputy Assistant Secretary of Defense for Drug Abuse and Alcohol Prevention and held at the White House in 1982— conferences that brought together nationally recognized experts in toxicology for the purpose of further refining and standardizing "minimal levels for both screening and confirmatory testing."[38]

Whereas events such as these would affect the entrenched culture of alcohol within the military, it is difficult to claim that they dramatically impacted televisual representations in programs concerning the United States armed forces.[39] For example, the critically lauded ABC war drama *China Beach* (1988–1991), centered on US medical staff stationed at the 510th Evacuation Hospital in Đà Nẵng, Vietnam, broached the subject of substance abuse on more than one occasion (see chapter 11, this volume). Like their predecessors in *M*A*S*H*, these beleaguered Army doctors and nurses frequently turned to the bottle to deal with daily setbacks and the trauma of incoming wounded. Although an ensemble series, one character—the camp's head nurse Colleen McMurphy (Dana Delany)—is often singled out, both narratively and critically, as someone whose many contradictions ("a woman proud of her composure and careful in her moral convictions, compassionate but capable of a scathingly condemning glance," according to one commentator) hints at the complexities of the wartime experience and the irrational rationale that leads people to drinking (Figure 9.4).[40] Referred to by Michael Saenz as a "feminized, Irish Catholic version" of Hawkeye, McMurphy is a central figure not only because she represents *China Beach*'s unusual focalization (shifting the narration from the war film's usual priorities, organized around displays of masculinity, to women), but also because she personified the "mordant irony" that had come to typify cultural productions concerned either with the dark legacy of Vietnam or with the enduring presence of alcohol in military life.[41] If *China Beach* succeeded in undermining "vainglorious heroism" and portraying war "as a vast and elaborate conceit," as Saenz and other critics claim, then a part of that success can be attributed to its televisual forerunner *M*A*S*H*, which made it possible for Americans to see and perhaps question their own complicity in the creation of a damaging and reductive social imaginary.

Figure 9.4 When one of the newly arrived female entertainers approaches her table, head nurse Colleen McMurphy (Dana Delany) takes a sip of alcohol and says, "I'm just one of the guys." Like the doctors from *M*A*S*H*, McMurphy is often shown nursing a bottle. From the pilot episode of *China Beach*.

Conclusion

According to Charles Taylor, the expression "social imaginary" refers to "the ways people imagine their social existence, how they fit together with others, how things go on between them and their fellows, the expectations that are normally met, and the deeper normative notions and images that underlie these expectations."[42] Common understandings and common practices, shared by many individuals, congeal into "normative" (ideologically entrenched) values and might lead to institutionalized forms of discrimination, exclusion, and othering. As Bill Nichols points out, once a "collection of prejudicial images [are] assigned to different groups within the social dynamics related to power and hierarchy," the social imaginary begins to look more and more like a means of licensing both institutional racism and sexism, among other things.[43] Similarly, thanks to televisual and other types of cultural representations (including, but not limited to, $M^*A^*S^*H$), a kind of alcoholic imaginary has come into existence over the past half-century, one that reflects the contradictory values that society attributes to drinking as both a recreational/relaxing pastime and a potentially addictive behavior to be stamped out. It is telling that TV viewing, another experience associated with both positive and negative effects, should be the means by which so many people's understanding of the alcoholic imaginary has been formed.

Wittebols asserts that, over the course of its 11-year broadcast, $M^*A^*S^*H$ reflected changes in the way that "real-world America" viewed alcohol consumption. Although such transformations "are probably evident in most programming of the 1970s," Gelbart and Reynolds' creation was particularly attuned to the attitudinal shifts occurring at a time when the negative consequences of substance abuse (among the nation's youth as well as within military contexts) were making headlines in US newspapers and magazines. However, as Wittebols also correctly claims, $M^*A^*S^*H$ "presents a nuanced perspective, neither underplaying nor exaggerating the fact that alcohol and drugs in general have problematic aspects."[44] This, I argue, is what distinguishes the series and makes it all the more relevant today, in a culture that has become ever more accustomed to televised images of inebriation (e.g., in contemporary network sitcoms such as *Two and a Half Men* [CBS, 2003–2015] and critically lauded cable dramas like *Rescue Me* [F/X, 2004–2011] and *Mad Men* [AMC, 2007–2015]).

Why do military personnel use alcohol? Often for the same reasons that non-military individuals partake in spirits: to relieve stress, to cope with boredom, to distract from one's loneliness or sense of isolation, to compensate for a lack of other recreational activities, or simply because they enjoy the taste and find its affects appealing.[45] However, the men and women serving in the US armed forces sometimes face challenges that few noncombatants and civilians are asked to endure and thus may turn more often to drink as a means of dealing with the psychic dislocation of war and familial separation. $M^*A^*S^*H$ presents viewers with a type of ritualized, militarily contextualized drinking that is unique to the wartime experience but understandable to anyone who has ever sought a source of relief from pain. Yes, sometimes alcohol is merely used for recreational purposes in the series, for instance, to spice up an otherwise boring game, as in the season two episode "George," when the surgeons play checkers with shot glasses—each jump entailing a throwback of the drink. And yet, although the clownish doctors may down bottles of beer in the Officers' Club and call out for sacramental wine at the sight of an attractive nurse, they are also "responsible professionals dealing with terrible causalities under great stress," an aspect of *M*A*S*H* that lifts it above many other examples of televisual insobriety, even as it contributes to a conflicting set of social values, that is, to an alcoholic imaginary that continues to change with each new cultural representation.[46]

Notes

1. Quoted in Jeremy Kuzmarov, *The Myth of the Addicted Army: Vietnam and the Modern War on Drugs* (Amherst: University of Massachusetts Press, 2009), 27.
2. "End Run," season 5, episode 17, *M*A*S*H: Season 5 Collector's Edition*, aired January 25, 1977 (Beverly Hills, CA: 20th Century Fox Home Entertainment, 2003) DVD.
3. James H. Wittebols, *Watching M*A*S*H, Watching America: A Social History of the 1972–1983 Television Series* (Jefferson, NC: McFarland, 1998), 53.
4. "Fallen Idol," season 6, episode 2, *M*A*S*H: Season 6 Collector's Edition*, aired September 27, 1977 (Beverly Hills, CA: 20th Century Fox Home Entertainment, 2004) DVD. "Bottle Fatigue," season 8, episode 16, *M*A*S*H: Season 8 Collector's Edition*, aired January 7, 1980 (Beverly Hills, CA: 20th Century Fox Home Entertainment, 2006) DVD. "Bottoms Up," season 9, episode 15, *M*A*S*H: Season 9 Collector's Edition*, aired March 2, 1981 (Beverly Hills, CA: 20th Century Fox Home Entertainment, 2008) DVD.
5. "L.I.P. (Local Indigenous Personnel)," season 2, episode 7, *M*A*S*H: Season 2 Collector's Edition*, aired October 27, 1973 (Beverly Hills, CA: 20th Century Fox Home Entertainment, 2002) DVD.
6. John Darrell Sherwood, *Officers in Flight Suits: The Story of American Air Force Fighter Pilots* (New York: New York University Press, 1998).
7. David Pratt, "Television," in *The SAGE Encyclopedia of Alcohol: Social, Cultural, and Historical Perspectives*, ed. Scott Martin (Thousand Oaks, CA: SAGE Publications, 2015), 1242.
8. Ibid.
9. Ibid., 347. See also Meredith H. Lair, *Armed with Abundance: Consumerism and Soldiering in the Vietnam War* (Chapel Hill, NC: University of North Carolina Press, 2011).
10. John Darrell Sherwood, *Officers in Flight Suits: The Story of American Air Force Fighter Pilots in the Korean War* (New York: New York University Press, 1998), 164–65.
11. Melinda L. Pash, *In the Shadow of the Greatest Generation: The Americans Who Fought the Korean War* (New York: New York University Press, 2012), 201.
12. For a discussion of the feature-length film *M*A*S*H*, see Robert T. Self, *Robert Altman's Subliminal Reality* (Minneapolis, MN: University of Minnesota Press, 2002), 22–44.

160 *David Scott Diffrient*

13. Michael B. Kassell, "*M*A*S*H*," in *The Guide to United States Popular Culture*, ed. Ray B. Browne and Pat Browne (Madison, WI: University of Wisconsin Press, 2001), 520.
14. "Rainbow Bridge," season 3, episode 2, *M*A*S*H*: Season 3 Collector's Edition*, aired September 17, 1974 (Beverly Hills, CA: 20th Century Fox Home Entertainment, 2003) DVD.
15. Reference to another unusual mixing of drinks is made in the episode "Deal Me Out" (season 2, episode 13) in which Radar alludes to the combination of Scotch, gin, and vodka contained in the same bottle of alcohol, a valued possession of Lieutenant Colonel Blake.
16. For more information about the series' mixing of tones and genres, see David Scott Diffrient and Hye Seung Chung, "TV Hybridity: Genre Mixing and Narrative Complexity in *M*A*S*H*," *Quarterly Review of Film and Video* 29, no. 4 (2012): 285–302.
17. "Old Soldiers," season 8, episode 18, *M*A*S*H*, aired January 21, 1980.
18. "Too Many Cooks," season 8, episode 1, *M*A*S*H*, aired September 17, 1979.
19. "Aid Station," season 3, episode 19, *M*A*S*H*, aired February 11, 1975; "The Grim Reaper," season 6, episode 11, *M*A*S*H*, aired November 29, 1977; "Stars and Stripes," season 8, episode 14, *M*A*S*H*, aired December 17, 1979; "Heroes," season 10, episode 18, *M*A*S*H*: Season 10 Collector's Edition* (Beverly Hills, CA: 20th Century Fox Home Entertainment, 2006) DVD.
20. "Hot Lips and Empty Arms," season 2, episode 14, *M*A*S*H*, aired December 15, 1973.
21. "Major Ego," season 7, episode 8, *M*A*S*H*: Season 7 Collector's Edition*, aired November 6, 1978 (Beverly Hills, CA: 20th Century Fox Home Entertainment, 2004) DVD.
22. "Bulletin Board," season 3, episode 16, *M*A*S*H*, aired January 14, 1975.
23. This unique way of "irrigating the innards" (to borrow a euphemism for drinking in "Check Up") apparently inspired Twentieth Century-Fox to license a unique novelty item during the original run of *M*A*S*H*: an IV liquor dispenser bearing both the title of the television series and the name of the studio. Among the most popular gift items related to the series was a set of shot glasses bearing the "M*A*S*H" logo. See David Scott Diffrient, *M*A*S*H* (Detroit, MI: Wayne State University Press, 2008), 4.
24. "Mr. and Mrs. Who?," season 8, episode 9, *M*A*S*H*, aired November 12, 1979.
25. "Some 38th Parallels," season 4, episode 19, *M*A*S*H*, aired January 20, 1976.
26. "Period of Adjustment," season 8, episode 6, *M*A*S*H*, aired October 22, 1979; "A Night at Rosie's," season 7, episode 23, *M*A*S*H*, aired February 26, 1979.
27. "End Run," season 5, episode 17, *M*A*S*H*, aired January 25, 1977.
28. "The Colonel's Horse" season 5, episode 11, *M*A*S*H*, aired December 7, 1976; "Last Laugh," season 6, episode 3, *M*A*S*H*, aired October 4, 1977.
29. Wittebols, *Watching M*A*S*H, Watching America*, 52–54, 107–11.
30. "Taking the Fifth," season 9, episode 9, *M*A*S*H*, aired January 19, 1981.
31. Ibid., 109.
32. "DUI," season 7, episode 5, *Quincy, M.E.*, aired December 2, 1981.
33. "Trick or Treatment," season 11, episode 2, *M*A*S*H*, aired November 1, 1982.
34. Jacques Normand and Richard O. Lempert, *Under the Influence?: Drugs and the American Work Force* (Washington, DC: National Academies Press, 1994), 129.

Drinking the War Away 161

35. Robert Bray, Mary Ellen Marsden, John F. Mazzuchi, and Roger W. Hartman, "Prevention in the Military," in Robert T. Ammerman, Peggy J. Ott, and Ralph E. Tarter, eds., *Prevention and Societal Impact of Drug and Alcohol Abuse* (Mahwah, NJ: Lawrence Erlbaum Associates, 1999), 349.
36. Ibid., 363.
37. Ibid., 350.
38. Ibid.
39. Genevieve Ames and Carol Cunradi claim that, although illicit drug use and cigarette smoking in the US military both "decreased significantly over the period from 1980 to 2002, heavy alcohol use did not show the same decline." Heavy drinking (consuming more than four drinks during a single occasion/session) was reported by 27 percent of young adults in the military. Genevieve Ames and Carol Cunradi, "Alcohol Use and Preventing Alcohol-Related Problems Among Young Adults in the Military," *Alcohol Research & Health*, 28, No. 4 (2004/2005): 252.
40. Michael Saenz, "China Beach," in *Encyclopedia of Television,* ed. Horace Newcomb (London: Routledge, 2013), 515.
41. Ibid., 516.
42. Charles Taylor, *Modern Social Imaginaries* (Durham, NC: Duke University Press, 2004), 23.
43. Bill Nichols, *Engaging Cinema: An Introduction to Film Studies* (New York, NY: W. W. Norton & Company, 2010).
44. Wittebols, *Watching M*A*S*H, Watching America,* 111.
45. Ames and Cunradi, "Alcohol Use," 252–57.
46. Daniel O'Brien, *Robert Altman: Hollywood Survivor* (New York: The Continuum Publishing Company, 1995), 36.

10 Small-Screen Insurgency

Entertainment Television, the Vietnamese Revolution, and the Cold War, 1953–1967

Scott Laderman

Forty years after it officially ended, there remains a remarkable dearth of scholarship on fictional television's wartime treatment of the conflict in Vietnam. At best, programs set in the Southeast Asian country show up in the literature sporadically and in passing. At worst, their existence is denied or they have been minimized to the point of irrelevance.[1] Julian Smith, while acknowledging that he had not made "a formal study of the extent to which Vietnam was the subject of television drama," wrote that a "casual poll of regular viewers" turned up only two instances in which the war appeared on fictional television: *Some May Live* (CBS, 1967) and *The Final War of Olly Winter* (CBS, 1967).[2] Rick Worland, whose insightful study of political fantasy in Cold War television addressed the war's brief appearance in *The Twilight Zone* (CBS, 1959–1964) and *The Outer Limits* (ABC, 1963–1965), wrote that "prime-time network television, which had largely succeeded in becoming America's chief medium of popular entertainment," followed Hollywood's lead in "similarly ignor[ing] Vietnam."[3] Daniel Hallin, meanwhile, maintained in the *Encyclopedia of Television* that, as the Vietnamese revolution unfolded, "it was virtually never touched in television fiction—except, of course, in disguised form on *M*A*S*H*."[4]

The reason for the networks' silence was presumably political. The war in Vietnam was controversial, and the American television industry, like its big-screen counterpart, more often chose to avoid controversy rather than explore it.[5] But even this statement minimizes the avoidance. The industry also shunned programs that could be *perceived* as echoing the imbroglio in Southeast Asia. Smith, for instance, reported the case of someone whose 1967 script for *The Virginian* (NBC, 1962–1971) was rejected by NBC. "No," the network told the writer about his episode featuring a Royal Canadian Mounted Policeman who "deserted to help the Indians fight the rape of their land. ... There is a desertion problem in Vietnam."[6] In the context of the twentieth-century's most controversial war, even this late-nineteenth-century allusion to imperial ambivalence might appear tendentious.

Although there were no fictional series devoted to the war before 1975—the oft-cited *M*A*S*H* (CBS, 1972–1983) was officially set in Korea and, in *Star Trek* (NBC, 1966–1969), the Vietnam War provided merely a subtext—the conflict did appear in several episodes of anthology series in the 1950s and 1960s.[7] It was also at the center of both a teleplay and a TV movie in 1967.[8] Some of these appearances, such as in a 1963 episode of *The Twilight Zone* and a two-part episode of *The Outer Limits* a year later, were admittedly marginal. This may explain the nearly wholesale absence of critical scholarship about such programs. Just as significant may be the difficulty in viewing the programs in the twenty-first century; of those addressed in greatest depth in this chapter, only one was released on VHS or DVD, and most of the major television archives lack copies.[9] But the programs are not simply historical curiosities. True, their influence was likely minimal— they probably did more to reinforce viewers' ideological convictions than to challenge them—and judging their contemporaneous reception is difficult. But the programs still matter. If nothing else, they are primary documents that illustrate how America's growing involvement in Vietnam was being imagined by the country's most popular cultural medium.

It was not always a given that television programs made in the anti-Communist 1950s and 1960s would firmly situate the Vietnamese insurgency within a Cold War context. When Vietnam first appeared on the small screen in 1953 in *Biff Baker, USA* (CBS, 1952–1953; syndication, 1954), the United States was committed to France's nearly 10-year effort to neutralize the Viet Minh. American aid had officially started flowing in 1950. But in the five years prior to that, Washington had struggled with the question of supporting the French reconquest of its longtime Indochinese territory.[10] The reason for this is rooted in a history with which most Americans are unfamiliar.

During the Second World War, the US Office of Strategic Services joined with the Viet Minh in opposing Japan, and there was a great deal of sympathy within the American intelligence agency for the Vietnamese desire for independence. US officials who worked in Vietnam respected the nationalist sentiments of Ho Chi Minh, and Ho admired the anti-colonial example of the United States.[11] Indeed, the Viet Minh revolutionary opened his September 1945 declaration of Vietnamese independence by citing America's analogous document from 1776. Despite this mutual admiration, however, the deepening of Cold War sentiment after World War II, together with American concerns about the US alliance with a politically divided France and the maintenance of resources and markets for occupied Japan, led Washington to increasingly turn against its Vietnamese ally. What had been a Communist-led coalition struggling for Vietnamese independence was transformed in American discourse into an instrument of "Red imperialism" threatening the Free World. Entertainment television's first foray into Indochina reflected this about-face.

Biff Baker, USA starred a relatively young, pre-*Gilligan's Island* Alan Hale, Jr. as its eponymous hero; Randy Stuart played Louise, his affable but jealous wife. Baker is an importer and sometime spy who, with Louise, sets out across the planet in search of goods. Given the show's setting in the early 1950s, he unfailingly brushes up against the Cold War, stumbling upon unexpected adventures from Paris and London to Istanbul, Cairo, and

164 *Scott Laderman*

Algiers. "The series was so effective," notes Fred MacDonald, "that business organizations criticized it for leaving the impression that all American businessmen working abroad were spies."[12] Baker's confrontations with America's Cold War enemies included the revolutionaries in Vietnam. Vietnam was at that time host to an anti-colonial war being fought by the Viet Minh. If most historians today recognize the conflict as a chapter in the long saga of the Vietnamese people's struggle to achieve or secure their independence, the CBS program's "Saigon Incident" episode framed the matter quite differently.

When the Bakers arrive in Saigon from Paris with the goal of purchasing rubber, Biff is confronted in a local bar by a "Madame Butterfly" who goes by the Chinese (as opposed to Vietnamese) name Lee Ming Toy (Marya Marco).[13] Told by this self-described "leader of the Viet Minh" that he must not purchase any rubber—that it is "national property" that "belong[s] to the Viet Minh," not to the white planters whose estates he intends to visit—Baker is incredulous. "Look, beautiful," he responds. "One thing we don't have in common is a favorite color. I'm not very partial to pink." The situation in Vietnam is thus coded as one of illegitimate Communist agitation, not genuine nationalist rebellion. The program assumes the absolute normalcy and benevolence of colonial exploitation, casting the white plantation owners tapping the local rubber trees as upstanding, moral figures resisting slow victimization by a shadowy band of Viet Minh "devils." These are guerrillas, viewers learn, who have not only killed white families but are engaged in "a campaign to frighten the [Vietnamese] workers," a campaign that has substantially slowed rubber production. Their tactics are wide-ranging and brutal: "raids on villages, burnings, wholesale slaughter, a lone planter murdered—stuff like that," Biff's planter friend explains.

There was thus little doubt in the program that Baker and the owners had every right to kill the insurgents. The Viet Minh did not represent a popular expression of Vietnamese hostility to French colonialism; it was instead a gang of ruthless "fanatics" plotting to kill peaceable whites and the "good Vietnamese" who served them. With the French army having failed to fully "clean ... out" the guerrillas, it becomes necessary for Baker and the planters to do so. In its representation of the ensuing violence, the program draws on one of the most powerful American archetypes of the frontier. When the plantation to which a number of planter families have retreated is attacked by the Viet Minh, the insurgents borrow a page from Hollywood's cowboys-and-Indians playbook, whooping it up like the loin-clothed savages of Western cinema. The planter families, in this scenario, represent the settlers. And, happily, the settlers—and cowboys—win. The Viet Minh/Indians are killed; Lee Ming Toy, who entered the compound disguised as a Muslim housekeeper (the Viet Minh are "geniuses at disguise," Louise was told) is detained, and, in the episode's final scene, Baker donates his share of the bounty for her capture to the family of Paul, a devoted Vietnamese "houseboy" who "hates the Viet Minh guerrillas like poison" and is killed by them while trying to alert the planters to the Communist threat. The message could not have been clearer. In the simplistic formulation of much Cold War-era television, Baker and the planters are the good guys, and the Viet Minh are the bad guys.[14]

Such representations mattered when the episode aired in 1953. France was, at that time, still more than a year from defeat in its war with the Viet Minh, a war that, by its end in 1954, would see the United States paying for roughly 80 percent of France's war costs. This was quite a departure from 1945. Less than a decade before *Biff Baker, USA* aired, the enlisted crewmen of at least eight US troopships assigned to transport French personnel to Indochina at the end of World War II protested the American facilitation of the putative French reconquest. Some wrote to the War Shipping Administration in Washington, others cabled President Harry Truman and Senator Robert Wagner, and still others drafted a petition in Saigon. The American crewmen were appalled, they wrote, by Washington's support for "the imperialist policies of foreign governments" attempting "to subjugate the native population."[15] The deepening of the Cold War would soon stifle such opposition, however. By the early 1950s, the news media was full of sympathetic portraits of the French campaign, and Hollywood fare such as *A Yank in Indo-China* (1952) only reinforced the prevalent anti-Communist framework. *Biff Baker, USA* did nothing to challenge it. Its "Saigon Incident" provided discursive support for Washington's embrace of French imperialism, in the process laying the groundwork for America's more direct military involvement in the years that followed.

Television viewers got their first fictional glimpse of how this involvement might look when the men of *Navy Log* (CBS, 1955–1956; ABC, 1956–1958), which offered fictional vignettes about American sailors navigating the real world of that era, arrived in Vietnam two years later. Sourcing "the dramas you see each week" to "official US Navy files," a narrator attested to the stories' authenticity. The producers, meanwhile, did nothing to disguise the series' military fealty, proudly notifying viewers that the program was "produced with the full cooperation of the Department of Defense and the Department of the Navy." *Navy Log* was, in almost every respect, fawning military propaganda. Its usefulness to US foreign policy was unmistakable.

This was certainly true of American priorities in Southeast Asia. In late 1955, in an episode entitled "The Bishop of the Bayfield," *Navy Log* presented its audience with the hopeful chaos of a recently divided Vietnam.[16] Essentially a narrative vehicle for the assertion of America's salvific mission, the story was loosely based on a March 1955 article by William J. Lederer in *Reader's Digest* called "They'll Remember the Bayfield." Lederer, who would go on to co-author *The Ugly American*, the bestselling novel of 1958 that is widely considered one of the major works of Cold War literature, was at the time a US Navy commander who accompanied some 2,000 Vietnamese from the northern port of Haiphong to Saigon aboard the USS Bayfield. The Vietnamese in his article arrive in Haiphong from the Vietnamese interior

166 *Scott Laderman*

as filthy, desperate, and emaciated Catholics wanting nothing more than "the right to worship in the religion of their choice"—a right that was allegedly denied them by "the Reds [who] took over North Vietnam last year"—but they leave the ship clean, well-fed, and grateful beneficiaries of American munificence. "The trip on the American ship was a sweet dream," a Vietnamese elder tells Lederer. "Never before were we treated with such kindness and dignity. ... We felt big."[17]

If Lederer's essay broadly discussed the experiences of numerous military personnel, the *Navy Log* episode opted to conjoin several of them within a single composite character. Deacon Jones (Peter Whitney), the fictional "bishop" whose honorific can be traced to the article's David Bollingham, is a hard-partying sailor who finds redemption through his service transporting Vietnamese "refugees" to Saigon. As the program begins, Jones is a disreputable slob. He drinks, gambles, and courts other men's girlfriends. He rejects rules, religion, and basic propriety, and his 15 years in the Navy have apparently been one long spell of aimless contentment. But Vietnam changes him. Jones's exposure to the hardships endured by those desperate souls fleeing Communism finally provides him with purpose.

Most Americans in 1955 would have been only vaguely familiar with the backdrop's geopolitical complexity.[18] When the Viet Minh defeated the French in 1954, the terms of the war's settlement were negotiated in a multilateral conference in Geneva. The accords that emerged out of that meeting temporarily divided Vietnam at the 17th parallel into two regroupment zones, with the Democratic Republic of Vietnam, the government established by the Viet Minh leadership in 1945, centered in the northern zone and the French-backed State of Vietnam, ruled by Emperor Bao Dai, in the southern. The zones were to be reunified two years later following nationwide elections. (It was the United States' refusal to honor that commitment to reunification that spawned what most Americans today call the Vietnam War.) For 300 days in the interim, Vietnamese would be free to travel between the two zones. Hundreds of thousands of Catholics in the north elected to "regroup" to the south, where in 1955 the US-backed Catholic despot Ngo Dinh Diem established an anti-Communist state called the Republic of Vietnam (RVN). Although there is little evidence that its efforts spawned the migration, Washington did everything it could to encourage the journey to the south.[19] Covert US operatives sabotaged buses in Hanoi, disseminated rumors of marauding Chinese Communists raping Vietnamese women, recruited astrologers to predict disasters, and hinted at the likelihood of a US atomic attack.[20]

These were the "refugees" that Jones and his compatriots were aiding. To lend the episode an air of authenticity, *Navy Log* drew on not only Lederer's account but also on actual footage of the operation. As archival scenes of haggard and desperate Vietnamese appear on screen, a narrator sets the appropriate context: "Time: Sunday. Place: the road from Hanoi to Haiphong. Objective: freedom." A banner in the footage of a Navy landing craft reinforces the point: "This is your passage to freedom," it reads. And the suggestion that viewers are witnessing a manifestation of the struggle between "freedom" and its antithesis is evident throughout the program. "The Vietnamese government has asked us to help evacuate some 50,000 refugees who are fleeing the Viet Minh Reds in the north," the ship's captain reveals to a subordinate. Some of the Vietnamese "have come over a thousand miles just to get away from them Reds," Jones says later. And when the "refugees" disembark in Saigon, they are greeted by "freedom messages in three languages, the first happy note in a long time." "Good luck on your passage to freedom," a sign tells them in English, French, and Vietnamese.

Viewers never actually see any Communists. They appear only indirectly, as when the Vietnamese grandfather (a middle-aged Richard Loo) of a young boy at the center of the story discloses to Jones in broken English that the "Communists tell everyone American sailors very bad, do cruel things," such as torture children, "cut off head, then throw into water." The episode demonstrates the absurdity of such propaganda, revealing American sailors—and by implication the United States—to be selfless humanitarians working to save the Vietnamese people. To do this, the show spins its tale around a conceit disclosed in Lederer's article: the Vietnamese children aboard the Bayfield believe the American sailors to be priests. Jones, in the article's small-screen translation, becomes the "bishop." At first dismissive of the presumed role, the wayward seaman eventually accepts it, leading a mass for the "refugees" while ensuring that only the most moral behavior is practiced by the crew; the "bishop" does not want to "set them kids a bad example." Jones, that is, gets religion. Vietnam thus offered what the program calls the "ship carrying a halo" an opportunity to illustrate American benevolence. Rather than undermine revolutionary claims to independence—which was in fact its intention—Washington wished to guarantee the Vietnamese people their "freedom." The kindness and generosity of the US Navy, at least as depicted in *Navy Log*, serves as a clear demonstration of this Cold War axiom.

For several years after Operation Passage to Freedom concluded, the United States for the most part limited its involvement in Vietnam to buttressing the embattled Diem regime. This happened at both the diplomatic and military levels, with a Military Assistance Advisory Group operating on the ground to develop and train the armed forces of the Republic of Vietnam. Then, in December 1960, a number of southern revolutionaries, backed by Hanoi, announced the formation of the National Liberation Front. With the growth of the NLF insurgency, it proved time, once more, to bring a fictional Vietnam to the American small screen. In January 1962, as the Kennedy administration was beginning to pour what would soon become thousands of military personnel into the country, an episode of Fred Astaire's *Alcoa Premiere* (ABC, 1961–1963) did just that. The series, which was narrated by the popular singer and actor, was hardly marginal; it was nominated for 13 Emmy Awards and drew considerable creative talent. Charlton Heston,

168   *Scott Laderman*

Robert Redford, Maureen O'Sullivan, Lee Marvin, James Stewart, Cliff Robertson, and John Wayne were among the actors who appeared in its episodes, and its directors, producers, and writers included John Ford, Alfred Hitchcock, and Ray Bradbury.[21] Nielsen estimated that the program averaged some 14 million viewers at the height of its second season.[22]

"The Hour of the Bath" was the name given to the 1962 episode set in Vietnam. Like the 1955 episode of *Navy Log*, "The Hour of the Bath" is a full-throated demonstration of American beneficence—although, in this instance, through a civilian volunteer in the nation-building project that sought to transform the Vietnamese countryside.[23] The plot centers on the capture by the "Viet Cong" of American agricultural advisor Henry Detweiler (Robert Fuller), a rural Pennsylvanian who has been living with and assisting the friendly residents of the village of Ban Hoa. Detweiler's presence, Fred Astaire reveals in his narration, was made possible "through the combined support of American foundations, private individuals, and industry long before the Peace Corps program became a reality." The village, Astaire says, is one in which "no one is rich" but "no one is hungry either, though for hundreds of years," he adds, "the people have not greatly changed their primitive methods of farming the rich delta land." Detweiler is there to fix that.

Yet even with his deep knowledge and considerable presence—the villagers affectionately refer to him as the "Giant American," an implicit suggestion of the paternalistic manner in which the United States viewed its Southeast Asian charges—Detweiler's methods are never assertive. He is not one to compel the Vietnamese to change their ways; he is there to persuade them. Detweiler simply explains the benefits his "Uncle Fritz" discovered when adopting some agricultural technique, and the Vietnamese farmers independently decide whether they wish to follow his lead. Detweiler's credibility rests on his humility and example. He immerses himself in the local culture. He has "learned the customs of the villagers, has adopted their manner of speech and even, to an extent, their Oriental philosophy," Astaire says. When the "hour of the bath" arrives—the regularly scheduled time every day when the people of Ban Hoa meet and bathe in the river—Detweiler respectfully stays back until invited by his hosts to join them. For two years, he has lived with the Vietnamese, "eating rice and sleeping on the ground, and working eighty-four hours a week for seventy-five dollars a month." Detweiler, in other words, is about as dissimilar as one could be from an "imperialist warmongering American," which a "Viet Cong" insurgent later calls him. His Americanness is hardly ugly.

If Detweiler comes off as a model of transnational amity, those insurgents prove to be the "imperialist warmongers" of their own denunciation. Astaire provides the necessary context:

> It's a lovely, peaceful life, the life of Ban Hoa. Yet these peaceful, hardworking, dignified people live in the shadow of dreadful terror lurking

Small-Screen Insurgency 169

in the jungle everywhere around them—a terror known as the Viet Cong. Trained in Red China to be the deadliest guerrilla fighters in the world and dedicated to the conversion of South Vietnam to Asian communism, they tie down ten times their number of army troops. They live off the rich land and kill without mercy all who dare oppose them. By day the jungle conceals them, and by night they strike.

Like beasts of the forest, the threat presented by what the program calls the "Viet Cong"—a propaganda contrivance intended to suggest the foreignness of the National Liberation Front—is omnipresent, at times manifesting itself in bizarre ways. When rumors spread about American-supplied fish causing impotence among Vietnamese men so that the Americans, pursuing a genocidal vision, may "control our population and ... deprive us of our children," Detweiler debunks such Communist-inspired nonsense. More immediately perilous, however, is the insurgents' physical threat.

An NLF patrol that materializes during the "hour of the bath" immediately demonstrates the Communists' brutality. One of the insurgents—played by a young George Takei—strikes a beautiful Vietnamese woman (Barbara Luna) with the butt of his rifle. Be Ky, the now-injured woman with whom Detweiler is smitten, soon works to spare his life. The "American pig" is "your enemy," the Communists announce to the villagers, "and he will come forth now and die." Knowing that the patrol includes a couple of injured men in need of serious medical attention, Be Ky pleads with the Communists to allow Detweiler, whom she desperately but dishonestly claims is a doctor, to try to save them. The fate of these wounded revolutionaries is a concern for the entire village, however, for the Communists announce that if either of their comrades dies, the patrol will return and "exact ten lives for one." Perhaps even more menacingly, the leader of the patrol (Viraj Amonsin) orders the villagers to tell the ARVN troops of "the imperialist Ngo Dinh Diem" that they "have not seen the Viet Cong here. If you do not, our comrades will inform us and then you must all die."

The stakes for Detweiler and the villagers could hardly be higher. "You're in an alien land," Astaire's narration interjects, calling on viewers to imagine Detweiler's predicament. "You're not allowed to stir up trouble, Henry, not even fight in your own defense. These Asian friends of yours are still so different from you. Because of their pride, you teach by indirection and a hundred little subterfuges. And because of their acceptance of the inevitability of death, they won't help you now, Henry. They will let you die." The question the rest of the program poses is whether the people of Ban Hoa will indeed "let" the American die. The suspense of course comes in not knowing. With scene after scene suggesting the villagers' utter lack of concern for Detweiler's fate, a twist at the end of the show—the villagers and the ARVN forces had set a trap for the NLF patrol but, for complicated reasons, could not disclose it to the American—reveals the deep affection they in fact feel for him.

170 *Scott Laderman*

"The Hour of the Bath" appeared at a propitious moment. The US intervention was deepening as the Diem regime was tottering. But in the fantasy spun by television, all was well. The episode denationalized the NLF insurgency, rooting it in Chinese expansionism rather than Vietnamese frustration. To the Chinese commander, Colonel Lee (Khigh Dhiegh), the insurgents are mere instruments; it matters not whether they live or die, so long as the insurgency succeeds. "You Americans are sentimental, idealistic," he spews. "We Orientals are practical, fatalistic." But, viewers learn, "Red China," unlike the United States, fails to understand the Vietnamese people. They actually love the Giant American. "In common with all the world," Colonel Lee tells Detweiler, "these people will take your money and despise you for offering it. But they will risk nothing to defend you or your ways. They fear us and respect us. No one fears or respects your country." It quickly becomes evident that Colonel Lee is deeply delusional. The villagers he thought his pawns, and whom he alone understood, actually despise him. "We who fear you have dared to set [a trap] for you," one tells the Chinese officer. "Yes, we fear you. But you have also boasted that we respect you. Do not confuse respect with hatred." Another says to him, "Yes, you boast to our American friend that you are as Oriental as we are. Yet you let it be known that you despise us. You taunt him with his difference. Yet you are far more alien to us than he."

If Colonel Lee is an exemplar of imperial hubris, Detweiler is its antithesis. "Knock it off," he shouts at the colonel. "You're right; it's not for me to do, because I'm a guest in this country. And it's not for me to oppose my hosts. And I won't. ... So get this straight, buster. Friends don't always agree on everything, but these are my friends. Understand?" Viewers soon learn that Detweiler's affection for the Vietnamese is mutual. The point is driven home to viewers in an expansive statement by Trong (Yuki Shimoda), a villager who, with his son, has been a recipient of the American's many kindnesses. "You are forever screaming that the Americans are decadent and finished, and it is your system that will replace theirs," he tells the Chinese commander:

> Perhaps it is. Heaven help us all. But we in Ban Hoa can do little to alter the course of events. We are simple, timid people. Content [to be] on our land and raise our families. We do not think overmuch of politics and systems. We in Ban Hoa have seen only one American. He does not seem rich to us, nor fat, nor lazy. And he's no coward, as even you have seen. He does not offer us money, though he eats as we do, sleeps as we do, and works twice as hard as any of us. And with kindness and wisdom he has taught us much and helped us greatly and asked for nothing in return. He does not even preach of his system nor complain of yours. It is therefore clear to us that the Giant American loves us all. Though it must be conceded that his affections are not equally distributed among us. And perhaps it is this one [Be Ky] for whom he shows a certain preference who will keep him forever among us. And all Ban Hoa would rejoice if this were so.

Viewers do not learn whether Detweiler stayed forever. But they do see that Be Ky proves irresistible. When she and Detweiler kiss, the villagers are ecstatic. The marriage of Vietnam and the United States has been consummated. The Giant American is one of them.

Not long after *Alcoa Premiere* celebrated the American commitment to Southeast Asia, the war made brief appearances in two popular science fiction series. The first was a September 1963 episode ("In Praise of Pip") of *The Twilight Zone* that opens in Vietnam with a gravely wounded private lying unconscious on a stretcher. The story quickly returns to the United States, where the remainder of the drama unfolds. To most Americans in 1963, the idea of what we know today as the Vietnam War would have been inconceivable. "Pip is dying," the soldier's father (Jack Klugman) says somberly when he receives the news of his son's injuries back home. "My kid is dying. In a place called South Vietnam. There isn't even supposed to be a war going on there. But my son is dying." To save him, the father sacrifices his own life, offering to die so that Pip might live (such trade-offs are possible in *The Twilight Zone*). The war then reappeared a year later in a two-part episode ("The Inheritors") of *The Outer Limits* featuring a young Robert Duvall. Like *The Twilight Zone*, it opens on "the Far Eastern front," which was quite clearly Vietnam, and like *The Twilight Zone*, the war quickly disappears. Viewers do glimpse American personnel in combat, and they learn from an ARVN officer that "these northerners" are "very sneaky," but the episode focuses far more on the intricacies of an extraterrestrial plot than the politics of the Vietnamese insurgency. In both programs, the war is a distant but notable conflict—worth acknowledging, but not really worth exploring.[24]

Meanwhile, other series began to feature Vietnam veterans, such as Lincoln Case, the character played by Glenn Corbett who first showed up in the drama *Route 66* (CBS, 1960–1964) in 1963. Yet it would be several years before the war itself appeared again in fictional programming. In 1967, it did so twice. *Some May Live* was a lackluster British telefilm shot in London and Saigon that aired without great fanfare across the United States. It was the first and most noteworthy of several made-for-TV movies at least partially set in the Southeast Asian country to air before 1975. *The Final War of Olly Winter*, conversely, was a highly regarded teleplay that inaugurated and drew favorable attention to the new series *CBS Playhouse* (CBS, 1967–1970). Airing almost precisely a year before the Tet Offensive, its storyline better reflected the growing disillusionment with the American campaign than did the far more conventional *Some May Live*.

The Final War of Olly Winter was, one contemporaneous critic wrote, an "unqualified success."[25] Starring black actor Ivan Dixon (who also appeared in the two-part episode of *The Outer Limits* addressed above) and with a script written by black playwright Ronald Ribman, the production, according to the *New York Amsterdam News*, was "the first time a Negro author has made it so big on television."[26] Praise for the program poured in

172 *Scott Laderman*

from all over the country. The *Christian Science Monitor* found the drama "gripping" and "poignant."[27] To the *New York Times*, it was "brilliant," the "most moving original television play of the season."[28] The *Washington Post* said it "had bite, humor, and the kind of vivid introspection that can move one to tears."[29] The appearance of this "excellent" drama, concluded the *Chicago Tribune*, contributed mightily to one of TV's "very best Sundays."[30] *The Final War* garnered five Emmy nominations, including for Outstanding Dramatic Program, and it was the only production from the 1960s to be included in William Kaufman's collection *Great Television Plays*.[31] It was also chosen for the Popular Library's *One Act Plays for Our Times*.[32]

The Final War is the moving story of an African American veteran (Dixon) of both World War II and the Korean War who, in 1963, finds himself trudging through the jungles of Southeast Asia.[33] He is in Vietnam as a military "advisor"—official American combat troops would not be introduced until 1965—which means he is accompanying Vietnamese, not American, personnel. The Vietnam War will be his last war, Winter insists, as he plans to leave the Army, return to New York, and go into the flower business. But he never makes it home. The program ends with his tragic demise.

The four-act teleplay opens with a Vietnamese refusal to heed American advice. Winter is accompanying an ARVN patrol that ignores his counsel on how to most safely cross a rice paddy. One might think the Vietnamese better understood local conditions—from the Philippines to the Mekong Delta, after all, the United States had hardly distinguished itself as an authority on counterinsurgency—but this refusal to defer to the American's expertise proves fatal. The NLF ambushes the patrol, and Winter, who chose to separate from the others, is the only survivor. In the three acts that follow, Winter attempts to make his way back to an American base. Along the way he is joined by a young Vietnamese woman (Tina Chen) whose family was massacred and village destroyed by the insurgents, a mangy dog, a baby whose parents were also killed by the NLF, and a young male guerrilla (Patrick Adiarte) whom Winter, given a deep humanitarianism attributed to his Christian worldview, takes prisoner rather than executes. By late in the production, Winter and the young woman have begun to fall for one another, and the captive insurgent has come to respect the American as a man of honor. When several NLF guerrillas liberate their comrade, they quickly attempt to disabuse him of this belief. "There is no question of honor with the Americans," a revolutionary officer (Soon Taik Oh) says. "They are fascist imperialists." But the prisoner demurs. Having earlier chastised the young woman accompanying Winter for "helping the imperialists enslave your people" in a "white man's war," he now says to his compatriot that "[t]his one was not. This one was a black man." But the NLF officer will hear none of it. Winter is merely "a trained dupe of the imperialists," he retorts.

The Final War is notable for its cynicism about the US military campaign. This should perhaps not be surprising. Although set in 1963, the teleplay was written years later. By that time popular misgivings had deepened, the anti-war movement had grown, and stirrings of dissent had begun to appear within the armed forces. To be sure, the production does not agree with the insurgents' clunky and rather doctrinaire characterization of the US intervention as imperialist aggression. Winter in fact disavows any imperial intent. "[N]obody wants this country," he insists. "The United States doesn't want it. What the hell would we want it for? Rice? Who the hell wants your rice? What the hell we got to be imperialistic about? The Chinese keep filling you with a lot of hogwash and you keep swilling it down." But neither does the teleplay celebrate the American campaign. "You think I wanna be here? You think I don't get tired of these stinking endless wars?" Winter asks his prisoner. His frustration is obvious. As for what accounts for his country's presence in Vietnam, he is alternately damning and vague. "Which brings us to the question why I'm here," he tells the captive. "There should be a reason for me being here. [He pauses.] I'm here to take helicopter rides. To see stupid lieutenants who don't know their tails from their elbows get killed. I'm here because I ain't in Yonkers. But there are other less obvious reasons, less obvious. Somebody's got this thing all figured out. Somewhere somebody's got charts and papers which makes all this killing worthwhile. Well, leave it go. This is my final war, man."

As viewers discover, Winter's disillusionment is not confined to Vietnam. He expresses deep misgivings about US foreign relations more broadly. Sparing the life of the belligerent NLF insurgent, Winter practices forgiveness ("[a] little Christian love")—the NLF, viewers learn, does not—and offers the prisoner food, as "provided for in the Geneva Convention." But he does so while delivering a stinging (if misguided) critique of American priorities. "What you guys wanna do is lose the war," he says to the young insurgent in his charge. "Then you'll be eligible for American aid."

In the end, *The Final War* appears ambivalent about US foreign policy. The United States is waging war because of "charts and papers," Winter says. But those it is battling are clearly a moral threat. The young insurgent had participated in the massacre of civilians and had threatened others who aided Winter. At the same time, there are hints that the guerrilla came to see the error of his ways. He apologized to Winter, for example, for having earlier plotted to attack him when he was asleep; his time spent in Winter's custody proved to him that his earlier impression of Americans had been mistaken. But the prisoner is just one cog in a larger machine. Other NLF guerrillas demonstrate a clear and cold brutality. As the teleplay approaches its end, they execute "without rancor" a village elder who assisted Winter, and they kill both Winter and the young woman he has protected. In essence, the invader becomes the victim while those resisting the invasion are either mistaken, misled, or inhumane.

CBS paid a price for placing this depiction of the Vietnam War on television. The network proved unable to secure a sponsor for *The Final War*, forcing it to sell one-minute spot commercials at a reported loss of $300,000. "Madison Avenue's supersalesmen apparently did not want to involve

174   *Scott Laderman*

themselves or their clients in anything so downbeat as a war story," wrote Hal Humphrey in the *Los Angeles Times*. "It doesn't sell automobiles."[34] Of course, this wasn't just any war story. It was a war story about probably the most controversial war of the war-laden twentieth century, and it took a dim view of American involvement. *Some May Live*, which quietly appeared in September 1967, suffered no such setback. When it aired, hardly anyone seemed to be paying attention. "*Some May Live* was obscure at the time of its release," noted Michael Lee Lanning in 1994, "and is even more so today."[35]

Some May Live is the story of a husband-and-wife spy team—she a civilian employee for the US military, he a foreign correspondent—who aid the Vietnamese revolutionaries before the wife begins covertly assisting the American effort to neutralize the global Communist conspiracy. Although it was a British production, it enjoyed its "world premiere" as a late-night feature film on American television, where, so far as I can tell, it did not generate a single review in a major newspaper.[36] Informal reviews that appeared years later were at times quite generous, with two contributors to IMDB calling the program "outstanding" and "typically great 1960's filmmaking."[37] A 2013 blog analysis was far more critical.[38] Perhaps the most notable legacy of *Some May Live* was its shooting location. To the best of my knowledge, it is the only fictional television program during the war to actually be shot (at least in considerable part) in Vietnam. Indeed, among its Hollywood feature-film counterparts, only two productions can make a similar claim: *The Quiet American* (1958) and *A Yank in Viet-Nam* (1964). Although the vibrant Saigon cityscapes certainly lend *Some May Live* an air of authenticity, its plot is so stale and moribund that CBS, not surprisingly, relegated it to the after hours.

For a program made during a period of growing anti-war sentiment, it is surprising how supine *Some May Live* appears. At its core is a basic anti-Communist story—the Americans are the good guys, the insurgents are the bad guys, and the brutal and opportunistic RVN authorities fall somewhere in between. The only dissent in its the-threat-is-global framework comes from a patronizing, abusive, middle-aged British journalist (Peter Cushing), devoted to world revolution, who cares so little for those around him that he does not shield his young son from the war's devastation, has his wife (Martha Hyer) try to sleep with an American captain (John Ronane) to gather information, and abandons his family to defect to "Red China." The war is "a savage conflict," as a narrator at the beginning says, but the film makes clear just who the savages are. By postponing a military offensive for six months, we are told, the United States wants to "save thousands of lives, ours and theirs," so that during the interim "a little sanity" might perhaps return to the situation in Southeast Asia. Conversely, an NLF bomb maker, providing his best automaton impersonation, regrets only that his weapon, hidden under dozens of flowers, will obliterate the delicate blooms. "Make them sleep and walk in fear, never knowing which man or woman carries death in a briefcase or basket," he robotically tells the flower seller who will

Small-Screen Insurgency   175

plant the bomb in a Saigon bar. He cares not at all that his explosive might claim civilian lives. His sole regret? "It is a shame such beautiful flowers must also be destroyed."

Some May Live was the last television fictionalization set entirely in Vietnam. With the war at its heart, its politics were quite explicit. The US intervention was a "magnificent ... effort" undertaken on behalf of the "South Vietnamese," a police inspector (David Spenser) claims. Those who oppose the American campaign, choosing instead to sympathize with the Vietnamese insurgency, are, according to a US military official (Joseph Cotten), "starry-eyed idealist[s] nursing a monster." These useful idiots "don't want a brave new world," the official shouts. "[They] want a mass new world that's scared to hell."

After the 1968 Tet Offensive, confronting the war's increasingly contentious politics on network television would prove difficult. It was better just to leave such controversy alone—and so the networks did. Apart from brief glimpses of the conflict in a handful of made-for-TV movies—among them, Aaron Spelling and Danny Thomas's *The Ballad of Andy Crocker* (ABC, 1969), the pseudonymously directed *The Challenge* (ABC, 1970), and Walter Grauman's *The Forgotten Man* (ABC, 1971)—the war did not again appear on fictional television before the conflict officially ended in 1975.[39] Veterans showed up occasionally in low-budget TV films in the years that followed. But for an extended treatment, small-screen viewers would have to wait for the CBS series *Tour of Duty* in 1987. And by then, the war—or, more accurately, the war's memory—had morphed into something else entirely.

Notes

1. For scholarship briefly addressing some of the fictional television programs, see Darrell Y. Hamamoto, *Monitored Peril: Asian Americans and the Politics of TV Representation* (Minneapolis: University of Minnesota Press, 1994), 107–09; Michael Lee Lanning, *Vietnam at the Movies* (New York: Fawcett Columbine, 1994), 315–16; J. Fred MacDonald, "The Cold War as Entertainment in 'Fifties Television," *Journal of Popular Film* 7, no. 1 (1978): 8, 14–15; J. Fred MacDonald, *Television and the Red Menace: The Video Road to Vietnam* (New York: Praeger, 1985), 108, 119; Julian Smith, *Looking Away: Hollywood and Vietnam* (New York: Charles Scribner's Sons, 1975), 22; and Rick Worland, "Sign-Posts Up Ahead: *The Twilight Zone*, *The Outer Limits*, and TV Political Fantasy 1959–1965," *Science-Fiction Studies* 23, no. 1 (March 1996): 117–18.
2. Smith, *Looking Away*, 22.
3. Rick Worland, "The Other Living-Room War: Prime Time Combat Series, 1962–1975," *Journal of Film and Video* 50, no. 3 (Fall 1998): 3.
4. Daniel Hallin, "Vietnam on Television," in *Encyclopedia of Television*, ed. Horace Newcomb, 2nd ed., vol. 4 (New York: Fitzroy Dearborn, 2004), 2447.
5. On Hollywood's contemporaneous treatment of the Vietnam War, see Scott Laderman, "Hollywood's Vietnam, 1929–1964: Scripting Intervention, Spotlighting Injustice," *Pacific Historical Review* 78, no. 4 (November 2009): 578–607.
6. Smith, *Looking Away*, 22.

176   Scott Laderman

7. On *Star Trek* and the Vietnam War, see H. Bruce Franklin, *Vietnam and Other American Fantasies* (Amherst: University of Massachusetts Press, 2000), 131–50.
8. A few later made-for-television movies at least briefly featured the war. These will be noted at the end.
9. Only *Biff Baker, USA* was released commercially; the "Saigon Incident" episode appeared on a DVD released by Alpha Home Entertainment in 2006. Of the four major archives whose catalogs I searched, the Museum of the Moving Image does not hold any of the programs addressed in the essay, the Paley Center for Media and the Wisconsin Center for Film and Theater Research hold only one (*The Final War of Olly Winter*), and the UCLA Film and Television Archive does not hold the *Navy Log* episode "The Bishop of the Bayfield."
10. See, for example, Mark Atwood Lawrence, *Assuming the Burden: Europe and the American Commitment to War in Vietnam* (Berkeley: University of California Press, 2005).
11. For a firsthand account of the OSS's favorable view of the Viet Minh, see Archimedes L. A. Patti, *Why Viet Nam? Prelude to America's Albatross* (Berkeley: University of California Press, 1980). On the United States in Vietnamese anticolonial discourse, see Mark Philip Bradley, *Imagining Vietnam and America: The Making of Postcolonial Vietnam, 1919–1950* (Chapel Hill: University of North Carolina Press, 2000), 10–44. Bradley also offers a nuanced analysis of Patti's (and the OSS's) views of the Viet Minh; see ibid., 134–45.
12. MacDonald, "The Cold War as Entertainment," 7–8.
13. That is the spelling given by IMDB for the character played by Marya Marco. The credits at the end of the episode do not identify the characters' names. See "Biff Baker, USA (1952–1954): Full Cast & Crew," IMDB.com, accessed September 26, 2014, http://www.imdb.com/title/tt0044238/fullcredits?ref_=tt_ov_st_sm. The name is pronounced "Tai" or "Thai" in the episode.
14. For a study complicating this simplistic Cold War binary, see Thomas Doherty, *Cold War, Cool Medium: Television, McCarthyism, and American Culture* (New York: Columbia University Press, 2003).
15. Franklin, *Vietnam and Other American Fantasies*, 50.
16. I am grateful to Fred MacDonald for providing me with a copy of both this episode and "The Hour of the Bath" episode of *Alcoa Premiere*.
17. William J. Lederer, "They'll Remember the Bayfield," *Reader's Digest* 67 (March 1955): 1, 8.
18. On the coverage of the exodus, see Seth Jacobs, *America's Miracle Man in Vietnam: Ngo Dinh Diem, Religion, Race, and US Intervention in Southeast Asia* (Durham, NC: Duke University Press, 2004), 127–71.
19. Peter Hansen, "Bac Di Cu: Catholic Refugees from the North of Vietnam, and Their Role in the Southern Republic, 1954–1959," *Journal of Vietnamese Studies* 4, no. 3 (Fall 2009): 182–92.
20. Marilyn B. Young, *The Vietnam Wars, 1945–1990* (New York: HarperPerennial, 1991), 45. See also Jacobs, *America's Miracle Man in Vietnam*, 132–33.
21. "Alcoa Premiere (1961–1963)," IMDb.com, accessed October 15, 2014, http://www.imdb.com/title/tt0054513/.
22. "Alcoa Moulds 'Hard Sell' TV Image with Hard News," *Sponsor* 17, no. 44 (November 4, 1963): 28.
23. For more on nation-building in Vietnam, see especially James M. Carter, *Inventing Vietnam: The United States and State Building, 1954–1968* (Cambridge: Cambridge

University Press, 2008); Jessica B. Elkind, "The First Casualties: American Nation Building Programs in South Vietnam, 1955–1965" (PhD dissertation, University of California, Los Angeles, 2005); Matthew Masur, "Hearts and Minds: Cultural Nation-Building in South Vietnam, 1954–1963" (PhD dissertation, Ohio State University, 2004); and Edward Miller, *Misalliance: Ngo Dinh Diem, the United States, and the Fate of South Vietnam* (Cambridge, MA: Harvard University Press, 2013).

24. For more, see Worland, "Sign-Posts Up Ahead," 117–18.

25. Jesse H. Walker, "Theatricals," *New York Amsterdam News*, February 11, 1967.

26. Ibid.

27. Louise Sweeney, "'CBS Playhouse' Curtain Rises on 'Olly Winter,'" *Christian Science Monitor*, January 30, 1967.

28. Jack Gould, "TV: 'The Final War of Olly Winter,'" *New York Times*, January 30, 1967.

29. Lawrence Laurent, "Quality Back in TV Drama," *Washington Post and Times-Herald*, January 30, 1967.

30. Clay Gowran, "TV Today: CBS' Top Story Editor Picks Plays," *Chicago Tribune*, October 30, 1967; Clay Gowran, "TV Has One of Its Very Best Sundays," *Chicago Tribune*, January 30, 1967.

31. William I. Kaufman, *Great Television Plays* (New York: Dell, 1969).

32. Francis J. Griffith, Joseph E. Marsand, and Joseph B. Maggio, eds., *One Act Plays for Our Times* (New York: Popular Library, 1973).

33. I have relied for this analysis on the illustrated script by Ronald Ribman published for CBS. *CBS Playhouse Presents:* The Final War of Olly Winter (New York: CBS Television Network, 1967). All quoted material comes from the script.

34. Hal Humphrey, "Playhouse to Air without Commercials," *Los Angeles Times*, October 15, 1967; Hal Humphrey, "'Olly Winter' Slow but Steady Drama," *Los Angeles Times*, January 30, 1967.

35. Lanning, *Vietnam at the Movies*, 48.

36. On its "world premiere," see "TV PREEM: Some May Live," *Chicago Defender*, September 16, 1967; Anna Nangle, "Movies," *Chicago Tribune*, September 30, 1967; "Saturday's TV Programs," *Los Angeles Times*, September 30, 1967.

37. Jamesbwill, "Excellent Spy Thriller," IMDB.com, last modified February 18, 2006, and michaeldouglas1, "Little Known Vietnam War Thriller," IMDB.com, last modified April 9, 2012, http://www.imdb.com/title/tt0062287/reviews?ref_=tt_urv.

38. "Film review: Some May Live (1967)," *Mistlake's Blog*, September 24, 2013, http://mistlake.wordpress.com/2013/09/24/film-review-some-may-live-1967/.

39. On these made-for-TV movies, see Jeremy M. Devine, *Vietnam at 24 Frames a Second: A Critical and Thematic Analysis of over 400 Films about the Vietnam War* (Austin: University of Texas Press, 1995), 57, 61, 69–71, 81–83.

11 *China Beach* and the Good Series Death

Christine Becker

All the movies, books, TV shows, they're becoming my memories now, pushing out the old one. The movies are ... better somehow, they seem to end up better than my messy old memory. Vietnam is just becoming a little war in history now, a little half page sandwiched between Kennedy's assassination and Watergate, and pretty soon all we'll have left is the cliché.

—Sgt. Bob Pepper, "Rewind," *China Beach*[1]

China Beach (ABC, 1987–1991) is one of only two dramas in American network television history about the Vietnam War. It is further set apart from nearly all other series by focusing on the frontline role of women in wartime. The show's creators and writers have explained that their primary mission for the series was to illustrate the emotional effects of the Vietnam War on the American women who participated in it and whose traumatic experiences were largely ignored in its wake.[2] But *China Beach* was not just about war or about trauma; it was also about the memory of Vietnam War trauma, the ways in which those who participated dealt with the mental anguish of the experience, especially in a home country that largely declined to acknowledge it. This exceptional focus culminated in a final season that combined the series' unique themes with a singularly innovative formal structure, providing an ending that has elicited effusive critical praise.[3] Such acclaim demands systematic analysis of how the series achieved such distinction, and a theory of television series finales advanced by media studies scholar C. Lee Harrington provides an intriguing template to apply in this regard.

In "The *Ars Moriendi* of US Serial Television: Towards a Good Textual Death," Harrington notes how often terms related to death arise in TV series finale discourse.[4] Fans speak of mourning a show and saying goodbye to its characters forever, and critics debate how a show's legacy could be affected in its afterlife by how it ends. Harrington took this discourse to its logical extension by applying theories of death and dying to television series finales, which led her to the 600-year-old Christian concept of the *ars moriendi*. The *ars moriendi* essentially took the form of an instruction guide to ensuring a person's "good death," with spiritual salvation and family comfort as the desired result. For the dying person, such factors as feelings of acceptance, control, comfort, and closure are essential to a good death, as are recognition that one is dying, affirmation of the value of one's legacy, the coherence of a life well lived relative to one's death, and optimized relationships with caregivers and family.[5]

Harrington accordingly applied these concepts to the termination of a television serial via the series finale. First, the notions of control, closure, and recognition translate into foresight and planning. A good death for a series can best be assured when the creative team knows a definitive end is coming, allowing them to strategically chart out a trajectory to the endpoint and leaving viewers in a position to prepare for this closure. A second translation of the *ars moriendi* to TV finales is judging the legacy and coherence of a text's life relative to its death. Here the focus is not on "death as the *end* of life but as a *part* of life" and as the connection between a beginning and an end: "one dies as one lives."[6] In television terms, this places value on internal coherence and continuity between a drama's storytelling patterns and its ending, such that closure feels satisfyingly circular and organic to the text, not discrete and arbitrary. Finally, Harrington argues that fan community satisfaction is also a relevant application of the *ars moriendi* to television finales, akin to a "final relational obligation" to loved ones. For long-running series especially, devoted viewers spend many hours connected to these story worlds and their characters, and the ending provides a powerful capstone through which they remember the series.

Figure 11.1 The first season cast of *China Beach* and the cover of the commemorative DVD edition. In its final season, *China Beach* openly memorialized the war and its veterans, thereby providing a "good death" for characters and audience alike.

180 *Christine Becker*

China Beach arguably confronted actual death as frequently and bluntly as any television series in US network television history, and its final season and series finale in particular dwell considerably on the regret, guilt, and pain felt by survivors and observers of war casualties. The writers understood that the program's fourth season would likely be the last, and this terminal notice allowed them to craft a set of episodes that delved even more strategically into these themes with a well-rounded sense of finality. That finishing run was very well received by critics and fans. *Boston Globe* critic Gail Caldwell wrote just prior to the series finale, "*China Beach* is going out with brilliant, sunset hues in the background; in keeping with Mickey Spillane's counsel about dying young, it's leaving a good-looking corpse."[7] Does this mean that *China Beach* fulfilled an *ars moriendi* of US serial television? If so, what are the implications of conferring a "good death" upon a representation of war trauma and a polemical conflict like Vietnam?

The Lifespan of *China Beach*

For its first three seasons, *China Beach* took place during 1967 and 1968 largely in Vietnam, with a few journeys back to the United States. The series' setting was based on an actual R&R outpost in Da Nang, nicknamed China Beach, and an adjacent hospital facility was added for the series. Co-creators John Sacret Young and William Broyles, Jr., a Vietnam veteran, set out to depict the role that women played as support staff during the war and took inspiration for the series from US Army Nurse Lynda Van Devanter's memoir *Home before Morning*, as well as recollections from other veterans.[8] Van Devanter's television counterpart is Colleen McMurphy (Dana Delany), an idealistic yet weathered nurse whose devotion and emotional attachment to her job are matched only by her despair at the horrific and often senseless conditions around her. She is equal parts dedicated and exasperated, stoic and vulnerable, earnest and pessimistic. Her primary foil across the series is K. C. Koloski (Marg Helgenberger), a cynical, savvy civilian residing at China Beach primarily to seek financial gain through prostitution (although only with officers) and business schemes. Whereas McMurphy is primarily maternal, K. C. is almost wholly self-serving. Another key female character is Major Lila Garreau (Concetta Tomei), the stern but sympathetic officer in command at China Beach, who is also a veteran of World War II and Korea. The male characters who appear regularly include Dr. Dick Richard (Robert Picardo), a cocksure, wisecracking surgeon who finds an understanding compatriot in McMurphy; Sergeant Evan "Dodger" Winslow (Jeff Kober), a brooding Marine who appears at China Beach between missions and often turns to McMurphy for emotional support; Corporal Boonie Lanier (Brian Wimmer), a lifeguard and bar manager devoted to providing troops with a brief escape from the war; and Private Samuel Beckett (Michael Boatman), the thoughtful, spiritual head of the

China Beach *and the Good Series Death*   181

Graves Registration Unit who sees it as his duty to send the battered bodies of soldiers home with the honor they deserve.

The pilot episode opens with McMurphy ostensibly at the end of her one-year tour of duty in 1967, readying to return home to her family in Iowa.[9] This means the main characters are presented with their camaraderie already established, whereas viewers arrive *in media res*, as do a pair of supporting characters, Laurette (Chloe Webb), a USO entertainer, and Cherry (Nan Woods), a Red Cross "donut dolly" recreation worker. Serving their pilot duty, these two are initially naive to the challenges China Beach will offer them, but they quickly learn, as do viewers. Pilots also typically indicate how a show will work on a weekly basis, and *China Beach*'s opening hours accordingly present motifs, plotlines, and themes that appear throughout the series run. Dodger's haunted stare, Boonie's bittersweet exuberance, the group's conviviality and flirtation amidst the carnage, all are evident at the start. So, too, is Beckett's spiritual connection with the dead soldiers that surround him, as he speaks to them as if they have not passed on. There are multiple monologues describing the difficulty of seeing so many mangled men come through the hospital every day, and there is a traumatic death scene, as Laurette comforts a soldier in his last moments. Most importantly, beginning the series with McMurphy on her way out activates one of the series' most central themes: the difficulty of letting go. The episode launches as a farewell, complete with a going-away party. But, in the final scene, McMurphy decides she cannot return to Iowa because China Beach, with all of its evident horrors, offers the family that needs her most.

Subsequent episodes unspool the show's distinctive genre mixture of war drama, medical drama, melodrama, and workplace comedy. Despite considerable critical acclaim for this narrative innovation, as well as 29 Emmy nominations, *China Beach* was never a Nielsen ratings hit. It was even close to cancelation at the end of its third season, but ABC brought it back for one last run. On the fall 1990 schedule, the network placed the series on Saturday night, pitting it against stiff competition from the popular sitcom *The Golden Girls* (NBC, 1985–1992). This resulted in a 42% ratings drop and an extended midseason hiatus.[10] The final seven episodes were burned off the next summer, with the two-hour finale airing in July 1991. Although this was an unfortunate scheduling end, it made possible an advantageous story-telling end, as the producers and writers went into the season expecting that it would be their last.[11] This afforded them a rare luxury in American network television: a planned, definitive conclusion, or the chance for a "good death."

Dying As One Lived in *China Beach*

As noted earlier, *China Beach*'s writers set out to confront the lingering effects of the Vietnam War, and the final season specifically explores post-traumatic stress tied to memories of the war and, as Sasha Torres describes, guilt

182   *Christine Becker*

stemming from "the impossibility of adequately remembering the Vietnam war."[12] In her article, "War and Remembrance: Televisual Narrative, National Memory, and *China Beach*," Torres further argues that the series repeatedly confronts three memory-related questions, which are crystallized in the final season: "Is it possible to remember Vietnam? How does the process of remembering the war transform the present? And what role does television itself play in the process of remembrance?"[13]

The first question relates to a systematic process of denial that followed Vietnam. Media scholar Peter Ehrenhaus notes that a nation typically feels obligated to remember what a war wrought once it comes to an end as a means of recovery. However, because Vietnam could be judged a "failed" war that called into question the legitimacy of core American myths, US authorities strove to suppress discussion of this past and turned a blind eye to its impact. Ehrenhaus writes, "Closure became impractical—if not impossible—for political institutions and public alike, when faced with the obligation to commemorate Vietnam and its veterans. When tradition called for acts of closure, the United Stated chose *not* to remember."[14] With no "greater good" justification for the war established as part of the official record, this left veterans bereft, with few available mechanisms for coming to terms with their wartime memories. According to Deborah Ballard-Reisch, "The profound moral guilt veterans felt, the same guilt felt by veterans of any war, could not be purged."[15] Ballard-Reisch notes that subsequent popular media representations of Vietnam have tried to address this psychological problem, as if to compensate for the lack of a satisfying ending in real life.

China Beach's final season offered one such media representation, and it covered Torres' second question—how remembering the war transforms the present—via a non-linear narrative. Season four opens in 1985, as we see Boonie and Richard well into their postwar lives.[16] Boonie's unexpected visit to Richard's house later prompts the doctor to awaken, unsettled, in the middle of the night. Rejecting comfort from his wife, Richard digs out an old box containing his war memorabilia and gazes at photos of his China Beach compatriots. One black-and-white photo of McMurphy dissolves into a color live-action shot of her at China Beach in 1967, and the narrative turns back to early interactions, both contentious and passionate, between McMurphy and Richard. The episode ends with a return to 1985, as Richard tries to call McMurphy, who answers with a lie and says he has a wrong number. Akin to a pilot, this episode sets forth a narrative and thematic template for the season: it skips between past and present and in doing so confronts the connective tissue between the two, with McMurphy, in particular, struggling to come to terms with the past and its reverberations in her present life.

Opening the season in 1985 also establishes a baseline for what past and present mean at this point in the series. In *China Beach*'s first three seasons, the Vietnam War years are the diegetic present, the current temporality for the characters. In the final season, due to its starting point, events

China Beach *and the Good Series Death*   183

that take place in Vietnam are marked as the diegetic past, meaning that footage is best characterized as flashbacks, which is crucial to how the final season explores memory and remembrance. In fact, this trope is distinctly televisual. Series television's long-form mode of narration allows for a variance of chronologies from episode to episode and for the accumulation of knowledge about characters and their emotions across time. This narrative capability enabled *China Beach* to work through a commemoration of Vietnam veterans' actions in a way that real-world events had evaded. As Torres describes, *China Beach* "offers the televisual image and televisual narrative in place of popular memory, as the solution to the memorial crises—collective and individual—that Vietnam initiates. For *China Beach*, memory is produced by, and ultimately coextensive with, televisual replay."[17]

The fourth episode of the final season, titled "Rewind," is a model illustration of this televisual representation of memory.[18] The story focuses on K. C.'s daughter, Karen (Christine Elise), who was born in Vietnam, raised by a Vietnamese nanny, and sent off by K.C. to live with Boonie when Saigon fell in 1975, an event depicted three episodes earlier. Now a college student in 1985, Karen sets out to make a documentary about the public memorialization of Vietnam, which soon turns into a film about China Beach and Karen's mysterious mother, as she travels around interviewing the main characters, except for the missing K.C. Thus, "man on the street" interviews with real people, a number of whom profess not to know much about the war, are progressively displaced by interviews with the main characters, who offer personal memories of China Beach and of K. C. The episode makes a point of frequently showing the documentary subjects through Karen's viewfinder lens and on TV screens, thereby visually underscoring the theme of "video as the only memorial technology capable of re-integrating recollected fragments into a tentative whole."[19]

The next episode, "Through and Through," explores such fragments through McMurphy's post-traumatic stress syndrome and her struggles to come to terms with her past experiences.[20] She begins the episode experiencing traumatizing flashbacks to a bombing at China Beach, the details of which are incomplete. In working through this memory with a therapist, McMurphy continually revises her conception of what happened. She finally fights her way to the accurate memory, which she had suppressed to avoid dealing with an agonizing recognition: she was angry with medic Ned Hyers, who was killed in battle shortly thereafter (an incident that regular viewers would recall from season three's "How To Stay Alive in Vietnam, Part 1" but which is not shown again here). Hyers had prevented McMurphy from attending to soldiers following the devastating bombing of a makeshift hospital ward because it wasn't safe to approach; she is tormented by the idea that she might have been able to save some of the men if he had let her go. Here again is McMurphy's central emotional conflict: she is unable to let go of the traumatic memory of a perceived failure to save enough lives.

184   *Christine Becker*

Crucially, the chronological jump forward via the non-linear structure of the final season enabled *China Beach* to explore this territory formally and thematically, and this was only possible because the writers expected that this season would be the last one. Critic Gail Caldwell effectively characterized this in her 1991 finale preview:

> The visual grammar that *China Beach* has mastered in its last season, so reflective of the war experience and yet so foreign to the medium, probably could have only happened when the end of the story was in sight. This is one of the black-hearted ironies of TV drama—that it rises above the constraints of its form only when threatened with the kiss of death. You can't bring home a bunch of war-damaged vets, facing rehab centers and second marriages, with the intent of dragging them all through it again for yet another season.[21]

The *ars moriendi* of proper planning for death thus enabled the season to dwell at great length on its main characters coming to terms with memories of Vietnam, providing a process of closure for them that their real-life counterparts rarely received.

The final season trajectory also adheres to the *ars moriendi* requirement of the coherence of a text's life relative to its death. In addition to the thematic relevance of the season to the rest of the series, the series' ending run also embodies the notion of a lifespan, specifically each character's Vietnam War lifespan. The early episodes of the season depict McMurphy's early weeks at China Beach, as well as those of other characters. We see McMurphy talk with Boonie for the first time, and we experience the formation of her intense bond with Richard. We also see K. C.'s first meeting with McMurphy and with Richard, as well as Beckett's first week at China Beach. This allows viewers to reflect back and better understand the war's impact on the characters' personalities, which they saw in a mature phase starting with the pilot episode. This underscores narratively what McMurphy states in the series finale about the day she left Vietnam: "Everything was exactly the same as the day I arrived. Except for me."

The fourth episode of the final season, "Escape," showcases this idea in terms of how Beckett came to relate to death and the soldiers' bodies so thoughtfully.[22] It opens in 1985 as Beckett sits in an empty church and quietly recites a Bible scripture from Corinthians about the resurrection of the dead: "How are the dead raised up, and with what body do they come?" The next scene takes place in the same church in 1957; Beckett is a young boy, his father is a preacher, and the setting is his mother's funeral. Beckett's father recites the resurrection scripture, and, as young Beckett approaches his mother's open casket, he drops his Bible and cries out for his mother to come back and not leave him. The episode then jumps ahead to 1967, as the adult Beckett arrives in Vietnam with a wholly different personality than viewers are accustomed to, flippant and disrespectful, rather than somber

China Beach *and the Good Series Death* 185

and thoughtful. This leads one to draw a connection back to 1957 and assume that young Beckett turned away from religion and his father upon his mother's death.

Beckett gets assigned to the Graves Registration Unit as punishment for disrespecting a dead body, and here we see a most anachronistic version of his character. He cracks jokes about the corpses, plays a prank with a body bag, and tells the dead soldiers they make lousy company. His turning point comes when a newly made friend, a tormented soldier portentously nicknamed Deadman, hangs himself. Beckett screams out the resurrection scripture in response, lamenting, "it doesn't work, it never works"; they never come back. While preparing Deadman's body for sending home, Beckett listens to his audio-recorded will; the voice of the dead man fills the morgue. The episode concludes back in 1985, as Beckett speaks at his father's funeral. He tells the gathered, "I hear my father's voice in this place, and I listen to it echoing. And know that he is alive, alive in me. They live in me. They live in all of us." He concludes by reciting the resurrection scripture. "Escape" thereby offers a profound retroactive deepening of Beckett's Vietnam identity and his most essential personality traits. In such a way, the final season enables viewers to reflect back on the characters they have followed across previous seasons and consider the implications of how the Vietnam experience changed their lives.

A further meshing of the season with the notion of a lifespan occurs due to the season's narrative structure. "Escape" closes off a four-episode first act that covers various beginnings, including Karen's birth. The subsequent second-act episodes of the season build in tension as various midlife crises unfold in both the past and present. For instance, episode seven depicts Vietnam at a crisis point in 1969, as drugs are rampant and chaos reigns at China Beach. McMurphy asks Lila if World War II had ever gotten like this.[23] Lila answers, "No, we didn't turn old in the middle of that one." The final five episodes stand as a third act, beginning with the characters at their lowest points. Episode 12, "The Always Goodbye," reveals McMurphy's descent into alcoholism in 1969, and in episode 13, "Quest," McMurphy attempts to overdose on pills in 1976. The next two episodes, "Rewind" and "Through and Through," present Karen and McMurphy respectively in their deepest throes of psychological turmoil about their pasts, with Karen suffering from feelings of rejection and McMurphy captive to traumatic flashbacks. "Rewind" ends with Karen saying, "This isn't finished, is it?" The final line of "Through and Through" is McMurphy asking, "Is this ever gonna stop?" These questions propel the season toward its definitive end.

Memorializing Death in the *China Beach* Finale

China Beach's final episode is entitled "Hello Goodbye," quite fitting for a season that transported viewers back to the start of the characters' time in Vietnam and at its end has them say farewell to it.[24] There is no punctuation

186   *Christine Becker*

between the two title words, which appear on screen at the start of the episode with the second word fading in as the first fades out. This implies a fluid connection between the beginning and ending, a graphic representation of what the final season itself played out. The finale is set in 1988 at a 20-year reunion of Vietnam veterans, thus cathartically bringing all of the characters together in the present for the first time in the season (except for K. C., who appears only at the end). Karen additionally records monologues from the main characters about their experiences, exactly as the series did with real veterans in a pair of previous episodes. Also, in keeping with the final season's narrative pattern, the past is intercut with the present via a combination of memorable scenes from across the series' run and new McMurphy flashbacks. In this way, as Sasha Torres deftly notes, the episode lets viewers relive the experience of China Beach and of *China Beach*.[25]

As a primary example, McMurphy's memories mesh with the viewers' own through a frame story. The episode opens with McMurphy sitting frontally but glancing slightly off-screen at Karen's camera as she describes, "There was one boy. Everyone has one. You think that you're gonna forget, and you don't. I promised that I would remember his name. I promised myself."[26] Her memories of the dying boy, a soldier nicknamed Lurch, are depicted via flashbacks intercut across the episode. Lurch is wearing compression pants to keep him from bleeding to death. As soon as the pants come off, he will bleed out instantly, so McMurphy has to prepare him for his impending death. Lurch insists McMurphy will remember him; she says she won't. This also happens to be McMurphy's final day in Vietnam. At the end of the ordeal, another doctor asks if she's ok, and she replies tearfully, "I'm going home." The footage that follows is set in her Iowa home, but it comes from the season two finale, when McMurphy was on leave in 1968. She gets angry at her mother for throwing out her clothes from Vietnam, which she insists represent "where I've been. It's who I am." Devoted viewers will remember this powerful moment well and, through reliving it in this context, better understand how McMurphy in 1988 is processing her own memory of Lurch's death in 1969. Like her soiled uniform, this is a past she refuses to let go of, even as it haunts her. By the end of the episode, though, viewers recognize that McMurphy is better able to cope with that past in 1988. Instead of angrily rebelling, as she did 20 years previously, she is able to accept the reality of what took place and understand how it affected her.

This concept is brought home in the episode's concluding act, which has the characters travel to Washington DC and gather together at the Vietnam Veterans Memorial Wall for a final goodbye. The Wall is an especially profound setting at which to end the series because it draws attention to how much the *China Beach* finale itself is like a memorial, a conduit for remembrance and a meditation on grief and loss. The Wall's designer Maya Lin has explained, "In the design of the memorial, a fundamental goal was to be honest about death, since we must accept that loss in order to overcome it."[27] It is such acceptance that McMurphy herself strives for across the season, and her ability to reconcile it in the finale resonates in a variety of ways with the Wall's design.

In her interpretation of the Wall's physical characteristics, Marita Sturken writes that "the black granite walls of the memorial act as a screen for innumerable projections of memory and history," and the reflective surface "allows viewers to participate in the memorial; seeing their own images in the names, they are thus implicated in the listing of the dead."[28] As *China Beach*'s characters approach The Wall, we see them reflected as a group. This is followed by contemplative close-ups of each character gazing at the structure, allowing viewers to think through their series memories and empathetically dwell on how the characters project their own histories into the memorial. These images and thoughts also directly call to mind the lyrics of the Supremes' "Reflections," the series' theme song: "Through the mirror of my mind / Time after time, I see reflections of you and me / Reflections of the way life used to be / Reflections of the love you took from me."

Further, the names on the Wall offer a link to a key *China Beach* motif. On the memorial, the names mark out each of the dead as an individual with a legacy to honor and a family that grieves, an acknowledgement of each loss as a component of a collective mourning suppressed in the aftermath of the war. Similarly, in *China Beach*, the names of the dead are often tied to the theme of deliberate memory suppression. The character who most boldly confronts death throughout the series, Beckett, is also the one most concerned with documenting soldiers' names. In the sixth episode of season three, Beckett asks for Dodger's help in identifying the full names of a group of dead soldiers, but he knows only their nicknames.[29] Beckett sighs, "Why don't you guys ever know last names?" Dodger looks toward the dead men: "This is why." Later that season, Dodger returns home upon completion of his tour.[30] The episode featuring this plotline is ironically titled "The Thanks of a Grateful Nation," as a running theme is the refusal to acknowledge Vietnam veterans' service. In the episode's final scene, Dodger walks through a military cemetery virtually devoid of other visitors. He approaches the Vietnam section and finds an anonymous gravestone labeled "an American soldier known but to God." Dodger remarks that he hoped to find a grave of someone he knew, but laments, "So many names, I can't remember them." He then yells out loudly toward the sky, "Don't you forget. Please, don't anybody ever forget us ... me. Please. Please don't forget. I won't forget. I promise."

Similarly, there are multiple instances in the final season of McMurphy remembering, or pretending to remember, a patient's name. Most tellingly, in "The Call," McMurphy writes soldiers' names in a notepad as they die, observing that the publicly announced tally of deaths in the military newspaper *Stars and Stripes* is clearly a deliberate undercount.[31] Dodger later questions what good it does to keep those names contained in a pad, for only her to see. At the end of the episode, McMurphy paints the names of the dead on the outside walls of the hospital ward. McMurphy says to

188 *Christine Becker*

Richard, "128 soldiers. Most of them believed in this. In all the lies. And they died. Was it worth it to them?" Richard responds that he doesn't know, and he asks McMurphy if she feels better. She answers, "Yes ... no." Meanwhile, gathering soldiers reach out and touch the painted names, much like their non-fictional compatriots would later at The Wall.

This name remembrance motif resounds strongly with the series' final lines of dialogue. As we watch McMurphy deposit at the Wall sand from China Beach, which she collected after overseeing Lurch's death, we hear her reunion monologue in voiceover: "I remembered his name. The boy in the pants. Lawrence F. McClintock. He was from Littleton, Colorado. And he loved football. They called him Lurch." The next image is from the monologue, but now McMurphy stares straight into the camera: "I couldn't save them all. But I saved some. I thought that I'd forgotten, but I remembered. He said that I would." McMurphy has clearly found a sense of peace in the vivid details of her memories, and her direct gaze at viewers leads them to find contentment with this ending as well, assurance of the *ars moriendi*.

The series also attempts to reassure viewers with multiple representations of departure. "Reflections" is the song that opened the series; the non-diegetic song that plays as the characters stand at The Wall is Michael McDonald's "I Can Let Go Now," and it has equally resonant lyrics to bookend the series: "It was so right, it was so wrong / Almost at the same time / The pain and ache a heart can take / No one really knows / When the memories cling and keep you there / Till you no longer care / And you can let go now." The characters themselves then explicitly let go, represented via a series of dissolves as they say goodbye to each other. McMurphy says to Dodger, "See you soon." He responds, "No, you won't." Here we have another meshing of character and spectator emotion, as viewers can recognize that Dodger's declaration applies to them, as well.

A Good Death?

Through these literal and metaphorical representations, viewers assimilate answers to the third question that Sasha Torres says *China Beach* explores: What role does television play in the processes of remembrance? In terms of finales, this also dovetails with Harrington's *ars moriendi* of television series finales in that "Hello Goodbye" provides a fitting remembrance of the series and satisfyingly organic closure to the experience the previous episodes offered. The episode offers a richly emotional, affective experience in this way by capitalizing upon the long-form story-telling mode of network television, which fosters deeply rooted bonds between viewers and characters. Viewers are taken through reminders of the four-season journey they have been on with the characters and are comforted with the relatively stable place of the characters in the present. There is pain in reliving scenes like Beckett's season two eulogy on behalf of a group of soldiers who have left nothing behind but their boots. There are continual reminders of the senselessness and ironies of death in Vietnam, such as a poignant montage of previous scenes both tragic and sentimental underscored by "America the Beautiful." There are character conflicts left open, such as K. C. once again walking away from Karen. But the finale ultimately aims to let the characters and viewers alike come to terms with those past circumstances, offering acceptance and redemption rather than regret, and it does so by underscoring the power of memory through its unique themes and televisual techniques.

One might question how appropriate this is as a remembrance for Vietnam specifically, however. Acclaimed writer and Vietnam veteran Tim O'Brien famously wrote in *The Things They Carried*: "If at the end of a war story you feel uplifted, or if you feel that some small bit of rectitude has been salvaged from the larger waste, then you have been made the victim of a very old and terrible lie. There is no rectitude whatsoever. There is no virtue."[32] *China Beach* arguably tries to offer a measure of rectitude in terms of the moral grounding of its characters' actions. McMurphy even openly voices one of the subtexts to the entire series in the finale, that despite the abominable nature of the war, it still offered personal fulfillment to some. She tells Karen: "All these old faces bring back memories. I miss it. I was alive. Things happened. Important things. Every day, every second. I mattered. We all did." She then yells out at the top of her voice, "I loved it!" There is tremendous guilt at the heart of this howl in that McMurphy misses something that tragically ended so many lives and brought pain to countless people. But it also undeniably acknowledges experiential pleasure, which in turn offered years' worth of spectatorial pleasure for viewers. This is almost unavoidable for the conventional serial television experience, based as it is on the gratification of spending countless hours immersed in a story world filled with compelling characters. But while *China Beach* apparently offers a "good death" to viewers, should anything tied to Vietnam leave the impression of a good death?

China Beach perhaps fulfills C. Lee Harrington's *ars moriendi* of television series finales as well as any network program ever has. Yet, one aspect of the Christian *ars moriendi* would prove impossible to translate to American TV: television programs do not truly die, never to be seen again. They are resurrected in syndication and in the bodies of home video formats. In fact, *China Beach* found a second-run home from 1992–1997 on the Lifetime cable channel, an irony in name that Private Beckett would relish. A complete DVD release took much longer, due to the expense of clearing the musical rights for the series, which used popular songs from the Vietnam era in nearly every episode. But in 2013, a deluxe collector's edition of the series arose from Time-Life. The DVD set was accompanied by a box containing commemorative scripts and cast photos. One could theoretically awaken in the middle of the night, and, like Dr. Richard, pull out the box and gaze wistfully at the photos contained inside. Then, after reminiscing about one's hours spent with the characters at China Beach, the still images could turn to live-action via the DVD player, allowing the memories to be reflected upon anew.

Notes

1. "Rewind," season 4, episode 14, *China Beach, China Beach: The Complete Collection*, aired July 9, 1991 (New York: Time-Life Video, 2013) DVD. All subsequent references are to this DVD collection.
2. "Bonus Features," *China Beach: The Complete Collection* (New York: Time-Life Video, 2013) DVD.
3. See Alan Sepinwall, "Review: Reflections of *China Beach* on DVD," *Hitfix*, December 9, 2013, http://www.hitfix.com/whats-alan-watching/review-reflections-of-china-beach-on-dvd and Bill Goodykoontz, "25 Years Later, *China Beach* Earns Your Respect," *USA Today*, May 19, 2013, http://www.usatoday.com/story/news/2013/05/28/television-china-beach/2367887/.
4. C. Lee Harrington, "The *Ars Moriendi* of US Serial Television: Towards a Good Textual Death," *International Journal of Cultural Studies* 16 (November 2013): 579–95.
5. For more on the "good death" concept, see Karen A. Kehl, "Moving Toward Peace: An Analysis of the Concept of a Good Death," *American Journal of Hospice and Palliative Medicine* 23, no. 4 (August/September 2006): 277–86.
6. Harrington, "Ars Moriendi," 585, 582.
7. Gail Caldwell, "Picturing Vietnam after Four Seasons, ABC's China Beach Says Farewell," *Boston Globe*, July 19, 1991, 23.
8. Lynda Van DeVanter, *Home before Morning: The Story of an Army Nurse in Vietnam* (Amherst, MA: University of Massachusetts Press, 1983).
9. "China Beach, Part 1," season 1, episode 1, *China Beach*, aired April 26, 1988.
10. Robert J. Thompson, *Television's Second Golden Age: From Hill Street Blues to ER* (New York: Continuum, 1996), 146–47.
11. Stephen Herbert, "*China Beach* Winds up Production," *Los Angeles Times*, February 15, 1991, http://articles.latimes.com/1991-02-15/entertainment/ca-1199_1_china-beach. Accessed on January 5, 2015.
12. Sasha Torres, "War and Remembrance: Televisual Narrative, National Memory, and *China Beach*," *Camera Obscura* no. 33/34 (May/Sep/Jan 1994/95): 147.
13. Ibid., 148.
14. Peter Ehrenhaus "Commemorating the Unwon War: On Not Remembering Vietnam," *Journal of Communication* 39, no. 1 (Winter 1989): 97.
15. Deborah Ballard-Reisch, "*China Beach* and *Tour of Duty*: American Television and Revisionist History of the Vietnam War," *Journal of Popular Culture* 25, no. 3 (Winter 1991): 140.
16. "History, Part 1," season 4, episode 1, *China Beach*, aired September 29, 1990.
17. Torres, "War and Remembrance," 151.
18. "Rewind," *China Beach*.
19. Torres, "War and Remembrance," 155.
20. "Through and Through," season 4, episode 15, *China Beach,* aired July 16, 1991.
21. Caldwell, "Picturing Vietnam," 23.
22. "Escape," season 4, episode 4, *China Beach*, aired October 27, 1990.
23. "One Giant Leap," season 4, episode 14, *China Beach*, aired November 17, 1990.
24. This is also a reversal of the pilot, which begins with a farewell that McMurphy turns away from in the end.
25. Torres, "War and Remembrance," 160.
26. "Hello Goodbye," season 4, episodes 16 and 17, *China Beach*, aired July 22, 1991. Dr. Richard started to offer similar words in "Rewind," but he got too

emotional to finish. McMurphy finishing the sentiment is another form of closure the episode brings.

27. Maya Lin, "Making the Memorial," *The New York Review of Books*, November 2, 2000. http://www.nybooks.com/articles/archives/2000/nov/02/making-the-memorial/. Accessed on January 7, 2015.
28. Marita Sturken, "The Wall, the Screen, and the Image: The Vietnam Veterans Memorial," *Representations* no. 35 (Summer 1991), 133, 120.
29. "Ghosts," season 3, episode 6, *China Beach,* aired November 8, 1989.
30. "The Thanks of a Grateful Nation," season 3, episode 17, *China Beach,* aired February 28, 1990.
31. "The Call," season 4, episode 9, *China Beach*, aired December 8, 1990.
32. Tim O'Brien, *The Things They Carried* (New York: Houghton Mifflin, 1990). E-book edition.

Part III

Contemporary Conflicts on the Small Screen

12 Imagining the New Military of the 1990s in *Babylon 5's* Future Wars

Kathleen Kennedy

Literary critic John Huntington argues that "a fictional war of the future can alert us to attitudes in the real world of the present."[1] These future wars served nationalist ends while simultaneously revealing the anxieties over American readiness to meet and even understand the real danger posed by the "enemy." From January 1994 to November 1998, J. Michael Straczynski wrote and produced *Babylon 5*, which aired on the Prime Time Entertainment Network and TNT. *Babylon 5* was a unique television series because it followed a five-year story arc and imagined how the introduction of powerful women and queer characters might influence future wars. *Babylon 5* later developed a cult following and has maintained a loyal fan base due to a continuing presence at science fiction conventions and its availability on DVD. Its broad premise is that after barely escaping a genocidal war with an alien race, the Minbari, the government of Earth created Babylon 5 as a diplomatic space station to settle disputes between civilizations. *Babylon 5* follows the efforts by the command staff to protect Earth from internal and external threats. It emphasizes that lasting peace and justice are only possible through the sacrifices and heroism of military men and women. *Babylon 5* was part of the cultural revival of soldiering and military values that took place in the years following the Persian Gulf War, even as it brought into our living rooms a military that allowed for greater participation by women and sexual minorities.

The future-wars imagined by *Babylon 5* engage with the changing composition of the US military during and in the years following the first Gulf War (August 12, 1990 to February 28, 1991). Specifically, *Babylon 5* uses the future-war narrative to explore how a military that includes women and lesbians, gays, and bisexuals (LGB) will uphold or fail to uphold traditional military values and effectiveness. In the years surrounding the first Gulf War, Americans grappled with policy changes that further diversified the military. President William Clinton opened previously closed military positions to women and promised to end discriminatory practices against LGB soldiers. The compromise of "Don't Ask, Don't Tell" (DADT) allowed LGB people to serve in the military but only if they kept their sexuality secret.

This chapter analyzes how *Babylon 5's* storylines involving Commander Susan Ivanova, (Claudia Christian) telepath Lyta Alexander (Patricia Tallman),

196 *Kathleen Kennedy*

and their interactions with the Psi Corps, a quasi-government bureaucracy that regulates the lives of telepaths and enforces the laws governing them, comment on how gender and sexual diversity would affect America's real-world military. *Babylon 5's* future-war scenario encouraged its viewers to imagine a military in which such diversity appeared unproblematic because it did not threaten traditional soldiering. In other words, *Babylon 5* relieved the audience's anxieties by promising that such soldiers would uphold conventional military values and remain the bulwark on which the American (now Earth) republic would survive. It did so in part through the dyad between "normals" (humans without telepathic ability) and "telepaths" (individuals with the ability to read other's thoughts), which symbolically defined a particular class of humans as dangers to the sense of moral justice held by good citizens and soldiers. By reserving the highest forms of heroism, sacrifice, and power for "normal" men and women allied with those men, *Babylon 5* reassured its audience that women's and lesbian and gay participation in the military would confirm rather than challenge traditional conceptions of soldiering.

Diversifying the Military Post-Gulf War

Due to women's increased participation in the military, the first Gulf War raised concerns over how Americans would react to the deaths and possible capture of female soldiers, even as it led to calls for opening combat positions to women.[2] Supporters of women's increased role in military operations contended that skill, not gender, should define who held what positions while opponents of change relied on the cultural impact that women's engagement with violence would have and the unwillingness of male soldiers to tolerate the effects of that violence. In the words of Lieutenant Cornel William Bryan, "I am not prepared to see American mothers and daughters paraded down the streets of Bagdad and subjected to abuse."[3] General Maxwell Thurman echoed these concerns arguing that "no people would want women to get victimized."[4] Bryan and Thurman could not imagine that male soldiers would see women in professional roles but only as "mothers and daughters" or "victims" of sexual violence. Each believed the protection of women was an essential American value that would be undercut if women served without restriction in the military.

Critics of women's military participation also argued that "woman's nature" and reproductive abilities compromised their fighting abilities. Members of the Presidential Commission raised concerns that menstruating pilots would make poor decisions and subsequently voted to uphold bans on female pilots.[5] Bowdoin College professor, Jean Yarborough, similarly argued that "it's not a good idea to try to obliterate concern about women's reproductive system and the kinds of humiliation she would be forced to endure" should women's role in combat be expanded.[6] Yarborough also claimed that because, "on the whole, men are more violent than women," women would be less effective in combat situations. Author David Evans

Imagining the New Military of the 1990s in Babylon 5's *Future Wars* 197

concurred, noting that "close combat involves the ability to engage in mass butchery, and maybe differences between the sexes in natural aggressiveness overwhelm concerns of equity and physical strength."[7] Although such arguments swayed members of the President's Commission to vote to keep most of the bans on women in combat, President Clinton rejected those recommendations. By 1994, the Clinton administration had revised these risk rules, reserving only the most elite special operations position for men. In 1998, women flew their first combat missions, and 90 percent of military positions were opened to women.[8]

President Clinton also attempted to remove barriers that prevented LGB people from serving in the military. The Cold War had institutionalized an ideology that equated homosexuality with disloyalty, disease, and chaos. LGB people were said to threaten national security because their "moral weaknesses" allegedly left them vulnerable to foreign influences, and their sexual "degeneracy" threatened appropriate male and female gender roles.[9] As had these Cold War commentators, critics of Clinton's plans framed homosexuality as a symptom of a more fundamental character flaw that made LGB people more susceptible to un-American ideas and influences than were heterosexuals. Their service made the nation vulnerable to Communist and, later, terrorist infiltration because LGB people's sexual deviance was symptomatic of an underlying unfitness for military service. For example, three law professors, writing soon after the passage of DADT for the *Dickerson Law Review,* defended excluding LGB people from the military because it would be an "onerous distraction for the military" to accept lesbian and gay soldiers because their immoral behavior eroded the integrity of soldiering.[10] More recently, Tim Duncan, writing for the conservative website *Renew America,* argued:

> Why would we think it a good idea to allow people who habitually lack self-control to openly flaunt the lifestyle, which is the *source* of their intemperance inside an institution whose success at its primary function is *dependent upon each individual exhibiting self-control?* Why sanction indiscipline within a military which requires discipline on the part of its members to accomplish its objectives? *That's* where the arguments about the destruction of group morale and unit cohesion come from. ... As experience and common sense tell us, people who don't control their behavior in one area tend to lack self-control in others, as well.[11]

Accordingly, critics claimed, the exclusion of LGB people from military service both maintained the cohesiveness of the military unit and protected heterosexual or "normal" men's sense of honor and dignity.[12] By their presence, LGB soldiers violated those soldiers' basic rights.

Proponents of DADT expected that the compromise would give the heterosexual public and service members an opportunity to become more

198 *Kathleen Kennedy*

comfortable with diversity and provide an opening for full recognition of lesbian and gay service members. Progressive critics feared the compromise made heterosexual soldiers comfortable with their prejudices and held LGB soldiers responsible for any discord their sexuality might create. Most significant for this discussion is that DADT held LGB soldiers responsible for maintaining secrecy.

Babylon 5 engaged debates about diversifying the military largely by ignoring them. Men and women, gay and straight, display leadership, courage, self-sacrifice, and fatal flaws that place them on trajectories toward heroic transcendence or personal annihilation. While this normalization of gender and sexual diversity is important, especially in the historical context of the 1990s, the show does not ultimately challenge the link among militarism, peace, and white, heterosexual, male leadership. Instead, *Babylon 5* reinforces a negative link between queer sex, that is, sex that breaks down the boundaries between gendered individuals, and anti-Western terrorism's threat to the liberal self.

"The Last Great Hope for Peace"

Babylon 5 takes place 10 years after humans were nearly wiped out during the Earth-Minbari war. Mysteriously, the Minbari stopped the war and surrendered. Later the Minbari religious caste discovered that their souls were being reincarnated into human bodies. To ensure peace between the Minbari and humans, Delenn (Mira Furlan), the Minbari ambassador on Babylon 5, undergoes the process of chrysalis in which she is reborn as half-Minbari and half-human. She later marries Captain John Sheridan (Bruce Boxleitner), who commands Babylon 5 until he is elected President of Earth at the end of season four. Together they lead the "conspiracy of light" against the twin dark forces of the Shadows, a seemingly indestructible alien foe, and President Clark, the increasingly dictatorial leader of Earth.

Babylon 5 is an archetypical quest narrative in which two male heroes, scarred by their participation in a recent war, find meaning in resolving the key conflicts of the postwar era.[13] As good soldiers and leaders of men and women, both Jeffrey Sinclair (Michael O'Hara) and Sheridan display honor, compassion, bravery, and a willingness to sacrifice all for the cause. Both are destined to transcend normal soldiering to establish humans and their alien allies as a force for freedom in a violent universe. To accomplish this goal, both must overcome powerful alien enemies and the evil President of Earth, who seeks to destroy constitutional government and replace it with a dictatorship.

Traditionally, male quest narratives place women in dependent roles and define the forces that the male hero must overcome as feminine. Thus, women are either peripheral or a threat to male heroism. *Babylon 5* was part of a movement in mid-1990s television to develop female characters capable of exercising the same command decisions and violence as men. As heroes of

Imagining the New Military of the 1990s in Babylon 5's *Future Wars*   199

their own stories, women like Xena, Warrior Princess, and Buffy the Vampire Slayer challenged men's exclusive claim on the quest narrative. Each, in her own way demonstrated women's mastery of violence, command decisions, and rational problem solving. Such characters captured the imagination of female audiences and feminist critics alike, although feminists debated whether placing women within this quest narrative truly undermined its patriarchal structure and glorification of violence.[14]

While *Babylon 5* represents women as powerful, ethical, and independent, women still play secondary roles in the larger quest narrative. Delenn comes closest to sharing equally with Sheridan in his quest. She is an influential member of the Minbari ruling Grey Council and a member of the religious class. Her new hybrid identity has eroded some of her influence among the Minbari, however, as members of the warrior class view her alliance with humans as disloyal. It is doubtful that Sheridan could have fulfilled his quest without Delenn's help. For example, it is due to Delenn's military and diplomatic interventions that Sheridan wins his first battle with Clark's forces and establishes Babylon 5 as the base for the "conspiracy of light." They share command of an elite Minbari-Human military unit, the Rangers, and future generations remember both as the founders of the Interstellar Alliance that brought relative peace to the Universe after the end of the Shadow wars and Earth's civil wars. Critics Sharon Ney and Elaine M. Sciog-Lazarov argue that when Delenn is with Sheridan, she defers to him, but when acting on her own, she "reclaims her status as a hero."[15]

Delenn is also responsible for the order that began the Earth-Minbari war, and her alliance with Sheridan is part of her search for redemption for what the show portrays as a rash decision. Central to this redemption is her marriage with Sheridan and the birth of their son. It is in her role as wife and mother of Sheridan's son that Delenn gives life to the future, reinforcing arguments that women best serve the community as wives and mothers. Their marriage and the role it plays in establishing the Minbari-Earth alliance is reminiscent of centuries-old traditions in which heterosexual couplings made families of past enemies. In this history, women and their children served as cultural mediators who brought peace between different cultural groups by developing hybrid identities. By placing their relationship at the heart of Sheridan's quest, *Babylon 5* underscores the importance of bio-politics to defining normality and the appropriate role that women play in the quest narrative.

"Death Incarnate"

While Delenn redeems herself through a conventional heterosexual plot device, the career military woman, as represented by Commander and eventually General Susan Ivanova, cannot. Ivanova serves as the second in command at Babylon 5 until season five when Elizabeth Lochley (Tracy Scoggins) takes over this role. Like many professionally successful women portrayed in popular culture, Ivanova's personal life suffers because of her career choices. Ivanova has no living blood relatives, and she is repeatedly unsuccessful in romance. In "The War Prayer," she discovers that an old boyfriend, who is courting her once again, has joined a racist organization bent on eliminating alien influences over humans. Later, in "Divided Loyalties," her new lover Talia Winters (Andrea Thompson) is revealed as a spy for Psi Corps, and in "Rising Star," Marcus (Jason Carter), a ranger and potential lover, dies before she responds in kind to his love for her.

Ivanova's career success stems from her military talents as well as her ability to be tougher than the boys. She joins the military after her brother is killed in the Earth-Minbari war and is one of the few characters who did not directly participate in that war. While committed in theory to peace, she believes that peace is often maintained through death and sacrifice. It is her voice that announces the change in Babylon 5's mission at the beginning of the third season: "The Babylon project was our last, best hope for peace. ... It failed. ... But in the year of the Shadow war it became something greater: our last, best hope ... for victory."[16] She participates in the "conspiracy of light," Sheridan's mission to overthrow Clark and reestablish constitutional government on Earth, because she shares with him a history of service and a core set of beliefs about honor, duty, democracy, and freedom.

Ivanova repeatedly distinguishes herself from "civilians" and aligns herself with military values. In her professional interactions, she displays the self-confidence forged through officer training and the mastery of violence it promotes. In "A Voice in the Wilderness, Part I," the commander of a scientific vessel places his ship in danger by disobeying her orders. After saving his ship, a frustrated Ivanova dresses him down: "I'd like you to take the time to learn the Babylon 5 mantra: 'Ivanova is always right. I will listen to Ivanova. I will not ignore Ivanova's recommendations. Ivanova is God. And if this ever happens again, Ivanova will personally rip your lungs out.' [To herself] Civilians. [Looking up] Just kidding about that God part. No offense."[17] Gruffness aside, Ivanova respects and grieves for those soldiers killed executing her orders. When Babylon 5 must defend itself against Earth Force, it is Ivanova who requests permission to go to the front lines, reminding Sheridan that "one of [them]" must accompany the troops into battle given the risks they are being asked to undertake.

Due to her skill and loyalty, Ivanova obtains the highest rank possible in the military. Upon Sheridan's death, 20 years after the action of the series, she takes command of the Rangers. Throughout the series, she participates in numerous battles, successfully directing important victories as well as commanding the respect of those who follow her. As the war with the Shadows intensifies, she contacts the "First Ones," the elders of the universe, to elicit their help in defeating the Shadows. She guides refugee populations to safety, arrests war criminals, keeps the station running on a daily basis, and knows everything that happens on Babylon 5. When President Clarke's forces capture and torture Sheridan, she leads the outgunned rebel forces

Imagining the New Military of the 1990s in Babylon 5's *Future Wars*   201

into battle with all the chutzpah of a leader confident in her ability to deal death. When told by an Earth-Force commander to surrender, she declines and explains to him precisely who she is:

IVANOVA: This is the White Star Fleet. Negative on surrender. ... We will not stand down.
EARTH-FORCE: Who is this? Identify yourself.
IVANOVA: *Who am I?* I am Susan Ivanova, Commander, daughter of Andrei and Sophie Ivanov. I am the right hand of vengeance, and the boot that is going to kick your sorry ass all the way back to Earth. ... I am Death incarnate, and the last living thing that you are ever going to see. God sent me.[18]

The battle ends with Ivanova sacrificing herself and her crew for victory. She attempts to ram an enemy cruiser and is mortally wounded. Her actions demonstrate that she is just as capable of dealing death and is just as willing to make the ultimate sacrifice to win the battle as are her male comrades. But her sacrificial death is preempted by Marcus. He attaches an alien-healing device to them to transfer his life force to her and dies in the process, which leaves a grief-stricken Ivanova to perpetually mourn his passing.[19]

Marcus' actions play into the fears that male soldiers will elect to protect women rather than carry out their duty because they will always view women as potential lovers or mothers, rather than soldiers. As critics Ney and Ciog-Lazarov point out, Marcus' actions override Ivanova's will and place her within the archetypical female romantic narrative that she had worked so hard to avoid, yet it is Ivanova whom the show punishes for Marcus' actions.[20] Because she failed to choose romance over duty, she must continue to mourn not only for Marcus but also for her choice to spurn him. As part of that punishment, Ivanova finds minimal satisfaction in her military career despite her promotion to general. When an aging Ivanova appears in the series' finale, she is, in Claudia Christian's words, "a curmudgeonly old Janet Reno ... bulldog. ... She is sick of her job [and] feels like she's just an old war horse."[21] The show leaves it unresolved as to whether her new role as head of the Rangers will revive her interest in her career or sense of self-worth.[22] As critics of women's equal participation in the military argue, when women act as "death incarnate," rather than as the mothers, daughters, and partners of those men who sacrifice, disaster follows. By choosing military valor over heterosexual romance, Ivanova has doomed both Marcus and herself.

"Divided Loyalties"

J. Michael Straczynski hoped to present a universe in which women's equal participation was expected and accepted, and he similarly deployed bisexual characters to imagine a future in which one's sexuality would not define one's

202 *Kathleen Kennedy*

fitness for service.[23] Its engagement with a lesbian subtext in Ivanova's friendship with Winters highlights problems with DADT and late twentieth-century constructions of normality and sexual deviancy. Nonetheless, debates in the wake of the First Gulf War about the ability of LGB soldiers to operate effectively within the American military are echoed in *Babylon 5*'s presentation of telepaths. As a class of people whose sexual practices and mind-reading abilities erode the autonomy of the liberal individual, telepaths occupy the subject position of deviant and dangerous queers who threaten the foundations of a free liberal society.

As the quintessential other in *Babylon 5*, telepaths define normality for humans. Normals are those humans who by their very nature cannot penetrate the minds of others and do not threaten the privacy and independence of the individual. Most of the civilizations represented in *Babylon 5* have clear laws that govern telepaths in order to protect the privacy of non-telepaths. Earth law requires human telepaths to choose one of three options: incorporation into the Psi Corps, which may happen at a young age, ingestion of sleeper drugs that repress their abilities, or imprisonment. While Psi Corps allows a few particularly potent telepaths to rise to power and influence, most are employed as commercial or political telepaths. Their primary role is to ensure honesty and fairness in commercial and diplomatic negotiations. On occasion, they may also scan criminals or help perform mind wipes: the process of destroying a criminal's personality and replacing it with another. The latter roles prove damaging for telepaths who must reach into the minds of the dying, mentally ill, or psychopathic, sharing their feelings and traumas. Earth law forbids telepaths from performing scans without the consent of the person scanned or orders from proper authorities. Telepaths must wear gloves and guard against accidental readings. They must also signal their consent to these rules by wearing a Psi Corps insignia on their chests. Most telepaths remain loyal to Psi Corps because that organization has raised them and protected them against the hostility of normals. Some telepaths, like Ivanova's mother, hide their abilities or go underground to escape Psi Corps. Others, like Lyta Alexander, have formed a resistance movement aimed at destroying Psi Corps and founding their own home world.

For the first season and a half, *Babylon 5* suggests that Ivanova's hostility toward Psi Corps results from their role in her mother's death. Her mother had hidden her abilities for years until discovery forced her to take sleeper drugs. As Ivanova explains to Winters:

> They caught up with my mother on her thirty-fifth birthday. She didn't want to join the Corps, didn't want to go to prison, so they gave her the treatment. For ten years, a man in a grey suit came to the door every week, and he gave her the injections. They were strong—terribly strong. Every day, we just watched her drift further and further away from us. The light in her eyes just went out, bit by bit. And when we thought she could go no further, she took her own life.[24]

Imagining the New Military of the 1990s in Babylon 5's Future Wars 203

Ivanova's description of the effects of her mother's forced suppression of her telepathy mirrors critiques of so-called reparative therapy, which claim that the forced suppression of homosexual desire alters a person's identity by altering and negating his capacity for intimacy. As the leader of a telepath resistance movement explains to Sheridan: "Do you know what a telepath has to do in order to avoid picking up stray thought? ... We have to kick down our natural abilities, run rhythms and little thoughts through our head, round and round."[25] Such self-policing, narcotization, and submission to the will of Psi Corps undermine telepaths' capacity for meaningful human relationships and self-development. These descriptions hint at the conflict in a liberal society when the rights of one group are negated to protect the rights of another. This conflict, I will argue, comes to fruition in season five in the story-arc of Lyta Alexander.

While the Psi Corps presents a benevolent face, in reality it controls the economic, social, and family choices of telepaths. It has its own police powers and conducts secret experiments on its members in a never-ending quest to increase their powers. The Psi Corps forces telepaths to surrender their individual will to the goals of the organization, creating soldiers who lack the honor of those who fight for a just cause; rather, they fight to protect the power of an individual or organization. When a Psi Corps officer shares with Ivanova his loss of a military career after discovering his telepathic talents, she dismisses him, noting that his choices violate her rights: "Mr. Gray, I'm grateful the Psi Corps gives you purpose in life, but when that purpose includes scanning my mind to prove my loyalty, it's not only an invasion of my privacy, but my honor. As for fear, if you enter my mind for any reason, I will twist your head off and use it for a chamber pot."[26] As long as Winters and other telepaths participate in Psi Corps, Ivanova views them as damaged individuals incapable of the independence necessary for democratic citizenship; thus, they constitute a threat to the integrity of others:

IVANOVA: What happened [to my mother] back then is not your fault. But it's part of what you are. And yet, you're as much of a victim as my mother.
WINTERS: I don't feel like a victim.
IVANOVA: No. And so far, I cannot tell if that is good or bad.[27]

Yet, her antipathy to Winters hides Ivanova's own secret, her latent telepathy, and she fears that the revelation of that secret will destroy her career and friendships. While her telepathic abilities are low, "barely a P1," she is still subject to laws that would require her to either take sleeper drugs or join the Psi Corps. She lives in constant fear of discovery and the prospect of making the same choices as her mother or Winters. Her struggles with keeping this secret, however, draw her closer to Winters, who is reconsidering her own relationship with the Psi Corps and the family relationships it represents.

204 *Kathleen Kennedy*

As Winters learns of Psi Corps secret experiments on telepaths, forced marriages, and other violations of telepaths' rights, she begins to doubt the morality of her participation in Psi Corps. This doubt creates an identity crisis for Winters because she was literally raised by the Psi Corps from the age of five. To her, the loyalty statement of the Psi Corps—"the corps is mother [and] the corps is father"—is to be taken literally. As Winters appears to cut ties with the Psi Corps, she turns to Ivanova for validation, support, and intimacy. Ivanova, in turn, accepts her gesture of friendship and eventually falls in love with her.

In "Divided Loyalties," Winters and Ivanova become lovers. Not coincidentally, the relationship begins just as Ivanova must confront the impact of her secret on the conspiracy of light. Rogue telepath Alexander arrives on Babylon 5 with information of a traitor among them. Because discovering the traitor involves sending a code into the minds of the command staff, uncovering the traitor threatens to also reveal Ivanova's secret. "After you tell someone you've been lying to them for years, maybe even put them in jeopardy, how are you supposed to look that person in the eyes again?" Ivanova asks Winters, who is aware that Ivanova is struggling with a secret but does not yet know that she is a latent telepath.[28] Winters promises Ivanova her complete trust, and the two spend the night together.

Faced with the prospect of being scanned and forever losing the trust of her colleagues, Ivanova confesses her secret to Sheridan:

IVANOVA: I am sorry. I thought I was ready for this. ... I'm a latent telepath.
SHERIDAN: Susan why didn't you tell me this before. I thought we could trust each other.
IVANOVA: It's got nothing to do with trust. I've spent my entire life hiding this, Captain. It's not something you just change overnight. It's hard enough telling you this now.
SHERIDAN: You're right. I'm sorry.
IVANOVA: For as long as I can remember, my mother drilled three words into my head—"tell no one." She taught me how to fool the tests. ... Always staying one step ahead of the Psi Corps. I'm probably not even a P1. I've never been able to read anyone except my mother. I can pick up on feelings sometimes. I can block a casual scan, and I know instantly if someone is doing it. But nothing more. But that's enough for the Psi Corps to pull you in. ... Sometimes I don't even know who I am anymore.[29]

Because it occurs simultaneously with her relationship with Winters, Ivanova's revelation invokes the LGB coming-out narrative. Her confession underlies the importance of the speech act in the construction of identity. Ivanova's "coming out" speech is less a confession of difference than an attempt at normalization. She frames her telepathy as a private concern between herself and her mother and assures the Captain that her powers do not jeopardize the privacy of others because, unlike other telepaths, she can easily control

Imagining the New Military of the 1990s in Babylon 5's *Future Wars* 205

her impulses. For this reason, she is more aligned with normals than with telepaths.

What differentiates Ivanova from normals is less her latent telepathy than her need to keep a secret. It is that need, created by the unjust policies of the Psi Corps, that shapes her interactions with normals, and it is the need for secrecy that distinguishes her from her colleagues. The revelation of her secret does not free Ivanova; rather, it increases her dependence on Sheridan. Despite his promise of protection, his knowledge of her secret gives him the power to take away her freedom and career. It is only his good will and personal loyalty that stand between Psi Corps and her. Her secret further subjects Ivanova to his will, potentially dividing her loyalties between the cause and the person.

Thus, it is possible to read Ivanova's dilemma as a critique of DADT and its requirement that LGB people keep their identities secret. In both the real and fictional military units, it is the necessity of the secret, rather than its content, that threatens the coherence of the group. As with LGB soldiers, the blanket laws regulating telepaths do not distinguish between the character and behavior of the individual and that person's orientation. Yet, *Babylon 5* also suggests that Ivanova's difference opens her to seduction and betrayal as is demonstrated by her doomed relationship with Winters. The danger is especially pronounced because of the queerness of sex between telepaths. "Do you know what it's like when telepaths make love, Commander?" Winter asks Sinclair in an earlier episode. "You drop every defense, and it's all mirrors: reflecting each other's feelings deeper and deeper—until, somewhere along the line, your souls mix."[30] Sex between telepaths has the potential to completely dissolve the boundaries between individual lovers, which is part of a Western romantic ideal, but one that is ascribed to the female subject position. Laws of coverture have historically protected the autonomy of the male subject. Sex between telepaths is queer because it threatens that autonomy, placing both parties in a female subject position, thus undermining the hegemony and authority of the male subject. *Babylon 5* reinforces this point when a former lover is able to gift Winters with his telekinetic powers because of the unique intimacy they established as lovers.[31] Ivanova and Winters' actual lesbian relationship is only the visible sign of this more radical queering.

By conflating bisexuality, telepathy, and betrayal, *Babylon 5* suggests a negative correlation between queer sex and the moral character of military personnel. Unknown even to Winters, she is the victim of a Psi Corps experiment that overrides her personality, turning her into a latent spy for that organization. It is Psi Corps that controls her desire and seduction of Ivanova, but Ivanova's own weakness that causes her to believe Winters' lies. Winters makes this connection explicit when she reveals to Ivanova the reason for their relationship: "Always the romantic. The program is complete. The Talia you knew no longer exists. There's just me. ... And you believed everything she said to you, all the things you wanted to hear, all the words I whispered

206 *Kathleen Kennedy*

in her thoughts while she lay sleeping, the words that would get her closer to you ... and to what you knew. You should see the look on your face ... my good ... and dear friend Susan."[32] Winters reminds Ivanova that it was her need for intimacy and her queer desire that made her vulnerable to seduction. Furthermore, because Winters' betrayal leads Ivanova to reject Marcus, her queer desire also preempts the future heterosexual relationship that might have led to Ivanova's happiness. Queer desire threatens both the coherency of the military unit and the promise of a normal family life. While *Babylon 5* opens the door to LGB people's equal participation in the military, then, it also reminds us of the dangers of queer desire and the dependency it creates.

"I Am an Orphan"

Babylon 5 further exploits these fears by linking telepaths' growing desire for independence with Middle Eastern politics through the story line of Lyta Alexander. If the Psi Corps is both mother and father, Alexander, as she explains to the head of Psi Corps, is "an orphan."[33] As an orphaned or homeless telepath, Alexander comes to occupy the subject position held by the Middle Eastern terrorist after the First Gulf War. As with queers and terrorists, Alexander's danger lies in her very nature and the ability of that nature to corrupt and control normals. Furthermore, Alexander and other telepaths are literally weapons, created by the Vorlons, one of the original species of the Universe, to resist the Shadows, another elder population. Afraid that their "little weapons," as Alexander characterizes most telepaths, would not be enough to defeat the resurgent Shadows, the Vorlons enhanced Alexander's powers to create a doomsday device. As a weapon with a will of its own, Alexander's loyalties to those like her and increasing willingness to direct violence against Sheridan's people, create an unresolvable conflict between herself and normals. That conflict, I argue, mirrors those between first- and third-world forces that continue to shape the post-Gulf War landscape.

Caught between an oppressive organization that eliminates their freedom in the name of protecting them, and the equally dangerous normals who distrust and often despise them, some telepaths like Alexander go rogue. Alexander's activities against Psi Corps initially lead her to side with the "conspiracy of light." Along with passing on intelligence about Psi Corps operations, she helps Sheridan defeat a Shadow ship. When Sheridan disappears on a planet controlled by the Shadows, Alexander volunteers to go to the planet to locate him. She is part of the party that rescues Sheridan from Clarke's forces and aids him in the climactic battle of the Civil War. Despite this cooperation, the command staff treats Alexander as a pariah. By the fifth season, Alexander is so disillusioned with normals that she charges hefty fees to help them in tasks she had previously done out of principle. She concludes that telepaths and normals are incompatible and fights not only to destroy Psi Corps but also for an independent homeland for telepaths. To this

Imagining the New Military of the 1990s in Babylon 5's *Future Wars* 207

end, she strikes a deal with the ambassador of Narn to funnel money and weapons to those telepaths revolting against the Psi Corps, which eventually leads to her arrest and a final confrontation with Lochley and Sheridan.

Alexander's journey toward violent resistance follows a path forged by revolutionary movements that have sought independent homelands after supporting Western powers in conflicts against common enemies, only to be disappointed when former allies or new governments maintain existing power structures or thwart those movements. She initially identifies with Sheridan, believing that his opposition to tyrannical organizations is similar to her own cause against Psi Corps' exploitation of telepaths. As Sheridan waivers in his support of telepath's independence from Psi Corps, Alexander comes to identify with Byron (Robin Atkins Downes), a pacifist leader who argues that telepaths should accept their unique identities and not attempt to control their talents as required by normals. Significantly, Alexander fully embraces a separatist identity through an act of queer sex with Byron, correlating her terrorist activities and separatist philosophies with her queerness.[34] When he dies for the cause, an angry but more self-confident Alexander searches for new allies and begins funneling weapons to rogue telepaths fighting Psi Corps.

As an independent and queer actor in possession of a weapon of mass destruction, Alexander is too powerful to coexist with normals. Due to her enhancements by the Vorlons, Alexander is capable of controlling the will of large groups and forcing them to act as she sees fit. She demonstrates her power by taking over the minds of an entire cafeteria when threatened with arrest by Lochley. Alexander's ability to override the will of normals, as well as to challenge the monopoly of violence and normality held by the state, threatens the basic premise of a liberal society in which the individual's will and ability to give meaningful consent governs relationships. In this respect, Alexander comes to occupy the subject position of the imagined queer terrorist, who destroys civilization by attacking the will of the most vulnerable and weak members of society and seducing them into her or his cause.

Just like American policy makers since the first Gulf War, the command staff is torn between supporting organizations and regimes that promise order by suspending the rights of certain populations and those, in a post-colonial world, who resist that oppression but seek to establish regimes that challenge the hegemony of Western normative structures, including the concept of equal rights for women and LGBT people.[35] Alexander's power poses problems for Sheridan, whose commitment to constitutional principles puts him in opposition to Psi Corps and prevents him from summarily executing Alexander despite her ability to destroy them all. Bound by those principles and aware that Alexander's terrorism is partly the result of his own policies, Sheridan chooses to exile rather than to kill her. While his actions are humane and appropriate, given the debt he owes Alexander and the fairness of her demand for a homeland for telepaths, by allowing her to live he only forestalls the inevitable conflict. It is left to the career

208   *Kathleen Kennedy*

military woman to suggest the action that the now civilian president cannot undertake: "I may hate myself for saying this," Lochley tells Sheridan, "but I almost wish you had blown her head off."[36] Lochley's realist sentiments prove prophetic when Alexander and the normals later go to war.

As the boundaries among soldiers, freedom fighters, and terrorists became blurred in the post-Gulf War world, *Babylon 5* reassured its audience that soldiers who accept the premise of a liberal military structure remain the truest heroes of republican government. They are the most unambiguously loyal to each other and the cause of democracy, and they have the will to do what is necessary to protect civilian populations from the messy decisions of wartime. Civilians are too easily fooled and manipulated by fascist regimes, such as those of President Clark and the Psi Corps, or by sentiment that masquerades as honor. For example, when INS, the news station in *Babylon 5*, becomes the propaganda machine of the Clark administration, Ivanova, a good soldier, serves as the voice of resistance by hosting an alternative news program dedicated to the truth. And while Sheridan's rebellion saves democracy, the show is clear that even those who fought for Earth Force were doing their duty. Lochley delivers a patriotic speech when critiqued for her decision to remain loyal during the Civil War. The applause she receives indicates that those at fault for the conflict were not the soldiers who fought on either side but the civilian leaders and bureaucrats who allowed democracy to be undermined. *Babylon 5* reinforces ideas that military men and women properly performing their duty, even if they occasionally make mistakes, are our best bulwark against tyranny. Because she is a civilian and freedom fighter, rather than a member of a formal military organization, Alexander lacks the credibility that soldiers have accrued, even if her cause and willingness to sacrifice mirrors their own. Unless she can assimilate into the liberal structures those soldiers defend, Alexander remains an orphan now exiled outside the boundaries of human space.

Conclusion

Babylon 5 brought into our living rooms a series of wars in which technological innovation made the physical bodies of soldiers less important than their embodiment of core military values. In this world, women and lesbian, gay, and bisexual people could embody the same heroic self-sacrifice as heterosexual men but only if they assimilated into the core structures of a liberal military establishment. In its promise of a more egalitarian future, however, *Babylon 5* signaled the core threats to Western values as those posed by gender and sexual queerness. Like the Middle Eastern terrorist or the queer body ravaged by AIDS, telepaths are literally doomsday weapons incapable of liberal democracy. *Babylon 5* also suggests that too much difference may be as dangerous to our future as not enough.

But this conclusion may be too hard on *Babylon 5*. In their analysis of women's roles in *Babylon 5*, Ney and Scoig-Lazaro argue that the show's

Imagining the New Military of the 1990s in Babylon 5's *Future Wars*   209

efforts to portray women are both hopeful and flawed. In particular, they argue that its presentations of independent and competent women open a dialogue "through which feminist thought and our patriarchal past can ultimately reach a compromise on the nature of gender, power, agency and identity."[37] In part because the writers and actors of *Babylon 5* intended to present a modern and diverse fighting force and to portray the ethical dilemmas faced by that fighting force as complex, *Babylon 5* has generated a conversation about those aspects of modern society and global relations that most threaten humanity's freedom. Those discussions continue on websites, discussion boards, and the occasional academic journal. As do Ney and Scoig-Lagaro, I argue that *Babylon 5's* ability to bring such discussions into our living room is its most important and hopeful legacy.

Notes

1. John Huntington, "Future Wars," *Science Fiction Studies* 40 (2013): 368–72, 368.
2. Linda Bird Francke, "Ground Zero," 648. Reprinted in *Women's America: Refocusing the Past*, 6th Edition, ed. Linda Kerber (New York: Oxford, 2003).
3. Ibid., 654.
4. Ibid., 654.
5. Ibid., 655.
6. Ibid., 654.
7. David Evans, "Women Have No Place in Military Combat," *The Daily Press*, January 21, 1990, http://articles.dailypress.com/1990-01-21/news/9001180208_1_place-in-military-combat-linda-bray-non-combat.
8. Franke, "Ground Zero," 648–55.
9. The literature on this topic is vast, see for example, Allen Bérubé, *Coming out under Fire: The History of Gay Men and Women in World War II* (Chapel Hill, University of North Carolina Press, 1990); K. A. Cuordileone, *Manhood and American Political Culture in the Cold War* (New York: Routledge, 2004); and David K. Johnson, *The Lavender Scare: The Cold War Persecution of Gays in Lesbians in the Federal Government* (Chicago: University of Chicago Press, 2004).
10. Arthur A. Woodruff, et al., "Gays in the Military: What about Morality, Ethics, Character and Honor," *Dickerson Law Review* (1995): 331–56, 356.
11. Tim Dunkin, "The Military Should Not Be Gay 'Positive-Liberty,'" *Renew America*, last modified December 30, 2010, http://www.renewamerica.com/columns/dunkin/101230.
12. See also, "H. Jefferson Powell to Associate Attorney General re: Policy Regarding Homosexuals in the Military," June 29, 1993, Clinton Presidential Library #655.
13. James F. Iaccino, "*Babylon 5's* Blueprint for the Archetypical Heroes of Commander Jeffrey Sinclair and Captain John Sheridan with Ambassador Delenn," *Journal of Popular Culture* 34, no. 4 (Spring 2001): 109–21.
14. See, for example, Elyce Rae Helford, ed., *Fantasy Girls: Gender in the New Universe of Science Fiction and Fantasy Television* (New York: Rowman and Littlefield Publishers, 2000); and Frances Early and Kathleen Kennedy, eds., *Athena's Daughters: Television's New Woman Warriors* (Syracuse: Syracuse University Press, 2003).

15. Sharon Ney and Elaine M. Scoig-Lazaro, "The Construction of the Feminine in Babylon 5," in *Fantasy Girls: Gender in the New Universe of Science Fiction and Fantasy Television*, ed. Elyce Rae Helford (New York, Boston: Rowman and Littlefield Publishers, 2000), 223–44, 239.
16. J. Michael Straczynski, "Matters of Honor," season 3, episode 1, *Babylon 5*, aired November 3, 1995, (Burbank, CA: Warner Brothers Home Video, 2009). All future references will be to this DVD set.
17. *Babylon 5*, "A Voice in the Wilderness, Part I," season 1, episode 18, aired July 27, 1994.
18. *Babylon 5,* "Between the Darkness and Light," season 4, episode 19, aired October 6, 1997.
19. *Babylon 5*, "Into the Fire," season 4, episode 6, aired February 3, 1997.
20. Ney and Scoig-Lazaro, "Feminine Identity in Babylon 5," 225–31.
21. Claudia Christian, quoted in Jane Killick, *Babylon 5: The Wheel of Fire* (New York: The Ballantine Company, 1999), 178.
22. Ibid.
23. J. Michael Straczynski, "Divided Loyalties," *The Lurker's Guide to Babylon 5*, accessed July 2, 2015. http://www.midwinter.com/lurk/countries/master/guide/041.html.
24. *Babylon 5*, "Midnight on the Firing Line," season 1, episode 1, aired January 14, 1994.
25. *Babylon 5*, "The Paragon of Animals," season 5, episode 3, aired February 4, 1998.
26. *Babylon 5*, "Eyes," season 1, episode 16, aired July 13, 1994.
27. *Babylon 5*, "Midnight on the Firing Line."
28. *Babylon 5*, "Divided Loyalties," season 2, episode 19, aired October 11, 1995.
29. Ibid.
30. *Babylon 5*, "Mind War," season 1, episode 6, aired March 2, 1994.
31. Ibid.
32. *Babylon 5*, "Divided Loyalties."
33. *Babylon 5*, "Epiphanies," season 4, episode 7, aired February 10, 1997.
34. Ney and Scoig-Lazaro, "Feminine Identity in *Babylon 5*," 231–36.
35. For a discussion of this problem, see Jasbir K. Puar, *Terrorist Assemblages: Homonationalism in Queer Times* (Durham, NC: Duke University Press, 2007).
36. *Babylon 5*, "Wheel of Fire," season 5, episode 19, aired November 4, 1998.
37. Ney and Scoig-Lazaro, "Feminine Identity in Babylon 5," 244.

13 *JAG*, Melodrama and Militarism

Stacy Takacs

The TV series *JAG* (NBC, 1995–1996; CBS, 1997–2005) focuses on the lives and adventures of US Naval and Marine Corps lawyers attached to the Judge Advocate General's Office, which investigates, prosecutes, and defends individuals charged with crimes under the Uniform Code of Military Justice. Helmed by journeyman producer Donald Bellisario, an ex-Marine who previously scripted series like *Baa Baa Black Sheep* (NBC, 1976–1978), *Magnum, P.I.* (CBS, 1980–1988), and *Air Wolf* (CBS, 1984–1986), the show was pitched as a cross between the action film *Top Gun* (1986) and the courtroom drama *A Few Good Men* (1992). Based on the cinema-quality, two-hour pilot ("A New Life"), NBC picked the series up for its 1995–1996 schedule on the condition that Bellisario recast the female lead for greater sex appeal and increase the action quotient.[1] Thus, season one focuses mostly on the virile exploits of Lieutenant Harmon "Harm" Rabb, Jr. (David James Elliott), a hunky pilot-turned-lawyer who brawls his way through most of his legal cases. Little attention is paid to developing the characters or their relationships, and virtually no attention is paid to the intricacies of the legal system. In the post-Tailhook, post-Anita Hill era,[2] this "guns, guts, and girls" formula proved a ratings loser, and NBC abruptly canceled the series.[3] This set off a bidding war between CBS and ABC, both of whom were eager to target "heartland" viewers and saw the series as a potential attractor.[4] CBS secured the series, gave Bellisario greater control over the show's development, and the rest is history.

Bellisario immediately recast the female lead, hiring Catherine Bell to play Marine Corps Major Sarah "Mac" MacKenzie—a woman with the backbone and service credentials to stand up to Harm's machismo, but whose statuesque figure and emotional vulnerability preempt any potential concerns about her femininity. Harm and Mac quickly become an item, and their on-again-off-again romance proves to be an enduring— and endearing—narrative runner. With the character-building, relationship elements restored, *JAG* generated a larger fan following and became something of a cult hit among older viewers (35+), Midwesterners, and military families. The show went on to become the longest running military drama in television history (to that point) and to spawn a billion dollar television franchise.[5] The *JAG* spin-off, *NCIS* (CBS, 2003-present), which

212 *Stacy Takacs*

centers on the military and civilian investigators attached to the Naval Criminal Investigative Service, has since surpassed *JAG* as the longest running military drama and fostered two additional spin-offs, *NCIS: Los Angeles* (CBS, 2009-present) and *NCIS: New Orleans* (CBS, 2014-present). In 2013, *NCIS* became the world's most watched TV drama with an average global viewership of 57.6 million.[6]

Like most conventionally successful broadcast series, *JAG* and its spin-offs have been largely neglected by television critics and scholars, who prefer to focus on innovative or "edgy" programming. Broadcast series that appeal to heartland viewers and values—series like *JAG* that promote a plain-spoken ethos of duty, honor, and respect for authority—are particularly disdained by critics, who address them only as examples of the aesthetic poverty of network television. Yet, the popularity and fan devotion *JAG* was able to sustain over 10 years begs for further analysis.[7] What factors—historical, institutional, social, cultural—account for this popularity, and, given this popularity, what ideological impact might a show like *JAG* have had on society? How, in particular, might it have contributed to a particular way of seeing, feeling, and thinking about topics like war and militarism?

As I have argued elsewhere, *JAG*'s producers worked closely with the Navy and Marine Corps to polish their depictions of military life, leading to a pro-military slant within the series.[8] Yet, *JAG*'s success is only partially explained by the authenticity, realism, or jingoism of its stories. The key to its success was the program's particular deployment of melodrama. *JAG* made audiences *feel* for the men and women who serve in uniform and successfully equated war and militarism with moral order. I am interested in how it achieved this equation.

JAG and Genre: A Conventional Look at War and Militarism

At first glance, *JAG* may seem more of a legal drama than a military series due to its courtroom setting and emphasis on crime, detection, and the intricacies of the law and legal work. However, it is a legal series set within the larger institutional context of the US military, and like most war films, it focuses as much on the "motivations, attitudes, and behavior of individuals preparing for or immersed in combat" as it does on legal matters.[9] Indeed, *JAG* often focuses *more* on military settings and combat or combat-like operations than on issues of crime and the law. Unlike its forebear, *Court Martial* (ABC, 1966–1967), which was set exclusively in the courtroom, *JAG*'s lawyers are dispatched to investigate cases on military bases and naval vessels located all around the world, and it regularly fetishizes military hardware, tactics, and discipline. *JAG*'s image of the military and its operations is both literally and figuratively constructed from the stuff of Hollywood war cinema. Savvy viewers can spot scenes from *Top Gun, The Hunt for Red October* (1990), and *Sands of Iwo Jima* (1949), among others, used as a substitute for actual combat operations. More importantly, the series recycles many of the formal and narrative conventions of the classic Hollywood war film.

For example, like the World War II combat film, *JAG* centers on the dynamic interaction of a warrior-hero, a group of mixed types surrounding him, and an objective they must attain.[10] The objective is only occasionally a military objective in *JAG*, but it is always a symbolic objective of strategic importance: to discover the truth about the military, its actors, and its actions. The *JAG* lawyers do battle with liars and the lies they tell, both within the parameters of the specific case and, more generally, with regard to the military and its people. Thus, while Harm is a fighter pilot and frequently participates in actual combat pursuits, even when he is not so engaged, he and his team are involved in metaphorical combat against the forces in civil society that seek to destroy the military. The suspects in *JAG* episodes are usually military officers and enlisted men and women, but the true villains of the series are the politicians, journalists, contractors, and businessmen who attempt to interfere with the military's smooth operations. The objective is to expose their tactics and destroy the threat. The voiceover prologue that introduced the series from years two through three makes the combat metaphor explicit:

> Following in his father's footsteps as a Naval aviator, Lieutenant Commander Harmon Rabb, Jr. suffered a crash while landing his Tomcat on a storm-tossed carrier at sea. Diagnosed with night blindness, Harm transferred to the Navy's Judge Advocate General Corps, which investigates, defends, and prosecutes the law of the sea. There with fellow JAG lawyer, Major Sarah MacKenzie, *he now fights in and out of the courtroom with the same tenacity that made him a top gun in the air* (emphasis mine).

While *JAG* may not *be* a World War II combat film, then, it certainly relies on the tropes of that (sub)genre to connect with its audience.[11]

In addition to mixing fictionalized combat with documentary footage of actual operations and using real life military incidents and personnel to shape its narratives, *JAG* includes most of the narrative elements film historian Jeanine Basinger defines as central to the WWII combat film: combat, death, enemy deception, outnumbered heroes, nature as the enemy (Harm and his partners are frequently abandoned in the wilderness and forced to survive), humor among heroes (a hallmark of a Bellisario production), a roll call at the end (the credits are overlaid on freeze frames of Harm and the other protagonists), the need to maintain equipment (a frequent plot driver), talk of loved ones (albeit not always wives and mothers), discussion of why we fight (constantly), and a big combat finale (at the end of every episode there is either a physical showdown or a courtroom conflagration). Bellisario and company even produced several special World War II-themed episodes in an attempt to connect directly with that tradition. "Port Chicago," for example, focused on the events leading to the explosion at the Port Chicago munitions depot in July 1944; Mac and Harm work to clear the African-American workers blamed for the incident of the charge of mutiny.[12] "Each of Us Angels" tells the tale of the nurses who tended the wounded at the Battle of Iwo Jima (Figure 13.1). A reenactment of films like *So Proudly We Hail* (1943) and *Cry Havoc* (1943), the episode features the cynical yet warm-hearted veteran nurse (played by Mac/Bell), the naïve recruit who must prove her mettle (Zoe McLellan, who also played Petty Officer Jennifer Coates), and the equation of romance with death (for Mac/Bell's character, who falls for a young seamen played by Harm/Elliott).

Figure 13.1 JAG patterned itself after the classic WWII combat film and often featured episodes commemorating those films, as well as the war. Actual footage of the Battle of Iwo Jima provides the backdrop for romance. From "Each of Us Angels"

It also ends with the same moral lesson as most WWII combat films: the best way to honor those who died is to live well. In fact, the episode cribs the frame story from Steven Spielberg's WWII epic *Saving Private Ryan*. An elderly WWII veteran tells the story of this brave-but-doomed nurse to a stranger he meets in Arlington National Cemetery; he ends by admonishing her "never to take a single moment for granted."[13]

One key difference between *JAG* and other combat films is the make-up of the combat team. In WWII films, the team is all-male and comprised of individuals from different races, ethnicities, and walks of life. This mixture is designed to prove that American values like liberty and equality are real and functional. Yet, it is usually the minority soldiers who are sacrificed in the cause and white men who remain standing in the end. Thus, the films indulge a sense of multicultural inclusion while ultimately affirming the centrality of whiteness to American society. *JAG* focuses more on gender integration than racial diversity, in part because it was a topical subject in the 1990s (about which, see chapter 12, this volume). "A New Life" was conceived in response to news reports of the first female pilots being deployed to battle carriers.[14] It told the story of a female pilot murdered by a jealous and resentful male service member. The JAG lawyers solved the crime, convicted the "bad apple," and restored faith in the Navy as an institution that neither discriminates nor condones discrimination against women. Just four years after the infamous Tailhook Scandal, "A New Life" promised that sexual harassment had no place in the new military and would be punished to the fullest extent of military law. Over the years, *JAG* included many competent women in its recurring cast and paired men and women on duty assignments with little friction.[15] Mac, in particular, is a highly capable individual with an unerring sense of justice, a dedication to truth, and the requisite training to kick butt with the boys (she is a martial arts devotee and a crack shot). She often spars with Harm in the courtroom, serving as the prosecutor to his defense attorney, and she gives as good as she gets. Bellisario and company treat Mac not as an appendage or a symbol but as a three-dimensional character. Like Harm, she has a personality, a colorful past, a sense of humor, and career ambitions, which she is not forced to renounce in favor of domesticity. The final episode ends with Harm proposing marriage and the two flipping a coin to determine who will resign his or her commission to join the other on a new assignment (Figure 13.2). The outcome is famously unresolved (although the producers purportedly pitched a *JAG* spinoff starring Mac/Bell).[16]

JAG also borrows the Vietnam War film's obsession with "daddy issues." As Lynda Boose notes, these films are often about generational abandonment or betrayal: "In the fictions of the filmmakers of the Vietnam generation the father-son rupture gets repeatedly narrated, always from the consciousness of the son. Figures of authoritative, compassionate leadership like John Wayne's Sergeant Stryker in *The Sands of Iwo Jima* are simply gone, their absence narrated into post-Vietnam movies as either the father's betrayal of the son or the son's quest to revalidate the father or

216   *Stacy Takacs*

both."[17] This has produced two types of Vietnam films: those, like *Platoon* (1986) and *Full Metal Jacket* (1987), that seem to blame the loss in Vietnam on the patriarchy—both the male military leaders who orchestrated the war and the hard, hyper-masculine models of heroism that the military life extols—and those, like *Top Gun*, that seek to redeem the manhood of fathers betrayed by the generals and the "feminized" culture of the Vietnam era. The aim of the sons in these films is to reclaim their patrimony as heroes, indeed to reestablish the equation between heroism and masculinity. Because *JAG* is modeled on *Top Gun*, it should surprise no one that Harm's "daddy issues" revolve around the project of reclamation, rather than critique. He is obsessed with finding his missing father, a pilot shot down over North Vietnam in 1969 and listed as Missing in Action. In episodes like "The Prisoner" (season 1, episode 20), "Ghost Ship" (season 3, episode 1), "King of the Fleas" (season 3, episode 5), "To Russia With Love" (season 3, episode 24), "Gypsy Eyes" (season 4, episode 1), and "Ghosts of Christmas Past" (season 5, episode 11) Harm is haunted by memories of the lost father and searches for clues to his whereabouts. At first, the goal is literally to redeem the father—to find and free the man, who Harm believes is still being held in captivity. Eventually, however, the quest becomes articulated to Harm's own mental and emotional health: He needs to find his father to become whole. When he does locate Harm, Sr., the man is long dead, but we discover that he refused to "break" under Soviet interrogation, escaped from prison, and died defending the honor of a local gypsy woman, who was being raped by Soviet soldiers. This story proves the father's mettle and establishes him as a heroic role model of whom Harm, Jr., and the audience can both be proud. In that way, it also redeems the military by casting it as an institution that "builds men" rather than destroys them.

Bellisario has described the series as a legal procedural set in the military, but its narrative structure, visual style, and use of sound, all clearly reference war-film conventions. Bellisario also admits his intention was to "depict the men and women of the US military as upholding the highest values of honor, commitment, and education."[18] Virtually transporting viewers to US military installations and battle groups around the world, the program made the need for these installations appear self-evident. Its legal premises also promoted a romanticized conception of the military as a moral institution— indeed, the last bastion of morality in a society sliding toward hedonism (as the discourse of the 1990s "culture wars" would have it). In that sense, it provided invaluable public relations for the Department of Defense. By keeping the military before the public's eye, the program implicitly argued for its continued necessity in a post-Cold War, pre-War on Terror world.

JAG and the War on Terror

Although the Department of Defense was reluctant to help the producers during the first season of the series, *JAG* eventually proved itself sufficiently pro-military to warrant official support. In addition to its civilian military advisor, Matt Sigloch, who was charged with ensuring the accuracy of the uniforms, haircuts, and salutes, *JAG* received material and script assistance from both the Navy and the Marine Corps liaisons' offices in Hollywood. This allowed the producers to enhance the authenticity of the series by shooting on Navy vessels and Marine Corps bases, using military personnel as extras in the show, and incorporating operational footage shot by the Navy and Marine Corps to enliven the action. For their part, these service branches used *JAG* to increase recruitment and help spread the "military message."[19]

As I've argued elsewhere, such cooperation increased in frequency and intensity after the September 11, 2001, terrorist attacks.[20] Bellisario used fictionalized stories of the War on Terror, often ripped from the headlines, to school the civilian audience in new military protocols and procedures. "The Mission" and "Friendly Fire," for example, focused on the rules of engagement and explained to audiences when it was ok to fire on suspected enemies (don't "exert caution beyond all reason," we are told).[21] Episodes like "First Casualty" and "Death at the Mosque" taught audiences to be skeptical of broadcast news coverage of the wars and, instead, to trust that the soldiers and their leaders know what they are doing.[22] "Camp Delta" defended the detention and interrogation tactics used at Camp Delta in Guantánamo Bay, Cuba, and "Tribunal" illustrated what the military tribunals proposed by the Bush administration to try enemy combatants might look like.[23] In the latter episode, the defendant is a high-ranking al Qaeda operative who is both unrepentant and obviously guilty. The standards of evidence in the tribunal are depicted as more rigorous than the standards used in civilian courts, and evidence obtained through waterboarding is excluded as "tainted." This fantasy construction served as propaganda for the Bush administration, which leaked details about the tribunal process to the show's producers in an effort to shape public opinion.[24] Finally, *JAG* interrogated the legality of the War in Iraq in an episode called "People v. SecNav," which placed the US Secretary of the Navy on trial for crimes against humanity when an Iraqi hospital was accidentally bombed by US forces.[25] Harm and Mac defend the secretary using what amounts to an exceptionalist argument for war. A Marine Corps Lieutenant and the Secretary both testify to atrocities committed by Saddam Hussein's regime and declare that the US had a "moral duty" to intervene. The judge is magically convinced by these appeals and finds the US not guilty of crimes against humanity, war crimes, and intentionally targeting non-combatants.

While *JAG* clearly offered support for the War on Terrorism, however, it did not offer its jingoism unalloyed. As expert dramatists, the producers knew they would have to accommodate a certain amount of conflict and debate. Every episode rehearses the counter-arguments before delivering a positive assessment of war and militarism. So, for example, Mac expresses outrage and disgust at the use of "harsh interrogation tactics" and

218 *Stacy Takacs*

actually calls them "torture" in both "Camp Delta" and "Tribunal" (she even litigates the question in "Touchdown"). The prosecuting attorneys in "People v. SecNav" call into question the legitimacy of the Bush doctrine of preemptive war and remind viewers of the importance of imminence and proportionality to the concept of "self-defense." They also challenge the morality of treating war prisoners as "enemy combatants," outside the normal jurisdiction of the law. A shipboard JAG officer in "First Casualty" defends a narrow interpretation of the rules of engagement, and "Camp Delta" reveals that CIA contractors, not soldiers, are to blame for the abuse at the prison (a story that the 2014 release of the Senate Intelligence report on CIA interrogation tactics seems to have confirmed).[26] Most interestingly, in "Fighting Words," a Marine Corps General and conservative Christian is indicted for dereliction of duty for publicly demeaning Muslims and Islam.[27] The trial gives the General a chance to defend his religious beliefs but also schools the audience in some of the finer points of Islam. Mac strongly condemns the General's words, introduces him to the true meaning of "jihad" (not "holy war" but "to struggle or to strive"), and explains that Islam shares with Judeo-Christian religions a prohibition against suicide and the targeting of unarmed women and children. In such cases, *JAG* may have served as a useful "Trojan horse," slipping more sophisticated interpretations of political events to a public increasingly uninterested in entertaining multiple perspectives. It is certainly possible that some viewers identified with the debates and counter-arguments and chose to ignore the (usually) pro-military outcomes.[28]

JAG also exhibited a certain schizophrenia regarding the portrayal of conservative politicking on the program. True, it regularly integrated conservative themes and characters into its episodes—the list of conservative guest stars included Fox News darlings Oliver North, Montel Williams, and Bill O'Reilly—but it also occasionally criticized conservative politicians and causes. In "Heart of Darkness," for example, a Marine Corps Captain goes AWOL from Iraq in order to pursue Osama Bin Laden in Afghanistan.[29] The episode implies that the Bush administration's pursuit of war in Iraq was a distraction that prevented the US from exacting justice for those killed on 9/11. In its early days, the series also featured running arcs about the meddling actions of two ultra-conservative "patriots": Lane Black (Vaughn Armstrong), a defense contractor who wants women and minorities out of the military, and Percival Bertram (Barry Corbin), a rightwing businessman who funnels money to terrorist groups in an effort to provoke US retaliation. Both gentlemen believe President Clinton's "weak" foreign policy has "emasculated" the nation, and they see a more aggressive military posture as the solution. Both are depicted as zealots, bigots, and villains, and their vigilante activity is explicitly condemned as such. Perhaps the most damning critique of conservative causes comes in the episode "Contemptuous Words."[30] When a letter to the editor maligning President Clinton is sent to the fictional *Washington Globe*, Harm is implicated, but it turns out that a politico with the Roanoke

Liberty Foundation, a conservative advocacy group, wrote the letter to make Harm a poster boy for the conservative cause. When the politico defends her actions, saying "organizations like this are trying to put the country back on the right track," Harm responds, "Then I'll stay on the wrong track, thank you." "But you don't even like [the President]," she replies, "It doesn't matter if I like him," Harm concludes, "He's my Commander in Chief." The next scene shows Harm being awarded a promotion. It is difficult not to see this as a cause-effect relationship and a lesson in proper civic discourse.

While Bellisario identifies as a Republican and a conservative, then, he is no ideologue. Rather, he is a pragmatist who knows that good drama requires a balancing of multiple perspectives. Although he has catered to the military in exchange for assistance, he has also inserted liberal arguments against war, domestic violence, gay bashing, and vigilantism into the series.[31] As he says, *JAG* is not *just* a "jingoistic military action-adventure show." It is a drama that tackles issues of relevance to the broader society and attempts to do so with "honesty and integrity."[32] The honesty and integrity of the series—its earnestness—is as much a draw for fans as the subject matter. Of course, honesty and integrity are relative terms related more to the style of narration than to a particular subject matter. So, to conclude, I want to consider how the aesthetic strategies used in the program, specifically its deployment of melodrama, may have shaped its ideological impact.

The Question of Melodrama

JAG's popularity was attributable to a mixture of good timing and topical, character-driven story telling. The growth of cable in the late 1980s fragmented and dispersed the mass audience, leaving advertisers increasingly unwilling to pay the high rates for advertising time demanded by the big four networks (ABC, CBS, NBC, and Fox). Most broadcasters responded by chasing smaller, "quality" audiences using specialized programming. For example, NBC's 1990s "Must-See TV" line-up of urbane comedies (*Seinfeld* [1989–1998], *Friends* [1994–2004], *Will & Grace* [1998–2006]) and sophisticated social dramas (*Homicide* [1993–1999], *ER* [1994–2009]) was designed for what TV historian Ron Becker calls the "slumpy" classes—socially liberal, urban-minded professionals.[33] Such well-heeled, highly educated, and discriminating viewers could be sold for higher rates than "ordinary" audiences could, so NBC tailored its programming to their tastes. The earnest *JAG* did not fit well within this plan. CBS took a different tack. It branded itself the last of the old-school broadcasters and sought to cater to the older viewers and "heartland" audiences abandoned by the other networks. *JAG*, with its emphasis on military life and respect for the values of honor, commitment, and dedication, fit right in with CBS's "old-school" branding strategy.[34]

James Poniewozik of *Time* magazine once described *JAG* as "a kind of *X-Files* for people who trust authority."[35] Although he meant that as a dig,

220 Stacy Takacs

there is a grain of truth to the comparison. Like *The X-Files* (Fox, 1993–2002), *JAG* was a fairly complex episodic serial that rewarded careful viewing. Each episode may have featured a new crime and a clear resolution, but the plots had a cumulative effect on the development of the characters and their relationships.[36] Indeed, the relationships drove the series and were radically open-ended. Each character was given a distinctive history, unique human foibles, and a clear growth-trajectory. Viewers watched them receive promotions (always rigorously registered on the "ribbon racks" on their uniforms), fall in and out of love, suffer triumphs and tragedies, and even die. *JAG*'s producers expected viewers to be familiar with the history of the series and to follow what one fan called its "interwoven plots, recurring actors, back references and subtle sub-plots."[37] In that sense, *JAG* was very much like *The X-Files* and other primetime serials in its scope and complexity. While the former was a critical darling, however, the latter was often maligned as "melodramatic." I want to end by briefly examining this charge: What do we mean by the term "melodrama," and why might it be useful for understanding the role of war fictions in the reproduction of a militaristic social order?

In the eighteenth century, the term melodrama described a type of play (*drama*) that was accompanied by music (*melos*). The definition has since been expanded to cover a certain type of content and style: stories about families and relationships, romance, and suffering rendered in an exaggerated visual and aural style. As film theorist Linda Williams notes, melodrama is often associated with "pounding music, pathetic victims, leering villains, florid acting, and the triumph of virtue in badly motivated happy endings."[38] *JAG* certainly fits many of these conventions. The action is structured around a nine-year romantic runner involving Harm and Mac, whose feelings are constantly discussed and then consciously suppressed (Figure 13.2).

Secondary characters like Bud Roberts (Patrick Labyorteaux) and Harriet Sims (Karri Turner) meet, fall in love, get married, have children, buy a house, experience the loss of a child and the loss of Bud's leg (in a combat mishap), and yet they go on living. They are all the consummate suffering subjects of melodrama: ordinary and beset by forces beyond their control, they persevere with "the grace of God" (as Harriet is wont to say). These themes, along with the serial structure of the program and the generally bad acting, make *JAG* feel a bit like a soap opera. The program also frequently uses entrapment and rescue scenarios to structure its action. Mac and Harm have each been stalked, kidnapped, held hostage, or otherwise beset by evil villains, both terrorists ("Code Blue," "Tiger, Tiger," "Embassy," "The Bridge at Kang So Ri," "Tangled Webb," "Persian Gulf") and simple sociopaths ("The Stalker," "People v. Mac," "Wilderness of Mirrors").[39] The producers do allow Harm and Mac to take turns rescuing each other, thereby defining heroism as compatible with femininity. However, they repeat the "victim-in-distress" trope so often that we might describe the show as "The Perils of Harm and Mac" (Figure 13.3).

Figure 13.2 JAG toyed with the romance between its two most prominent characters for 10 seasons before finally consummating the relationship. The series famously ended on a coin toss to determine which of the lovers would resign to facilitate the union. From "Fair Winds and Following Seas"

Convoluted plots and magical resolutions are also a hallmark of melodrama and a specialty of *JAG*. For example, "Death Watch" involves the murder of Harm's former lover and Mac look-a-like Diane Schonke (also played by Catherine Bell), a naval lieutenant stalked and killed while on shore leave.[40] The episode was originally slated to be the final episode of season one ("Skeleton Crew") but was never aired. For "Death Watch," Bellisario and company repurposed the footage and gave it a slightly different ending. Instead of implicating Harm in the murder (as in the original cliffhanger), "Death Watch" implicates the ship's Executive Officer (XO). Rather than apprehend the man, Harm grabs his gun and heads to the ship to exact a violent vengeance. Before he can shoot, however, Mac emerges

Figure 13.3 JAG frequently placed its protagonists in peril so that they could rescue one another. Mac (Catherine Bell) was rescuer as often as rescued. From "Gypsy Eyes"

from the fog. The XO believes she is Diane Schonke returned from the grave and backs over the lip of the pier. He is crushed between the pier and the hull of the ship, conveniently sparing Harm the need to strike the fatal blow. The twist allows viewers to choose their own ending. Those who want to believe that violent retribution constitutes justice are permitted to invest in the fantasy of Harm as avenging angel. Those who view law and order as sacrosanct get to retain Harm as a hero because justice was done without implicating him in illegal activity. In this case, the coincidental death obfuscates questions of moral duty, but plot twists are more often used in the series to clarify matters of guilt or innocence. In "Death at the Mosque," for instance, the JAG officer assigned to defend the Marine accused of killing an unarmed prisoner on live television discovers a suicide vest hidden under the floorboards of the mosque. This retroactively reclassifies the murder as self-defense, and the Marine is exonerated. Likewise, in "Camp Delta," the JAG lawyers conveniently uncover a videotape that implicates a CIA interrogator in the "harsh treatment" of prisoners at the Guantánamo Bay prison.

Certainly, *JAG* is guilty of stylistic excess and emotive story telling, and it is not improperly likened to a soap opera. To dismiss *JAG* for such excesses, however, is to fail to grapple with the appeal of melodrama. As Williams argues, the essence of melodrama is not its style but its thematics, specifically "the dramatic recognition of good and/or evil and in that recognition the utopian hope that justice might be done."[41] In a secular society, melodrama makes the moral order—and the processes of moral ordering—legible. By "offer[ing] the contrast between how things are and how they could be, or should be," it works to promote a sense of justice.[42] This sense of justice is never objectively just, however. It is a particular construction of morality, generated through the manipulation of the formal elements of the story, which, in turn, manipulate the emotions of the audience. Put simply, melodrama is about advocacy, about pressing for a certain understanding of what is right, true, and just.

As a type of "masculine melodrama," Hollywood war films vividly illustrate the way melodrama may be used to promote a narrow sense of the moral good.[43] As Guy Westwell explains, the conventional war film constructs a "moral universe ... in which the battle, or campaign, or wider war is posed as a struggle between elemental forces of good and evil."[44] Americans are generally identified with the good, and the "enemy," whoever it may be, is associated with evil (often using derogatory racial stereotypes). Like other forms of melodrama, the war film also personalizes abstract social forces (governments, military institutions, war itself) and aligns viewer sympathy with the subjects who suffer from the injustice of those forces, in this case the soldiers. The emotional trajectory of the film is from pity (for the suffering soldiers) to admiration (for their endurance or triumph). Even if the soldiers are killed, their devotion to duty, collaborative labor, and self-sacrifice ("it's about the man next to you") may arouse admiration and generate a sense of moral redemption. Arguably, it is this conversion of pity into admiration that explains both the appeal of the genre and the difficulty of creating a truly anti-war film.

As a series designed for the more intimate medium of television, *JAG* is simply more explicit about its melodramatic roots than most war stories are willing to be. It succeeded so well with audiences because it offered precisely the sort of moral elevation viewers seek from war stories. Every episode dramatized a conflict between good and evil, right and wrong, and rarely was the outcome of the struggle left to the imagination. With regard to the War on Terrorism, *JAG* presented military action as a necessary and just response to both the brutal victimization of US citizens on 9/11 and the ordinary suffering of peoples oppressed by Middle Eastern dictators, religious zealots, and terrorists. Fans certainly responded to the program's thematic of moral elevation. As one fan noted, "This program's main characters (men and women) display high ethics and don't sway under pressure. It shows respect for superiors and authority and portrays the military as an attractive, highly intelligent organization."[45] Even the Navy cites the program's "moral clarity" in its rationale for lending support: "We're fine with [seeing military personnel as villains] as long as the bad guys are caught and punished, and the institution of the Navy is not the bad guy."[46]

224   *Stacy Takacs*

Donald Bellisario was quite open about his intention to shape popular perspectives about the military and its operations: "People always forget the military until there's a crisis. That's why I've always been trying to show the military and tell stories about the military."[47] While *JAG*'s first priority may be to entertain viewers, then, its melodramatic presentation of war and militarism is also designed to persuade the public to continue supporting the troops, both emotionally and monetarily, in perpetuity. "The problem with seeing and thinking about war in this [melodramatic] way," as Westwell argues, "is that it blocks properly historical understanding of American strategy or political purposes."[48] In favoring personal stories of good and evil, suffering and triumph, *JAG* reassured viewers that they had nothing to worry about and no need to raise questions. If the promise of melodrama is that it raises the question of moral order, then, the peril, especially of simplistic melodramas like *JAG*, is that it resolves the question too quickly and decisively. Bellisario virtually dares us to root against the increased militarization of US society, and we feel happy (literally) to capitulate. Emotional elevation mistaken for moral elevation can be a dangerous thing, indeed.

Notes

1. According to Bellisario, the order was to hire "a blonde, good-looking, big cabasas." In response, they hired novice actress Tracey Needham, who perfectly fit that bill. James L. Longworth, "Donald Bellisario: Leatherneck Optimist," in *TV Creators: Conversations with America's Top Producers of Television Drama*, ed. James L. Longworth (Syracuse, NY: Syracuse University Press, 2002), 148.
2. The 1991 Senate confirmation hearings for Supreme Court Justice Clarence Thomas fostered a public debate about sexual harassment in the workplace when Anita Hill accused Thomas of having harassed her during her time at the Equal Employment Opportunity Commission. Also in 1991, dozens of witnesses reported being groped, harassed, and assaulted by Navy and Marine Corps personnel attending the Tailhook Symposium that year. The incident caused the Navy to institute new, more stringent policies on sexual harassment and gender equity in the service. See Neil A. Lewis, "Tailhook Affair Brings Censure of 3 Admirals," *New York Times*, October 16, 1993.
3. *JAG* ended the season in 79th place in the Nielsen ratings with only about 10 million regular viewers. While that would be a robust number in today's competitive market, in 1996 it was considered poor. "JAG (TV Series)," Wikipedia. com, accessed December 26, 2014, http://en.wikipedia.org/wiki/JAG_(TV_series).
4. On the "heartland" in the programming calculations of TV executives, see Victoria Johnson, *Heartland TV: Prime Time Television and the Struggle for US Identity* (New York: New York University, 2008).
5. Bill Carter, "CBS Is a Network on a Roll," *New York Times*, October 10, 2010. http://www.nytimes.com/2010/10/11/business/media/11cbs.html?_r=0& pagewanted=print.
6. Rick Kissell, "'NCIS' Has Become World's Most-Watched TV Drama," *Variety. com*, June 11, 2014, http://variety.com/2014/tv/news/ncis-most-popular-drama-in -worldwatched-tv-drama-1201218492/.

JAG, *Melodrama and Militarism*   225

7. TV scholar Greg Smith raised precisely this point at the 2006 Flow TV conference: "Where is the analysis of *JAG*, a popular show that flew under the critical radar for 10 seasons? ... What of texts that are square and yet immensely popular by the standards of broad viewership?" For more on the discussion, see Henry Jenkins, "On Blogs, Lost and JAG Studies," *Confessions of an Aca-Fan*, December 17, 2006, http://henryjenkins.org/2006/11/on_blogs_lost_and_jag_studies.html.

8. Stacy Takacs, *Terrorism TV: Popular Entertainment in Post-9/11 America* (Lawrence, KS: University of Kansas Press, 2012), 122–43.

9. David Slocum's definition of the war film. See J. David Slocum, "General Introduction: Seeing through the War Cinema," in *Hollywood and War: The Film Reader*, ed. J. David Slocum (New York: Routledge, 2006), 8.

10. On the form of the World War II combat film, see Jeanine Basinger, *The World War II Combat Film: Anatomy of a Genre* (Middletown, CT: Wesleyan University Press, 2003).

11. Basinger insists WWII combat films are a genre unto themselves, but I agree with Steve Neale and others that the WWII incarnation of the combat film is not as self-contained as Basinger suggests. I view it, and combat films in general, as a subgenre of war films. See Steve Neale, "War Film," in *Hollywood and War: The Film Reader*, ed. J. David Slocum (New York: Routledge, 2006).

12. "Port Chicago," season 7, episode 20, *JAG*, aired April 9, 2002 (Hollywood, CA: Paramount Home Entertainment, 2008), DVD. All subsequent episode citations will refer to this DVD collection.

13. "Each of Us Angels," season 8, episode 14, *JAG*, aired February 4, 2003.

14. Richard Huff, "After 10 Seasons, 'JAG' Is Discharged ..." *New York Daily News*, 24 April, 2005.

15. In "War Stories" (season 4, episode 13), Admiral Chegwidden (John M. Jackson), who is serving as military advisor to a Hollywood film crew, suggests to the producer that she consider a female for the role of a Navy lieutenant in the film: "I'm a little surprised by your old-fashioned ideas about the military," he says. We are to believe the Admiral is more of a feminist than the female director.

16. "JAG (TV Series)," *Wikipedia*.

17. Lynda Boose, "Techno-Muscularity and the 'Boy Eternal': From the Quagmire to the Gulf," in *Hollywood and War: The Film Reader*, ed. J. David Slocum (New York: Routledge, 2006), 280.

18. *Donald P. Bellisario and Belisarius Productions v. CBS Studios Inc*, no. BC460417, 2011 Superior Court of the State of California, County of Los Angeles.

19. "The Guide to the Navy JAG Corps" recruitment brochure references the television program as having been "inspired by our profession." Gerry J. Gilmore, "Why I Serve: Officer Explains Military Life to Hollywood," *American Forces Press Service*, September 9, 2004. http://www.defense.gov/news/newsarticle.aspx?id=25364.

20. Takacs, *Terrorism TV*, 122–43.

21. "The Mission," season 7, episode 16, *JAG*, aired February 26, 2002; "Friendly Fire," season 8, episode 15, *JAG*, aired February 11, 2003.

22. "First Casualty," season 7, episode 19, *JAG*, aired March 26, 2002; "Death at the Mosque," season 10, episode 18, *JAG*, aired April 1, 2005.

23. "Camp Delta," season 10, episode 7, *JAG*, aired November 19, 2004; "Tribunal," season 7, episode 21, *JAG*, aired April 30, 2002.

24. Katherine Seelye, "Pentagon Plays Role in Fictional Terror Drama," *New York Times*, March 31, 2002. The US Supreme Court ruled the procedures unconstitutional before they could be employed.
25. "People v. SecNav," season 9, episode 14, *JAG*, aired February 6, 2004.
26. Senate Select Committee on Intelligence, "Committee Study of the Central Intelligence Agency's Detention and Interrogation Program," declassified revisions December 3, 2014. For a breakdown of the findings, see "Senate Intelligence Committee: Study on the Central Intelligence Agency's Detention and Interrogation Program," Council on Foreign Relations, December 9, 2014, http://www.cfr.org/terrorism/senate-intelligence-committee-study-central-intelligence-agencys-detention-interrogation-program/p33919.
27. "Fighting Words," season 9, episode 20, *JAG*, aired April 30, 2004.
28. Although most fans do not seem to question the pro-war stance of the series—indeed, they celebrate it—some *JAG* fan fiction betrays an interest in the moral dilemmas, rather than just the characters or their relationships. See, for example, "It's The End of the World" by Visual IdentificationZeta at https://www.fanfiction.net/s/7069192/1/It-s-The-End-Of-The-World, which suggests nuclear annihilation is a logical outcome of rampant militarism of the sort touted by *JAG*.
29. "Heart of Darkness," season 10, episode 13, *JAG*, aired February 4, 2005.
30. "Contemptuous Words," season 5, episode 9, *JAG*, aired November 23, 1999.
31. On Bellisario's work with the military liaisons, see David Robb, *Operation Hollywood: How the Pentagon Shapes and Censors the Movies* (Amherst, NY: Prometheus Books, 2004), 133–36; Takacs, *Terrorism TV*, 122–43.
32. Longworth, "Donald Bellisario," 137.
33. Ron Becker, *Gay TV and Straight America* (New Brunswick, NJ: Rutgers UP, 2006).
34. Johnson, *Heartland TV*, 203.
35. James Poniewozik, "Battlefield Promotion," *Time.com*, December 2, 2001. http://content.time.com/time/magazine/article/0,9171,186616,00.html.
36. Bellisario's work is so associated with the accumulation of detail that TV scholar Horace Newcomb even coined a term—"cumulative narrative"—to describe it. Although he was referring to Bellisario's earlier *Magnum PI* series, the description applies equally well to *JAG*. Horace Newcomb, "Magnum: The Champagne of TV," *Channels of Communication* (May-June 1985): 23–26.
37. DJ, "About," *The JAG Episode Summary Website*, accessed December 23, 2014, http://jag.djmed.net/about/. DJ's television literacy perhaps proves the show was right to count on the intelligence of its fans.
38. Linda Williams, *On the Wire* (Durham, NC: Duke University Press, 2014), 107.
39. "Code Blue," season 2, episode 13, aired April 5, 1997; "Tiger, Tiger," season 3, episode 18, aired March 24, 1998; "Embassy," season 4, episode 2, aired September 29, 1998; "The Bridge at Kang So Ri," season 5, episode 18, aired February 29, 2000; "Tangled Webb," season 8, episode 24, aired May 20, 2003; "Persian Gulf" season 9, episode 16, aired February 20, 2004; "The Stalker," season 3, episode 17, aired March 17, 1998; "People v. Mac," season 4, episode 9, aired November 17, 1998; "Wilderness of Mirrors," season 4, episode 21, aired May 4, 1999.
40. "Death Watch," season 3, episode 19, *JAG*, aired March 31, 1998.
41. Ibid., 113.
42. Ibid.

43. Steve Neale, "Aspects of Ideology and Narrative Form in the American War Film," *Screen* 32, (Spring 1991): 53.
44. Guy Westwell, *War Cinema: Hollywood on the Front Line* (New York: Wallflower, 2006), 113.
45. Susan to ChristianAnswers.net, accessed December 26, 2014, http://www.christiananswers.net/spotlight/tv/2001/jag.html.
46. Commander Bob Anderson, qtd. in "*JAG*," in *Encyclopedia of Television Law Shows: Factual and Fictional Series about Judges, Lawyers and the Courtroom, 1948–2008*, ed. Hal Erikson (Jefferson, NC: McFarland Publishing, 2009), 129.
47. Maureen Ryan, "Why 'JAG' Came to an Abrupt End," *Chicago Tribune*, April 29, 2005. http://articles.chicagotribune.com/2005-04-29/features/0504280344_1_jag-fans-military-drama-jag-donald-p-bellisario (Accessed December 24, 2014).
48. Westwell, *War Cinema*, 113.

14 Political Amnesia Over Here and Imperial Spectacle *Over There*

Anna Froula

Over There (F/X, 2005) was the first scripted series about a contemporary war to be broadcast on US television during the conflict it depicted. By the time it aired, however, a radical insurgency and torture scandal had made the war a tough sell to American audiences, which may explain in part why F/X ran only 13 episodes. The series debuted to mostly positive reviews, praising its gritty visuals, provocative story lines, and, as one critic remarked, the way it "crashes through television's complacency like a Humvee with the pedal to the metal."[1] Yet, it failed to find an audience and was canceled after only one season.[2] Still, despite its short run, *Over There* functions as what one critic described as "a first TV draft of history."[3] It remains a grim index of the consequences and controversies associated with the US-led invasion of Iraq and, following Scott Laderman (chapter 10, this volume), a "primary document" animating both American fantasies about the US occupation of Iraq and its controversies. What the Bush administration promised would be a short, decisive, and profitable invasion was quickly undermined by corporate and military scandals involving bribery and corruption, as well as moral scandals related to the sidestepping of the Geneva Conventions on torture and the reduction of dead and injured Iraqi civilians to "collateral damage." Perhaps most disastrously, the US failed to find the Weapons of Mass Destruction used to rationalize the invasion.[4] Put simply, the war did not turn out at all as planned.

F/X initially approached Executive Producer Steven Bochco to develop the series and convinced him that because he had created the successful *Hill Street Blues* (NBC, 1981–1987) without having police experience he could do the same thing for a war series without having been a soldier.[5] Like his police dramas, *Over There* focuses on the mundane, everyday experiences, this time of soldiers in Iraq.[6] After bringing Chris Gerolmo on board as writer, who used Evan Wright's *Generation Kill* as source material, Bochco assembled a team who wanted to make a show that mattered and honored the troops; nonetheless, the Department of Defense provided no material support.[7] As Keith Robinson, who plays Pvt. Avery "Angel" King put it, "It was a story that was going untold, that we just kind of live with, kind of get desensitized to. ... And for the first time, this show ... brought it to your doorstep and showed you exactly what it's like to be under fire [and for]

Political Amnesia Over Here and Imperial Spectacle Over There 229

that person to hold a machine gun to be the kid next door ... the guy in high school, the gang member, the aspiring musician ... that's what art is supposed to do. It's supposed to wake you up, make you think ... to promote change."[8] Even though the show deserves critical attention for being the first attempt to depict an on-going war, the production team's earnest aims did not pay off in a political climate already disenchanted with the war. More pointedly, Paul Rieckhoff, who completed a tour in Iraq and is the Executive Director and founder of Iraq and Afghanistan Veterans of America (IAVA), criticized Bochco and F/X for not donating any of the show's proceeds to veterans or family charities.[9]

Bochco repeatedly stated that the series did not have a political agenda, that "a young man being shot at in a firefight has absolutely no interest in politics."[10] Such a depoliticized approach is familiar to Americans from decades of Vietnam combat films and can have the effect of situating the Iraq War as something inflicted *on*, rather than *by*, the US military. *Over There*'s soldiers do not personify what went wrong in Iraq; rather, they are emblems of an insufficient strategy. They are the fictional players in what Michael Gordon and Bernard Trainor characterize as a "chronicle of illusions expensively pursued" and a reality of military occupation "only reluctantly accepted."[11] By August 2005, when the series was airing, General George Casey had realized that the US strategy to stabilize the Iraqi government in the face of the growing insurgency was failing. Also, throughout August 2005, grieving mother and anti-war activist Cindy Sheehan camped outside Bush's vacation ranch in an attempt to make the president answer truthfully why her son died in Iraq.[12] While the series does not explicitly mention politicians, protests, or contemporary foreign policies, and Saddam Hussein appears only as a poster and a portrait under cracked glass, many episodes raise questions about the long war's myriad controversies, from the legitimacy of US detention, torture, and rendition policies to the scandal of corporate war profiteering and shoddy work by Halliburton, Blackwater, and other private contractors who outnumbered military personnel on the ground by 2006.[13] It also indicted American citizens on the home front for being out of touch with policies enacted in their names. Each episode of the series took up a focus on a particular controversy, although, in most cases, the show moved on to another problem in the next episode. The episodic structure raised complex questions about the US military strategies and tactics that were narratively concluded for the series' squad but not ideologically so. *Over There* comments on but reaches no conclusions about the war in Iraq, which allows viewers to entertain both pro- and anti-war messages.[14]

Lessons Unlearned

Ironies, both mundane and tragic, appear briefly, such as when one soldier, eating his Meal Ready to Eat (MRE), notes that it is 10-percent digestible plastic and that the squad is "sitting on top of eight percent of the world's oil reserves eating petroleum."[15] Another episode features a soldier who lost his leg to an IED explosion being charged $2,500 by the Army for equipment he didn't return while being treated stateside. The series articulates the folly of the United States' adventure in Iraq, much as *Rambo III* (1988) anticipated the failure of the military occupation of Afghanistan.[16] Speaking to one of the "gallant" Mujahadeen the film is dedicated to, Rambo (Sylvester Stallone) notes that Afghanis "will never stop fighting" invaders because "you guys don't take no shit." Col. Trautman (Richard Crenna) similarly mocks the USSR's imperial ambitions to the Soviet commander in charge of a prison known for its torture. It was a speech that could have provided an important lesson for Americans in the wake of 9/11 about arming and training revolutionary fighters who could turn around and fight the United States:

> You know there won't be a victory. Every day your war machines lose ground to a group of poorly armed, poorly equipped freedom fighters. The fact is that you underestimated your competition. If you studied your history, you'd know that these people have never given up to anyone. They'd rather die than be slaves to an invading army. We tried. We already had our Vietnam.

The Taliban grew from one faction of "gallant Mujahadeen" whose conquest of Afghanistan succeeded in 1996 and who gave al-Qaeda and Osama bin Laden sanctuary; *Rambo III*'s cautionary tale went unheeded.[17] As Lynn Spigel points out, American popular cultural production in the wake of 9/11 recycled soothing American myths instead of encouraging American citizens to learn more about the world.[18] In 2005, analysts such as Mark Jacobson, who worked in the Office of the Secretary of Defense, defined al-Qaeda as a "global insurgency," implying that to "engage in a war on violent extremism anywhere, and thus fight an open-ended global campaign *everywhere*—[is] a classic recipe for imperial overstretch."[19] A cultural acceptance of such imperial overreach pervades much of the televisual flow of *Over There*, as I discuss in the last section. Yet, the series does suggest some of the costs and limits of a militarized foreign policy.

The show runners likewise could have involved more veterans in the writing room. A *New York Times* survey of veterans and soldiers revealed an "almost universally negative" response to the show for sacrificing accuracy for drama.[20] Many decried the "bogus" scenes that made service members seem like "idiots" or "monsters," such as when one soldier removed his helmet during a firefight or when another slit the throat of a child.[21] In the special features of the series' DVD, the show's military advisor explains that he advised how military training would take effect in combat, but the show runners' concern for story "overrode that level of military realism."[22] However, some saw the show's attempt to bring more awareness of soldiers' experiences in Iraq. "This is a war that does not immediately affect most of the country," said Robert Timmons, who served in Iraq in 2003. "People here see yellow ribbons on cars, but they see very little of the reality of the war other than short stories on CNN when American soldiers die. This series is over the top, but anything that brings attention to a war that is not getting much coverage is helpful."[23] Still, more criticisms were leveled at Bochco's use of stereotypical, yet generic, investments in war movie tropes, such as the cliché-ridden characters that populate the unit of the Third Infantry Division.[24] I would add that Bochco's grounding the series' tropes primarily in his generation's war—the Vietnam War—undergirds much of these criticisms, intentional or not.

The show's characters derive from the diverse-but-unified squad trope of the World War II film—a representation of the American "melting pot," updated for the Vietnam era and beyond.[25] These throwbacks to past wartime characters resonate with the broader national goal to depict the 9/11 attacks as on par with the Japanese bombing of Pearl Harbor and, thus, portray the ensuing "war on terror" as a similarly "good" and necessary war. Iraq War veterans criticized the pilot for having the squad members meet in the heat of battle, which was more applicable to short-term Vietnam tours of duty, instead of training together before deployment.[26] *Over There*'s soldiers are familiar remixes of the combat genre: Ssg. "Scream" (Erik Palladino), a World War II-era tough-but-caring squad leader who has been stop-lossed due to his would-be replacement's illness; Pvt. "Dim" Dumphy (Luke MacFarlane), a watered-down version of *Full Metal Jacket*'s Private Joker who is Cornell educated yet culturally ignorant; Pvt. Maurice "Smoke" Williams (Kirk "Sticky" Jones), who is a stereotype of the joint-smoking urban "gangsta" from "the god-damned combat zone" of Compton, California; Pvt. Angel King, a paradoxically Christian sharp-shooter; Pfc. Bo Rider (Josh Henderson), an earnest Texan who loses his leg to an IED in the pilot and spends the rest of the series determined to return to his squad, much to the dismay of his wife; his replacement Pfc. Tariq Nassiri (Omar Abtahi), an Iraqi-American from Detroit; and their drivers/mechanics, West Virginian Pvt. Brenda "Mrs. B" Mitchell (Nicki Aycox), who displays a curious combination of Jessica Lynch looks and Lynndie England sadism; and Pfc. Esmeralda "Doublewide" del Rio (Lizette Carrion), a mother and wife whose husband (Lombardo Boyar) strays with a member of his spousal support group.[27]

Over There provided characters as canvasses on which to screen the perplexed—and changing—face of America at war. While, as the documentary *Lioness* (2008) shows, women skillfully fought in combat before the Pentagon's ban was lifted in January 2013, *Over There* is both ambivalent and nonchalant about its female soldiers.[28] Overburdened by depicting as many women-involved scenarios as possible, Doublewide and Mrs. B begin the season as a virgin/whore dichotomy, demonstrating that women can be as depraved or as betrayed by their spouses at home as men. Yet, even though the pilot depicts the women as not quite combat ready—Mrs. B shrugs off assistance digging a trench, requiring a male soldier to push her head

232 *Anna Froula*

down to avoid being shot and in a later episode loses her weapon to a prisoner she is guarding—they are routinely involved in the men's missions and receive relatively little gender-based flak from the men, who are themselves mash-ups of Vietnam-era characters. Despite his Ivy League credentials, Dim Dumphy is unaware that Iraqis speak a different language than Iranians, an ignorance emblematic of many Americans concerning Middle Eastern nations. Yet, he occasionally voices more profound ideas about the war, such as when he points out that the squad's enemies "are willing to die for what they believe in, and we're just trying to live through the day." Dim also troublingly personifies the show's clumsy race relations with his elitist and racist banter with Smoke, frequently and condescendingly commenting on his ignorance. This trope of troubling race relations derives from Hollywood's Vietnam and highlights *Over There*'s investment in earlier war representations, an investment that neglects the realities of the twenty-first century military. In one attempt to update the racial trope, Smoke himself refers to the newly arrived Tariq as "a goddamned A-rab" and refers to Iraqis as "sand niggers" or "goat people."

Despite Gerolmo's claim that the show was committed to depicting "an enemy we could respect on the ground," *Over There*'s enemy lacks clear motivation for why it attacks US soldiers.[29] Like the politicians who would label all Arabs trying to kill Americans in Iraq "terrorists," "insurgents," or "dead-enders," the squad fights the "bad guys" who are skilled at mixing with civilians. According to Bochco, the show defined "the enemy as those individuals who are trying to kill us, who are shooting at us. And we don't put names on them or labels on them. They are just trying to hurt us, and they are the bad guys."[30] Or as Tariq describes a couple of wealthy Syrians the squad kills, they are kids fighting jihad against America for excitement—it's their "Woodstock." As David Swanson notes, in the show's exclusively American point of view, "the Iraqis in this show have no names and for the most part no faces, no stories, no families, no nicknames, no annoying and endearing habits, no motivations or regrets, no NOTHING."[31] *Over There*'s flattening of the complex players in Iraq into a simplistic portrait of "the enemy" resembles similar tactics in Hollywood's Vietnam films and, perhaps unintentionally, reinforces this connection with Bo's encounter with a young girl at home when he trains on his prosthetic leg at a local track. She explains that her grandfather's false limb came courtesy of "some Viet Cong." This evasive response links the Iraq War to Vietnam and implies that both wars are properly remembered as tragedies that happen to American soldiers. Similar to Hollywood's versions of the Vietnam War, *Over There* depicts war as an "American" story aimed at an American audience that is already nostalgic in its fascination with a vicarious experience of war.[32] Such forms of entertainment silently endorse the US's highly controversial occupation of Iraq as a surrogate front of the "war on terror" and a reasonable diversion of resources from the Afghanistan theater and the pursuit of al-Qaeda leader Osama bin Laden.

Political Amnesia Over Here and Imperial Spectacle Over There   233

As many American scholars have argued, the conventional understanding of the Vietnam War is an American tale of lost national innocence that fails to consider Vietnamese history, culture, and peoples. Whereas Vietnam's jungles served as an allegorical stage for American "cowboys" against the enemy "Indians," Bochco's Iraq desert functions as a rearticulated frontier for war profiteers and multinational corporations alike, its agents the grunts on the ground. The soldiers' unavoidable complicity with the military-industrial complex becomes clear in "I Want My Toilets" in which they put their lives on the line for the toilets delivered for the private contractors making 20 times their monthly salaries, or, in the series finale when the unpopular Lt. Alexander "Underpants" Hunter (Josh Stamberg) sacrifices four of his soldiers in his mission to guard a truck carrying freshly-minted Iraqi dinar.[33] Yet, in another example of older war tropes overwhelming the realities of the Iraq War, *Over There* fails to end the scene with moral outrage. The truck comically explodes, sending the currency soaring through smoke and debris. Soon after, the bad lieutenant—who has consistently endangered the squad with poor decisions—is killed in a friendly fire incident, likely by the kind of "fragging" associated with the Vietnam War.

"It's Not Ours to Reason Why"

The title of the series and its theme song are yet additional throwbacks to an earlier war, this time World War I's "Over There," penned by George Cohan in 1917. Chris Gerolmo wrote the show's version in 2003 on the eve of the US-led invasion and then performed it as a rock ballad over the closing credit sequence. Gerolmo's "Over There" is a melancholy, existential tune about wars gone by, in which "there's mothers cryin' ... fathers sighin'. ...[and] trains are filling up with boys ... putting away their favorite toys. They're goin' over there." The final lyrics, however, highlight the show's nonpartisan intent: "It's not ours to reason why. But someone has to die." These lyrics, which end each episode over slow-motion images of the squad completing its duty of the week, discourage engagement with why this squad is "over there" and highlight *Over There*'s use of the melodramatic mode. As Stacy Takacs describes, the melodramatic mode encourages identification with the personal experiences of the soldiers as an act of citizenship: "Social concerns are approached through personal narratives that foreground the traumatic aspect of experience and promote a sentimental identification with suffering individuals. Viewers are invited to become involved emotionally, but are rarely mobilized politically. The melodramatic structure of broadcast television fare thus works against the sort of political awakening that shocking images might otherwise engender."[34] In the pilot, the song is credited to Angel, who sings it for his bunkmates and enables the squad to take up the subject position of the song's "ours." For viewers interested in understanding why people are dying in

234 *Anna Froula*

Iraq, however, the lyrics chafe, particularly when played over visuals such as close-ups of the bloody uniform of an American soldier who has just committed suicide.[35]

To be sure, the series makes more explicit references to some of the controversial aspects of the war, such as the presence of CIA torture enthusiasts, the exorbitant salaries of private contractors (especially as compared to the much lower soldiers' pay), the rising number of veteran suicides, and the presence of military women in combat before it was legal. The series also conveys the chaos of battle, the boredom of waiting, the longing for the niceties of home, and the obsessive anxiety over what loved ones might be doing at home. Both Dim's wife and Doublewide's husband engage in extramarital affairs, thereby driving home the toll war takes on service members' marriages. The squad occasionally discusses the moral conundrum of when—and whom—it's ok to kill, as in "I Want My Toilets" when the squad, under the orders of a pill-popping general, must eliminate a mortar spotter in a small village to clear the Coalition's supply route for a delivery of 1200 American Standard toilets. The unit's reliance on Angel's sniper talents forces him to make the ultimate decision of whether his target is indeed their insurgent spotter. "I'm a soldier, not a judge," answers a frustrated Angel to his team's increasing demands that he shoot the man, whom they have observed playing in the village with his young son. Scream effectively makes the decision for him, explaining, "Either you shoot him, or we all do and probably kill the wife and child too. It's your only two choices." After Angel makes the kill shot, the subsequent mortars hit wildly off the mark, confirming the righteousness of his trigger finger, though his lone tear underscores his regret.

Because the squad is tasked with a range of post-invasion clean-up missions, they allegorize the conditions that inform President George H. W. Bush's decision not to invade Baghdad in 1991 for fear that doing so:

> would have incurred incalculable human and political costs. ... We would have been forced to occupy Baghdad and, in effect, rule Iraq. The coalition would instantly have collapsed, the Arabs deserting it in anger and other allies pulling out as well. ... Had we gone the invasion route, the US could conceivably still be an occupying power in a bitterly hostile land. It would have been a dramatically different—and perhaps barren—outcome.[36]

Indeed, *Over There*'s squad encounters the frustrations and problems of a collapsing coalition in a hostile land and does so without reasoning why.

As Marita Sturken explains, series such as *Over There*, can "exert significant influence in the construction of national meaning in the United States" because, for many Americans, particularly younger viewers who may know little about the war, they "are a primary source of historical information" and can work to "smooth over" discomfiting histories of traumatic events

Political Amnesia Over Here and Imperial Spectacle Over There 235

that can take on new meanings as a result.[37] In one example, the shocking, gory visual of a young Iraqi girl's head blown open by the squad as it guards a roadblock in "Roadblock Duty" horrifies Dim and the viewer alike, yet her violent death is superseded by the next car that approaches the roadblock carrying a middle-aged Iraqi couple.[38] Just as Tariq allows them to proceed, he hears a cell phone ringing in their trunk, prompting the squad to shoot and kill the couple, open the trunk, and discover an insurgent, who reminds the squad, "I am your prisoner. You are bound by the Geneva Conventions." Because four people—including the young girl—died for him, they are redefined as "collateral damage," and their sacrifice suggests both how important the prisoner is and how degraded human life is to the insurgents, who used these folks as "human shields."[39] Because the enemy put her in danger in the first place, the episode's narrative contains any potential fallout from the girl's death and Dim's anguish over it. The final shot is of the squad leading away their prisoner in a pyrrhic victory; in the subsequent episode, "The Prisoner," the squad will assist, although unwillingly, in his interrogation at a CIA black site.[40]

"Roadblock Duty" opens with a torture dream sequence of Bo, who had been transported to Landstuhl Regional Medical Center in Germany. Tellingly, Bo embodies the fantasy perpetuated by entertainment media that Americans can withstand the enemy's torture techniques, which include dangling him from chains cuffed to his arms, beating him, and injecting him with acid (which turns out to be his phantom limb pain when he screams himself awake). His dreams continue to haunt him in "The Prisoner," prompting his decision to wean himself off morphine. The rest of the episode crosscuts his torturous withdrawal with the squad's encounter with US torture policy. However, even if "The Prisoner" references how US policymakers authorized the treatment of "enemy combatants" and the political debates about that decision, it legitimizes the interrogation techniques—because, as the plot progresses, they are shown to work.

Colonel Ryan (Michael Cudlitz) forces the squad to assist him in the interrogation by shooting their Humvee after they deliver the prisoner Hassan (Rami Malek). In this episode, *Over There* questions the logic of the "Bybee memo," which argued the legality of sidestepping the Geneva Conventions that Hassan keeps mentioning.[41] Ryan informs Hassan that because he has no name, rank, nor serial number, he is not a legitimate Prisoner of War who would otherwise be protected. Moreover, the episode uses the "ticking time bomb" trope—Hassan knows where insurgents have stashed Stinger missiles—to inform the squad's debate about whether it's ever right to torture. Smoke voices Vice President Richard Cheney's opinion that torture is justified if it saves "one American ass" while Tariq ironically personifies American anti-Iraqi racism.[42] After Dim voices some praise of the prisoner's ability to withstand the stress position for hours, Tariq tells him, "If you get taken prisoner, they're gonna crush your balls in a garlic press and post it on the internet for your mom to see" because their Iraqi

Figure 14.1 Over There explores the controversies surrounding US interrogation policies in "The Prisoner."

enemies are "living in the middle ages." After Hassan calls Tariq's mother a "whore," Tariq beats him, defending the abuse as "a conversation, bro. You just didn't know how to talk." Since Ryan knows that Hassan would rather be a dead martyr than give up his intel, he orders Hassan's 15-year old sister brought in and warns him that if he doesn't give up the missiles he will transfer her to a black site in Pakistan where they will beat and rape her "until her skin turns black, until she is too sick to touch, and then they'll stick rifles in her." Broken, the prisoner reveals where the stinger missiles are and pleads that they not kill the family who has innocently, perhaps unwittingly, stored the missiles on their farm. The episode ends with US bombers approaching the farm and a hyper-realistic CNN-style tracking shot to the target, although we never see the expected explosion. Because viewers do not bear witness to the material destruction, the show's audience can maintain a virtual distance from the bombing and its repercussions.

Many other visually discomfiting moments point to, if not underscore, US foreign policy and its attendant controversies, such as when Mrs. B casually steps on a dead Iraqi's hand to hear the bones crunch, when Lt. "Underpants" shoots a kid trying to wave his convoy over, or when the team pulls guard duty for a Dubai-based, US-owned oil company.[43] Significantly, however, such moments often relieve the audience of its collective complicity in the exercise of American corporatized military imperialism. For instance, in "Situation Normal" a wealthy, arrogant, white private contractor in a cowboy hat, who seems like a stand-in for the Bush administration's energy connections, is portrayed as culturally ignorant.[44] Yet, in comparison to the Imam in charge of the valley where the US contractor's oil pipeline will run, he seems downright progressive. The Imam is depicted as an intolerant,

Political Amnesia Over Here and Imperial Spectacle Over There   237

backward hick who rules with an iron fist, backed by a harshly conservative interpretation of Islam. The contractor will build a structure of the community's choice in exchange for running an oil pipeline through the valley; the Imam requests a mosque while his wife, who has already drawn his ire for smiling at Dim, requests a school. The Imam perceives her request as disobedience and retaliates by calling his dangerously progressive wife a "whore" and inciting her death via a village stoning, which the episode suggests will undoubtedly occur after the Americans pull out.

Much like its audience, the series was ambivalent about the impact of Americans on the lives of Iraqis. Late in the season, the "Orphans" episode starkly contrasted the fate of Iraqi children orphaned by the war to the children of the occupying nation.[45] Sgt. Scream's squad must inform Sophie (Serena Scott Thomas), the French caretaker of an Iraqi orphanage, that the Iraqi interim government has ordered the children out of their building in order to house a police station. As Scream explains the situation to Sophie, his squad hands out a meager supply of candy to eager hands. "I beat you America," intones a little boy holding a box with a timer that was revealed to be a chess set, but only after the squad nervously shot it to pieces because IEDs also have timers. After Scream later gives him his own set, Dim over-confidently takes his challenge to play, and viewers are encouraged to relish the child's imminent victory over him. Yet this rare moment of identification with a humanized Iraqi character is short-lived: He dies a violent death later in the episode after a car bomb explodes in the vicinity.

This episode is particularly critical about the US mission and strategy in Iraq, contrasting the orphans' lives in which war carnage is a regular occurrence with the lives of most American children, on which the war has little to no impact. Earlier in the episode, as Sophie lists American offenses to her wards, such as how she has watched "her" children die from infection because Americans prevented their access to antibiotics via sanctions, she leads Scream down a darkened hallway under the large, watchful eyes of the orphans. "That boy your men are playing chess with," she angrily informs, "his parents were walking into a school when they were caught in a battle. They covered him with their bodies. They bled to death on top of him." She graphically depicts the carnage of war that has been censored from US domestic consumption, decrying that children have died because Americans wouldn't let medicine through "ever since the sanctions." "Every time the Americans have a helpful idea," she concludes, "Iraqi children die." In the face of this explicit moment of critique, Scream's response is an oblique reference to pro-war American anger toward France for not joining the "Coalition of the Willing" to invade Iraq and to Vichy France's cooperation with Nazi rule: "It's a collaboration, which as a French person, you should be able to understand."

The scene's visuals drive home this moment of censure, particularly when the episode cross-cuts from Sophie and Scream standing in a barren room with one mat and one bowl set for each orphan to a children's birthday party in America. Brightly colored helium balloons crowd hovering parents, while

Figure 14.2 In "Orphans," *Over There* contrasted the plight of Iraqi orphan children. ...

Figure 14.3 .... with the abundance enjoyed by children in the United States.

vibrant piñatas and crepe decorations float over tables full of cupcakes and punch. The titillating attraction between Doublewide's husband Sergio and Army wife Anna (Ana Ortiz) takes center stage in the kitchen as they awkwardly discuss their feelings for each other and the moral dilemma the feelings present. A harried woman looking for sprinkles interrupts their interlude. "Little monsters," she grumbles. "They see some cupcakes with sprinkles, now everybody has to have them. Here. Thank God." Her irreverent prayer hollowly echoes the insurgent's praise to Allah before the car bomb explodes at the orphanage and underscores Americans' cognitive dissonance regarding

Political Amnesia Over Here and Imperial Spectacle Over There 239

the war and its lack of impact on much of everyday life. The parallel editing of these two scenes is critical of home-front consumption, but what ultimately effaces the condition of the orphans is that the sexual tension between Anna and Sergio culminates in the coupling of Sophie and Scream, who reenlists in order to save the orphanage and move the police station. In "Orphans" Scream is the focal point for viewer identification: the noble American grunt who will put his own well-being on the line to do orphans one good turn and be rewarded for his gesture and sacrifice with a romantic interlude with a beautiful woman whom he will never see again. *Over There* indeed indicts Americans for behaviors that highlight the gap between civilian and soldier-at-war; however, the episodic structure of the squad's experiences and shifting responsibilities does not allow these indictments to compound.

Perhaps the most poignant issue of soldiers' experiences is addressed in "Suicide Rain" when the squad's delivery of supplies to clamoring villagers is disrupted by a female suicide bomber.[46] The resulting carnage mimics *Saving Private Ryan* (1998) with its spectacular realism, and the explosions result in American and Iraqi casualties alike. Lt. "Underpants" insists that the Americans receive the attention of a troubled medic, Corporal Shaver (Currie Graham) despite his intentions to treat the most badly wounded first. When a concussed Pvt. Dana (Ken Luckey) is taken hostage by a father whose son's leg was blown off, the show touches on American exceptionalism wanting it both ways: The CO wants Americans treated first while Shaver, Smoke, and Angel want to rescue one American hostage. Shaver and an unarmed Angel work on the boy but are ultimately unable to save him, and both Shaver and the father weep. Yet, because they did not emerge with the hostage in the Lieutenant's allotted time frame, he sends in two of his men, guns blazing, ignoring Angel's pleas not to shoot. The anguished father points a gun at Dana, but Angel quickly neutralizes the threat with a body block, telling Underpants' men, "I said it was OK!" After the smoke clears, Angel asks Shaver, "Are you, OK, brother?" "Oh yeah," he replies, before sticking his pistol in his mouth and blowing his head off, a chilling reference to veteran suicides. A shaken Angel leaves the house and receives Scream's understanding nod as the theme song begins over the end of the episode before cutting to commercial. War television can tell complex stories about war experiences, but televisual flow can complicate its own reception. This sobering reminder of how war trauma can shatter soldiers doesn't leave viewers contemplative in a darkened theater. Rather, this moment slides into F/X's programming flow selling Sam Adams beer and Chevy trucks, promoting more consumption and less engagement.

Over There and Televisual Flow

In 2005, only seven percent of Americans with televisions had digital video recording technology, so viewers had more exposure to commercial advertising.[47] The programming's flow in many ways captures the disconnect

240 *Anna Froula*

between civilian and soldier. Flow, as Raymond Williams defines it, takes into consideration how stations broadcast commercials within television shows and how shows are scheduled in time slots, resulting in blurred "viewing strips," rather than discrete texts.[48] As a part of TV's commercial "flow," *Over There* allowed spectators to consume the spectacle of war as another commercial product for sale. The juxtaposition of representations of war and alcohol was only one ironic piece of the show's viewing strip. Alcohol for military personnel was banned in Iraq, although, as *Over There*'s pilot episode depicts, the ban wasn't always effective. More egregious examples include the advertisements for war video games run during the original broadcast of the series, such as *Delta Force: Black Hawk Down* (NovaLogic, 2003) and *Tom Clancy's Rainbow 6: Lockdown* (Ubisoft, 2005), which features civilian players playing against a team of Navy Seals. Such commercials created a strip in which viewers could consume the scripted war drama and then alternately imagine fighting the enemies of the country virtually over here while actual Americans literally fought over there.[49] Similarly, the repeated broadcast of the commercial for the WWII first-person shooter war game, *Brothers in Arms: Earned in Blood* (Ubisoft, 2005) enabled spectators/gamers to wage "the good war" at a safe temporal, geographical, and imaginary distance, perhaps after enjoying the show, followed or preceded by extreme, rock-n-roll-laden Armed Forces recruitment commercials. This ad opens to a squad of US servicemen crouched behind a wall in a bombed-out European city. Voyeuristically, the viewer overhears one soldier bragging about a recent sexual conquest. "I told her I was a general," he announces, laughing raucously, "and she believed it!" Before the squad can congratulate him for deceiving a woman for sex, a bomb explodes, and a street battle ensues. "It's my job to lead these men," the sergeant's voiceover informs, "and none of them are gonna die on my watch." In the chaotic barrage of ads for alcoholic beverages, credit cards, hybrid vehicles, and gas-guzzling Hemi engines, this first-person shooter tribute to the Greatest Generation emphasizes the military values that *Over There* encapsulates (camaraderie, battle readiness) and lacks (a clear mission with a definable enemy).

Another video game advertisement entitled *Conflict Global Terror* (Pivotal Games, 2005) more directly underwrote the series by beginning with a deep male voice urging viewers to understand the war on terror as "global, from the city streets to the jungle. You and your elite special-ops squad are the last line of defense between annihilation and freedom." Its fast-paced visual montage features the squad fighting in a variety of environments before a helicopter leaves an explosive trail of napalm in the vibrant jungle below, as if anticipating how military operations in Iraq would outlast those in Vietnam. The synergistic relationship between the video game advertisements and the television show promises the viewer a safe, virtual, and sufficiently patriotic participation in the global war on terror—a fantasy of supporting the troops through a Playstation controller that provides the further fantasy of being able to control the war on terror. While I do not

Political Amnesia Over Here and Imperial Spectacle Over There   241

assign intent on the part of the show runners, these two examples highlight one of the troubling ways that Americans can consume and safely "experience" the spectacle of war through television and be simultaneously militarized. As David Annandale points out, games that "cheerlead" the US at war provide players access to "the satisfaction in dishing out the kind of fantasy justice that the Bush administration promised but could never deliver."[50]

Ultimately, the flow throughout *Over There*'s only season creates a visual tableau of a show—and an occupation—destined to fail. The American strategists' lack of a clear mission finds expression in the squad's series of objectives that lead to no discernible victory or strategic gain—and in the series' ultimate cancelation. However, the show is useful as a snapshot of some of the ways Americans imagined the realities of war. Contrary to the theme song, it *is* ours to reason why, and we *ought* to consider how we commit our troops to combat.

Notes

1. Quotation from Aaron Barnhart in Dana Stevens, "Steven Bochco's *Over There* Can't See the Quagmire for the Trees," *Slate,* July 27, 2005, http://www.slate. com/articles/news_and_politics/surfergirl/2005/07/war_in_a_general_sense_is_ hell.html. See also Robert Bianco, "*Over There* Brings the Iraq War Home," *USA Today,* July 26, 2005, http://usatoday30.usatoday.com/life/television/ reviews/2005-07-26-over-there_x.htm; Gillian Flynn, "*Over There*" (review), *Entertainment Weekly,* July 25, 2005, http://www.ew.com/article/2005/07/25/ over-there.

2. "F/X Withdraws from *Over There,*" 1 November 2005, *TV.com.* Bill Keveney, "Provocative *Over There* Didn't Go over Big Here," *USA Today,* October, 25, 2005, http://usatoday30.usatoday.com/life/television/reviews/2005-10-25-over- there_x.htm. While the pilot episode garnered 4.1 million viewers, the remainder averaged 2.1 million, and only 1.35 million tuned in for the season finale. Reuters, "FX Network Ends Iraq War Drama *Over There,*" *TV.com,* November 2, 2005, https://www.tv.com%2Fnews%2Ffx-network-ends-iraq-war-drama-over- there-2218%2F&usg=AFQjCNHrIjI1srirYy1bXiwh9uvozKkyzQ&sig2=pic QHh4rs73gaHq7Y1Qefg.

3. James Poniewozik, "Missing in Action: FX's Daring New Iraq War Drama Is Violent and Provocative, but Filled with Clichéd Characters," *Time,* August 1, 2005, 58.

4. As Stacy Takacs notes, the series illustrated the limitations of the Revolution in Military Affairs (RMA), which aimed to use war as a form of political persuasion. See *Terrorism TV: Popular Entertainment in Post-9/11 America* (Lawrence, KS: University Press of Kansas, 2012), 146–48. For bribery and corruption, see, for example, *Quarterly Report and Semiannual Report to the United States Congress,* prepared by the Special Inspector General for Iraq Reconstruction, (Washington, DC: 2009), especially 234–44. For the faulty rationale for invasion, see Jonathan Stein and Tim Dickinson, "Lie by Lie: A Timeline of How We Got into Iraq," *Mother Jones,* September/October 2006, http://www.motherjones. com/politics/2011/12/leadup-iraq-war-timeline.

5. Carter Harris, "Q+A: Steven Bochco," *Esquire* 144, no. 2 (August 2005): 38.

242   *Anna Froula*

6. François Debrix reads Bochco's attention to the banal as part of his strategy to create "an existential drama about the 'grunts' out there who could easily be one of them" (773). See "The Sublime Spectatorship of War: The Erasure of the Event in America's Politics of Terror and Aesthetics of Violence," *Millennium: Journal of International Studies* 34, no. 3 (2006): 767–91.

7. Evan Wright, *Generation Kill: Devil Dogs, Iceman, Captain America and the New Face of American War* (New York: Berkeley Caliber, 2004). Takacs, *Terrorism TV,* 145.

8. "Tour of Duty: Filming *Over There,*" directed by Keith Clark, *Over There* (Century City, CA: Twentieth-Century Fox, 2006), DVD.

9. David Carr, "Iraq Veterans Question *Over There,*" *New York Times,* August 24, 2005, www.nytimes.com/2005/08/24/arts/television/iraq-veterans-question-over-there.html.

10. Stevens, "Steven Bochco's *Over There.*"

11. Michael Gordon and Bernard Trainor, *The Endgame: The Inside Struggle for Iraq from George W. Bush to Barack Obama* (New York: Pantheon, 2012). Quote from John Barry, "*The Endgame* Is a Well Researched, Highly Critical Look at US Policy in Iraq," *The Daily Beast,* September 25, 2012, http://www.thedailybeast.com/articles/2012/09/25/the-endgame-is-a-well-researched-highly-critical-look-at-u-s-policy-in-iraq.html. See also Takacs, *Terrorism TV,* chapter 5.

12. For further analysis, see Debrix, "Sublime Spectatorship," 788–89.

13. For outsourcing, see *Hard Lessons: The Iraq Reconstruction Experience,* prepared by the Office of the Special Inspector General for Iraq Reconstruction (Washington, DC: 2009), 38. For an example of shoddy work, see Scott Bronstein, "'Multiple' Failures Led to Electrocution, Pentagon Says," *CNN.com,* July 27, 2009, http://www.cnn.com/2009/US/07/27/military.electrocutions/.

14. Horace M. Newcomb and Paul M. Hirsch, "Television as a Cultural Forum: Implications for Research," *Quarterly Review of Film Studies* 8, no. 3 (1983): 49.

15. "Weapons of Mass Destruction," season 1, episode 12, *Over There* (Century City, CA: Twentieth-Century Fox, 2006), aired October 19, 2005. All subsequent episode references are to this DVD collection.

16. As of December 2014, nearly 5,000 troops remain on the ground to confront the Islamic State, or ISIS, which has been capitalizing on the fractured country. Phil Stewart, "US General Says Allies to Send about 1,500 Troops to Iraq in Training Role" *Reuters,* December 8, 2014. http://www.huffingtonpost.com/2014/12/08/coalition-troops-iraq_n_6289264.html?utm_hp_ref=iraq.

17. Zachary Laub, "The Taliban in Afghanistan," *Council on Foreign Relations,* updated July 4, 2014, http://www.cfr.org/afghanistan/taliban-afghanistan/p10551.

18. Lynn Spigel, "Entertainment Wars: Television Culture after 9/11," *American Quarterly* 56, no. 2 (2004): 235–70.

19. "Interview: Mark Jacobson," *Frontline,* July 13, 2005, http://www.pbs.org/wgbh/pages/frontline/torture/interviews/jacobson.html. Italics in original. Audrey Kurth Cronin, "The 'War on Terrorism': What Does It Mean to Win?" *The Journal of Strategic Studies* 37, no. 2 (2013): 1–25, 6.

20. "There are a few bad war movies and TV shows, but this one takes the cake," complained an active duty Army soldier in Iraq. "If the inaccuracies they made in this new show was to keep the real enemy from watching and knowing our real tactics, then they did a SUPERB job." Carr, "Iraq Veterans Question *Over There.*"

Political Amnesia Over Here and Imperial Spectacle Over There   243

21. M.L. Lyke, "These Soldiers Say *Over There* Is Bogus," *Seattle PI*, July 25, 2005, http://www.seattlepi.com/ae/tv/article/These-soldiers-say-Over-There-is-bogus-1179094.php.
22. "Tour of Duty: Filming *Over There*."
23. Quoted in Carr, "Iraq Veterans Question *Over There*."
24. Carr, "Iraq Veterans Question *Over There*."
25. Jeanine Basinger, *The World War II Combat Film: Anatomy of a Genre* (Middletown, CT: Wesleyan University Press, 2003), 30.
26. Lyke, "These Soldiers Say."
27. For analysis of representations of Jessica Lynch and Lynndie England, see Anna Froula, "Lynch 'n England: Figuring Females as the US at War." *Global Media Journal* 5.9 (2006).
28. *Lioness*, directed by Meg McLagan and Daria Sommers, (2008; Sausalito, CA: RoCo Films International) DVD.
29. "Tour of Duty: Filming *Over There*."
30. Bochco defines the enemy when pressed by *Hardball* host Chris Matthews. "*Over There* Brings Battlefield Home," *NBC News*, July 29, 2005, http://www.nbcnews.com/id/8741886/#.Vh0v5aLeP3U.
31. David Swanson, quoted in Danny Schechter, "It's Time for a Sequel: 'Over Here,'" *Commondreams.org*, http://www.commondreams.org/views05/0801-20.htm.
32. On nostalgia, see Marita Sturken, *Tangled Memories: The Vietnam War, the AIDS Epidemic, and the Politics of Remembering* (Berkeley: University of California Press, 1997), 76.
33. "I Want My Toilets," season 1, episode 4, *Over There*, aired August 17, 2005; "Follow the Money," season 1, episode 13, *Over There*, aired October 26, 2005.
34. Stacy Takacs, "The Body of War and the Management of Imperial Anxiety on US Television," *International Journal of Contemporary Iraqi Studies* 3, no. 1 (2009): 85–105, 87.
35. "Suicide Rain," season 1, episode 9, *Over There*, aired September 28, 2005.
36. George H. W. Bush and Brent Snowcroft, *A World Transformed* (New York: Knopf, 1991) 3.
37. Sturken, *Tangled Memories*, 85–86.
38. "Roadblock Duty," season 1, episode 2, *Over There*, aired August 3, 2005.
39. Kathleen T. Rehm, "US Military Works to Avoid Civilian Deaths, Collateral Damage," *US Department of Defense*, March 5, 2003, http://www.defense.gov/news/newsarticle.aspx?id=29337.
40. "The Prisoner," season 1, episode 3, *Over There*, aired August 10, 2005.
41. For more on the United States' use of torture, see Nick Wing, "Here Are the Most Horrific Details from the Senate Torture Report," *HuffingtonPost*, December 9, 2014, http://www.huffingtonpost.com/2014/12/09/senate-torture-report-details_n_6295396.html. The memo itself can be accessed at http://www.justice.gov/sites/default/files/olc/legacy/2010/08/05/memo-gonzales-aug2002.pdf.
42. "Cheney: I'd Do It Again in a Minute," *USA Today*, December 15, 2014, http://www.usatoday.com/story/opinion/2014/12/15/dick-cheney-senate-meet-the-press-editorials-debates/20459735/.
43. "Pilot," season 1, episode 1, *Over There*, aired July 27, 2005; "Mission Accomplished."
44. "Situation Normal," season 1, episode 8, *Over There*, aired September 14, 2005.
45. "Orphans," season 1, episode 11, *Over There*, aired October 5, 2005.

244 Anna Froula

46. "Suicide Rain," season 1, episode 10, *Over There*, aired September 28, 2005.
47. David Bauder, "Execs: People with DVRs Watch More TV," *Washington Post*, November 16, 2005, http://www.washingtonpost.com/wp-dyn/content/article/2005/11/16/AR2005111601756.html.
48. Raymond Williams, *Television, Technology, and Cultural Form* (New York: Schocken, 1971), 86. On "viewing strips," see Newcomb and Hirsch, "Television as Cultural Forum," 51. Viewing strips vary according to which commercial sponsors advertise in different regions of the country.
49. For war shows habituating citizens to see themselves as soldiers, see Takacs, *Terrorism TV*, 101.
50. David Annandale, "Avatars of Destruction: Cheerleading and Deconstructing the 'War on Terror' through Video Games," in *Reframing 9/11: Film, Popular Culture, and the "War on Terror,"* ed. Jeff Birkenstein, Anna Froula, and Karen Randell (New York: Continuum, 2010), 97–106, 101.

15 *Generation Kill* and the New Screen Combat

Magdalena Yüksel and Colleen Kennedy-Karpat

No one could accuse the American cultural industries of giving the Iraq War the silent treatment. Between the 24-hour news cycle and fictionalized entertainment, war narratives have played a significant and evolving role in the media landscape since the declaration of war in 2003. Iraq War films, on the whole, have failed to impress audiences and critics, with notable exceptions like Kathryn Bigelow's *The Hurt Locker* (2008), which won the Oscar for Best Picture, and her follow-up *Zero Dark Thirty* (2012), which tripled its budget in worldwide box office intake.[1] Television, however, has fared better as a vehicle for profitable, war-inspired entertainment, which is perhaps best exemplified by the nine seasons of Fox's *24* (2001–2010). Situated squarely between these two formats lies the television miniseries, combining seriality with the closed narrative of feature filmmaking to bring to the small screen—and, probably more significantly, to the DVD market—a time-limited story that cultivates a broader and deeper narrative development than a single film, yet maintains a coherent thematic and creative agenda.

As a pioneer in both the miniseries format and the more nebulous category of quality television, HBO has taken fresh approaches to representing combat as it unfolds in the twenty-first century.[2] These innovations build on yet also depart from the precedent set by *Band of Brothers* (2001), Steven Spielberg's WWII project that established HBO's interest in war-themed miniseries, and the subsequent companion project, *The Pacific* (2010).[3] Stylistically, both *Band of Brothers* and *The Pacific* depict WWII combat in ways that recall Spielberg's blockbuster *Saving Private Ryan* (1998). Involving Spielberg and his DreamWorks studio also forges natural connections between Hollywood cinema and HBO content—which, to be fair, has always been deeply entwined with the movie business thanks to a pre-series business model built on airing feature films for subscribing TV audiences. The channel's turn to serial television with *The Sopranos* (1999–2007) marked a departure from this film-centered model, yet it remains significant that in terms of production, HBO's *Generation Kill* (hereafter *GK*) lacks the cinematic pedigree of Spielberg's WWII miniseries.

Still, co-creators David Simon and Ed Burns were no strangers to HBO when they began filming *GK*, which they started immediately after wrapping up their previous HBO series *The Wire* (2002–2008), a landmark of recent quality TV. The success of *The Wire* helped win Simon the status of an auteur, presumed to be the most important factor in creating a show's unique vision. While in film, "auteur" refers most often to the director, television tends to treat directors as skilled craftspeople rather than creative lynchpins, reserving authorship status for the producer (which, significantly, was also Spielberg's role for *Brothers*). Simon's role as the public face of his television work directs the shows' metanarrative and separates him from his credited co-creator Burns, thereby promoting Simon alone to the realm of TV auteurship.[4]

When *GK* was released, television critics seemed eager to capitalize on the momentum that had gathered around *The Wire*'s later seasons. Positive reviews would generally mention *The Wire* and its co-creators within the first two paragraphs, including *USA Today*'s suggestion that HBO's recipe for future success would be to "let David Simon and Ed Burns do whatever they want."[5] Indeed, most critics praised the show, noting both an unusual resistance to romanticizing warfare and a "faithful" adaptation of Evan Wright's book of the same name—although the latter point was also made by the series' most fervent detractors.[6]

However, like many Iraq War films made for the big screen, *GK* never amassed a significant audience, prompting *Variety* to reiterate its endorsement mid-run under the faintly incredulous headline: "*Generation Kill*: Folks, you're really missing out."[7] Yet, even *Variety*'s initial review muses that *GK*'s mid-summer release indicates a lack of confidence that an Iraq War miniseries will attract a devoted audience, let alone win any industry plaudits at the distant Emmys. For his part, Simon committed to the long view, telling an interviewer in 2008 to "check back in about five, six years" to determine the real impact of *GK*.[8] Almost on cue, in 2012 Simon told *Salon* that *GK* was selling twice the DVDs it had turned out four years earlier, crediting the power of word of mouth and, in particular, the endorsement of "guys at Camp Pendleton in the Marines for two years telling their families, their brother, whoever else, 'You've just got to see this miniseries. Because these guys got what we do.'"[9]

What the Marines do in *GK* is kick off the war in Iraq. The miniseries follows the men of First Recon Battalion from the war's first day through its third week, the same unit and time frame that Wright wrote about in his 2004 book. Wright's fictionalized counterpart in the film (Lee Tergesen) is never named, but the soldiers call him "War Scribe" or "Reporter" on the rare occasions they engage with him. Those soldiers, poised on the front lines of a nascent conflict, are the beating heart of *GK*, with high-ranking officers largely absent from the action on screen. As many critics concede, it takes a few episodes to pick out the protagonists, but several individuals emerge as key players. Sgt. Brad Colbert (Alexander Skarsgård), known to his comrades as "Iceman," leads the vehicle charged with protecting the Scribe, and Cpl. Ray Person (James Ransone) runs communications alongside him; filling out the vehicle is Lance Cpl. James Trombley (Billy Lush), who appears the most eager for combat regardless of its moral dilemmas. Farther up the chain of command, First Lt. Nathaniel Fick (Stark Sands) distinguishes himself as a competent leader and a voice of reason, particularly compared to the overzealous Capt. Dave "Captain America" McGraw (Eric Nenninger) and the lunkheaded Capt. Craig "Encino Man" Schwetje (Brian Patrick Wade). Even First Recon's most visible, high-ranking commander, Lt. Col. Stephen "Godfather" Ferrando (Chance Kelly), seems more interested in gaining favor with Maj. Gen. James Mattis (Robert John Burke) than in maintaining attentive leadership on the ground. *GK* traces the battalion's complicated political workings in part to comment on the problems inherent in military hierarchy, but also to critique the deployment of First Recon as what Iceman calls "semi-skilled labor," used for purposes beyond (that is, beneath) their highly specific training.

Instead of promoting individuation by highlighting characters one at a time, *GK* recreates the sensation of sudden immersion, leaving viewers to "feel the movie" rather than focus on who says what.[10] Unlike *Brothers*, which carefully individuates the soldiers and their experiences (see chapter 6, this volume), *GK* tends to crowd the screen by framing the protagonists alongside secondary or unnamed tertiary characters in the same shot. Just as Wright was thrown into the dynamics of a well-established unit, viewers must comprehend the soldiers' personalities over time, through repeated exposure rather than belabored exposition. Although this approach might preclude character development (a drawback noted by several critics), it emphasizes the shared experience of war. The sheer number of people with significant screen time combines with a visual style inspired by documentary filmmaking to suggest an ethnographic sensibility, reinforcing the sense of authenticity introduced by *GK*'s source text—an eyewitness account of life on the front lines—and further supported by Simon's background as a journalist. These aesthetics indicate a quiet refusal to bow to typical requirements for the genre and medium while underscoring Simon's effort to immerse his characters in the historical reality of the Iraq War.

GK was neither the first nor the only foray into the Middle East for HBO, and more than most media outlets post-9/11, the channel has shown a keen awareness of how not to fall into the ideological trap of framing warfare as entertainment that supports a neoconservative agenda. Chronologically and ideologically, *GK* falls between two made-for-TV movies set during the US wars in Iraq and aired on HBO. *Live from Baghdad* (2002), based on Robert Wiener's memoir, centers on CNN's corporate cynicism and exposes how journalists exploited the first Gulf War. But whereas *Live from Baghdad* can be interpreted as a self-critical interrogation of media objectivity, *Taking Chance* (2009) draws on more familiar tropes of patriotic sacrifice set against a disingenuously apolitical home front. *Live from Baghdad* showcases the media's contribution to the perception of the war, while *Taking Chance* narrates a home front drama of patriotic martyrdom. What *GK* brings to HBO is the missing element in each of these TV movies: the soldiers

248 *Magdalena Yüksel and Colleen Kennedy-Karpat*

on the front lines. Not coincidentally, each of these three HBO productions was "based on a true story," with Wright himself participating in the adaptation of his reportage for *GK*.

Authenticity and the Combat Genre

As a genre rooted in history, the combat film has been subjected to pointed criticism of its accuracy and authenticity, both of which draw upon the complex notion of the "true story." For war narratives, the notion of truth plays a significant role, and these texts connote truth in a variety of ways. Early WWII combat films incorporated documentary footage into their fictional stories (e.g., *Sands of Iwo Jima* [1949]) and often cast veterans as actors; *GK* also puts veterans on the screen, combined with a documentary-like characterization and cinematography that reflects the creators' desire for "obsessive verisimilitude" in depicting combat.[11]

Drawing on eyewitness accounts as source material also conveys a desire to hew closely to the truth, as Spielberg did with *Brothers* by adapting historian Stephen E. Ambrose's interviews with WWII veterans. The elapsed time between WWII and its retelling, along with the pervasiveness of preformed war narratives in American culture, allows legitimate skepticism to qualify *Brothers*' claim to truth. Although Holocaust scholars have questioned the reliability of memory, Cathy Caruth observes that referencing trauma in film and television aims not to eliminate history, but rather to help others understand an event by resituating it onto the screen.[12] Although much less time separates soldiers' and journalists' experience in Iraq from its mediated adaptation, memory scholars assert that the veracity of any eyewitness account remains inherently disputable. War reportage like Wright's also raises the issue of reliability. Like memoirs, first-person journalism is subject to tension that "arises between factual truth and the discovered or imposed pattern of meaning."[13] Putting lived experience into writing involves selection, manipulation, and reorganization; the practice of adaptation then initiates the process again, with the added concern of molding the source material to fit the demands of a different medium.[14]

With any appeal to *truth* rendered problematic, then, the more flexible concept of *authenticity* might better serve an analysis of how war narratives on film and television try to respect the ebbs and flows of lived history. What does it mean for a film to be authentic, to lay claim to its own veracity? Textually, *GK* connotes its authenticity through its attention to historical accuracy and in its commitment to televisual verisimilitude. But, perhaps most importantly, much of *GK*'s claim to authenticity comes from adaptation and auteur discourses. Wright's role as a reporter invokes a certain responsibility when relating the facts, and the miniseries retells his "true story" through TV adaptation. Although Wright's book frames the author and narrator as a single figure, the miniseries complicates this unified vision by delegating these roles to a team of directors, writers, and actors who relay events they never witnessed.[15] By adopting

Wright/Scribe's point of view, the "understanding of events could bring an audience closest to some emotional truth of the character's experience."[16] However, film and television both have the power to carry multiple points of view, so *GK* shows conversations happening outside the Scribe's purview, e.g., between General Mattis and Godfather. Simon's claim that Wright's book was his bible bolsters this discourse of authenticity, which is reinforced by *GK's* collaborative authorship under Simon's auteur brand.[17] Presenting the miniseries any other way would have risked alienating audiences familiar with the book.

Another issue of authenticity is related to the way journalists like Wright reflected contemporary politics. As Stacy Takacs has noted, the media presented the first stages of the Iraq War in ways that echoed the government's neoconservative attitudes.[18] Although many TV series complied with the Bush administration's propaganda goals, niche programming like *GK* departed from this formula by voicing doubt, making soldiers the mouthpiece for disaffected citizens who saw the Iraq War as futile and unnecessary. As Takacs argues, *GK's* producers made an unusually strong effort to leave its viewers the work of producing their own "moral judgments about the war."[19] Wright's account introduced anti-propaganda messages that added much-needed complexity to war narratives circulating in the media; as a miniseries, *GK* sought a perspective that differed from the one championed by pro-government media outlets by drawing on Wright's perceived authenticity and, as discussed below, by innovating the combat genre.

These innovations must be understood alongside films depicting earlier wars, as the combat genre evolves within its own category over time. Jeanine Basinger writes, "Genre will be stronger than truth. It will use truth, take it in, incorporate it. This is how genre stays alive."[20] As a TV miniseries, *GK* assumes the conventions of the combat film by embracing the mélange of platforms implicit in the tagline: "It's not TV. It's HBO." Framed by Basinger, the combat film has established a number of familiar conventions beyond the historical setting of war. Typically, a combat film features a male, military protagonist who interacts with a socioeconomically and ethnically diverse group of soldiers under the eye of a commentator or observer: a reporter, his own or a comrade's diary, omniscient voice-over narration, etc. Collectively, these soldiers experience interpersonal conflict within the unit, bond over their struggles, and (eventually) engage the enemy. Thematically, the combat film also celebrates the machismo of war, characterized by a precarious combination of agony and exhilaration, as well as the potential for cathartic sacrifice. The story is infused with concomitant references to military life: insignia, flags, military songs, military objectives, enemy presence, and at least one climactic, cinematic battle.[21]

Films about WWII draw on these conventions to build sympathy for Allied soldiers, even if the "good guys" are not always well intentioned or valorous. Vietnam films, however, often eschew a polarizing view of "good" and "bad," instead establishing motifs including the "feminization of the enemy, the demonization of the media and the valorization of patriarchy."[22]

250   *Magdalena Yüksel and Colleen Kennedy-Karpat*

These differences have brought Vietnam films into dialectical tension with WWII films, because the loss of soldiers' lives in Vietnam cannot be balanced by the posthumous compensation of military victory.[23] As Robert Eberwein explains, during WWII Americans killed Nazis, while in Vietnam the Americans ended up killing each other, thereafter changing "the nature of the war film genre." Contrary to the righteousness and purpose of WWII films, Vietnam films "ripped apart the union of the combat squad, and turned within to confront the true enemy."[24] Films about the Iraq War push several tendencies of Vietnam War films even further: by replacing long, realistic, necessarily climactic battle scenes with shorter, intermittent violence; by portraying local populations with compassion and including their criticism of the US military operations on their soil; and by de-emphasizing the casualties and fatalities among US troops that WWII films use to heighten audiences' emotional involvement. Whereas Basinger emphasizes that the resolution of a typical WWII film involves "either ... victory or defeat, death or survival," Iraq War films such as *Redacted* (2007), *In the Valley of Elah* (2007), or even *American Sniper* (2014) question what it means to kill civilians in the name of the mission—is this defeat or victory?[25]

While adopting some longstanding conventions, in many respects *GK* and other visual entertainment narratives of the Iraq War underscore generic developments that reflect changes in how war has been fought. In *GK*, as in WWII films, a heterogeneous mix of soldiers bond as "brothers" and fight a telegenic battle sequence in nearly every episode. As in Vietnam films, these soldiers confront a problematically othered enemy under the command of officers whose motives and competence are increasingly called into question. Departing from both the "good war" narratives of WWII films and the absurdist narratives of Vietnam War films, *GK*'s ideological framework comes from Wright and Simon's desire to showcase the soldiers' feelings about war. The miniseries also breaks with post-9/11 news media's depiction of bloodless combat, a strategy that misleadingly suggests that technology has stripped warfare of both its inherent violence and its human costs. The ethos of skepticism that *GK* builds around the US mission challenges many established conventions of the war genre: most pointedly, the dual notion of military service as patriotic sacrifice and the character-building nature of combat.

Narrating Combat: Characters and Conflicts

Echoing WWII-era combat film conventions, *GK* establishes a clear parallel between the military unit and family dynamics. Basinger describes the "father figure" in a military narrative as "the best educated" among the soldiers, and he usually dies in action.[26] Simon expands and explains his version of these parallels, naming Iceman as the "father," Person as the "mother," and Trombley as the "child"—even assigning the less conventional role of "weird uncle" to the reporter.[27] But *GK* also twists this structure by

Generation Kill *and the New Screen Combat* 251

showing multiple father figures, yet pushing none of them to make the ultimate sacrifice. In fact, these military "fathers" distinguish themselves within the narrative and within the military unit by overtly expressing doubt that this war might be worthy of such a sacrifice in the first place. Nevertheless, these leaders look out for their men, take responsibility for their behavior, and often keep their own feelings muted. One example of this is Iceman's reaction to Trombley's shooting of two Iraqi children early in the series. Although Iceman is stumped by Trombley's seeming indifference to the incident, he does not join the unit in condemning Trombley for negligence; instead, Iceman reassures him that the standing order to consider all persons in the area as hostile will protect him from prosecution. Like an honorable father, Iceman assumes responsibility for the incident himself.

In the wider network of this military family, the characters also use humor to diffuse the tensions of combat, especially through Ray Person. This humor tends toward the political: The soldiers not only mock the US for bringing "freedom" to the oppressed—Espera often mentions the US's similar "help" for Native Americans—but also criticize their own situation with jokes about the lack of food, lack of sex, lack of supplies, and an apparent lack of common sense, as when one captain requests that soldiers mark a minefield at night. Similarly, the long-running series *M*A*S*H* (CBS, 1972–1983) offers morbid and self-critical humor but tempers its bite by setting the action in Korea when the real target was clearly Vietnam.[28] *GK* might not mix comedy with combat drama as comfortably as *M*A*S*H*, but its humor mordantly criticizes the framing and execution of the ongoing conflict. For example, in "A Burning Dog," Ray Person admits to suggesting that the US entered Iraq for NAMBLA (North American Man/Boy Love Association) and insinuates that the soldiers are actually clearing the way for Starbucks.

The solidarity in *GK*, however congenial and familial, is forged in an aggressive atmosphere and shaped by commanders who clearly take pleasure from the fight itself. Similarly, Basinger observes that WWII combat films convey ambivalence about battle, showing that "war is hell" and that glory is never unmitigated. A film that portrays war as thrilling to watch, she says, "denies its own message" while "a film that says war is fun, but shows too much violence and death, may not deliver [the emotional relief] it intends."[29] *GK* shows combat as exhilarating, yet often reveals its purpose to be dubious or self-serving. In the series, Mattis overlooks Godfather's mistakes and his failure to address the ineptitude and mental illness that Captain America inflicts on his men. Godfather's misplaced priorities bring undue punishment to Lieutenant Fick, who faces sanctions after urging conduct that is more principled.

This problematic hierarchy and its flawed assessment of competence produce one of the most common conflicts in the Iraq War combat film: interpersonal friction among American comrades. *GK* sets up adversarial relationships between Godfather and Fick, between Fick and Encino Man, and between Captain America and the unlucky men under his command. These conflicts inspire bonding when it comes to understanding the rules of engagement, standard operating procedure, and, most broadly, the execution of maneuver combat. For example, in "Screwby" Fick confronts Encino Man over calling in an airstrike that would endanger their own unit. When Encino Man misreads the grids, and Fick refrains from correcting him, the unit doctor (Jonah Lotan) grumbles that "for once, our asses get saved by sheer incompetence." Fick's will to speak out—or not—in order to safeguard the unit also earns Iceman's trust. But their most intense adversaries are officers set farther up the chain; although many orders are questionable and/or irrelevant to the work of the mission—like Major Sixta's (Neal Jones) meticulous grooming standards—the soldiers find ways to address them so as not to seed discord in the battalion. Major Sixta finally admits that his attention to the soldiers' moustaches aims to boost morale by redirecting dissatisfaction with the higher command toward himself ("Bomb in the Garden"). When the battalion can focus on the banality of shaving after a haphazardly planned mission, he suggests, they bond over a common, internal "nemesis" instead of dwelling on each other's mistakes.[30]

Battlefield Contact

GK also complicates the dichotomy between the trauma and exhilaration of the combat experience in ways not seen in other combat films, because the nature of combat, redesigned for the new century, does not allow soldiers to "get some" in the same way they could in preceding conflicts. This "new" warfare started with the Gulf War (1990–1991), often labeled the first postmodern war because it blended technological progress with unprecedented media saturation in alignment with the Cold War-era concept called the Revolution in Military Affairs (RMA).[31] In 2001, the September 11 attacks provoked further changes, shifting the boundaries between enemy and ally, between civilian and military domain. In Philip E. Agre's view, post-9/11 nation-states at war—primarily the US—focus on damaging "enemy" infrastructure rather than on direct combat; technology, he continues, has nearly "eliminated [soldiers'] zone of professional autonomy" within the sphere of combat. By subjecting the men of First Recon to the orders of technophilic, trigger-happy superiors, *GK* tries to apprehend this postmodern warfare.[32]

The RMA changed the way soldiers experienced war and how they understood the "imagined" (represented) war in which they could never participate. Men in *GK* seem well versed in military history, comparing their mistakes with those made in Vietnam or—even more tellingly—in European colonies, but their most tangible point of reference is their own experience in Afghanistan, where the RMA was also applied. Those who had tours of duty there show nostalgia for it, implicitly holding up Afghanistan as a more "legitimate" war, and certainly one *better fought*—that is, a war

Generation Kill *and the New Screen Combat*   253

with rules that were followed; a more purposeful distinction between allies and enemies; and a far more effective targeting of the latter ("Cradle of Civilization"). Beyond the critique of the Iraq War couched in these comparisons, *GK*'s characters also show frustration about their current mission, which grows deeper over the course of the series. Indeed, this ability to build the soldiers' dissatisfaction gradually underscores one of the advantages that television offers the war narrative. An episodic structure allows time not only to develop multiple and complex points of view, but also to invite viewers to immerse themselves in the virtual world of war through week-to-week viewing or binge watching. Extended and/or repeated exposure to the characters builds viewers' trust in their perspective, and showing these soldiers' personal evolution invites audiences to adjust their own outlook according to the characters' mounting disillusionment about the war, including the problems and effects of the RMA.

This creeping discontent, justified through cause and effect, builds a feeling of failure that complicates any sense of military victory. In the beginning (of both the series and the war), the Marines are stoic, yet regret lingers on their faces when they release surrendered Iraqis under orders, already silently questioning the logic of their superiors' decisions. The sense that the Marines have abandoned those they were sent to help magnifies their disillusionment, and the gaps and contradictions in military strategy become so glaring that the soldiers begin to speak out against them. In "A Burning Dog," First Recon is ordered to drive past piles of ordnance lying in an open field just outside the city en route to the area's only school, which is slated for detonation because the Republican Guard "took over every classroom." Ray Person comments on how "weird" it is that two injured servicemen convinced their superiors to "level half the town" when abandoned weaponry provokes no such extreme reaction.

Perhaps most poignantly, the final episode "Bomb in the Garden" shows the troops entering Baghdad and coming face to face with the US military's failures. The soldiers are forbidden to provide security to local neighborhoods and cannot restore the water or electricity systems that were destroyed during the US bombing, constraints that Fick describes as "madness." In the same episode, Iceman tries to safely detonate US bombs that have fallen, intact, into urban areas; he deals with one lodged in a garden where children would play, but Fick orders him to stop before he can detonate a second bomb. Iceman's frustration only worsens after a BBC radio report describes kids playing on a tank who were shot by "newly arrived grunts" for "having a weapon"; in response, Iceman declares, "We keep killing civilians, we're gonna waste this fucking victory." Ever the professional soldier, Iceman still follows orders, but this episode delivers frank criticism from the miniseries' most sympathetic characters, emphatically underscoring the poor planning that brings them, at best, a pyrrhic victory.

The most compelling and frequently recurring evidence of combat mistakes in *GK* comes in its portrayal of death, a burden the series shows to be borne almost exclusively by non-combatants.[33] This marks a complete departure from connoting death as either patriotic sacrifice, a framing prevalent in WWII combat films, or as punishment for involvement, as seen in Vietnam War films. For the soldiers in *GK*, death is omnipresent yet kept at arm's length, entering their orbit when they kill Iraqis—"enemy" and civilian alike—or when they hear about Marine casualties with no attachment to First Recon. The Iraqi bodies that appear in nearly every episode highlight America's gruesome failure to "win hearts and minds," as the series focuses more intently on civilian casualties than on insurgents killed in action. This stark imbalance points to the strategic shortcomings of US policy, and the lack of fatalities in First Recon denies characters and viewers alike the catharsis that accompanies an American death in other war films. Death in *GK* aims not to convey heroism to fallen soldiers, but rather the full apprehension of the meaning of "collateral damage." Allied deaths in WWII combat films are presumed to serve the good of society, but American deaths in *GK*, which occur rarely and never among the protagonists, are treated with indignation among the troops, as they clash with their superiors over decisions that they find irrational.

The *purpose* of death in the WWII film thus marks a sharp contrast with the pointlessness that *GK* ascribes to the casualties in Iraq, whether suffered by US forces or by civilians guilty only of being in the wrong place at the wrong time. From the beginning, the soldiers of First Recon grapple with an inability to absorb these casualties into a coherent narrative, as illustrated in Iceman's comment about "wasting" the victory. The soldiers pass civilian corpses on the roads, mistakenly kill children and women, and repeatedly witness their superiors' glaring incompetence, like ordering an airstrike on empty desert. Although most of the main characters are keenly aware that US forces are inflicting unnecessary damage on the Iraqi people, *GK* shows that tensions run high for any combat situation, no matter how hastily or carelessly ordered, even though each incident further inures them to the act of killing.

The gory display of Iraqi corpses in *GK* draws attention to how American forces outmatch the insurgents in training and technology. The Allied and Axis powers in WWII had comparably trained soldiers and access to similar technologies; in Vietnam, the US had technological superiority but lacked its opponents' knowledge of the territory; in Iraq, the US had superior technology, training, and tactical information while Iraqi insurgents fought with improvised weapons and little to no training. These imbalances demonstrate the RMA's conception of battlefields that contrast First World technology with outmoded, Third World warfare. The RMA foresaw a short-operational victory, and as Takacs notes, only in these terms did it succeed; the RMA failed to create a long-term strategy to finish the conflict.[34] Without a plan to bring closure to the war, the drawn-out US military presence alienated and angered the Iraqis, obscuring the ultimate goal of bringing broader peace to the region.

Generation Kill *and the New Screen Combat* 255

In *GK*, the failure of the RMA to prevent collateral damage takes a heavy toll on the soldiers' morale and on the US goal to win "hearts and minds," compounding the traumatic experiences discussed above. The soldiers see tough combat in every episode, nearly all of it dogged by fatal or near-fatal mistakes: In "A Burning Dog" the Recon soldiers observe a calm Iraqi village with kids playing in the garden and women cooking then witness its annihilation after an erroneously ordered airstrike (Figure 15.1).

Figure 15.1 *Generation Kill* highlights the military's failure to prevent collateral damage in the Iraq War and its consequent wearing down of the soldiers' morale. In one example, members of First Recon witness the annihilation of an Iraqi household that they had determined harmless.

After watching the destruction, Iceman can only stutter that they cannot know what their superiors saw, but they must have found something to justify the attack. The war, pitched as necessary and preventative, thus

256   *Magdalena Yüksel and Colleen Kennedy-Karpat*

transforms before viewers' eyes into a war of provocation. Beyond battles with insurgents, the soldiers raid villages, homes, and schools, killing innocent civilians and transforming the war zone into a no-man's-land, open to criminals who disregard the laws of war.

The Iraqis are not the only ones under surveillance in *GK*; as Agre observes, the US soldiers have no "zone of professional autonomy," as every decision about where to move and whom to shoot is discussed beforehand with their superiors.[35] Unlike WWII and Vietnam films, in which soldiers have little to no contact with the officers who organize the battle, *GK* shows soldiers in Iraq as under near-constant supervision. Leaders like Godfather operate at a remove from their soldiers and engage in combat not for strategic gain but for the thrill of combat itself. For example, in "A Burning Dog" the battalion is ordered to cross a bridge where the insurgents have set up an ambush. Forced down the most dangerous road, in darkness, the soldiers continue under the lights of Cobra helicopters to drive over a booby-trapped bridge. These orders introduce a parallel between Iraqi civilians and US combat troops, both of whom are subject to the power of distant but violent others. In a war where air strikes can replace almost any direct combat situation, commanders still push their soldiers into unnecessary engagements, forcing confrontation for its own sake, regardless of its target or effects.

Media Presence in Combat

By portraying combat during an ongoing conflict, *GK* also connects to contemporary, non-fictional representations of the Iraq War, even contributing to the heated debate over the war's effectiveness that involved Americans at the home front. Unlike *GK*, *Brothers* and *Pacific* take a nostalgic perspective on the notion of WWII as a "good war" and reiterate established conventions of the WWII film. *GK*, on the other hand, takes a more ironic stance toward the combat genre by showing how its established assumptions are poorly suited to the reality of postmodern warfare. *GK* thus illustrates how the new mode of engagement has unmoored itself from the generic expectations established by combat films based on previous wars.

The role of the media in the soldiers' lives marks yet another aspect of warfare in the new century. Technology allows journalists to share images of war almost instantaneously with soldiers, civilians, and other journalists, leading to the immersion and entrapment of soldiers within images of war. Observing photographs of the World Trade Center collapse and prisoner abuse at Abu Ghraib, Jean Baudrillard contends that war now takes place virtually; it is, for example, in a photo of an American soldier forcing an Iraqi to sodomize a pig that true violence exists, for these images neutralize conflict just as pornography neutralizes sex.[36] These photographs not only become viral, leading to one side "extinguishing" the other through such

Generation Kill *and the New Screen Combat* 257

images, but they also amass their own power to reduce the fact of the event to mere spectacle.

Baudrillard claims that it is no longer important whether these war images are false or true; rather, it is the way images are immersed in the war that measures their impact, making events synonymous with their pictures and turning them into a parody of violence, a reality show that is in fact "a desperate simulacrum of power."[37] He also claims that "embedded" journalists, like Wright, are no longer necessary; the soldiers themselves can circulate their own imagery. *GK* acknowledges that soldiers now narrate their own war experience by adding a concluding scene, without precedent in Wright's book, in which the unit gathers together to watch a video montage they created. As Baudrillard describes, while watching their own video, the soldiers observe how their virtual identities have become of a piece with the dead bodies, the explosions, the battered landscapes. In the beginning, the soldiers perceive these images as exultant and triumphant, similar to the scene in *Jarhead* (2005) when Marines cheer at an attack on a Vietnamese village in *Apocalypse Now* (1979). Anthony Swofford, ex-Marine and author of the Gulf War memoir from which Sam Mendes' film was adapted, has discussed the perception of "anti-war" Vietnam films as exhilarating rather than appalling, emphasizing that, for a young man thirsty for combat, these films cannot avoid becoming pro-war.[38] In *GK*, however, the accumulation of these images shifts the Marines' perspective, and one by one, the soldiers of First Recon stop egging on their virtual selves, then turn and walk away from the screen in silent acknowledgment of the bitterness that comes with this experience of war. By the end, the only soldier left is Trombley, for whom these images are "fucking beautiful." As Takacs notes, Trombley's vocal, visible approval leaves viewers with the notion that men like Trombley would most probably be responsible for the next, doomed phase of the already botched war.[39]

In Baudrillard's words, "those who live by the spectacle will die by the spectacle"—meaning a figurative death for most, but the relationship between soldiers and the media reveals different implications.[40] Although post-9/11 news coverage tended to assume a pro-military perspective, with time the media began to turn its back on the war. The soldiers in *GK* seem quite aware of the American media's duplicity, treating the BBC as trustworthy—in "Get Some," someone claims that even Godfather gets war news from the BBC—while dismissing CNN in "Cradle of Civilization" as purveyors of "drama" lacking any useful information.

Perhaps the postmodern news media—that is, media outlets invested in the simulacrum of war—will soon be disregarded when it comes to Iraq. As historian Michael Anderegg once said of Vietnam, "cinematic representations seem to have supplanted even so-called factual analyses as *the* discourse of the war, as the place where some kind of reckoning will need to be made and tested."[41] The potential for entertainment television like *GK* to assert historical knowledge is already here, reflecting a postmodern tendency to render history indistinguishable from its representations, even in

258 Magdalena Yüksel and Colleen Kennedy-Karpat

conflicts whose conclusions and repercussions have yet to play out. These events, after all, need distance to be assessed as history, so that, in Simon's words, citizens can become "more fully aware of what it means to engage in modern state-sponsored warfare."[42] But cloaking war discourse in the guise of entertainment brings with it the risk that "the conversion of war, especially specific wars, can escape recuperation in America as long as war and militarism remain such deeply ingrained features of social life."[43] The Iraq War combat genre is relatively young, yet it presents the potential to avoid both romanticizing warfare and generating celebratory "war porn."

Notes

1. Financial information for *Zero Dark Thirty* from Box Office Mojo, accessed July 3, 2015: http://www.boxofficemojo.com/movies/?id=binladen.htm.
2. For an analysis of the rising esteem of television, including the designation "quality TV," see Michael Z. Newman and Elana Levine, *Legitimating Television: Media Convergence and Cultural Status* (New York: Routledge, 2012).
3. On *Band of Brothers*, see chapter 6, this volume.
4. This is just one theory of Simon's rise to auteur status despite repeated collaboration with Ed Burns. The focus on Simon as auteur has evidently reached the level of received wisdom; a book dedicated to *The Wire* mentions Simon on nearly every page, whereas Burns's name appears only a handful of times. Tiffany Potter and C. W. Marshall, *The Wire: Urban Decay and American Television* (New York: Continuum, 2009).
5. Blanco, Robert, "HBO scores a direct hit with *Generation Kill*," *USA Today*, July 11, 2008, http://usatoday30.usatoday.com/life/television/reviews/2008-07-10-generation-kill_N.htm.
6. According to review aggregator Metacritic.com, *Generation Kill* has a better-than-respectable score of 80 out of 100. But this high grade masks how polarizing the miniseries was for critics; *The New Yorker* and *Slate* published negative reviews that countered fairly unbridled praise from *Variety*, *Entertainment Weekly*, *The Washington Post* and other venues.
7. Brian Lowry, "Review: *Generation Kill*," *Variety*, July 9, 2008, http://variety.com/2008/scene/markets-festivals/generation-kill-1200508469/ and Stuart Levine, "*Generation Kill*: Folks, you're really missing out," *Variety*, August 13, 2008, http://variety.com/2008/tv/news/posted-by-stuar-19768/.
8. Richard Beck, "Beyond the Choir: An Interview with David Simon," *Film Quarterly* 62, no. 2 (2008): 44–49.
9. Willa Paskin, "David Simon: Most TV is unwatchable," *Salon*, September 23, 2012, http://www.salon.com/2012/09/23/david_simon_most_tv_is_unwatchable/.
10. Beck, "Beyond the Choir," 47.
11. Jacob Weisberg, "The Wire on Fire," *Slate*, September 13, 2006, http://www.slate.com/articles/news_and_politics/the_big_idea/2006/09/the_wire_on_fire.html.
12. Cathy Caruth, *Unclaimed Experience: Trauma, Narrative, History* (Baltimore: The John Hopkins University Press, 1996); see also Marita Sturken, "The Remembering of Forgetting: Recovered Memory and the Question of Experience," *Social Text* 57 (1998): 103–25.
13. Ibid., 292.

Generation Kill *and the New Screen Combat* 259

14. William Mooney, "Memoir and the Limits of Adaptation," in *The Literature/ Film Reader: Issues of Adaptation*, ed. James M. Welsh and Peter Lev (Maryland: Scarecrow, 2007), 292.
15. Ibid., 286.
16. Ibid., 288.
17. Beck, "Beyond the Choir," 46.
18. Stacy Takacs, *Terrorism TV: Popular Entertainment in Post-9/11 America* (Lawrence, KS: University of Kansas Press, 2012), 167.
19. Although she still finds that *GK* echoes neoconservative ideology in its portrayal of the invasion as "botched" but not irredeemable. Ibid., 160.
20. Jeanine Basinger, *The World War II Combat Film: Anatomy of a Genre* (New York: Columbia University Press, 1986), 170.
21. Ibid., 73–75.
22. Michael Anderegg, *Inventing Vietnam: The War in Film and Television* (Philadelphia: Temple University Press, 1991), 8.
23. Robert Eberwein, *The Hollywood War Film* (West Sussex: Wiley-Blackwell, 2010), 94.
24. Ibid., 96.
25. Basinger, *Combat Film*, 75.
26. Ibid., 54.
27. Beck, "Beyond the Choir," 48.
28. For more on *M*A*S*H*, see chapters 8 and 9, this volume.
29. Basinger, *Combat Film*, 95.
30. Beck, "Beyond the Choir," 48.
31. Melani McAlister, *Epic Encounters: Culture, Media, and US Interests in the Middle East Since 1945* (London: University of California Press, 2005). McAlister argues that the Gulf War was both "a major military action and a staged media event," describing coverage as intensified and dramatic, yet not very informative (239). The RMA's innovations aimed to reform the American military with a clear focus on deterrence and efforts to minimize collateral damage. According to Andrew Bacevich, until the Gulf War, the RMA tried to move war out of the industrial age and into the information age, aiming "both to render the battlefield and the enemy's order of battle transparent and to make it possible to hit and kill anything anywhere on the planet at any time." Andrew J. Bacevich, *The New American Militarism* (New York: Oxford University Press, 2005), 167–68.
32. Postmodern in the sense that the twenty-first century soldier, much like an audience glued to a screen, experiences war primarily as a simulacrum of itself. Philip E. Agre, "Imagining the Next War: Infrastructural Warfare and the Conditions of Democracy," September 15, 2001, http://polaris.gseis.ucla.edu/pagre/war.html.
33. For an extended conversation on casualties from opposing sides of the Iraq war, see Judith Butler, *Precarious Life: The Powers of Mourning and Violence* (London: Verso, 2004), and Butler, *Frames of War: When Is Life Grievable?* (London: Verso, 2009).
34. Takacs, *Terrorism TV*, 147–48.
35. Agre, "Imagining the Next War."
36. Jean Baudrillard, "War Porn," in *The Conspiracy of Art*, ed. Sylvère Lotringer, trans. Ames Hodges (New York: Semiotext(e), 2005), 205–209.
37. Ibid., 206.

38. Andrian Kreye, trans. "An Interview with Anthony Swofford, Author of the Gulf War bestseller *Jarhead*," originally published in *Das Magazin* (12/03), accessed July 2, 2015, http://www.andriankreye.com/Swofford1.html.
39. Takacs, *Terrorism TV*, 159.
40. Baudrillard, "War Porn," 208.
41. Anderegg, *Inventing Vietnam*, 1.
42. Beck, "Beyond the Choir," 46.
43. Takacs, *Terrorism TV*, 167.

16 "Don't Ask, Don't Tell" and Its Repeal in Showtime's *The L Word* and Lifetime's *Army Wives*

Liora Elias

This essay will examine the representations of the "Don't Ask, Don't Tell" (DADT) policy on US television in two series, one before the repeal and one after. While they embody decidedly different tones, both programs avoid critiquing the military and subsequent DADT policy outright. The essay begins with a brief introduction to the history of DADT, then examines *The L Word* (Showtime, 2004–2009) and *Army Wives* (Lifetime, 2007–2013) to show that in both cases the history of violence and homophobia against gays and lesbians in the military is underscored by each show's pro-military, patriotic, and normative sensibilities. In the case of *Army Wives,* the show uncritically celebrates military family life—but unique to much of the television archive centered on the military in the past, it features same-sex soldiers and their domestic as well as professional aspirations in the US military. Unlike *Army Wives, The L Word* does examine the difficulty lesbian soldiers face under the DADT policy. However, it does this at the same time that it maintains a commitment to normative forms of service and patriotism. In its depiction of life on base post-repeal, *Army Wives* promotes an unrealistic, idealized version of what lesbian life in the military is like within an uncharacteristically neat and tidy story-arc that was influenced by military oversight. Before discussing the way the television shows *The L Word* and *Army Wives* take on military policy of DADT before and after repeal, I will provide a brief history of DADT.

The History of Don't Ask, Don't Tell

Although hard data is difficult to find, one can assume that as long as the US military has existed, gay people have been involved in service.[1] Surprisingly, the military has not always had a policy excluding gays and lesbians from service.[2] The first time that gays were officially banned from service was during World War II. The reasons the military gave included concerns about men having feminine bodily characteristics and "effeminacy in dress and manner."[3] Other reasons included the perception that homosexuals would become "bad" soldiers, and cost the military money in the long run. The irony of the ban on gays in the military during WWII was that this was the first time in US history that the gay and lesbian community started to form

262   *Liora Elias*

a public identity. Military ports in places like San Francisco inspired the beginnings of gay urban life. In 1964, five years before the now-famous Stonewall riots, one of the first gay rights demonstrations took on the military's ban on gay service members as its central issue.[4] In 1992, Bill Clinton made a presidential campaign promise to repeal the ban on gays in the military. In fact, Clinton claimed at the time that he would lift the ban by Executive Order, if necessary, much like President Truman did when he desegregated the military in 1948. However, once Clinton was installed in the presidency, he met vocal opposition to lifting the military ban from the religious right, social conservatives, and military personnel. On the first day Clinton took office, The White House received 434,000 calls in favor of continuing the ban.[5]

The most prominent argument against lifting the ban heard at the 1993 Senate hearings had to do with "unit cohesion" (for examples, see chapter 12, this volume). Many years later, retired soldiers admitted to making up this particular rationale for the exclusion of gays from the military when they discovered that there was no legitimate reason to limit service in the military.[6] Interestingly, in 1957 the Navy commissioned the Crittenden Report, which is the first known study about gay people serving in the Armed Forces. The report concluded that gays and lesbians posed no security threat and could serve as effectively as anyone else. As the Crittenden Report states, "No factual data exists to support the contention that homosexuals are a greater [security] risk than heterosexuals."[7] It is key to note that the Crittenden Report only addresses the question of security risks (as in, whether LGBT soldiers are more susceptible to blackmail than heterosexual soldiers), not fitness for duty or "unit cohesion."

In 1993, after five months of hearings, the "Don't Ask, Don't Tell" policy was instituted by the Clinton administration in lieu of lifting the ban on gays and lesbians serving in the military. In theory, the implementation of DADT was to enforce effective military participation based on conduct rather than sexual orientation. Gay service members (former and active) have since reported that they were asked about their personal lives on a daily basis, from "what are you doing this weekend?" to "why aren't you married yet?" and often gay soldiers who attempted to keep their private lives private were disciplined for being "anti-social."[8] Despite the purported aim of the DADT measure, then, it actually failed to protect the privacy of gay and lesbian service members. In *Virtual Equality*, Urvashi Vaid called the DADT policy a product of "mainstreaming" and noted that it concretized the continuation of the "closet" for LGBT members of the Armed Forces. The ambiguous language of the policy made such soldiers susceptible to dismissal merely for arousing the suspicions of their commanding officers. The upshot, as Vaid put it, is that "no matter how straight-acting, patriotic, normal-looking, accessible, and heroic [gays and lesbians] are, the straight world resists our open integration into its society."[9]

One of the widespread consequences of the passage of DADT included the reporting of soldiers as gay or lesbian by psychiatrists (there is no patient confidentiality on base) or by parents and friends. In a number of cases, private journals were confiscated and used as a basis for discharge. If DADT was created to make sexuality a "non-issue" that was clearly not the result. As an anonymous gay service member says about living on base under DADT, "the Army continues to ask, continues to pursue, and continues to harass."[10] As a measure to assist with educating enlisted soldiers about the ins and outs of the DADT policy, the Pentagon issued a pamphlet that stated, "Don't ask means that a soldier will not be asked to divulge or discuss their sexual orientation unless there is credible information of homosexual conduct."[11] Of course, the vague language leaves much room for interpretation. What exactly is credible information? Who has the discretion to decide what is credible and what is not? Moreover, under the DADT policy, there were no options for legal remedy available to gay or presumed gay soldiers who experienced harassment from their fellow soldiers. The consequences of this omission became clear in 1999, when PFC Barry Winchell was harassed and eventually murdered because he was suspected of carrying on a relationship with a transgender woman (a story recounted in the 2003 Showtime movie *Soldier's Girl*). In all, according to the Servicemembers Legal Defense Network, an advocacy organization, over 14,000 service personnel were discharged under the policy from 1994 to 2003.[12]

The DADT measure seems to have had a disproportionate impact on women and especially women of color. Women were discharged under DADT at a rate that was approximately twice their representation in the military.[13] Sheridan Embser-Herbert called DADT's effect on women a "double whammy" and argued that:

> "Don't Ask, Don't Tell" provides service members a mechanism for harassing women in a way that virtually insures that they won't complain about the harassment. There are hundreds, if not thousands, of documented instances in which women who were harassed by being targeted as a lesbian did not complain because they feared that such a complaint would trigger an investigation of their sexual orientation.[14]

Black women, in particular, suffered under the measure. According to a Task Force Study of the 2000 US Census, black women were discharged under DADT at a rate that was three times their representation in the military. Black women reportedly were less than one percent of the military population, but they were discharged under DADT at a rate of three point three percent.[15] The same report notes that black women were discharged under DADT even if they were not lesbians. There were cases in which men brought charges against black women because they refused sexual advances (this likely applies to women generally, as well). In other cases, women were discharged under DADT simply for being in positions of power that threatened men who were not interested in serving under black women.

264   *Liora Elias*

Most infamously, between 1994 and 2003, over 54 Arab linguists were discharged from the military simply for being gay.[16] This set of discharges garnered significant news coverage because the lack of available Arab linguists meant that key intelligence about the 9/11 attacks was not translated until a day or so after the event.[17] By 2003, the US was involved in two overseas wars, and, as a result, the enforcement of DADT shifted. Starting in 2001, the discharge figures begin to decline (from 2001 to 2004 discharges fell from 1227 to 653).[18] Starting in 2009, support for the repeal of DADT was initiated by the US Military. At this time, the military leadership shifted from not supporting the repeal to determining how to implement it. On December 22, 2010, President Barack Obama signed the repeal of DADT into law, and, in September of 2011, the repeal began to be implemented. Unfortunately, the result would be unsatisfying for many gays and lesbians who were discharged during the enforcement of DADT. As trial lawyer Dan Woods notes, the repeal of DADT did not reinstate those who were discharged under the policy. Although those discharged are able to re-apply or re-enlist, many people have "aged out" and are no longer eligible for service. There is no provision in the repeal for monetary compensation or benefits to those discharged under the DADT policy.[19]

The repeal of DADT is considered one of the major accomplishments of the Obama administration, and, in some ways, it is. Yet, it is important to recognize both the progressive and regressive aspects of the repeal. Although inclusion in the Armed Forces is a boon for gay and lesbian civil rights, it fundamentally fails to challenge the normative assumptions associated with participation in, and the taken for granted "rightness" of, the US military.

The L Word: DADT on TV Prior to Repeal

The L Word featured the plight of a lesbian soldier under the DADT provision. Unlike *Army Wives*, *The L Word* is not largely focused on military life or military families. Nonetheless, the series introduced Tasha Williams (Rose Rollins) in season four in what would unravel into a two-season-long storyline that pits Williams' lesbian identity against her aspiration to make a life-long career out of military service. As opposed to *Army Wives*, where the lesbian storyline appears on the show after the repeal of DADT, in *The L Word* Tasha's struggles with military life occur under the enforcement of the DADT provision. Where *Army Wives* reflects back on the DADT measure, *The L Word's* real-time temporality offers a different perspective.

In 2007, *The L Word's* creators introduce two women of color characters, Tasha Williams, and Papi (Janina Gavankar), in what appeared to be an effort to diversify the primarily white cast. Although Tasha and Papi came to have a significant place within the ecology of the television show, they remained outsiders for a number of reasons. Their racial difference as black women, their "masculine" performance of gender, and their socio-economic status as working class set them apart from the rest of the characters.

In particular, Tasha's status as working class becomes a contentious issue a number of times in the context of her relationship with Alice Pieszecki (Leisha Hailey). For example, when the couple apartment hunts together, Tasha's salary cannot support Alice's proposed standard of living. It is significant that working-class status, black female "masculinity," and the desire to serve in the US Army converge in the character of Tasha. Tasha's patriotic stance is unwavering, in line with traditional working class values.

Lesbians on television have rarely been presented as anything other than feminine. This is true of Ellen DeGeneres' character on *Ellen*, which featured a coming out storyline that Anna McCarthy describes as a media event.[20] It is also true of the newer iteration of Ellen's personality on her daytime talk show. Although today's Ellen dresses in masculine clothing and sports a short haircut, she also maintains an appeal to traditional femininity, for example, by agreeing to be the ambassador for CoverGirl makeup.[21] When looking to prime-time broadcast and cable television, the feminine lesbian trope abounds. Examples include Emily on *Pretty Little Liars*, Brittany and Santana on *Glee*, Willow on *Buffy the Vampire Slayer*, Stef and Lena on *The Fosters*, and Callie and Arizona on *Grey's Anatomy*. The prominence of the feminine lesbian makes sense for the industry in that the appearance of feminine lesbians will attract the widest possible audience. As Candace Moore and Kristen Shilt point out, female masculinity is an identity position that challenges current ideas about masculinity and what it means to be a man. Therefore, television shows that desire a crossover audience are generally unwilling to feature "butchness" or female masculinity in any prominent way out of fear that it would have an adverse effect on the ratings.[22]

The coupling of feminine women on television is presumed to be the most likely way to attract a hetero-patriarchal gaze. *The L Word's* second season was renewed more quickly than any other show on Showtime's lineup. In fact, Showtime's vice-president for original programming, Gary Levine, banked on the show's appeal to heterosexual men telling the *New York Daily News* that "lesbian sex, girl-on-girl, is a whole cottage industry for heterosexual men."[23] This is reiterated by Sarah Warn who notes that the overtly feminine lesbians in *The L Word* are meant to attract both straight and gay viewers.[24] The cultivation of what Candace Moore calls a "polymorphous audience" was endemic to *The L Word* from the start.[25] Showtime's top executive Bob Greenblatt is quoted as saying, "We want people everywhere to buy it. So yes, the women are all attractive and we make no apologies about that."[26] It is notable that Greenblatt conflates attractiveness with femininity—a conflation that is true to Hollywood but less true to life (especially in queer communities where female masculinity is more normalized). In addition to appealing to straight men, *The L Word* has crossover appeal for straight women by presenting attractive feminine lesbians that straight women might aspire to be. Also, the marketing of the show appeals to straight women's desire to be seen as "heteroflexible" with the T-shirt slogan "I'd go gay for Shane."[27] That the show, at least early on

266 *Liora Elias*

in the series, is hesitant to introduce masculine female characters speaks to the history of unease about "butchness" and female masculinity among professional, middle-class, gender conforming lesbians, as well as the straight audiences the producers hoped to attract.[28]

Thus, Tasha and Papi represent a modest (though only modest) development in the depiction of lesbian identity on television. In terms of DADT, however, the progress is mixed. On one hand, *The L Word* offers a critique of what comes to be thought of as an unfair policy (DADT). However, the inflection of sexual politics comes in the form of conforming to homonormative performances of citizenship—or in other words, aligning with post-gay sentiment. Post-gay politics assumes that civil rights for gays and lesbians have been achieved and continued activism is no longer needed. In season four of *The L Word*, Alice and Tasha begin dating. Alice is working in media at the time, and Tasha is just back from a tour in Iraq. Although Tasha is hesitant to get involved, careful about public displays of affection because of the DADT policy, she is seen with Alice at the race track and is reported to her superiors for engaging in "suspicious behavior."[29] This instance sets off a series of events that result in an investigation and subsequent trial under the DADT provision. Tasha enlists the assistance of an Army lawyer, Captain Curtis Beech (Ted Whitthall), who initially refuses to defend her. He eventually comes around with the encouragement of his wife, who insists that Tasha and Alice are not unlike the two of them. The appeal to sameness is a key factor in legitimating Tasha as worthy of assistance. Or as Kellie Burns and Christyn Davies put it, "The conventional attractiveness of the women, their harmonious management of their class and racial differences, and the recontextualization of their performances of gender within a conventional heteronormative framework, allows Captain Beech to produce an account of Tasha as an adequately patriotic citizen."[30] It is key that Tasha is only validated as a soldier through the acceptance of her male heterosexual lawyer. Tasha's sense of patriotic duty seems to trump her identity as a lesbian at numerous junctures in the investigation. As Tasha proclaims, "I'm not fighting to allow gays to serve openly in the military. I'm not even trying to overturn DADT." Tasha's disavowal of politics is one of the ways the show inflects post-gay sentiment into this particular narrative. By positing Tasha as pro-military, at whatever the cost, *The L Word* avoids critiquing DADT outright.

In the end, Tasha is dishonorably discharged, but only after she publicly announces her "truth" at the DADT discharge hearing. In other words, Tasha is not discharged on the Army's terms but on her own. Interestingly, the woman prosecuting Tasha's case is revealed to be a lesbian herself. This is made known in subtle gestures, like watching her check out other women in locker rooms. But the subtlety is not lost on Alice, who threatens to use her media connections to out Tasha's prosecutor, who is also at risk of separation from the military. Alice's actions provide Tasha with an opportunity to resume her military career, as the prosecutor agrees to drop the case because of Alice's threat. However, it is Tasha's allegiance to "duty," to the military code of conduct, that instead inspires her to be truthful about her romantic relationship with Alice. The subtle critique of DADT, as well as the forwardness of female same-sex attraction present in *The L Word,* may account for the military's refusal to work with the series' producers, who did approach them for assistance. This is unlike the television show *Army Wives*, which received financial support from the military. As the following section reveals, however, financial support does come with a certain amount of strings attached.

Enter Lifetime's *Army Wives*

Toward the end of season six, about seven months after the repeal of DADT, the Lifetime show *Army Wives* introduced Charlie Mayfield (Ryan Michelle Bathe), the female director of the community center on base and her life-partner Captain Nicole Galassin (Kellie Martin). Charlie and Nicole were the first lesbian characters to have a reoccurring presence on *Army Wives*. Clearly inserted as a response to the repeal of DADT, Charlie and Nicole's portrayals of ideal patriotic and post-gay citizens is designed to resolve the US military's culpability in the history of homophobia and violence against gay and lesbian soldiers, which has been a disappointingly real experience for many such soldiers under DADT and post-repeal.

The show began its run in 2007 and, at the time, focused on the fictional lives of Army spouses Claudia Joy Holden (Kim Delaney), Pamela Moran (Brigid Brannagh), Roxy LeBlanc (Sally Pressman), Denise Sherwodd (Catherine Bell), and Roland Burton (Sterling K. Brown), and their interactions with their respective spouses and the US Army as an institution. Consistent with the soap opera genre familiar to the Lifetime network, the show interweaved the dynamics of military family life with soldiers' experiences before, during, and after battle. After seven seasons, Lifetime Television canceled *Army Wives*, the networks' most popular and longest running show to date. The show attracted primarily women and "propelled Lifetime to be the #1 ad-supported cable network in the 10–11 time period."[31] The seventh and final season saw ratings fall from 3.2 million average viewers to 2.5 million.[32] That and the loss of star Kim Delaney, as well as a reduced role for co-star Sally Pressman, may have contributed to the show's demise.

Like *JAG* and other military-themed shows, *Army Wives* received financial assistance and access to film on location at Army bases by entering into a partnership with the Department of Defense (DoD). Since season two, *Army Wives* issued their scripts to the Pentagon in exchange for filming at Charleston Air Force base and for the use of Air Force reservists as extras.[33] As a cultural text, *Army Wives* is instructive on a number of accounts, especially regarding the politics of gender and sexual identity. Mary Vavrus' research on *Army Wives* highlights the show's "constitution of two different marriages." The first partners individuals to the Army while

268   *Liora Elias*

the second weds the Lifetime network to the military-industrial complex.[34] This is not the first time that the Lifetime network has partnered with governmental institutions and private organizations, however. Eileen Meehan and Jackie Byars report that part of Lifetime's branding as "women's television" includes partnerships with liberal feminist organizations such as the National Organization of Women (NOW) and the MS Foundation (2000). The result, as Meehan and Byars note, is "telefeminist programming formulae that defuse any basic structural challenges to patriarchy and its institutions."[35] Lifetime Television brands itself as a network for "women" but resists the feminist label. As Byars and Meehan put it, "By not challenging the assumptions about labor, sexuality, and power that underlie the model of 'having it all,' Lifetime remains commercially viable presenting television that provides role models for a way of life made possible by second wave feminism, but which Lifetime defines as feminine, never feminist."[36]

Feminist sociologist Cynthia Enloe's research has shown that women are less drawn to the military than men are.[37] By presenting women in positions of power within the military, *Army Wives* and the US Army arguably worked to overcome this resistance. And, by portraying lesbian women thriving within military culture, *Army Wives* also helped the military extends its outreach efforts to lesbians.

Despite the introduction of the lesbian storyline in season six, however, virtually nothing changed about the way the show invests in the marriage partnerships of its characters. Charlie and Nicole marry each other and marry the Army, and by extension the viewer is asked to invest in these same ties. The emphasis on sameness between straights and gays resembles the normalizing discourse of homonormativity, which has been critiqued by social historian Lisa Duggan, among others. Homonormativity refers to a sexual politics that upholds dominant heteronormative assumptions. Homonormative gay culture is both demobilized and depoliticized; it is fueled by the values of primarily privileged, white, upwardly mobile individuals concerned with issues of domesticity (marriage rights, adoption rights) and consumption. She suggests homonormativity has brought shifts in the priorities of gay and lesbian equality movements including an emphasis on "access to institutions of domestic privacy, the 'free' market, and patriotism."[38] Duggan continues:

> This new homonormativity comes equipped with a rhetorical recoding of key terms in the history of gay politics: "equality" becomes narrow, formal access to a few conservatizing institutions, "freedom" becomes impunity for bigotry and vast inequalities in commercial life and civil society, the "right to privacy" becomes domestic confinement, and democratic politics itself becomes something to be escaped. All of this adds up to a corporate culture managed by a minimal state, achieved by the neoliberal privatization of affective as well as economic and public life.[39]

"Don't Ask, Don't Tell" 269

Charlie and Nicole embody the achievement of the narrow ideal of gaining access to the conservative institution of marriage. In that way, they align perfectly with homonormative ideals. The idealized version of lesbian soldiering and service presented on *Army Wives* is a compelling fantasy. However, at the same time Charlie and Nicole assimilate perfectly into the fantasy of the unquestioning patriotic soldier and doting wife, the depictions of these characters fail to explore what it might mean to value the unique qualities and complexities that comprise the reality of life as a same-sex military family.

Army Wives' Brief Lesbian Storyline

The story-arc of this lesbian couple is contained within seven episodes during season six, after which they disappear from the show never to be heard from again. Although *Army Wives* made common practice of introducing new characters and storylines, in most cases the new characters had a long-term presence or recurred throughout the remainder of the series. Uncharacteristically, Charlie and Nicole's story-arc is neatly self-contained. The lesbian storyline also comes approximately six months after the real-life repeal of DADT, which is not coincidental. Charlie and Nicole are excused from the cast of *Army Wives* once the audience is convinced that the Army will "play by the rules" with regard to lesbian and gay service members. Post-repeal, the discrimination and harassment that have been regular features of Army life for gays have basically disappeared. Evidence of how Charlie and Nicole function as post-DADT props can be seen in the series' sendoff episode *Army Wives: A Final Salute*. The two-hour finale included commentary from the cast as well as "real-life" Army wives, and Charlie and Nicole are nowhere to be seen—not in flashback or in the commentary about what the show has meant to "real-life" Army wives. Moreover, the investment in the politics of sexual difference among the creative team of *Army Wives* is completely absent in *Under the Sabers: The Unwritten Code of Army Wives* by Tanya Biank, the book that inspired the television series.[40] Biank's book follows the real-life stories of four women married to Army men stationed at Fort Bragg between late 2000 and 2003. It includes almost no evidence that lesbian soldiers, gay soldiers, or "Don't Ask, Don't Tell" was part of military life in Fayetteville, North Carolina, where her exposé is set. Except for two casual mentions, both of which are offensively dismissive, gays and lesbians are an unknown entity in *Under the Sabers. Army Wives* creators and writers clearly invented Charlie and Nicole's (lesbian) storyline for the purpose of addressing the Army's long history of homophobia and anti-gay persecution. Charlie and Nicole are inserted, on the heels of the repeal of DADT, to resolve in fantasy form the Army's culpability in creating a hostile climate for gays and lesbians in service.

Via the coupling of Nicole and Charlie, *Army Wives* links post-feminist, post-racial, and post-gay discourses into a thorny knot, which viewers

270   *Liora Elias*

are encouraged not to unravel. These "post" discourses all masquerade as celebrations of difference when in fact they depend upon and reinforce sexualized, racialized, and gendered hierarchies of power. Although Nicole and Charlie are same-sex, for example, they otherwise fit a very specific historically safe-for-television paradigm as middle-class professionals and stereotypically feminine lesbians.

Nicole is not only depicted as a lesbian soldier, but is also granted a leadership role on an international mission to the fictional African country of Narubu where she proves herself a worthy hero. In Narubu, the troop's mission is to resolve a violent dispute between warring tribes. After her male colleague fails to communicate with one of the warring tribes, Nicole recognizes that the tribes are matriarchal and will respect her expertise. She thus uses her (feminine) skills to extract herself and a number of American soldiers from danger. Gender saves the day, and Nicole is declared a war hero. Nicole proves herself to be an invaluable resource to the US Army. However, before she can be publicly recognized for her bravery, a male colleague approaches General Clarke, a man who had spoken in favor of DADT before its repeal, about Nicole's lesbian identity. General Clarke replies,

> Do you have any idea the kind of courage it took for Captain Galassin to do what she did? She saved lives that day, Major. Most likely prevented an international incident. We should thank God we have soldiers like her. But instead you want me to penalize her because she happens to be gay. I don't care how I have been quoted, the Army has clearly stated its policy, and I will not tolerate anyone in my command that tries to undermine that policy.[41]

The homophobic soldier functions as a "problem case" in need of reform. By dismissing the soldier's concerns, *Army Wives* implies that institutionalized homophobia in the US Army is a thing of the past, a sin absolved by General Clarke's change of heart.

As Charlie and Nicole's plotline continues, they express their shared desire for marriage and kids. These options, which in many "real-life" circumstances are difficult for lesbian and gay couples to pursue, are readily available in *Army Wives*. In a telling scene, Nicole and Charlie are invited to have dinner at the house of Captain Joan Burke and her husband Roland. As a couple, the Burkes represent a model heterosexual family with two beautiful children. We learn that Nicole, because of the pressures of her career in the Army and the enforced silence of DADT, has been hesitant to commit to the relationship with Charlie long term. But, directly after Nicole and Charlie have dinner with Joan and Roland, Nicole is in the street proposing marriage, a proposal that is happily accepted by Charlie. In this case, gay life is only measured in comparison to the heterosexual norm. It is literally the model of a heterosexual union that inspires the gay one. Their plan to marry is only problematized once by Nicole's meddling mother, who seems

"Don't Ask, Don't Tell" 271

to have been against Nicole and Charlie's relationship from the start. Yet, even she quickly comes around and proudly agrees to attend the wedding she threatened to boycott. The couple's shared desire to have children is also only briefly problematized before a friend of a friend's baby fortuitously falls into their laps. The lenses offered by *Army Wives* display a world where wedded bliss and babies are easily acquired by all, highlighting the illusion that post-gay sentiment would have us believe: that all lesbian and gay individuals aspire to the heteronormative ideal of domestic bliss and have access to it right at their fingertips. In other words, the television characters Charlie and Nicole are allowed to be same-sex, as long as they are both feminine lesbians. Nicole and Charlie are allowed a primary same-sex relationship, as long as they aspire to conventional forms of patriotism, marriage, and family life. In this way, *Army Wives* constructs the military as a possible caring entity, providing a very enticing fantasy of the love relationship (with the Army).

Conclusion

In both *The L Word* and *Army Wives*, pre-DADT and post-DADT, same-sex coupledom and soldierdom is legitimized only in relation to the heterosexual norm. In *The L Word* Tasha's legal case is only taken seriously by Army lawyer Captain Beech when his wife insists that Tasha and Alice are the same as they are. Tasha's allegiance to the US military and her stated disinterest in seeing the DADT policy repealed leads to a missed opportunity to critique the discriminatory policy. In *Army Wives* post-repeal, the DADT policy is erased from the blemished past of the US Army, as Charlie and Nicole are inserted into the *Army Wives* community, gain friends and allies, and achieve their American Dream. Nicole is an Army Captain and an openly gay woman; the couple gets legally married, and when they decide they want to start a family, there are no impediments placed in their way. *Army Wives* showrunner Jeff Melvoin is quoted as saying, "It was our intent during this season to introduce a lesbian couple in an unexpected and natural way. In this manner, we felt we were reflecting the reality that we've observed researching the military since the repeal of the 'Don't Ask, Don't Tell' policy.[42] However, contrary to Melvoin's claim, outside of the televised universe of *Army Wives,* the struggles of gay and lesbian couples, married to the Army or not, are very different from heterosexual pairings on the issues of marriage and family.

Military bases in conservative states still refused to issue military IDs to same-sex spouses a year and a half after the repeal of DADT, and many same-sex military couples were ruled ineligible for military sponsored housing. In January 2013, Ashley Broadway, the spouse of Army Lt. Colonel Heather Mack, was denied membership in the Fort Bragg Officers' Spouses' Club.[43] The organization went so far as to change the rules to require an official military ID for entry even though the club had no such rule previously. After

272 *Liora Elias*

much ado, and much bad press for Fort Bragg, the administration of the Fort Bragg Officers' Spouses' Club finally allowed Mack entry.

The disconnect between what is possible for gay and lesbian military couples on television and in real-life, prior to and post-repeal of DADT, is a reflection of today's post-gay era. On *The L Word* and *Army Wives*, normative gays and lesbians are rewarded for maintaining a conservative and assimilationist ideological frame. The possibilities for identity expression on *The L Word* and *Army Wives*, as well as the values asserted by gay and lesbian civil rights activists in today's political era, only cater to the few and further marginalize those on the outskirts of mainstream gay and lesbian civil rights activism. Contrary to Melvoin's hope that *Army Wives* "reflected the reality" of military life post-repeal of DADT, instead, the show presented a post-gay fantasy and a dangerous one at that.

Notes

1. Randy Shilts, *Conduct Unbecoming: Lesbian and Gays in the US Military Vietnam to the Persian Gulf,* (New York: St. Martin's Press, 1993).
2. Melissa Sheridan Embser-Herbert, *The US Military's 'Don't Ask, Don't Tell' Policy: A Reference Handbook* (Wesport, CT: Praeger Security International, 2007).
3. Allan Bérubé, *Coming out under Fire: The History of Gay Men and Women in World War Two* (New York: The Free Press, 1990), 29.
4. *The Strange History of Don't Ask, Don't Tell,* directed by Fenton Bailey and Randy Barbato (HBO Documentary Films, 2011), DVD.
5. Ibid.
6. Ibid.
7. Captain S.H. Crittenden, *Report of the Board Appointed to Prepare and Submit Recommendations to the Secretary of the Navy for the Revision of Policies, Procedures and Directives Dealing with Homosexuals,* Navy Department, United States Government, March 15, 1957.
8. *The Strange History of Don't Ask, Don't Tell.*
9. Urvashi Vaid, *Virtual Equality: The Mainstreaming of Gay and Lesbian Liberation,* (New York: Anchor Books, 1995), 148.
10. *The Strange History of Don't Ask, Don't Tell.*
11. Ibid.
12. This number may be inaccurate, as it relies on self-reporting. More reliable data collected by The Palm Center, another advocacy group that studies issues of gender, sexuality and the military, has determined that 6,273 discharges could be associated with DADT from 1998–2003, the only years for which reliable data exist. They have provided a breakdown of the discharges by base and occupation at: http://www.palmcenter.org/resources/dadt/discharge_data.
13. Sheridan Embser-Herbert, *The U.S. Military's 'Don't Ask, Don't Tell' Policy,* 45.
14. Ibid., 47.
15. Alain Dang and Somjen Frazer, *Black Same-Sex Households in the United States* (Washington, DC: National Gay and Lesbian Task Force Institute, 2000).
16. "Testimony Relating to the 'Don't Ask, Don't Tell' Policy," *Hearing before the Committee on Armed Services, United States Senate* (Washington, DC: US Government Printing Office, 2010).

"Don't Ask, Don't Tell" 273

17. *The Strange History of Don't Ask, Don't Tell*.
18. Ibid.
19. William D. Araiza and Dan Woods, *Understanding the Repeal of Don't Ask Don't Tell: An Immediate Look at Policy Changes Allowing Gays and Lesbians to Openly Serve in the Military*, (New York: Thompson Reuters/Aspatore, 2011), 16.
20. Anna McCarthy, "Ellen: Making Queer Television History," *GLQ: A Journal of Lesbian and Gay Studies* 7, no. 4 (2001): 593.
21. Not being beholden to advertisers for funding, premium cable and Internet TV providers have recently started to introduce masculine lesbian characters, including the later seasons of *The L Word, Transparent* (Amazon, 2014-present), and *Orange Is the New Black* (Netflix, 2013-present).
22. Candace Moore and Kristen Schilt, "Is She Man Enough? Female Masculinities on The L Word," in *Reading The L Word: Outing Contemporary Television*, eds. Kim Akass and Janet McCabe (New York: I.B. Tauris, 2006), 169.
23. Eve Kosofsky Sedgwick, "'The L Word': Novelty in Normalcy," *The Chronicle of Higher Education*, January 16, 2014, http://chronicle.com/article/The-L-Word-Novelty-in/13751.
24. Sarah Warn, "Introduction," in *Reading the L Word: Outing Contemporary Television*, eds. Kim Akass and Janet McCabe (New York: I.B. Tauris, 2006), 4.
25. Candace Moore, "Getting Wet: The Heteroflexibility of Showtime's The L Word," in *Third Wave Feminism and Television: Jane Puts It in a Box*, ed. Merri Lisa Johnson (New York: I.B. Tauris, 2007), 121.
26. Ibid., xix.
27. Ibid., 121. The character of Shane McCutcheon (played by Katherine Moennig) is talked about as the most "butch" of the central characters. However, I agree with Moore and Schilt when they note that Shane is only contextually "butch" when compared to the lack of masculinity in the remainder of the main cast. Moore and Schilt, "Is She Man Enough?.
28. Margaret Kennedy and Elizabeth Davis, "I Could Hardly Wait to Get Back to that Bar," in *Creating a Place for Ourselves: Lesbian, Gay, Bisexual Community Histories*, ed. Brett Beemyn, (New York: Routledge, 1997), 64.
29. "Little Boy Blue," season 4, episode 10, *The L Word*, aired March 11, 2007 (New York: Showtime Networks, 2007), DVD. All subsequent references are to this DVD.
30. Kellie Burns and Cristyn Davies, "Producing Cosmopolitan Sexual Citizens on The L Word," *Journal of Lesbian Studies* 13, no. 2 (2009): full page run, 184.
31. Lifetime Press Release, "Lifetime's Drama 'Army Wives' Concludes Historic Run," *The Futon Critic*, September 24, 2013, http://www.thefutoncritic.com/news/2013/09/24/lifetimes-drama-army-wives-concludes-historic-run-355413/20130924lifetime01/.
32. Lesley Goldberg, "Lifetime Cancels 'Army Wives' After Seven Seasons," *The Hollywood Reporter, September 24, 2013, http://www.hollywoodreporter.com/live-feed/lifetime-cancels-army-wives-seven-635552*.
33. Mary Douglas Vavrus, "Lifetime's Army Wives, Or I Married the Media-Military-Industrial Complex," *Women's Studies in Communication* 36, no. 1 (2013): 103.
34. Vavrus, "Lifetime's Army Wives," 93.

274 *Liora Elias*

35. Eileen R. Meehan and Jackie Byars. "Telefeminism: How Lifetime Got Its Groove, 1984–1997," *Television & New Media* 1, no. 1 (2000): 34.
36. Jackie Byars and Eileen R. Meehan, "Once in a Lifetime: Constructing "The Working Woman" Through Cable Narrowcasting," *Camera Obscura* (May/September/January 1994–1995): 36.
37. Cynthia Enloe, *Maneuvers: The International Politics of Militarizing Women's Lives* (Berkeley: University of California Press, 2000).
38. Lisa Duggan, *The Twilight of Equality? Neoliberalism, Cultural Politics, and the Attack on Democracy* (Boston: Beacon Hill Press, 2003), 51.
39. Ibid., 66.
40. Tanya Biank, *Under the Sabers: The Unwritten Code of Army Wives* (New York, NY: St. Martin's Press, 2006).
41. "After Action Report," season 6, episode 10, *Army Wives*, aired April 29, 2012.
42. Sara Bibel, "'Army Wives' Showrunner Jeff Melvoin Shares His Favorite Episodes," *Xfinity TV Blog,* November 21, 2012, http://xfinity.comcast.net/blogs/tv/2012/11/21/army-wives-showrunner-jeff-melvoin-shares-his-favorite-episodes/.
43. Mark Thompson, "Same-Sex Marriage: Army's Not Budging," *Time*, January 17, 2013, http://nation.time.com/2013/01/17/same-sex-marriage-armys-not-budging/.

List of Contributors

Christine Becker is an Associate Professor in the Department of Film, Television, and Theatre at the University of Notre Dame specializing in film and television history and critical analysis. Her book *It's the Pictures That Got Small: Hollywood Film Stars on 1950s Television* (Wesleyan University Press, 2009) won the 2011 IAMHIST Michael Nelson Prize for a Work in Media and History. She is currently working on a research project comparing contemporary American and British television production and programming.

Kelly J.W. Brown is a PhD student in History at Ohio University where she is currently researching the intersections of popular culture, gender, and disability in the twentieth century. In 2013, Brown served as a Fellow at Ohio University's Contemporary History Institute. Brown previously attended The University of Tulsa, where she received her Master's degrees in both History and Museum Science and Management.

Todd Decker is an Associate Professor of Music at Washington University in St. Louis and the author of three books: *Who Should Sing Ol' Man River?: The Lives of an American Song* (Oxford, 2014), *Show Boat: Performing Race in an American Musical* (Oxford, 2013), and *Music Makes Me: Fred Astaire and Jazz* (California, 2011, winner of the Society for Cinema and Media Studies Best First Book Award). His articles have appeared in *Music, Sound and the Moving Image* and *Daedalus*, among other journals. Decker has lectured at the Library of Congress. His current project, under contract with University of California Press, examines music and sound in post-Vietnam combat films.

David Scott Diffrient is the William E. Morgan Endowed Chair of Liberal Arts and Associate Professor of Film and Media Studies in the Department of Communication Studies at Colorado State University. His articles have been published in *Cinema Journal, Historical Journal of Film, Radio, and Television, Journal of Fandom Studies, Journal of Film and Video, Journal of Popular Film and Television, New Review of Film and Television Studies, Quarterly Review of Film and Video*, and *Post Script*, as well as in several edited collections about film and television topics. His most recent book is *Omnibus Films: Theorizing Transauthorial*

276 *List of Contributors*

Cinema (Edinburgh University Press, 2014), and he is the co-author of *Movie Migrations: Transnational Genre Flows and South Korean Cinema* (Rutgers University Press, 2015). He is the co-editor of the *Journal of Japanese and Korean Cinema.*

Sam Edwards is a Senior Lecturer in American History at Manchester Metropolitan University and a former Fulbright Distinguished Scholar at the University of Pittsburgh. His research engages with transatlantic relations, commemoration and memory, and the cultural history of conflict. His most recent article—published in the *Journal of Transatlantic Studies*—examined twentieth-century efforts to 'Anglicize' Abraham Lincoln, and he is co-editor of a new volume exploring the place of D-Day in international remembrance, *D-Day in History and Memory: The Normandy Landings in International Remembrance and Commemoration* (University of North Texas Press, 2014). He is the author of *Allies in Memory: World War II and the Politics of Transatlantic Commemoration* (Cambridge University Press, 2015) and is lead editor for a new volume exploring the use of film and television as historical sources (*Histories on Screen: The Past and Present in Anglo-American Cinema and Television,* forthcoming with Bloomsbury Academic in 2016). Recently, Edwards has worked with BBC radio and television, and he is keenly involved in community engagement and school outreach.

Liora Elias is a Lecturer in the Department of Communication Studies, with a focus on Critical Media at the University of Minnesota in the Twin Cities. She received her BA from the University of Minnesota in Women's Studies and her MA in Gender and Cultural Studies at Simmons College in Boston, Massachusetts. Elias' current research interests include queer film and television, gay marriage, LGBTQ bullying, "Don't Ask, Don't Tell," mediated discourses of madness, transgender representation on television, queer theory, and feminist theory, as well as critical race theory.

Anna Froula is an Associate Professor of Film Studies in the Department of English at East Carolina University. She is the co-editor of *Reframing 9/11: Film, Popular Culture, and the "War on Terror"* (Continuum, 2010) and of *It's a Mad World: The Cinema of Terry Gilliam* (Wallflower, 2013). She has published on gendered representations of war and on zombies in a variety of journals and edited collections, including the *Journal of War and Cultural Studies* and *Cinema Journal.* Froula is the Associate Editor of *Cinema Journal,* the journal of the Society for Cinema and Media Studies.

Kathleen Kennedy is Head of the History Department at Missouri State University. She has published several articles on violence and American culture, *Xena: Warrior Princess* and Joan Jett. She is the co-editor of *Athena's Daughters: Television's New Women Warriors* and *Sexual Borderlands:*

Constructing an American Sexual Past. She is also the author of *Disloyal Mothers and Scurrilous Women: Gender and Subversion during World War I.*

Colleen Kennedy-Karpat is an Assistant Professor in the Department of Communication and Design at Bilkent University, where she has taught film and media studies since receiving her PhD in 2011 from Rutgers University. A specialist in French cinema, she is the author of *Rogues, Romance, and Exoticism in French Cinema of the 1930s* (Fairleigh Dickinson UP, 2013), winner of the Northeast Modern Language Association Book Award, and a number of short pieces on French films and stars, including an essay on the 1934 film *Itto* that appeared in the *Directory of World Cinema: France* (Intellect, 2013). Beyond France, she also wrote an essay about Bill Murray for *The Films of Wes Anderson* (Palgrave, 2014). Current research interests include pre-World War II European cinema, media adaptations, genres, and stardom.

Scott Laderman, who received his PhD in American Studies from the University of Minnesota, Twin Cities, in 2005, is a professor of History at the University of Minnesota, Duluth. He is the author of *Tours of Vietnam: War, Travel Guides, and Memory* (Duke University Press, 2009) and *Empire in Waves: A Political History of Surfing* (University of California Press, 2014). His co-edited collection, *Four Decades On: Vietnam, the United States, and the Legacies of the Second Indochina War* (Duke University Press, 2013), was named a *Choice* Outstanding Academic Title for 2013. Among the issues explored in his articles and book chapters are federal Indian policy, film history, and war propaganda.

Lisa M. Mundey is an Associate Professor of History at the University of St. Thomas in Houston, Texas, where she has taught since 2007. She received her doctorate in history from Kansas State University in 2006. She is the author of *American Militarism and Anti-Militarism in Popular Media, 1945–1970* (McFarland, 2012). Dr. Mundey also worked at the US Army Center of Military History, researching the US Army's experiences in Afghanistan. This study was published with Brian F. Neumann and Jon Mikolashek in 2013 as *The United States Army in Afghanistan: Operation Enduring Freedom, March 2002-April 2005.* Dr. Mundey contributed a chapter on "The Combatants' Experiences" about service members in Iraq and Afghanistan to *Understanding the US Wars in Iraq and Afghanistan* (NYU Press, 2015). She has given numerous conference presentations, most recently on her book at the US Army Heritage and Education Center in Carlisle, Pennsylvania, in August 2013.

Sueyoung Park-Primiano received her PhD in 2015 from the Department of Cinema Studies at New York University. Her dissertation narrates the development of South Korean cinema in the aftermath of World War II, under the US occupation and during the rise of the First Republic before

278   *List of Contributors*

and after the Korean War. She is a contributor to *Popular Culture in Asia: Memory, City, Celebrity* (Palgrave, 2013) and teaches courses on film and new media at NYU, FIT, and Parsons, New School.

David P. Pierson is an Associate Professor of Media Studies in the Department of Communication and Media Studies at the University of Southern Maine. He currently teaches courses in film and television criticism, field video production, and broadcast writing. He has published book chapters and articles in the *Journal of Communication Inquiry, Journal of Popular Culture* and *Film and History* on *C.S.I.: Crime Scene Investigation, Combat!, Mad Men*, and *Seinfeld* The Discovery Channel and Turner Network Television made-for-TV westerns. He has recently published a monograph on the 1960s TV series *The Fugitive* (2011) for Wayne State University Press and an edited collection *Breaking Bad: Critical Essays on the Contexts, Politics, Style and Reception of the Television Series* (2013) published by Lexington/Rowman and Littlefield.

Robert R. Shandley is a Professor of German and Film Studies and Head of the Department of International Studies at Texas A&M University. In addition to his contribution to the TV Milestones book series at Wayne State University Press (*Hogan's Heroes*, 2011), he is the author of *Runaway Romances: Hollywood's Postwar Tour of Europe* (2009) and *Rubble Films: German Cinema in the Shadow of the Third Reich* (2001). *Rubble Films* was also translated into German and published in 2010.

Stacy Takacs is an Associate Professor and Director of American Studies at Oklahoma State University and an associate member of the faculty in Screen Studies. Her research focuses on the intersections of popular and political cultures in contemporary American society. Her work has appeared in *Cultural Critique, Cultural Studies, Quarterly Review of Film and Video, Feminist Media Studies, Critical Studies in Television,* and *Spectator: Journal of Film and Television Criticism*, among other journals. She is also the author of two books: *Terrorism TV: Popular Entertainment in Post-9/11 America* (U of Kansas Press, 2012) and *Interrogating Popular Culture* (Routledge, 2014).

A. Bowdoin Van Riper is a historian whose work focuses on depictions of science and technology in popular culture and the intersection of film and television with history and memory. He received his BA from Brown University and his MA and PhD from the University of Wisconsin—Madison. He is the author, editor, or co-editor of 11 books to date, including: *Imagining Flight: Aviation and the Popular Imagination* (Texas A&M Press, 2003), *Rockets and Missiles: The Life Story of a Technology* (Johns Hopkins UP 2004; rpt. 2007), and the co-edited collection *Horrors of War: The Undead on the Battlefield* (Rowman & Littlefield, 2015; with Cynthia J. Miller). His article on Hollywood films about the Manhattan Project appeared in the edited collection *The Adaptation of*

History (McFarland, 2012) and his article on the WWII-themed dramas *Piece of Cake* and *Danger—UXB* in the edited collection *Upstairs and Downstairs: The British Historical Costume Drama on TV* (Rowman & Littlefield, 2014). He is the founding editor of the Rowman & Littlefield book series "Science Fiction Television" and Web Coordinator for the Center for the Study of Film and History.

Magdalena Yüksel is a doctoral student in Cinema Studies at the University of Toronto. She holds a double BA in Polish and English Philology from Nicolaus Copernicus University, Poland and an MA from Bilkent University in Media and Visual Studies. She presented a paper at the 2013 NECS conference in Prague on the mediation of non-organic memory through the body in *Black Mirror*. She has worked on other projects involving postcolonial studies, dystopian film, multicultural England in films and television, and the effects of globalization on third world countries as shown in films.

Index

9/11, see September 11, 2001
12 O'Clock High: film 36, 79–80, 86, 87; TV series 5, 8, 31, 46–59, 63, 76, 79, 130

ABC 1, 30–33, 43, 52, 55, 57–9, 63–4, 89, 118, 181, 211, 219
Alcoa Premiere 10, 167–71; see also Vietnam War
alcohol: alcoholism 119, 144, 146, 152, 154–5; DOD policies and 146, 156, 161 n.39, 240; in *China Beach* 156–7, 185; in *M*A*S*H* 9, 144–59; in *Over There* 240; as social ritual 149, 151, 153, 158–9; social attitudes about 145, 155–6, 158; as trauma buffer 149, 151, 154, 158
alcoholic imaginary 9, 145, 152, 158–9
Alda, Alan 129, 139, 144, 147, 153; as Captain Benjamin Franklin "Hawkeye" Pierce on *M*A*S*H* 131–2, 135–40, 141 n. 11, 145, 147, 148–9, 152–3, 155, 157
Alexander, Lyta: see Patricia Tallman
Altman, Robert 37–8, 130, 147, 152
Ambrose, Stephen 94, 96–7, 100–1, 258
American air power 8, 46–59
American Forces Korea Network (AFKN) 119–25; see also American Forces Network-Korea
American Forces Network-Korea (AFN-Korea) 124–5; see also American Forces Korea Network
American Forces Radio and Television Service 111–20; American Forces Korea Network 120–5; American Forces Vietnam Network 146; see also Armed Forces Radio and Television Service
anthology series 7, 10, 162–73
anti-communism 20, 34, 50, 163, 166; in anthology programs 162–175; Armed Forces Korea Network

(AFKN) and 111–13, 122–4; in *Combat!* 38–41; effect on gays and lesbians 197–8, 261–2
anti-militarism 5, 7, 17–27, 72–5, 246
anti-war themes 9, 38, 44 n. 37, 59, 65, 72, 130, 147, 173–4, 223, 229, 257
Arbus, Allan 132; as Dr. Sydney Freedman on *M*A*S*H* 136–7, 138, 139–40, 141 n. 11
Armed Forces Korea Network (AFKN) 9, 111–25; see also American Forces Korea Network, American Force Network-Korea
Armed Forces Radio and Television Service (AFRTS) 111, 114–119, 123–124; see also American Forces Radio and Television Service
Army Wives 11, 261, 264, 267–72
Army of the Republic of Vietnam (ARVN) 169–72

Baa Baa Black Sheep 4, 5, 8, 77–90, 211; see also World War II
Babylon 5 10, 195–209; as future war scenario 195–6; see also Bruce Boxleitner, Claudia Christian, Persian Gulf War, Patricia Tallman, Andrea Thompson
Band of Brothers 9, 31, 77, 93–108, 245
Bartlett, Sy 48, 50
Basinger, Jeanine 3, 32, 34–6, 43–4, 79, 213, 225 n. 11, 249–51
Battleground 30–1, 36, 78, 80, 91 n. 9
Baudrillard, Jean 256–7
BBC 253, 257
Bell, Catherine 211; as Major Sarah "Mac" MacKenzie in *JAG* 221, 267
Bellisario, Donald 90, 211, 213, 215–17, 219, 224, 225 n. 18
Biff Baker, USA 10, 163–5, 176 n. 9; see also Vietnam War
Black Sheep Squadron, see *Baa Baa Black Sheep*

282 *Index*

Boxleitner, Bruce 198; as Captain John Sheridan on *Babylon 5* 198–200, 203–4, 206–8
Boyington, Major Gregory "Pappy" 77, 81–2, 86; played by Robert Conrad 81–2 85–9
Burns, Major Frank, see Larry Linville

Catch-22 46, 50
CBS 1, 18–9, 42, 56, 63–5, 72, 118, 164, 173–4, 211–12, 219
CBS Playhouse 171–3
China Beach 5–6, 10, 156–7, 178–89; alcohol in 156–7, 185; memorialization and 178, 182–3, 185–9; as quality television 6–7, 156–7, 178–89; trauma and 178–89; see also serial narrative, Vietnam War
Christian, Claudia 195, 201; as Commander Susan Ivanova on *Babylon 5* 199–206, 208
Churchill, Winston 41, 68
CNN 231, 236, 247, 257
Cold War 2, 4, 7, 8, 40, 197, 252; doctrine of air power and 49–51, 58; in anthology series 162–175; in *Combat!* 31, 34, 38–41; combat films and 36, 46–7, 79–81, 112–114; gays and lesbians and 197–8, 261–2; in *Hogan's Heroes* 63, 68–72; in *The Phil Silvers Show* 21, 24, 26; politics and 7, 31, 34, 38–41
Combat! 5, 7, 8, 30–42, 58, 63, 77, 93, 122; Cold War in 38–41; disability and 130, 134; World War II in 30, 33–38; see also anti-communism, communism
Combat Sergeant 31, 43 n. 7
Command Decision 48–9, 52–3, 56, 88
Conrad, Robert, see Major Gregory "Pappy" Boyington
communism 20, 34, 39, 111–12, 163, 166–7, 169; in anthology programs 162–175; in *Combat!* 38–41; in *Hogan's Heroes* 63, 68–72; in *M*A*S*H* 149, 153; and programming on Armed Forces Korea Network (AFKN) 111–13, 122–4
Cronkite, Walter 56, 72–3

D-Day 30–1, 33–5, 52, 56, 58, 80, 102, 105, 276
de Gualle, Charles 40–1

death, "good" or "clean" 10, 54, 56, 178–80, 185–9; "bad" 11, 19, 31, 33–4, 41, 44 n. 37, 57, 87, 130, 135, 169–70, 174–5, 252–6
Department of Defense (DOD), see United States Department of Defense
disability 9, 129–34, 137–139, 141; in *M*A*S*H* 129–41; see also trauma
Don't Ask, Don't Tell Policy (DADT) 195, 196–8, 261–4; on television 264–72; campaign to repeal 262–4; effects of repeal 271–2
Dr. Strangelove or How I Learned to Stop Worrying and Love the Bomb 8, 46, 50–1, 54, 58

Elliott, David James 211, 214; as Lieutenant Harmon Rabb, Jr. on *JAG* 211–17, 219–22
episodic series 4, 6–7, 32–4, 130, 229, 239

feminism 199, 209, 225 n. 15, 268–9; see also post-feminism
femininity 25–6, 157, 198–9, 211, 216, 220; and lesbianism 265–8, 270–1; in music 93–4; as threat to masculinity 25–6, 216, 249, 261; see also gender and masculinity
The Final War of Olly Winter 171–3; see also Vietnam War
First Gulf War, see Persian Gulf War
flow 239–241
Fox network 29 n. 55, 77, 218–19
Fox Television Productions 46, 51–2
Freedman, Dr. Sidney, see Allan Arbus
future war scenario 10, 195–6; doctrine of air power and 54–9

The Gallant Men 5, 31, 90 n. 1, 130
Garrison's Gorillas 5, 31, 42, 81, 90 n. 1
Geneva Conventions 74, 228, 235
gender 17, 25–6, 52, 107, 130, 132–3, 138, 153, 157, 196–8, 208–9, 215, 224 n. 2, 232; and genre 3, 25–6, 34–5, 93–4, 99, 198–9, 211, 216, 220, 223, 270; and sexuality 261, 265–7, 268–70, 272 n. 12, 273 n. 27; see also feminism, femininity, masculinity, and post-feminism
Generation Kill: book 228, 246; see also *Generation Kill* television series, *Over There*

Generation Kill: TV series 2, 6, 7, 11, 31, 228, 245–58; as quality television 245–7, 257–8; trauma and 248–9, 252–6; see also Iraq War, serial narrative, War on Terror(ism)
Gomer Pyle, USMC 4, 63–4, 147, 152
"Greatest Generation" 9, 90, 95, 132, 146, 240; sentimental representation of 94, 99–100, 103, 107, generational obligation to 94, 97, 99–100
Guns of Navarone 32

Hell is for Heroes 30, 36
Heller, Joseph 46–7, 50–1, 57, 59
heteronormativity 12, 266–71
Hersey, John 46–7, 50–1, 57, 59
Hiken, Nat 18, 19, 20
Hogan's Heroes 4, 7–8, 33, 63–75, 78, 147; Cold War and 68–72; Vietnam War and 63–72; World War II and 63, 66, 68, 70
Holocaust 103, 105–106, 248
Home Box Office Television (HBO) 8, 9, 11, 31, 77, 93–4, 245–8, 249
homonormativity 266, 268–9
Houlihan, Major Margaret, see Loretta Swit

Iraq War 4, 7, 11; *Generation Kill* and 245–58; *JAG* and 216–19; *Over There* and 228–41; veterans of 229–31, 234, 239, 248
Ivanova, Susan, see Claudia Christian

JAG 6, 7, 10, 211–24; Iraq War and 216–19; War on Terror(ism) and 216–19; as serial narrative 219–20; see also David James Elliott, Catherine Bell

Kennedy, John F. 31, 34, 38–9, 44, 88, 167
Kennedy, Robert F. 72
King, Jr., Martin Luther 72
Korea, Republic of 7–9, 47, 119–25, 130, 131, 147, 152, 162, 251
Korean War 8–9, 33, 36, 47, 50, 59, 64, 112, 146–7, 172; American Forces Network and 9, 112, 114–16, 119–24; anti-militarism and 19, 21, 36, 172; *The Big Picture* and 115–16; post-Korean War society 8, 19, 21, 33, 36, 130–1, 146–7; as setting for *M*A*S*H* 6, 140, 144,

146, 251; veterans of 146, 149, 172, 180
Kubrick, Stanley 46 7, 50–1, 55, 57, 59

The L Word 11, 261, 264–7, 271–2
Lay, Jr., Beirne 48, 50, 52
Lederer, William J. 165–7
The Lieutenant 5, 130
Lifetime channel 11, 189, 262, 267–9
Linville, Larry 134, 144; as Major Frank Burns in *M*A*S*H* 134–5, 150
The Longest Day 32, 46, 51–2, 56, 80–1, 102

MacDonald, J. Fred 12, 33, 164, 176 n. 16
MacKenzie, Major Sarah "Mac," see Catherine Bell
The Man from U.N.C.L.E 63–4
Martin, Quinn 52, 57–8
masculinity 107, 132, 138, 153, 157, 216; in music 93, 99; as performance 264–6; as threatened by femininity 25–6, 216, 249, 261; in war film 3, 223; see also femininity and gender
M*A*S*H: film 26, 130
M*A*S*H: TV series 26, 78, 90, 92 n. 30, 129–41, 144–59, 251; alcohol in 9, 144–59; communism and 149, 153; as quality television 6–7, 129–131, 140–1, 144–145, 148–9, 158–9; trauma and 129–141, 148–9, 151; Vietnam War and 129–41, 144–59, 251; see also Alan Alda, Allan Arbus, Larry Linville, serial narrative, Tom Sullivan, Loretta Swit
McHale's Navy 4, 26, 33, 63
The Memphis Belle 48, 57–8
melodrama 10, 99, 101, 105, 181, 212, 219–24, 233
memorialization 6–7, 32, 49, 139–40, 149, 153, 213–15; in *Band of Brothers* 93–107, 108 n. 33; in *China Beach* 178, 182–3, 185–9
militarism 21, 106, 198, 211–227, 258
Montagne, Edward 20, 26
musical genres: march 93, 102; waltz 93, 98–99, 101–103

National Liberation Front (NLF) 167–74
narrative (dis)equilibrium 148, 150, 152–3

284 *Index*

Navy Log 1, 10, 31, 176 n. 9; Vietnam War and 165–7
NBC 1, 2, 12 n. 3, 64, 77, 89, 112, 118, 162, 211, 218–19
NCIS 211–12
North Atlantic Treaty Organization (NATO) 2, 40, 45 n. 52, 59

Office of Armed Forces Information and Education (OAFIE) 113–115, 123
O'Brien, Tim 189
The Outer Limits 162–3, 171
Over There 2, 4, 7, 11, 31, 229–41; alcohol and 240; trauma and 233–9; see also Iraq War, War on Terror(ism)

Pacific theater of war 8, 26, 49, 77, 81–83
patriotism 3, 51, 67, 114, 208, 212, 217–19, 240–1, 247, 250, 254, 261, 262, 265–7, 268–9, 271
Persian Gulf War 247, 252, 257, 259 n. 31; *Babylon 5* and 195, 196–8, 202, 206–8
The Phil Silvers Show (TV series) 4, 7–8, 17–23, 25–26, 85
Pierce, Captain Benjamin Franklin "Hawkeye," see Alan Alda
Pirosh, Robert 30–1, 36
Platoon 96, 106, 216
Pork Chop Hill 30–1, 36, 38
post-gay politics 11, 266–7, 269–71, 272
post-feminism 198–9, 209, 215, 268–70; see also feminism

quality television 6–7, 55, 74–5, 76 n. 17, 93–4, 211, 219–20, 228–9, 245–7; *China Beach* and 6–7, 156–7, 178–89; *Generation Kill* and 245–7, 257–8; *M*A*S*H* and 6–7, 129–131, 140–1, 144–5, 148–9, 158–9; "non-quality" TV 4, 6–7, 57, 117–18

Rabb, Jr., Harmon, see David James Elliott
race 18, 119, 130, 145–6, 195, 232, 267–9
racism 145, 158, 200, 232, 235–6,
Radio Corporation of America (RCA) 1, 112, 115, 121–2
The Rat Patrol 5, 31, 42, 77, 90 n. 1
Revolution in Military Affairs (RMA) 251–2
Rieckhoff, Paul 229

Sands of Iwo Jima 78, 86–7, 91 n. 9, 212, 215
satire 5, 9, 46, 50, 148–9
Saving Private Ryan 90–1 n. 6, 95–6, 106, 215, 239, 245
September 11, 2001 9, 94–5, 218, 223, 230–1, 247, 250, 252, 257, 264
serial narrative 6, 12, 77, 85, 129, 238 n. 36, 246; *Band of Brothers* and 77, 93–107; *China Beach* and 178–180, 182–4, 189; *Generation Kill* and 245–6, 248, 253–4; *JAG* and 219–220; *M*A*S*H* and 129–31, 136–7, 15–1
sex 10, 105, 148 153; censorship of 119, 125
sexuality 10, 198, 201–6, 208–9, 240, 251, 261, 265–7, 268–70, 271–2
Sheridan, Captain John, see Bruce Boxleitner
Showtime channel 11, 261, 263, 265–7
Silent Service 1, 31
Silvers, Phil 17–20
Simon, David 249–50, 258; as auteur 245–8; see also *Generation Kill*, quality television
social ritual: drinking as 145, 149–51, 153, 158; Hollywood war film as 2–3; television as 5–6, 12, 21–2, 34, 74–5, 129–31, 138, 140–141, 158–9, 218, 222–4, 233, 258
Some May Live 162, 171, 174–5
Spielberg, Steven 91 n. 6, 94–5, 101, 106, 215, 245–6, 248
Strategic Air Command (SAC) trilogy 49–52
Sullivan, Tom 139; as Tom Straw on *M*A*S*H* 132
Swit, Loretta 133, 150; as Major Margaret Houlihan in *M*A*S*H* 150, 154

Tallman, Patricia 195; as Lyta Alexander on *Babylon 5* 206–8
terrorism 198, 206–8; see also War on Terrorism
The Thin, Red Line 95–6, 100
Thompson, Andrea 200; as Talia Winters on *Babylon 5* 205–6
Top Gun 211, 212, 216
Tora! Tora! Tora! 32, 80
torture 70, 167, 200, 218, 228–30, 234–5
Tour of Duty 5, 10, 31, 42, 175

Index 285

trauma 8, 10, 36–7, 54, 202–4; *China Beach* and 178–89; *Generation Kill* and 248–9, 252–6; *M*A*S*H* and 129–141, 148–9, 151; *Over There* and 233–9

Twelve O'Clock High, see *12 O'Clock High*

The Twilight Zone 162–3, 171

United States Air Force 21, 49–51, 115, 117–18, 121; Army Air Force (precursor) 19, 23, 25, 79; in *Baa Baa Black Sheep* 77–8, 81–90; in *Twelve O'Clock High* 47–9, 51–8

United States Army 1, 88, 111, 113–14, 115–116, 119, 180; and American Forces Radio and Television Service 111–120; and American Forces Korean Network 120–5; in *Army Wives* 261, 267–71; in *Band of Brothers* 96–7; in *Combat!* 3–42; in *The Final War of Olly Winter* 171–4; in *Hogan's Heroes* 64–75; in *The L Word* 261, 264–7; in *M*A*S*H* 129–41, 144–59; in *Over There* 228–241; in *The Phil Silvers Show* 17–27; in *Twelve O'Clock High* 47, 49, 51–8; see also American Forces Radio and Television Service

United States Department of Defense 52, 112–114, 146, 156, 228; as TV programmer 1–2, 111–25, 165, 216–19, 267–8; as Department of War 111–13

United States military: gays and lesbians in 195–8, 261–4, 267, 271–2; policies of 1, 112–125, 146, 156, 158–9, 161 n.39, 240, 250, 253–4; support for 212, 216, 224, 229, see also patriotism; women in 11, 17, 25–6, 52, 107, 130, 132–3, 138, 153, 157, 196–8, 208–9, 215, 232; see also Cold War, Iraq War, Korean War, Persian Gulf War, United States Army, United States Air Force, United States Department of Defense, United States Marine Corps, United States Navy, Vietnam War, War on Terrorism, World War II

United States Marine Corps 8, 113, 133, 156, 180, 224 n. 2, 246 ; in

Baa Baa Black Sheep 77–90; in *Generation Kill* 252–6; in *JAG* 211–224; Marine Corps Hymn 93

United States Navy 1, 10, 21, 80, 84, 87, 107, 113, 116, 133, 156, 240, 262; in *JAG* 211–224, 224 n. 2, 225 n. 15; in *McHale's Navy* 4, 26, 33, 63; in *Navy Log* 1, 10, 31, 165–71, 176 n. 9;

"universal platoon" 3, 79, 84–5

Viet Cong 59, 66, 168–9, 233

Viet Minh 163–5, 167

Vietnam War 5, 6, 7, 8, 9, 10, 26, 30, 33, 38, 77, 88, 92 n. 30, 162–4; *Alcoa Premiere* and 167–71; *Apocalypse Now* and 92 n. 33, 257; *Biff Baker, USA* and 163–5; *China Beach* and 5–6, 10, 156–7, 178–89; combat film cycle 11, 96, 106, 181–2, 189, 215–16, 229–33, 240, 249–50, 254, 256–7; the doctrine of air power and 47–51, 55, 58–9; *The Final War of Olly Winter* 171–3; *Hogan's Heroes* and 63–75; *M*A*S*H* and 129–41, 144–59, 251; *Navy Log* and 165–7; science fiction series and 162–3, 171; *Some May Live* and 171, 174–5; *Tour of Duty* and 5, 10, 31, 42, 175; veterans of 129, 131, 134–7, 171–2, 175, 180, 182–3, 186–7, 189

The War Lover 46, 50, 54–5, 57

War on Drugs 156

War on Terror(ism) 2, 11, 107, 223, 231–2, 240; *Generation Kill* and 245–58; *JAG* and 216–19, 223; *Over There* and 229–41

war profiteering 229, 233

Williams, John 95, 220, 223

Williams, Linda 220, 222–3

Winters, Talia, see Andrea Thompson

Wittebols, James 137, 145, 155, 158

Women's Army Corps (WAC) 17, 25–26

Worland, Rick 32–4, 162

World War II 1, 5, 8, 47, 114, 132, 163, 165, 185, 213–14, 261–2; *Baa Baa Black Sheep* and 77–8, 81–90; *Band of Brothers* and 93–107; *Combat!* and 30, 33–8; doctrine of air power and 47–9, 56, 58–9; *Hogan's Heroes* and 63, 66, 68, 70; *The Phil Silvers Show* and 19–21, 23, 25–7; veterans

286 *Index*

of 19–21, 24–5, 32, 48–9, 80, 86, 94–7, 100–02, 112, 114; 130, 143 n. 45, 172, 180, 214–15; 248
World War II combat film 3, 32, 34, 36, 78–81, 86–7, 213–14, 225 n. 11, 231, 249–51; *Why We Fight* 114

Wright, Evan 228, 246; see also *Generation Kill, Over There*

The X-Files 219–20

Zanuck, Daryl F. 48, 51–2